MICROBIOLOGY OF FERMENTED FOODS

Volume 1

MICROBIOLOGY OF FERMENTED FOODS
Volume 1

Edited by

BRIAN J. B. WOOD

Department of Bioscience and Biotechnology,
University of Strathclyde, Glasgow, Scotland, UK

ELSEVIER APPLIED SCIENCE PUBLISHERS
LONDON and NEW YORK

ELSEVIER APPLIED SCIENCE PUBLISHERS LTD
Crown House, Linton Road, Barking, Essex IG11 8JU, England

Sole Distributor in the USA and Canada
ELSEVIER SCIENCE PUBLISHING CO., INC.
52 Vanderbilt Avenue, New York, NY 10017, USA

British Library Cataloguing in Publication Data

Microbiology of fermented foods.
Vol. 1
1. Food industry and trade   2. Fermentation
3. Food—Microbiology
I.   Wood, B. J. B.
630′.2′76   TP370.5

ISBN 0-85334-332-2 (Volume 1)
ISBN 0-85334-334-9 (The set)

WITH 59 TABLES AND 49 ILLUSTRATIONS

© ELSEVIER APPLIED SCIENCE PUBLISHERS LTD 1985

Printed in Great Britain by Galliard (Printers) Ltd, Great Yarmouth

To the memory of my parents,
who encouraged and supported me
through a long education

Preface to Volume 1

When I was first approached by Elsevier Applied Science Publishers with the suggestion that I consider editing a text on fermented foods, my immediate reaction was that the field had been covered by several other books which have appeared recently. However, a more detailed appraisal resulted in the conclusion that there was a place for a text which sought to cover the food fermentations of both the developed and the developing worlds. There is, inevitably and happily, a great deal of overlap between the fermentations practised in various parts of the world and division of this text into two volumes owes more to publishing convenience than to an exclusiveness between the two sets of topics.

A number of the overseas contributors, in their replies to the invitation to write sections for the book, mentioned varying degrees of concern over the adequacy of their written English. This created for me a difficult dilemma. Should I edit very heavily so as to achieve a uniform and cohesive style, or should I accept as far as possible compatible with clarity, the individual approaches to the presentation of written English? Most of my overseas authors asked me to do whatever was necessary with their English, and I elected for the minimum interference compatible with this request. The result, I hope, has preserved the diversity of approaches which is a continuing fascination of work on food fermentations, particularly those of the less developed parts of the world. I asked that as far as possible the lists of references cited in the chapters should include the title of each paper, since this is of value to people in less developed countries who frequently need to send abroad for reprints, having very limited access to journals. For various reasons this could not always be complied with but I hope that the book's users will be forgiving in this matter.

The topics covered in this first volume will in general be familiar throughout most of the world, although even here there are many exceptions. For example, most British people regard pickles as preserves with vinegar, i.e. acetic acid, as the principal acidulant; most Europeans are well aware that many vegetables can be preserved by spontaneous lactic fermentation, although not all people in (for example) the olive-growing areas appreciate that the inevitable result of immersing olives in brine under farm conditions will be a lactic fermentation essential to production of the preferred organoleptic qualities.

Again, the farther East one goes across Europe, the more diverse (it seems) is the range of fermented milks and cheeses. The United States has many of these available on at least a local basis, a reminder of the great diversity of traditions to which it is heir.

Progress in food fermentation will draw upon many other disciplines in addition to microbiology. Tony Godfrey's chapter shows the increasing importance of enzymes in both fermented and non-fermented foods. In this case the contribution of a class of microbial products to the production of non-fermented foods is, in economic terms, very substantial.

The ability of fermented food to supply vitamins to the diet is perhaps not very important in the more developed parts of the world where a reasonable diet is normally available to all. Even here, however, certain groups, such as vegans, may be at risk to particular deficiencies, such as that of vitamin B_{12} in a dietary regime free of all animal products. The demonstration of the presence of substantial amounts of vitamin B_{12} in tempeh will have importance to people whose diets exclude animal products. As Keith Steinkraus' chapter shows, fermented foods can also make other significant vitamin contributions to the diets of people in less developed countries.

Vinegar is a case where there is a need for appropriate, small-scale technology for local use in the developing countries. The Tropical Development and Research Institute (TDRI) has been active in the development of technologies on a scale and with the raw materials appropriate to these countries. Martin Adams' chapter bridges the gap between the large-scale operations often found in the more industrialised countries and the TDRI's work on production methods for tropical countries. Of course, countries such as France continue (happily) to produce what most gourmets still regard as the finest vinegar in the world by the slow and laborious Orleans method, a very primitive technology by most standards.

Bread, in its origins a food of the higher latitudes, has been taken into all parts of the world by the early explorers and has become as commonplace in the moist tropics as it is in Northern Europe. The development of specialised strains of wheat and of the new, hybrid grain, triticale, will extend the range over which bread-making grain can be grown. Pressed and dried yeast preparations offer the baker simplicity and reliability in bread-making, but they are the products of a fairly sophisticated microbial technology. Dried yeast can be exported to developing countries but this represents a further drain on their inadequate supplies of 'hard' currency. Frank Sugihara shows that sourdough leavens can be easily maintained in a wide variety of climatic conditions, and can probably give satisfactory results with a bigger range of flours than can dried yeast. This technology is therefore of potential interest to developing countries. Its use has already undergone great expansion in the USA of recent years, with 'San Francisco Sourdough Bread' on sale right across the country, and in other industrialised countries sourdough breads are becoming more readily available, being valued both for their organoleptic qualities and as part of the movement to return to a supposedly simpler way of life.

With some fermented foods the movement has been from East to West. Soy sauce, although a static market in Japan, is rapidly expanding in Europe and North America. Its success in the USA is shown by the growth of the Kikkoman Co.'s offshoot in Wisconsin. The dietary value of soy sauce is such that it is developing this market penetration at a time when there is a vigorous campaign against the use of high levels of sodium chloride in the diet. Tamotsu Yokotsuka's article shows how the Japanese have succeeded in developing a very ancient and highly traditional technology into a very modern, highly mechanised process, without losing the qualities, both organoleptic and almost mystical, which make soy sauce unique.

With mushroom cultivation there is movement in both directions. The techniques developed in Western Europe and the USA for cultivation of *Agaricus*, are being more widely adopted elsewhere and there is a developing interest in the West in some of the techniques for growing Eastern fungi such as the padi-straw mushroom and certain tree fungi, as Fred Hayes demonstrates.

If you, the reader, have comments, criticisms, or a complaint that some important area has been omitted, I shall be most pleased to receive your comments, etc., for action should the opportunity present itself.

Brian J. B. Wood

Acknowledgements

To those authors who submitted their manuscripts on time, my thanks for their forbearance. To Miss Elizabeth Clements and Mrs Jean Winter for typing many letters and my contributions to this text. To Mr George Olley of Elsevier Applied Science Publishers, for his patience when it seemed as though we would never get this into its final form.

B.J.B.W.

Contents

VOLUME 1

xiii

VOLUME 2

List of Contributors

VOLUME 1

M. R. ADAMS

Tropical Development and Research Institute, 56–62 Gray's Inn Road, London WC1X 8LU, UK. Present address: Department of Microbiology, University of Surrey, Guildford, Surrey GU2 5XH, UK

R. J. M. CRAWFORD

The West of Scotland Agricultural College, Education Division, Department of Dairy Technology, Auchincruive, Ayr KA6 5HW, Scotland, UK

J. H. GALLOWAY

The West of Scotland Agricultural College, Education Division, Department of Dairy Technology, Auchincruive, Ayr KA6 5HW, Scotland, UK

A. GODFREY

Managing Director, Biocatalysts Ltd, Grand Metropolitan Biotechnology Division, 430 Victoria Road, South Ruislip, Middlesex HA4 0AF, UK

W. A. HAYES

Department of Biological Sciences, University of Aston in Birmingham, Gosta Green, Birmingham B4 7ET, UK

MARY M. HODGE

Department of Bioscience and Biotechnology, Division of Applied Microbiology, University of Strathclyde, Royal College Building, 204 George Street, Glasgow G1 1XW, Scotland, UK. Present address: Department of Microbiology, University of Surrey, Guildford, Surrey GU2 5XH, UK

HELENA OBERMAN

Institute of Fermentation Technology and Microbiology, Technical University, ul. Wólozańska Nr 173, 90-530 Łódź, Poland

KEITH H. STEINKRAUS

Professor of Microbiology, Institute of Food Science, Cornell University, Geneva/Ithaca, New York 14456/14853, USA

T. FRANK SUGIHARA

Agricultural Research, Western Regional Research Center, United States Department of Agriculture, 800 Buchanan Street, Berkeley, California 94710, USA

REESE H. VAUGHN

Department of Food Science and Technology, University of California, Davis, California 95616, USA

BRIAN J. B. WOOD

Department of Bioscience and Biotechnology, Division of Applied Microbiology, University of Strathclyde, Royal College Building, 204 George Street, Glasgow G1 1XW, Scotland, UK

TAMOTSU YOKOTSUKA

Kikkoman Corporation, 339 Noda, Noda-shi, Chiba-ken 278, Japan.

VOLUME 2

C. G. BEDDOWS

School of Health and Applied Science, Leeds Polytechnic, Calverley Street, Leeds LS1 3HE, UK

J. G. CARR

Formerly Long Ashton Research Station, Long Ashton, Bristol BS18 9AF, UK. Present address: 24 Hill Burn, Henleaze, Bristol BS9 4RH, UK.

G. R. HRUBANT

Northern Regional Research Center, Agricultural Research Service, United States Department of Agriculture, 1815 North University Street, Peoria, Illinois 61604, USA

JOHN R. JOHNSTON

Department of Bioscience and Biotechnology, Division of Applied Microbiology, University of Strathclyde, Royal College Building, 204 George Street, Glasgow G1 1XW, Scotland, UK

NAPHA LOTONG

Department of Microbiology, Faculty of Science, Kasetsart University, Bangkok 10900, Thailand

FRIEDRICH-KARL LÜCKE

Institut für Mikrobiologie, Toxikologie und Histologie der Bundesanstalt für Fleischforschung, E.-C. Baumann-Strasse 20, D-8650 Kulmbach, Federal Republic of Germany

S. A. ODUNFA

Department of Botany and Microbiology, University of Ibadan, Ibadan, Nigeria

W. R. STANTON

Formerly Professor of Botany, University of Malaya, Pantai Valley, Kuala Lumpur, Malaysia. Present address: 73 Main Street, Stanbury, Keighley, West Yorkshire BD22 0HA, UK

BRIAN J. B. WOOD

Department of Bioscience and Biotechnology, Division of Applied Microbiology, University of Strathclyde, Royal College Building, 204 George Street, Glasgow G1 1XW, Scotland, UK

MICHAEL K. WOOLFORD

Grassland Research Institute, Hurley, Maidenhead, Berkshire SL6 5LR, UK. Present address: Agil Agriculture, Fishponds Road, Wokingham, Berkshire RG11 2QL, UK

Chapter 1

Vinegar

M. R. ADAMS*

*Tropical Development and Research Institute,
London, UK*

1. INTRODUCTION

Vinegar is a dilute solution of acetic acid produced by a two-stage fermentation process. In the first stage fermentable sugars are converted into ethanol by the action of yeasts, normally strains of *Saccharomyces cerevisiae*, while in the second bacteria of the genus *Acetobacter* oxidise the ethanol to acetic acid. An outline of the overall process is presented in Fig. 1.

The subject of vinegar production has been periodically reviewed from various points of view, but normally stressing the most modern, most sophisticated procedures used (Conner & Allgeier, 1976; Greenshields, 1978; Ebner, 1982). While it is hoped that the present chapter does not neglect this important area, some attempt is made to give greater emphasis to traditional methods still widely practised and which, in certain cases, may be more appropriate to local conditions and requirements.

2. THE ORIGINS OF VINEGAR PRODUCTION

The production of vinegar can occur as a spontaneous fermentation. Both types of micro-organism necessary for its production are commonly associated with plant products as part of their natural microflora, and at

* Present address: Department of Microbiology, University of Surrey, Guildford GU2 5XH, UK.

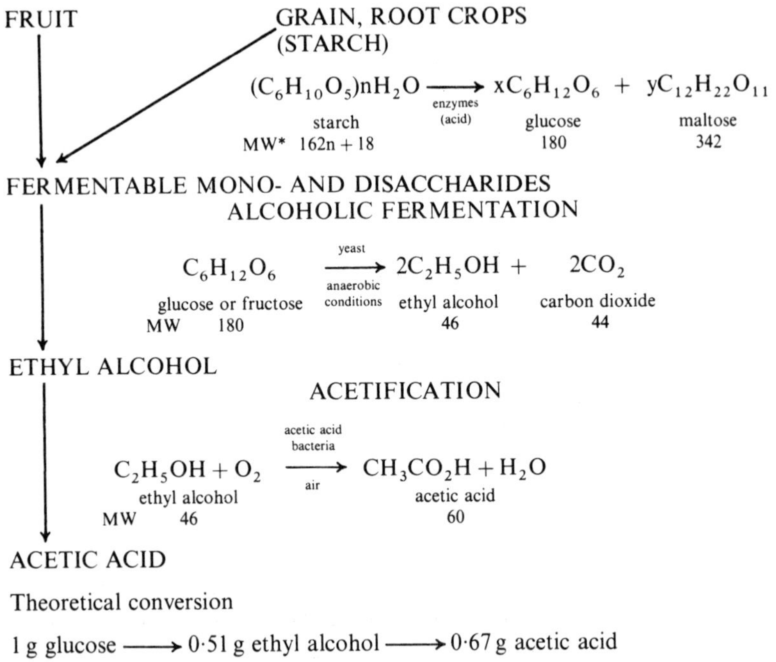

FRUIT   GRAIN, ROOT CROPS
                         (STARCH)

$$(C_6H_{10}O_5)nH_2O \xrightarrow[\text{enzymes}]{} xC_6H_{12}O_6 + yC_{12}H_{22}O_{11}$$

          starch   (acid)   glucose   maltose
        MW* 162n + 18   180   342

FERMENTABLE MONO- AND DISACCHARIDES
             ALCOHOLIC FERMENTATION

$$C_6H_{12}O_6 \xrightarrow[\text{anaerobic conditions}]{\text{yeast}} 2C_2H_5OH + 2CO_2$$

      glucose or fructose   ethyl alcohol   carbon dioxide
      MW   180   46   44

ETHYL ALCOHOL
                         ACETIFICATION

$$C_2H_5OH + O_2 \xrightarrow[\text{air}]{\substack{\text{acetic acid} \\ \text{bacteria}}} CH_3CO_2H + H_2O$$

        ethyl alcohol   acetic acid
      MW   46   60

ACETIC ACID

Theoretical conversion

1 g glucose $\longrightarrow$ 0·51 g ethyl alcohol $\longrightarrow$ 0·67 g acetic acid

Note: *MW = Molecular weight.

Fig. 1.   Schematic outline of vinegar production.

each stage in the process conditions are in some way restrictive to microbial competition. An initially high sugar concentration, typically 10 % w/v or more, and an acid pH favour the production of ethanol by yeasts. During alcoholic fermentation, anaerobic conditions are created, the pH drops further and the ethanol concentration rises. At the end of yeast fermentation when the sugars have been consumed, aerobic conditions are re-established at the surface of the liquid permitting the growth of ethanol utilising acetic acid bacteria. These produce high levels of acetic acid (between 0·7 and 1·7 M in most commercial vinegars) decreasing the pH still further to a value of 3 or below. Thus, a suitable substrate left open to the environment will, in many cases, undergo a natural fermentation to produce first ethanol and, in time, a product resembling vinegar. This, in all probability, is why vinegar was an early discovery of Man, preceding recorded history but succeeding the discovery of alcoholic beverages perhaps by only a matter of days!

Because of this close relation between alcohol and vinegar, it is probably a fair assumption that both products were discovered at about the same time, possibly independently in several places. One problem in dating the recognition of vinegar as a distinct commodity, noted by Conner & Allgeier (1976), is the absence of any precise definitions to help distinguish between terms such as wine, old wine, sour wine and vinegar. One instance of this confusion is the use of the word vinegar in a passage in the King James Bible (Ruth 2, 14) and its replacement by wine in the subsequent Revised Standard Version.

The brewing of beer and wine were well known in ancient Egypt and Mesopotamia several millenia BC (Corran, 1975). In Mesopotamia between 3000 and 2000 BC it has been estimated that 40 % of the total cereal crop was used for brewing and there was considerable concern about the problems of over-indulgence (Corran, 1975; Roberts, 1980). It was known in Egypt that the fermentation would proceed further to produce vinegar, and Egyptian vinegar was much esteemed by the Greeks and Romans at a later date (Derry & Williams, 1960; Soyer, 1853). The Babylonians produced several different types including those from palm sap, dates and malted grain, raw materials used for vinegar production to this day (Huber, 1927).

Knowledge of vinegar and its production appears to have spread to other countries from the Middle East and perhaps China. The Japanese techniques of vinegar making, believed to have originated from China, were introduced between AD 369 and 404 (Masai, 1980). Vinegar could have reached Britain around the first century BC when it was known to be in use by the Celts along the French Atlantic coast (Wilson, 1976). It is possible that British production of the malt-based product started in Roman times, but the etymology of the word vinegar, from *vin aigre* (Fr. sour wine) suggests that continental sources remained important for a considerable period. Indeed, the early use of the related term alegar to describe malt vinegar supports this.

3. WORLD PRODUCTION OF VINEGAR

Vinegar production is never more than a comparatively small industry in the economy of industrialised countries. Nevertheless, substantial quantities are produced and the average, annual, *per capita* consumption in the non-communist, industrialised world is more than 2 litres of 5 % acidity vinegar. Some recent data on the production of vinegar in these countries are presented in Table 1.

TABLE 1

Vinegar Production in Major Industrialised Countries (all Volumes in Hectolitres, hl)

Year	European Community[1]								Canada[2]	Japan[3]	USA[4]
	Belgium	Denmark	W. Germany	France	Ireland	Italy	Netherlands	UK			
1978	76 645	119 291	1 022 810	961 160	7890	517 500	140 517	674 950	244 890	2 696 000	—
1979	97 166	119 472	1 079 330	1 051 420	12 150	522 000	164 178	640 200	230 530	2 855 000	—
1980	101 878	132 510	992 830	987 340	13 400	522 000	129 900	660 550	—	2 877 000	4 210 000
1981	121 562	136 350	1 080 880	1 021 330	13 000	522 000	107 030	583 500	—	—	—

[1] All figures as 10% w/v acidity vinegar. Source: Vinegar Brewers Federation (M. C. Ainley, personal communication).
[2] All figures based on proof litre of 117·5 grains (grain strength = concn acetic acid w/v × 10). Source: Statistics Canada, Fruit and Vegetable Processing Industries (G. D. Cooper, personal communication).
[3] Figures usually supplied at 4·2% w/v acetic acid. Source: Japanese Dept. of Agriculture, Forestry and Fisheries (H. Masai, personal communication).
[4] All figures converted to 10% w/v acetic acid. Source: Ebner (1982).

Some developing countries are also producers of vinegar, although detailed production figures are not available. Others meet their requirements through imports. In 1980 exports of vinegar from the European Community and the USA to developing countries totalled 7900 tonnes, to a value of US $4 million. Although its impact should not be overstated, the introduction of vinegar production based on locally available raw materials in these countries could have several benefits. It would conserve foreign exchange, create some local employment and provide the opportunity for making use of a range of tropical fruits and their wastes. Expansion of domestic food processing industries could also lead to an increase in demand for vinegar and offer increased incentive for local production.

4.   USES

4.1. Non-food Uses

Vinegar was the strongest acid known in antiquity and as such its unique properties found various applications. In civil engineering it was reportedly used in fire-setting where large rocks to be cleared were heated and then rapidly cooled. Although water was more often the coolant of choice, Pliny states that vinegar was also used. Both Plutarch and Livy (and every reviewer of vinegar production since) give the story of Hannibal's use of vinegar for this purpose in his march across the Alps to Rome (Partington, 1935). Several authorities regard it as highly unlikely that vinegar was, in fact, used for this purpose (see, for example, Singer *et al.*, 1956), but it is interesting to note that independent accounts of its use in fire-setting in China have been recorded (Needham, 1971a).

Vinegar and distilled vinegar were both given their own symbols by the alchemists (Mitchell, 1926), and feature prominently in their lists of materials purchased (Singer *et al.*, 1956). Among its uses in alchemy was in conjunction with nitrate (saltpetre) when it forms a very dilute solution of nitric acid. This was used for the preparation of aqueous solutions of minerals that were otherwise insoluble (Needham, 1971b). During the Middle Ages verdigris (a basic acetate of copper) was made by moistening metallic copper with vinegar and exposing it to the air (Singer *et al.*, 1956).

An important industrial application of vinegar was in the production of the pigment ceruse or white lead. This basic lead carbonate was widely used in paints and cosmetics and has been found at Indus Valley sites, ancient Egyptian remains, and is mentioned in Chinese writings of the 4th Century BC (Needham, 1971c). It was prepared by the Dutch or stack process in which sheets of lead were laid over the top of small earthenware pots containing vinegar. The pots were sunk in a layer of horse manure or spent tanning bark up to a metre thick. This maintained the temperature at around 30 °C and supplied the carbon dioxide gas which, with the acetic acid fumes from the vinegar, converted the lead to white lead over a period of 8–16 weeks. At the end of this period the white lead was scraped off, washed, recrystallised and dried (Raistrick, 1973). By laying boards over the lead sheets another layer of manure, pots and lead could be placed on top and a stack built up. In 18th Century England one manufacturer had stacks containing 1600 pots and 4 tons of lead (Campbell, 1971).

Nowadays readily available acetic acid from petrochemical sources has largely replaced vinegar in its non-food uses. Although the distillation of vinegar to produce acetic acid as an industrial chemical has been reported in modern times (Conner & Allgeier, 1976), the more usual routes employed for its production from renewable resources have been extraction from pyroligneous acid and the chemical oxidation of fermentation ethanol (Adams and Flynn, 1982).

Under certain conditions, however, vinegar can still be used as a local source of acetic acid. During the Second World War, for instance, it was produced from molasses in East Africa for use as a latex coagulant in rubber production (Hansford & Martin, 1943).

4.2. Food Uses

As well as the sharpness conferred by acetic acid, individual vinegars each have their own particular flavour. This reflects the process by which it was made and the raw material used. Both characteristics have been employed since the earliest times to enliven food, particularly where a diet has a tendency to monotony or blandness. A good example of this was its role as an ingredient in 'black broth', the staple food of the Spartans (Tannahill, 1973). Here though, it seems that the limits of vinegar's improving qualities were reached, for a Sybarite once declared, after dining in a Spartan mess, that he now understood why they had no fear of death! (Kitto, 1951).

Vinegar is a good solvent for the essential oils of herbs and spices and has been a ubiquitous sauce ingredient throughout history (Tannahill, 1973). The Babylonians are known to have added a wide variety of herbs to the vinegars they used in food preparation and preservation (Huber, 1927) and frequent mention is made of its use in the only cookery book to survive from the imperial Roman period, Apicius' *Artis magiricae libri X* (Wilson, 1976). Today, vinegars flavoured with tarragon, chilli, garlic, rosemary, and the like, are produced commercially for use in home-produced marinades and salad dressings (Binsted *et al.*, 1962).

The range of other food products that can be prepared using vinegar is enormous, including mayonnaise, ketchups, sauces, chopped pickles and brined vegetables (see, for example, Binsted *et al.*, 1962; and Poultney, 1949).

Pickling foods in vinegar is one of the traditional technologies of food preservation, along with solar drying, salting and smoking. A common characteristic of these techniques is that the product frequently resembles the fresh raw material to only a very limited extent. This is in contrast to procedures such as canning or freezing where the aim is to retain the character of the fresh or freshly cooked product as far as possible. Although it is largely the taste which accounts for the continuing popularity of traditionally preserved foods in the developed world, the importance of such low-cost techniques for food preservation in less developed countries remains (see, for example, Bachman, 1981).

The preservative action of vinegar is due to its acetic acid content. As little as 0.1% of the undissociated acid will inhibit the growth of most food poisoning and spore-forming bacteria and 0.3% will prevent the growth of mycotoxigenic moulds (Baird-Parker, 1980). In vinegar preserves the effect of the acetic acid is frequently enhanced by the presence of salt (sodium chloride) and other solutes which reduce the water activity of the product to below the optimum for most spoilage and food poisoning organisms.

The types of micro-organism capable of growing under such conditions are extremely limited. A survey of 84 samples of spoiled vinegar preserves in the UK isolated representatives of the bacteria (*Lactobacillus* spp.), yeasts (*Saccharomyces acidifaciens* and *Pichia membranaefaciens*) and a fungus (named *Moniliella acetoabutans*) as the primary agents of infection (Dakin & Day, 1958; Dakin & Radwell, 1971; Stoik & Dakin, 1966).

The antimicrobial activity of acetic acid is not simply a pH effect. When acetic acid was used as the acidulant in a synthetic medium, the initiation of growth by *Salmonella* spp. was inhibited by pH values below 5.4, but if hydrochloric acid was used growth initiation occurred down to 4.05 (Chung & Goepfert, 1970). The mechanism of acetic acid's antimicrobial action is thought to be broadly similar to that of the other organic acids used as food preservatives. Activity is associated with the unionised, lipophilic molecule which can penetrate the cell membrane, disrupting membrane transport processes, and dissociating within the cell to increase acidity and produce toxic levels of the anion. The pK_a of the acid therefore indicates the pH range over which it is effective.

The pK_a of acetic acid is 4.75 (Weast, 1975). How this influences the percentage of undissociated molecules at different pH values is illustrated in Table 2. Acetic acid pickles and preserves normally contain enough acid

TABLE 2
Effect of pH on the Dissociation of
Acetic Acid

pH	Percentage of acetic acid undissociated
7·0	0·6
6·5	1·7
6·0	5·3
5·5	15·2
5·0	35·7
4·5	64·3
4·0	84·8
3·5	94·7
3·0	98·3

to overcome any buffering effect of the raw materials and reduce the pH to below 3·5, when more than 95 % of the acetic acid is in the undissociated form (Binsted *et al.*, 1962). Empirical rules have been formulated to determine the amount of acetic acid necessary to achieve satisfactory preservation of a pickle or sauce. These attempt to make some allowance for the preservative effect of other solutes. Work at the British Food Manufacturing Industries Research Association indicated that a minimum of 3·6 % acetic acid, calculated as a percentage of the volatile constituents of the product, is necessary (Binsted *et al.*, 1962).

$$A = \frac{3·6}{100} \times VC$$

where A is the percentage acetic acid on the whole product and VC is the percentage of volatile constituents, defined as the percentage weight loss from a sample dried for 5 h at 70 °C at approximately 1–2 in of mercury pressure.

Bell & Etchells (1952, cited by Binsted *et al.*, 1962), working with sweet cucumber pickles, derived a different formula which provides for a slightly higher acetic acid content.

$$A = \frac{80 - S}{20}$$

where A is the percentage acetic acid on the whole product and S is the percentage sugar (sucrose) on the whole product.

Products made according to either of these formulae are likely to be stable for long periods but will have rather a strong acid flavour. This is an appreciated feature of many pickled products, although in some cases milder pickles are preferred.

Where the acetic acid content is decreased below the level recommended, some pasteurisation treatment of the product is necessary. Even after opening in the home and storage at UK ambient temperatures these products have been found to have a good shelf life despite their lower acidity (Dakin, 1957). This, no doubt, reflects the fact that the source of the rather specialised vinegar preserve spoilage organisms is more likely to lie in the factory where conditions are selective. It also emphasises the need for the exercise of high standards of hygiene during production of both pasteurised and unpasteurised products.

Although they are still often made on the domestic scale, vinegar products can also be the subject of large-scale commercial production. This is particularly true for the developed world where the proportion of total vinegar production used in such enterprises ranges from around 25% in Japan, up to 70% in the United States (Ebner, 1982; Masai, personal communication; Nickol, 1979).

Vinegar, diluted with water, was commonly used as a refreshing, non-intoxicating drink in Roman times (Brothwell & Brothwell, 1969). Its antibiotic activity probably also proved useful with water supplies of doubtful quality. Vinegars flavoured with flowers, fruits and honey, and diluted with water were drunk in Britain from the 17th Century and blends of cider vinegar with honey and with raspberry juice are still produced and marketed in the UK today.

4.3. Medicinal Uses

Several interesting historical examples of the use of vinegar in medicine have been recorded (Conner & Allgeier, 1976). Although today the quantities used for this purpose are probably insignificant, vinegar remains a popular remedy in some circles. Cider vinegar is widely sold in health food shops and a book has been published describing the alleged beneficial effects of rice vinegar on a remarkable range of ailments (Kuroiwa, 1977). Undoubtedly, vinegar is often simply a nostrum but, in some cases, there does appear to be some basis for its use in its antibacterial and solvent properties. An example of the latter would be the consumption of 'stone swallows' in ancient China, where calcium dissolved in vinegar from the shells of the brachiopod, *Spirifer*, may have been a useful supplement to a diet from which dairy products were absent (Needham, 1971a).

5. RAW MATERIALS

Vinegar can be made from any non-toxic raw material that furnishes a juice or solution containing fermentable sugars. Ideally these should be present in levels sufficient to produce a vinegar that accords with any local standards regarding acetic acid content. With low sugar juices, however, exogenous sugar can be added or the juice concentrated by evaporation or reverse osmosis.

Theoretically 1 g of glucose will produce 0·67 g of acetic acid (see Fig. 1), but as this figure is never achieved in practice at least 2% w/v sugar is required for every 1% w/v acetic acid in the final product.

Normally a vinegar takes its name from the raw material used, frequently the same as is used to produce the indigenous alcoholic drink. Examples of this are the preponderance of malt vinegar in England and wine vinegar in continental Europe. Preference is also sometimes shown for the techniques as well as the raw materials of alcoholic beverage production. In Scotland, home of Scotch Whisky, distilled malt vinegar (distilled after acetous fermentation) accounts for around 70% of the market.

Since vinegar itself is an inexpensive commodity, its economic production requires that a relatively low-cost raw material is used. This has prompted numerous investigations into its manufacture from sources such as sub-standard fruits, seasonal agricultural surpluses and various food processing wastes or by-products. By way of illustration a selection of these is presented in Table 3.

The product known as spirit vinegar in the UK and distilled vinegar in the United States uses purified ethanol as substrate. It can be produced in higher strengths than is normally possible for other vinegars (up to around 13–15% w/v acetic acid), is widely used in the food processing industry and is probably the single most commonly produced type of vinegar. Published figures indicate that spirit vinegar production accounts for about 9% of ethanol usage (excluding potable spirits) in the USA, 5% in Japan, 5% in France and 7% in the Federal Republic of Germany (Adams & Flynn, 1982). In the UK only the alcoholic distillate from fermented mashes can be employed in spirit vinegar production but petrochemical ethanol is frequently used in the USA. To prevent ethanol abuse and to avoid the payment of duty, the alcohol is usually denatured to some special formula. This may involve mixing with finished vinegar but in the United States the formulation known as SDA 29 (1 gallon of ethyl acetate to every 100 gallons of 190° proof ethanol) is commonly used. In the course of acetification the ethyl acetate is hydrolysed and contributes to the overall yield of acetic acid (Allgeier et al., 1953).

TABLE 3
Selective Bibliography of Raw Materials Used in Vinegar Production

Raw material	Reference(s)
Apple (Cider)	Lamb & Wilson (1923), Lawyer (1928), LeFevre (1924), Hallack (1921), Nagarathnama (1964), Vandecaveye (1926)
Banana	Adams (1978, 1980), Benon (1972), Eggebrecht (1939), von Loesecke (1929)
Banana skins	Cerasari & Botteri (1953)
Cashew apples	Adams (1980), Maldonado *et al.* (1975), Nagarathnama *et al.* (1964)
Cocoa sweatings	Adams *et al.* (1982)
Coconut water	Diokno-Palo & Vilela (1967)
Coffee pulp	Freise (1931)
Dates	Das & Sarin (1936), Samiullah & Ara (1969)
Ethanol	Arnstein (1923), Wustenfeld (1923)
Honey	Fabian (1929)
Jack-fruit	Datta & Biswas (1942)
Jamun	Datta & Biswas (1942), Virmani (1950)
Kaki (persimmon)	Cauda (1924), Junior & Aquarone (1981), Kim *et al.* (1980), LeFevre (1924)
Malt	Greenshields (1975a, b), Hassack (1929), White (1970)
Mango	Adams (1980), Beerh *et al.* (1976)
Maple products	LeFevre (1924)
Milk (whey)	Bean (1928), Hadorn & Zurcher (1973), Kosikowski (1979)
Molasses	Arnstein (1923), Hansford & Martin (1943)
Oranges	Maldonado *et al.* (1975), McNary & Dougherty (1960), Poore (1920)
Palm saps	
Buri	Robillos (1978)
Coconut	Anon. (1971), Nathanael (1952a, 1952b, 1958)
Nipa	Florenzani & Balloni (1969), Paivoke *et al.* (1982), Adriano & Banzon (1933)
Palmyrah	Varma (1959)
Peach	LeFevre (1924), Wyant (1919)
Pears	LeFevre (1924)
Pineapple	Anon. (1973), Maldonado *et al.* (1975), Richardson (1967), Spurgin (1964)
Prickly pear	Juritz (1920)
Prune	Wyant (1919)
Rice	Kuroiwa (1977), Masai (1980)
Sugar cane juice	Datta & Biswas (1942)
Sweet potatoes	Tsukahara & Nakamura (1946, 1950)
Tamarind	Maldonado *et al.* (1975)
Tea	DeSilva & Saravanapavan (1968)
Tomato	Wyant (1919)
Watermelon	Khattak *et al.* (1965a, b)
Wine	Hoffman (1926), Llaguno (1971)

In most cases the raw material used in vinegar production contains sufficient nutrients to support the growth and metabolism of acetic acid bacteria. In spirit vinegar production, however, some nutrient supplementation is necessary. Many vinegar breweries have their own particular recipes for such supplements but normally they consist of glucose, ammonium nitrogen, inorganic phosphate, sulphur, calcium, magnesium and some source of vitamins and growth factors such as yeast extract. Proprietary brands of nutrient mixtures are marketed under trade names such as Acetozym (Frings, W. Germany) and Aceto-pep (Industrial Alcohol Co., USA). One published formulation developed at the United States Industrial Chemical Company replaces the complex natural source of vitamins with calcium pantothenate (Beaman, 1969).

6. THE PRODUCTION OF VINEGAR STOCK

Originally the alcoholic stock used by vinegar breweries was failed batches from the production of alcoholic beverages. With improvements in the understanding of the process of fermentation failures became less frequent so that the vinegar brewer had to resort to producing his own alcoholic stock. Understandably, therefore, there are many similarities between the processes used in both industries.

6.1. Raw Materials Preparation

Procedures for the preparation of a sugar solution for alcoholic fermentation depend upon the nature of the raw material.

Substrates with a low sugar content have been used only occasionally because of the difficulties associated with storage and the need to concentrate the sugars. However, the technique of reverse osmosis has been claimed to offer cost savings over conventional concentration techniques and this may lead to the more widespread exploitation of materials such as whey (Kearsley, 1974; Philliskirk & Yates, 1978).

Products with a high fermentable sugar content such as molasses, corn syrup and honey must first be diluted with water to an appropriate strength (usually 10–15 % w/v sugar). To reduce the risks of infection the medium may then be acidified to pH 4·5–5·0 with sulphuric acid and pasteurised. In some cases yeast nutrient in the form of ammonium sulphate is added.

The extraction of juice from most fruits (including apples and grapes) involves the chopping or crushing of the fruit followed by pressing. Preparations of pectinolytic enzymes may be added to the crushed material since the partial degradation of fruit pectin often facilitates pressing and improves the juice yield (Rombouts & Pilnik, 1980). In a method for the preparation of banana vinegar, pectinolytic enzymes are added to a slurry of the ripe pulp but the separation of the liquid is deferred until after the alcoholic fermentation is complete, as in rice vinegar production (Adams, 1978).

Starchy materials such as the cereal grains must be processed to convert the starch into fermentable sugars. This can be done by acid hydrolysis or by the use of starch-degrading enzymes, either in the form of malted grain or as preparations produced using micro-organisms. In the case of malt vinegar in the UK, only malted barley is used as the saccharifying agent, although 30 % or more unmalted cereal may be added as an adjunct. These are milled together before mashing with hot water in a false-bottomed vessel known as a mash tun. Usually what is known as an infusion mashing system is used where the process is carried out at a single, uniform temperature of 65 °C. During this process 90–95 % of the malt starch is solubilised along with about 35–40 % of the malt protein (Palmer, 1980). The liquid drawn off from the bottom of the mash tun at the end of mashing is known as sweet wort. In the case of beer brewing this would then be boiled with hops, thus inactivating any residual amylolytic activity. Hop flavour is not a requirement in malt vinegar so the sweet wort is not boiled and the degradation of dextrins into fermentable sugars continues through into the alcoholic fermentation stage. An outline of the complete process for malt vinegar production is presented in Fig. 2.

The mould *Aspergillus oryzae* is grown on steamed rice in Japan to produce *koji*, the source of amylolytic enzymes in rice vinegar production. In the final mash prepared for alcoholic fermentation the *koji* is mixed with steamed rice in a ratio of about 1 to 3. Unlike the malt vinegar process, the mash is not filtered prior to fermentation and its high solids content is thought to be one of the factors responsible for the alcohol concentrations achieved. Other moulds, notably *Rhizopus* and *Mucor* spp., are used as saccharifying agents in China.

Commercially produced concentrates of the microbial amylases, α-amylase and amyloglucosidase are now widely used in industrial starch conversion processes, including the production of much of the grain ethanol used for spirit vinegar.

6.2. Alcoholic Fermentation

Normally the yeast used in alcoholic fermentation is a strain of the species *Saccharomyces cerevisiae*, although the fission yeast *Schizosaccharomyces*

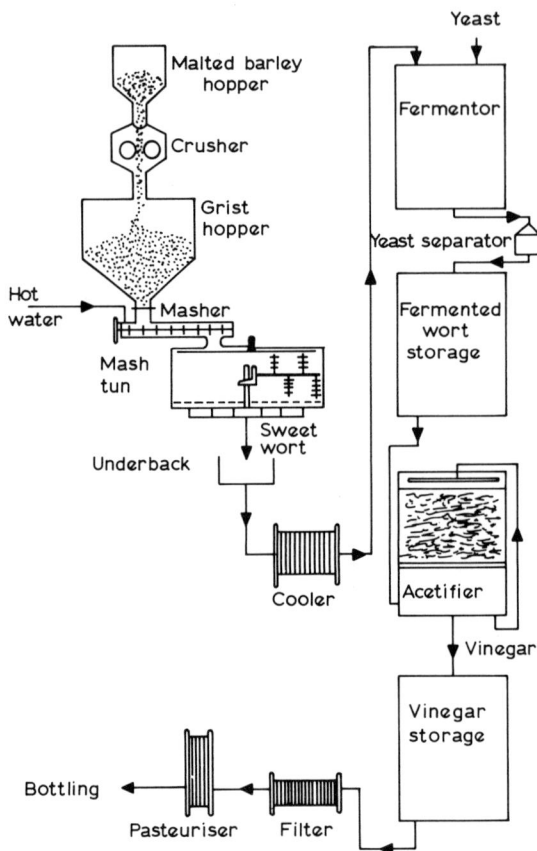

Fig. 2. An outline of malt vinegar production.

pombe has been associated with some molasses fermentations in the Caribbean. When whey is the substrate, a lactose fermenting yeast such as *Kluyveromyces fragilis* or *Candida pseudotropicalis* must be used.

The transformation of a hexose by *S. cerevisiae* can be represented chemically by the Gay–Lussac equation:

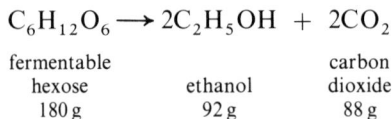

$$C_6H_{12}O_6 \longrightarrow 2C_2H_5OH + 2CO_2$$

fermentable hexose	ethanol	carbon dioxide
180 g	92 g	88 g

Since the catabolism of sugar provides the yeast with a source of biosynthetic intermediates as well as energy, not all the sugar is converted to ethanol. Some is diverted to the production of yeast cell biomass, glycerol and succinic acid. This leads to a decrease in ethanol yield: a more realistic theoretical yield would be 95 %, and a good practical yield 90 % of the figure indicated by the equation.

The fermentations in vinegar production are less susceptible to microbial contamination than many other industrial fermentations. The factors responsible for this were outlined on page 2. It is, therefore, possible to carry out the alcoholic fermentation in relatively simple vessels such as open vats of wood or concrete, or earthenware pots. Although elaborate procedures to preserve sterility are unnecessary, alcoholic fermentations are rarely free from some level of contamination which can become a problem unless adequate levels of hygiene and containment are observed. In particular, the alcoholic and acetous fermentation stages should be physically well removed from one another. Premature acetification can cause serious losses by inhibiting the yeast and terminating the alcoholic fermentation while substantial quantities of sugar still remain unfermented.

Several different techniques of yeast inoculation are used. In the fermentation of palm saps the yeasts are initially introduced from the environment, but in subsequent batches the collection vessels serve as the primary source of the inoculum (Child, 1964). To collect a sweet, unfermented sap or toddy the vessels used are thoroughly cleaned or the inside surfaces sterilised by inverting the collection pots over an open fire. A similar 'spontaneous' fermentation occurs in the production of cocoa sweatings (Adams *et al.*, 1982).

To overcome the sometimes unreliable character of such natural fermentations, most vinegar breweries use a large inoculum of active yeast either grown up in-house from a pure slope culture or bought in as active dried or pressed yeast. In the past some malt vinegar breweries used spent brewer's yeast but this practice has been largely discontinued because of the large numbers of dead cells and bacterial contaminants in these inocula.

It is possible to run the alcoholic fermentation without any form of temperature control, particularly when small vessels are used and the ambient temperature is suitable. In many cases though, the fermenting mash is maintained at around 30 °C by cooling coils, an external heat exchanger or by simply spraying water on the outside of the fermentation vessels. Progress of the fermentation can be monitored visually by observing the rate of carbon dioxide evolution, but more reliably by determining the specific gravity or alcohol content of the mash. The absence of sterility in the uninoculated wort has meant that the commercial application of continuous culture techniques to vinegar stock brewing has not proved practicable, so that batch fermentation remains the norm. The time for a fermentation to go to completion is variable but is normally of the order of 48–72 h. When fermentation is complete the stock may be centrifuged to remove yeast cells and mixed with a proportion of raw vinegar before being transferred to storage.

7. ACETIFICATION

Acetification is the oxidation of ethanol by bacteria to produce acetic acid and water. The process can be represented chemically by:

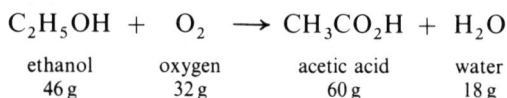

$$C_2H_5OH + O_2 \longrightarrow CH_3CO_2H + H_2O$$

ethanol	oxygen	acetic acid	water
46 g	32 g	60 g	18 g

From the stoichiometry of the equation it is apparent that 1 litre of ethanol should produce 1·036 kg of acetic acid and 0·313 kg of water. The slight increase in volume that occurs during fermentation, in the range of 1–3 % for the ethanol concentrations generally used, means that approximately 1 % v/v of ethanol should produce 1 % w/v of acetic acid. This relationship, which holds best at ethanol concentrations around 9·2 % v/v, is used as the basis for forecasting the eventual acidity of the vinegar and calculating the fermentation yield. It implies that, in the absence of losses due to evaporation and over-oxidation, the sum of the concentrations of ethanol (% v/v) and acetic acid (% w/v), known as the total concentration or GK (Ger. *Gesammte Konzentration*), should remain constant throughout acetification. The GK yield is the GK of the final vinegar expressed as a percentage of the original vinegar stock GK.

An alternative procedure is the calculation of the acid yield which is the change in acid concentration during fermentation expressed as a percentage of the original alcohol content of the vinegar stock (Hromatka & Ebner, 1959). This is always lower than the GK yield since it takes no account of residual alcohol in the vinegar.

The oxidation of ethanol to acetic acid is an exothermic reaction producing around 8·4 MJ for every litre of ethanol oxidised. The heat output in acetification is slightly lower than this since allowance should be made for the biomass produced and its heat of combustion (approximately 23 MJ/kg dry weight) (Pirt, 1978). This correction factor will vary depending on the fermentation technique and substrate used.

Also apparent from the equation is the need for oxygen, supplied as air. Since it is only sparingly soluble in aqueous media (8·1 mg/litre in water at 25 °C, and less as the temperature and solute content increase), oxygen availability is often the rate limiting factor in acetification. The different approaches to this problem of oxygen mass transfer are one of the distinguishing features of the various techniques used.

7.1. The Acetic Acid Bacteria

The taxonomic history of the bacteria responsible for acetification is complex, and much of it is of little but academic interest to the vinegar brewer since pure cultures are not widely employed in the industry. The use of mixed or, at least, undefined cultures is probably not essential, it is simply that the process can be operated quite satisfactorily without strict and costly sterility controls. Shimwell (1954) has, however, used a single species (*Acetobacter mesoxydans*), in pure culture, to satisfy the 4 criteria of Henle and Koch and establish a causal relationship between the organism and acetification.

The fact that the film formed on acetifying wine was a living organism was established by Persoon (1822) who gave it the name *Mycoderma* (viscous film). Kutzing (1837) realised the relationship between the film and the process of acetification but identified the organism as *Ulvina aceti:* an alga. Acetification also became part of the controversy between the vitalists and the chemists such as Berzelius and Liebig who maintained that the process was purely chemical, analogous to the oxidation of ethanol by platinum black. It was the experiments of Pasteur on the Orleans process that finally established the relationship between the microbial film, oxygen and acetification, although he failed to recognise its bacterial nature, describing it as 'a little plant, a microscopic fungus: the *Mycoderma aceti*' (Vallery-Radot, 1937). He presented his results in a lecture given in Orleans in 1867 at the request of the Mayor and the President of the Chamber of Commerce. 'A great many vinegar manufacturers, some doctors, apothecaries, professors, students, even ladies (*sic*)', came to hear him (Vallery-Radot, 1937). The results were also published as his 'Etudes sur la vinaigre' (1868).

Hansen isolated three bacterial species from vinegar which he named *Bacterium aceti, B. pasteurianum* and *B. kutzingianum* while Brown characterised the cellulose forming species *Bacterium xylinum* (Jorgensen, 1900). In 1900 Beijerinck proposed that the generic name *Acetobacter* be given to these species.

Asai (1968) gives a comprehensive account of the taxonomic history of acetic acid bacteria, including his proposal in 1935 to divide the genus *Acetobacter* into two, *Acetobacter* and a new genus *Gluconobacter*. This was based on a study that included isolates from fruits as well as those from the usual source, vinegar. Among the characteristics of the *Gluconobacter* were the ability to produce large amounts of gluconic acid from glucose, inability to form films in liquid media and poor growth in ethanol-containing substrates such as saké and beer.

A similar division, but this time based on morphology, was proposed by Leifson (1954). Those with peritrichous flagella (and non-flagellated species with similar physiology) retained the name *Acetobacter*. Those with polar flagella (and non-flagellated species with similar physiology) were placed in a new genus *Acetomonas*. Species of the latter also displayed the characteristics ascribed to *Gluconobacter* spp. by Asai.

Further support for the existence of two types of acetic acid bacteria came from work on their nutrition and biochemistry by Rainbow and co-workers (Rainbow & Mitson, 1953; Brown & Rainbow, 1956; Rainbow, 1961). The *Acetobacter* were classed as being lactaphilic in their nutrition. They grow well on lactate, in many cases with ammonium salts as the sole nitrogen source, but relatively poorly on glucose. Only one of the lactaphilic species examined required exogenous growth factors. Glycophilic acetic acid bacteria (*Acetomonas/Gluconobacter*) were nutritionally more fastidious. They grow well on glucose and certain sugar alcohols but not on lactate. They require preformed amino acids in synthetic media as well as the growth factors nicotinic acid, pantothenate and sometimes *p*-amino benzoate.

In the latest edition of the authoritative *Bergey's Manual* two genera of acetic acid bacteria are described, *Acetobacter* and *Gluconobacter* (De Ley & Frateur, 1974a, b). The principal characteristics of these are presented in Table 4. The article by Carr & Passmore (1979) is a particularly valuable supplement to *Bergey* on this subject since it is less ambiguous in its description of some characteristics and gives practical details of the various tests.

A useful summary of techniques for the maintenance and purification of cultures for practical vinegar production is given in the review by Nickol (1979).

As indicated in Fig. 1, the oxidation of ethanol proceeds via the intermediate aldehyde. The basic pathway of ethanol oxidation was demonstrated very early on by trapping the intermediate acetaldehyde with sulphite (Neuberg & Nord, 1919). Exogenous NAD was shown to stimulate ethanol oxidation by *Acetobacter suboxydans* (Lutwak-Mann, 1938), and later an NAD-dependent alcohol dehydrogenase was isolated from the same species (King & Cheldelin, 1954). Both NAD and NADP could act as co-enzyme for the acetaldehyde dehydrogenase isolated from the same source, although the latter displayed four times the activity in the most highly purified preparations obtained (King & Cheldelin, 1956). Nakayama (1959) investigated the oxidation of ethanol by a strain of *Acetobacter* used in commercial vinegar production in Japan. The organism was described as being similar, but not identical, to *Acetobacter suboxydans* and the characteristics mentioned would also fit *Acetobacter aceti* subsp. *orleanensis* (see Table 4). The enzymes responsible for acetic acid production were found to be tightly bound to cell fragments and strongly inhibited by cyanide and carbon monoxide, suggesting that a cytochrome oxidase operated as the terminal oxidase. Spectrophotometry showed that the cytochromes present in the cells were immediately reduced by an addition of ethanol or acetaldehyde. Since the cyanide inhibition was not removed by the addition of an alternative electron acceptor such as methylene blue, Nakayama postulated that the whole system was acting as a tightly organised multi-enzyme complex.

In subsequent papers the same author described the solubilisation, purification and the properties of an NADP-dependent aldehyde de-hydrogenase (Nakayama, 1960), a co-enzyme independent aldehyde dehydrogenase (Nakayama, 1961a), and a new type of alcohol dehydro-genase—cytochrome 553 reductase (Nakayama, 1961b).

As a result of this work, Nakayama proposed the scheme outlined in Fig. 3. Ethanol is oxidised by the cytochrome 553-reductase (E_1). The acetaldehyde produced is then oxidised to acetate by either E_2 or E_3. The former transfers the liberated electrons to cytochrome 553 which is, in turn, oxidised by cytochrome oxidase, while E_3 generates NADPH. The reduced NADP was thought to inhibit further oxidation of the acetic acid through the TCA cycle by upsetting the cell's NADPH–NADH equilibrium.

More recently, Ameyama & Adachi (1982a, b) have described the isolation and properties of two enzymes similar to E_1 and E_2 from *Acetobacter aceti* IFO 3284. Both are localised on the outer surface of the cytoplasmic membrane with substrate oxidation linked to the organism's respiratory chain. The alcohol dehydrogenase (MW 149 000) is composed of four sub-units, the largest two being the dehydrogenase and a cytochrome c containing component. Like Nakayama's E_1, it is not specific for ethanol and will oxidise several other primary alcohols. It also has a similar K_m, $1·6 \times 10^{-3}$ M (E_1 $2·1 \times 10^{-3}$ M) and pH optimum (around 4). Spectroscopic data suggest the presence of pyrroloquinoline quinone (PQQ) as a prosthetic group.

The aldehyde dehydrogenase (Ameyama & Adachi, 1982b) resembles

TABLE 4

Characteristics of the Acetic Acid Bacteria (based on tables in Bergey's Manual, see De Ley & Frateur, 1974a, b)

	Acetobacter	Gluconobacter
Gram stain	−	−
Morphology	Ellipsoidal to rod-shaped Peritrichous flagella or none	Ellipsoidal to rod-shaped Polar flagella or none
Growth at pH 4·5	+	+
Oxidn of ethanol to acetic acid	+	+
Acetate to CO_2	+	−
Lactate to CO_2	+	−
Krebs cycle	+	−
Catalase	+	+

	A. aceti				A. pasteurianus					A. peroxydans	G. oxydans
Sub-species:*	a	b	c	d	a	b	c	d	e		
Ketogenesis in glycerol	+	+	+	+	+	+	+	+	−	−	+

Formation of:	A. aceti				A. pasteurianus				
	a. aceti	b. orleanensis	c. xylinum	d. liquefaciens	a. pasteurianus	b. lovaniensis	c. astunensis	d. ascendens	e. paradoxus
5-ketogluconate	(+)	(+)	(+)	(+)	-	-	-	-	+
2-ketogluconate	(+)	(+)	(+)	(+)	d	-	-	-	+
Gluconate	+	+	+	+	(+)	+	-	-	+
Growth on ethanol/ammonium salts	+	-	(-)	+	+	+	-	+	-
Produces cellulose	-	-	+	-	+	+	-	-	-
Produces gamma-pyrones	-	-	+	-	-	-	-	-	-
Produces brown pigment	-	-	-	+	-	-	-	-	+
G+C moles %	59-65	60-61	62-63	64	55-62	62	55-56	61-64	60-64

Key to symbols: +, >90% positive; -, >90% negative; d, 11–89% positive (among the isolates tested). ( ), delayed reaction.

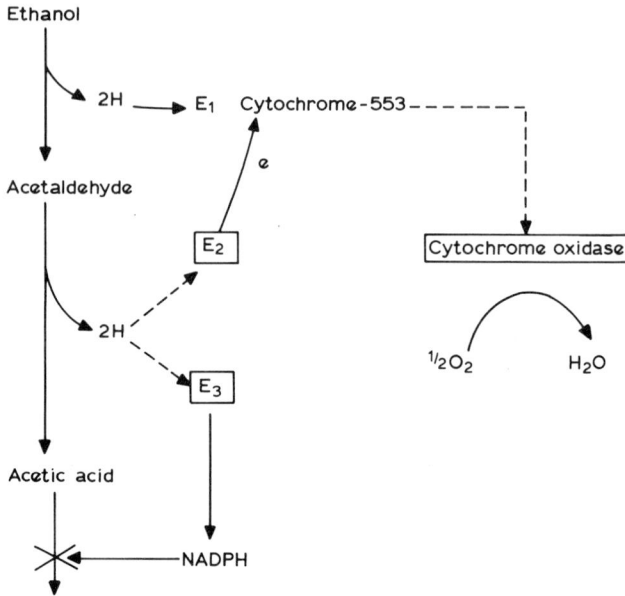

Fig. 3. Nakayama's scheme for ethanol oxidation.

Nakayama's E_2 in so far as it does not require NAD or NADP as an electron acceptor and displays a broad substrate specificity for aliphatic aldehydes. The enzyme (MW 137 000) was shown to dissociate into 3 components, the largest two being the dehydrogenase and cytochrome c containing units. It did not, however, display the same affinity for acetaldehyde as E_2 (K_m 2.9×10^{-3} M as compared with 8.7×10^{-5} M for E_2).

Some evidence has been presented to suggest that the ethanol oxidising capacity and acetic acid resistance may be linked to a plasmid (Ohmori *et al.*, 1982). However, the only *Acetobacter* plasmid isolated to date, pTA 5001, seems to have no connection with these properties.

7.2. Surface Culture

The growth of acetic acid bacteria on an alcoholic liquid in an open vessel will produce a surface film of bacteria which will convert stock into vinegar.

In the procedure described as the 'let-alone' process by Cruess (1958) the vinegar stock, in partially filled barrels or similar vessels, is left to acetify spontaneously. The process is operated batchwise and so the bacterial film has to be reformed each time, wastefully consuming substrate. If relatively clean vessels are used and chance environmental contamination is relied upon for the inoculum then the process can be particularly slow and inefficient.

Some improvement is possible through the use of a good inoculum of *Acetobacter*. The vessels used for acetification can themselves act as the source of an inoculum as in the production of Nipa palm sap vinegar in the Philippines. The palm sap, which has undergone a spontaneous alcoholic fermentation in the bamboo collection vessels, is transferred to large earthenware jars called *tapayan*, covered with wooden boards and set aside to acetify, usually for about 3 weeks (Adriano & Banzon, 1933). Acetic acid bacteria adhering to the inside of the vessel and suspended in residual vinegar remaining from previous batches act as the inoculum. Since there is no chemical monitoring of the progress of fermentation, acetification is often incomplete with substantial quantities of ethanol remaining in the product (Gibbs, 1911; Florenzani & Balloni, 1969). Alternatively, a large inoculum of *Acetobacter* may be added in the form of unpasteurised 'mother' vinegar. This is a common practice in household production and is used commercially in Pakistan (Wahid & Chughtai, 1969) and, in particular, in Japan where about 60–70 % of vinegar production is by surface culture techniques (Masai, personal communication).

The delays and losses which result from the need to re-establish an active surface film are overcome in the semi-continuous technique known as the Orleans process. Partially filled casks are allowed to acetify until the acidity reaches an appropriate level, determined by the initial alcohol concentration or GK. At this stage a proportion of the vinegar is removed and replaced with fresh vinegar stock and the process restarted. Casks are usually fitted with a pipe which passes through the top of the barrel and the liquid to rest on the bottom (see Fig. 4). This enables fresh stock to be added to the vessel without disturbing the film. Holes, often covered with muslin to prevent insects entering, are drilled above the liquid level to allow air circulation.

The Orleans process, applied to the production of Nipa palm vinegar in Papua New Guinea, has largely eliminated the problems associated with this product in the Philippines (Paivoke *et al.*, 1982). It has also formed the basis of methods recommended in the United States for small-scale production of vinegar in the home and on the farm (Wyant, 1919; Lamb & Wilson, 1923; LeFevre, 1924).

Only a small proportion of the world's vinegar is produced by this method today, although it is reputed to give the finest quality vinegars (Vaughn, 1942; Conner & Allgeier, 1976). A detailed account of how this

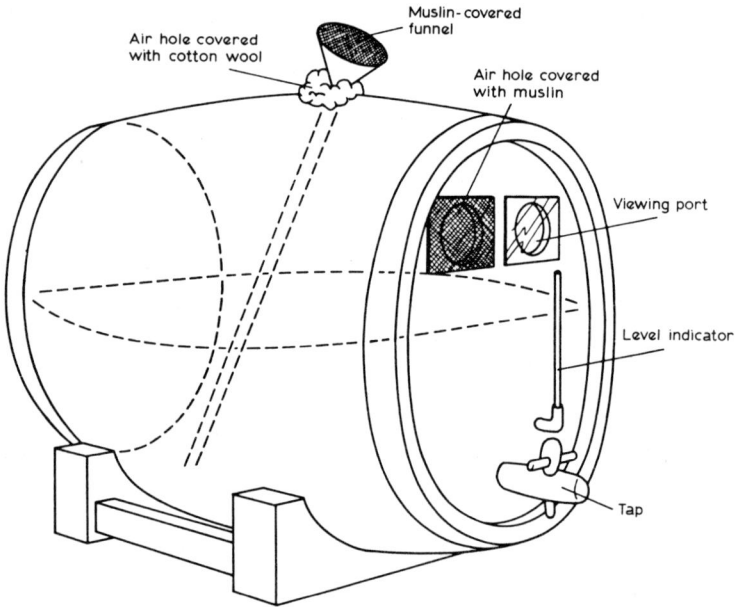

Fig. 4. Acetification by the Orleans process. (Source: Adams, 1980. © Crown Copyright, 1980.)

process was operated on a large scale in the 19th Century is provided by Muspratt (1877). The casks used, known as 'mothers', each holding 50–100 gallons, would rest on strong wooden frames, supported by pillars of wood or stone 18 in. in height. Several such casks were arranged in rows, and when acetification was carried out in the open air, 8, 10, 15 or 20 such ranks constituted a vinegar field. In the Orleans region of France, from where the process derives its name, casks were often stacked in warmed cellars. To start a new 'mother' the cask was filled $\frac{1}{3}$ full with strong vinegar and $2\frac{1}{2}$ gallons of wine were added at 8 day intervals to allow for acetification. When the cask was more than half full, $\frac{1}{3}$ of its content were siphoned off and the cask was recharged as before. At temperatures in the range of 24–27 °C a cask would usually work off double its contents of vinegar annually. It would last 25 years, requiring emptying and cleaning every 6–8 years.

The use of shallow trays for surface acetification is not a new idea (see, for example, Hoeppner, 1866). In Japan, however, their use has been revived in various continuous surface acetification techniques (Masai, 1980).

Acetifying liquid is passed at a constant rate through a series of trays in sequence using methods that minimise disturbance to the bacterial film. Conversion rates intermediate between those of the quick vinegar process and submerged acetification are claimed for these procedures (Kewpie Jozo Kabushiki Kaisha, 1973).

Generally, the technique of surface culture is far slower than the other techniques of acetification, although considerably faster than is sometimes claimed. Using the Orleans process a vessel can produce about $\frac{1}{2}$ its volume of vinegar each month with GK yields of up to 94 % or more (Desrosier & Desrosier, 1977; Adams, 1978). The technique uses simple, relatively low-cost equipment and can be operated on a wide range of scales simply by varying the size or number of acetifying vessels. A vinegar brewery in Turkey, visited by the author, has 96 casks with working volumes of 3–5 tonnes and a production capacity of 5 tonnes of vinegar per day (see Fig. 5). Because the rate of acetification is slow, the use of cooling water is unnecessary and the power requirement is minimal. Surface culture techniques do, however, have a substantially larger requirement for land and personnel than other methods. This is broadly in line with the results of a study conducted on the relative costs of surface and submerged culture as applied to the production of citric acid (Messing & Schmitz, 1976; Schierholt, 1976). In areas where labour and land costs are relatively low,

Fig. 5. A vinegar brewery in Turkey using the Orleans process.

for instance in many developing countries, surface acetification by methods akin to the Orleans process may still have an important role to play.

7.3. The Quick Vinegar Process

The quick vinegar process achieves faster rates of acetification than surface culture techniques by increasing the area of bacterial film and by improved oxygenation of the stock. Like the Orleans process, much of the active biomass is retained in the fermenter between runs thus reducing the lag phase. The fermenter, more commonly known as a generator, is a fixed bed microbial film reactor in which a film of bacteria grows on an inert support medium packed in a false-bottomed tower. The acetifying wash is trickled down over the support against a counter current of air which is either pumped up the tower, or drawn up by the heat of reaction within it. The basic features of the quick vinegar generator are illustrated in Fig. 6.

The earliest known record of this type of process cited by Mitchell (1926), occurs in the *Philosophical Transactions of the Royal Society* for 1670 (**5**, 2002), entitled 'The way of making vinegar in France'. Two large casks each with a false bottom were packed with vine twigs and rape (the foot stalks of grapes and light vine branches). One vessel was filled with wine while the other was only half-filled. Each day half the contents of the full vessel were removed via a stop-cock and added to the half-full barrel. After a few days the onset of acetification was signalled by a rise in temperature in the half-full vessel. The time taken for acetification was variable. During summer, it was completed in about 15 days and more frequent transfers between casks were often necessary in order to control the rise in temperature. In the cooler winter months, however, it took considerably longer. This process is essentially the same as that described by, and often credited to, the Dutch chemist and physician Boerhaave some 60 years later.

Between 1820 and 1830 several major improvements to the process were described and introduced. Schutzenbach, in 1823, used a wooden vat instead of the usual cask and fitted it with means for the repeated distribution of stock over the packing material (Mitchell, 1926). In 1824 a British patent was issued to Ham describing all the principal features of the quick vinegar process as applied today. It included recirculating of the acetifying stock, its distribution over the packing by means of a sparge arm, control of the temperature and forced aeration of the fermenter (Ham, 1824). Numerous minor modifications and variations of this basic process were tried in subsequent years, but, as Bitting points out in his review of US patents covering vinegar production, not all have genuinely sought to improve the procedure. Many were obviously impractical, and others simply intended

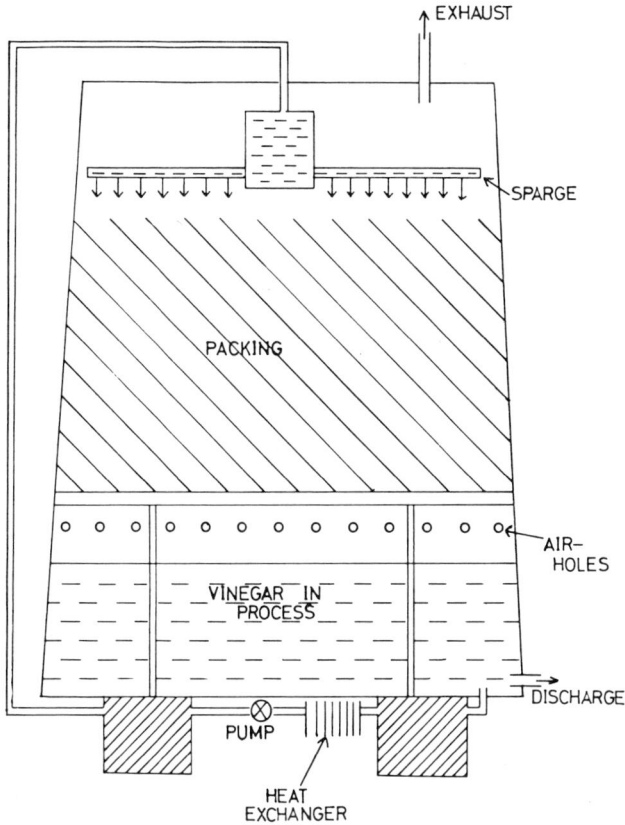

Fig. 6. The quick vinegar process.

to evade existing patents and achieve the same result by a slightly different means (Bitting, 1929). In addition to the review by Bitting, those interested in this particular topic are referred to the works by Brannt (1890) and Mitchell (1926).

The design and construction of a simple quick vinegar generator is relatively straightforward and outline designs have been published on several occasions (Anon, 1971, 1973; Nathanael, 1958). The Frings company of the Federal Republic of Germany has for many years offered the complete unit, improving on its original model by the incorporation of additional automatic control facilities (Hansen, 1935; Lowy, 1941). Many vinegar breweries, however, assemble their own semi-automatic generators from bought-in components.

The most efficient and most commonly used method for distributing stock on to the bed of packing material is the rotating sparge arm. The tipping trough which alternately floods each side of the bed is still used in some cases (see, for example, Nathanael, 1958), but the wick distribution system developed by Wagenmann (Mitchell, 1926) has been largely abandoned.

Nowadays the forced air flow through a generator is usually carefully controlled and monitored, but in simpler generators relying on natural air flow some element of control is achieved by the opening and closing of vents. Theoretically the oxidation of 1 litre of ethanol requires about 430 litres of oxygen at 30 °C. Since oxygen comprises only about 20 % of air and its consumption by bacteria is not quantitative, at least ten times this volume of air is necessary. An air flow rate of around $0.8–0.9\,m^3\,h^{-1}$ for every cubic metre of packing is normally adequate (Nickol, 1979).

Although some control of temperature is possible through variations in the wash and air flow rates, it is usually more effectively achieved by passing the circulating wash through an external heat exchanger. In the Frings automatic generator the wash temperature is adjusted to around 28 °C in order to maintain a temperature profile through the bed increasing from around 28 °C at the top to a maximum of 35 °C at the bottom. In some UK vinegar breweries considerably higher temperatures are maintained, around 40–43 °C.

Micro-organisms generally have a great facility for adhering to surfaces, so the choice of support medium for vinegar generators is large. Usually some form of ligno-cellulosic material is used; birch twigs, vine twigs, rattan, corncobs and numerous types of wood shavings have all been mentioned in the literature. Coarse bagasse from sugar cane processing was used in vinegar production in Barbados during the 1940s (Coppin, personal communication). Wood charcoal, ceramic materials and coke have also been used on occasion. Although the performance of different packing materials does vary, availability and cost are usually the principal considerations in making a choice. Some of the factors involved in obtaining the optimum performance from packing materials other than wood shavings have been described (Allgeier et al., 1954). The productivity of a quick vinegar generator based on its packing material is usually 2–5 kg of acetic acid per m^3 of packing every 24 h.

Eventually packing becomes compressed and tends to clog, particularly if excessive growth of the cellulose producing species, Acetobacter xylinum, occurs. Replacement of packing material in a generator can be a labour intensive and unpleasant task, particularly in large generators, but the frequency with which it is required is low. Stock poor in nutrients such as that used in spirit vinegar production restricts microbial growth and allows the same packing to be used continuously for many years. With more nutritious media, bacterial growth can be restricted by working at high temperatures and high GK values.

Normally the quick vinegar process is operated semi-continuously so that by adding alcoholic stock to finished vinegar the ethanol concentration is not so high as to retard acetification (less than 4–5 %). Acetification is terminated while around 0·3 % ethanol remains in the wash. It is sometimes claimed that this is to allow esterification to take place during storage and improve vinegar aroma. A more important reason, however, is the avoidance of over-oxidation when, in the absence of ethanol, *Acetobacter* spp. oxidise acetic acid to carbon dioxide and water causing a loss of acidity. This pathway is repressed by the presence of ethanol (Shimizu *et al.*, 1977) but does not appear to be readily reversible, once operating. The only remedy for excessive over-oxidation in a vinegar generator is its complete shutdown, and sterilisation.

The size of quick vinegar generators and their efficiency of operation is obviously extremely variable. In a typical, moderately large vinegar brewery a generator may contain 50–60 m^3 of packing material and have a sump or reservoir holding about 14 m^3 of acetifying stock. Depending on the degree of sophistication of the generator (and the skill of its operators) a stock with a GK of 10 and an ethanol content of 4 % should be acetified in about 4–5 days in yields of 85–95 %.

Laboratory trials of a modern variation of the quick vinegar process have been reported to give production rates of up to 10·4 g of acetic acid litre^{-1} h^{-1} (Ghommidh *et al.*, 1981, 1982a, b). Cells were immobilised on a ceramic support material, Cordierite, packed in a column, and wash and air passed up through the column by a pulsating pump. This is not, however, the basis of any commercial process, as yet.

7.4. Submerged Acetification

Aerated deep culture has been used since the late nineteenth century in the production of bakers' yeast and the amylo process (Grove, 1914; Burrows, 1979). It was, however, the development of the penicillin fermentation during the Second World War that prompted investigations into other submerged culture, aerobic processes, including vinegar production.

Several methods for submerged acetification have been described and patented, but undoubtedly the most successful has been the Acetator®, arising from the work of Hromatka and Ebner and marketed by Heinrich

Frings GmbH & Co. of Bonn (see Fig. 7) (Hromatka & Ebner, 1959). Units are supplied with capacities ranging from 750 litres of 10 % acidity vinegar per day (2500 hl p.a.) up to 12 000 litres per day (40 000 hl p.a.). Since 1954 some 350 have been sold around the world, together capable of producing about 500 million litres of 10 % acidity vinegar annually (Greenshields, 1978).

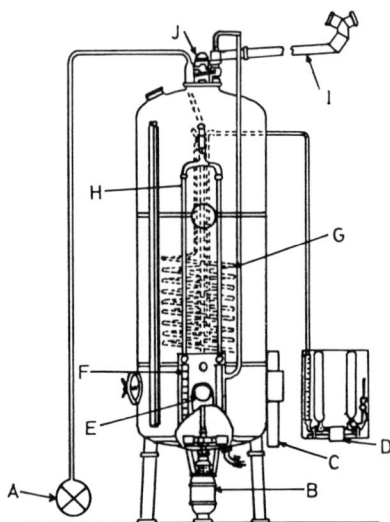

Fig. 7. The Frings Acetator (reproduced by kind permission of Heinrich Frings GmbH, Bonn). A, charging pump; B, aerator and motor; C, Alkograph; D, cooling water valve; E, thermostat controlling D; F, rotameter; G, cooling coil; H, air line; I, air exhaust line; J, defoamer.

The vessels themselves can be of stainless steel or wood, although all fittings are of stainless steel or plastic. The most important design feature of the Acetator is its self-priming aerator (Ebner *et al.*, 1967). It consists of a bottom drive, hollow turbine surrounded by a non-rotating stator. The turbine, turning at 1450–1750 rpm, draws air down a central inlet tube and releases it into the wash via a series of radially distributed holes that open against the direction of rotation. Liquid is sucked in from above and below the turbine, mixed with the air and forced outwards through the stator. The stator comprises an upper and a lower ring connected by a series of vertical plates set at an angle of about 30° to the radius. These serve to improve dispersion of air in the liquid and to direct it to all parts of the tank.

In a comparative study of the aerobic propagation of bakers' yeast, a 15 000 gallon capacity fermenter fitted with a Frings aerator had an oxygen absorption coefficient (k_La) of 1740 ml O_2 100 ml^{-1} h^{-1} atm^{-1}, whereas the k_La of a similar vessel fitted with a compressor and turbine was 1200 (Enenkel & Ebner, 1970).

A series of papers by Hromatka, Ebner and coworkers have presented the results from a detailed study of the different factors affecting submerged acetification (for a review of much of this work, see Allgeier & Hildebrandt, 1960). Foremost amongst these was the sensitivity of acetic acid bacteria to oxygen deficiency. They established that if bacteria from the quick vinegar process were held in an oxygen-deprived atmosphere for varying periods, when the process was resumed the rate of acetification depended on the length of time the bacteria had been starved of oxygen. Acetification was slightly affected if the period was short (1 h), but was almost completely suppressed by 7 h of oxygen limitation. This effect was considerably more pronounced in submerged culture. An interruption of the air supply for 1 min or longer completely stopped acetification in a wash with a GK of 11·35, and there was no significant recovery when aeration was resumed. At lower GK values though, longer interruptions of the air supply caused less damage. For instance, a 2 min pause in a wash with a GK of 4·80 produced only a 34% reduction in the subsequent rate of acetification (Hromatka *et al.*, 1951; Hromatka & Exner, 1962). If the GK was held constant, the degree of damage increased with increasing acidity. From this it would appear that oxygen starvation leads to a breakdown in the mechanism of acid resistance in the bacteria, possibly through a rapid depletion of intracellular ATP pools required to prevent acetic acid penetrating the cell (Ebner, 1982).

Aeration accounts for most of the Acetator's power consumption which ranges from 1·2 to 20·0 kWh h^{-1} depending on the model. A reliable power supply is, therefore, essential and where this is not available an auxiliary generator is necessary.

The fermentation is usually run semi-continuously, each run taking 24–48 h. The temperature is maintained at around 30 °C by cooling coils which circulate water at a rate of 500–8000 litres h^{-1}. Cooling towers or a refrigeration plant are sometimes included to enable the cooling water to be recycled.

To avoid over-oxidation a run is terminated when the wash contains 0·1–0·3% v/v alcohol. The wash is analysed periodically and with experience, the time for discharging the vinegar can be predicted with some accuracy. To eliminate any problems that may arise from this procedure and to facilitate automatic control, the Frings company also produce an instrument for the continuous, automatic monitoring of ethanol content. The Alkograph is based on the ebullioscopic method for ethanol determination. The boiling point of the wash from the fermenter is compared with that of the wash freed from alcohol by distillation. The difference is proportional to the ethanol content. In the continuous model wash flows at about 9 ml/min through a preheating vessel into two boiling vessels connected in series. The first is fitted with a reflux condenser so the temperature of the wash is maintained at its boiling point. In the second vessel, the ethanol is distilled off and the difference between the boiling points is measured by a thermocouple and displayed on a recorder. Adjustable contacts are fitted to allow automatic process control by the Alkograph (Ebner & Enenkel, 1969).

At the end of fermentation up to half of the fermenter's contents are pumped out and replaced with fresh vinegar stock. This is introduced into the fermenter just above the aerator so that the stock is swiftly and efficiently mixed with the rest of the vessel's contents.

Foam resulting from the presence of surfactant biomolecules is a perennial problem in submerged aerobic fermentations. It can lead to liquid losses, the blockage of air outlets, increased risk of infection and a decrease in oxygen transfer rates. Foaming can be controlled by the addition of antifoam chemicals such as silicones, but these increase the size of air bubbles and thereby decrease the oxygen transfer rate. Various mechanical defoamers have been designed (see, for example, Solomons, 1969), including one for use in Acetators (Ebner *et al.*, 1967). The unit is fitted at the top of the Acetator and as foam builds up it is forced into a rotor chamber where centrifugal force breaks the foam and separates it into liquid and gas. The liquid and any unbroken foam is pumped back into the tank down a return pipe and the gas escapes through a vent stack. The belt-driven rotor runs at 1000–1450 rpm with an average power consumption of 0·01–0·04 kWh m^{-3} of air in foam.

Several factors have to be balanced when choosing between the quick vinegar process and submerged acetification. The Acetator operates faster than the quick vinegar process, generally with a higher conversion efficiency (around 94% on average). The plant is relatively simple to operate and control, requires less labour and occupies about half the area of an equivalent capacity quick vinegar factory. It does, however, have a higher capital cost, it consumes cooling water and power at a faster rate and the process is particularly susceptible to power failures. The vinegar produced by submerged culture is also very cloudy and requires some fining process to clarify it.

Several other processes for submerged acetification have been used. The Yeoman's Cavitator was developed by Meyer and manufactured by the Yeoman Brothers Company of Illinois (Mayer, 1963). Circulation of the fermenter contents is achieved by the use of a central draught tube down which the acetifying wash cascades. A top-drive, hollow turbine also passes down the draught tube and its rotation mixes air with the wash, forcing it out to the sides of the vessel, thus maintaining circulation. This plant is no longer produced although some are still operational in the USA and Japan (Conner & Allgeier, 1976; Nickol, 1979).

The Bourgeois process was supplied by the Swiss firm Bourgeois Freres & Cie and is used in Spain and Italy (Ebner, 1982; Nickol, 1979). It uses two fermenting vessels, one supplying inoculum to the other, and a compressor for aeration. Acetification is allowed to proceed until all the ethanol is removed and some ethanol is added to the final vinegar to restore its aroma. The process is slow and suited only for low acidity vinegars (Nickol, 1979).

The Fardon process (White, 1970) achieves aeration by withdrawing wash from the fermenter and returning it via a Venturi nozzle. The process has been described as having a low productivity and high energy consumption, although several units are still operating in South Africa (Ebner, 1982).

The use of aerated tower fermenters has received considerable attention (Shimwell, 1955; Simonin & Bernard, 1958; Greenshields, 1972) but has had only very limited commercial application.

The Vinegator is a submerged culture fermenter produced by the Swiss company Chemap. It uses a self-aspirating stirrer coupled with an additional air supply from a compressor. The latter is controlled by a polarographic oxygen electrode and is switched on when the dissolved oxygen tension falls below a set value. It is claimed that this produces a more efficient use of energy. The fermenter is also fitted with a mechanical foam breaker (Muller, 1978).

8.   PROCESSING OF VINEGAR

After acetification, vinegar is usually matured in full, closed vats of wood or stainless steel for periods of up to a year. During this time it develops its characteristic flavour and aroma and some settlement of unstable colloids takes place.

Raw vinegar is normally cloudy with suspended bacteria and other particles, the degree of turbidity depending on the process used. It is generally less of a problem with Orleans process vinegars which undergo some settlement during acetification and can often be bottled without any further treatment. Vinegars from the quick vinegar process are usually clarified by passage through a plate and frame filter press using a diatomaceous earth filter aid. In submerged acetification, all the active biomass is suspended in the vinegar and a preliminary fining treatment is necessary. Isinglass, casein, gelatin with tannin can all be effective, but the most commonly used fining agent is bentonite clay (O'Neal & Cruess, 1951; Cruess, 1958). It is added as a suspension to the vinegar at a rate of about 5 kg/10 000 litres of vinegar, mixed thoroughly in and left to settle. The clear supernatant is then racked or filtered off. A procedure for clarifying vinegar by ultrafiltration has been patented (Ebner & Enenkel, 1976).

An occasional, non-bacterial contributor to vinegar cloudiness is the vinegar eel, *Anguillula aceti*. This harmless nematode worm is a common inhabitant of quick vinegar generators and Orleans process casks but occurs less frequently in submerged acetification. Readily removed by pasteurisation and filtration, it is generally regarded as having no effect on acetification, although some workers have claimed that it improves the quick vinegar process by scavenging surplus bacterial growth (Zalkan & Fabian, 1953). Higher standards of factory hygiene have meant that it is no longer the ubiquitous inhabitant of vinegar it once was. In the 17th century it was a common belief that the sourness of vinegar was due to the eels pricking the tongue with their tails! (Mitchell, 1926).

A haze or precipitate may form in vinegars that have been in contact with non-acid-resistant materials. This is usually due to the formation of iron and copper casses which spoil the appearance of the vinegar and make it unsuitable for use in pickling. The high levels of metal ions present may also have a deleterious effect on taste (Vaughn, 1954). The obvious remedy is the use of correct grades of material for plant and equipment, but where it does occur the problem can be alleviated by precipitation of the iron and copper with tannin (Campbell, 1928) or by very carefully controlled treatment with potassium ferrocyanide or a special preparation such as Cufex (Scott Laboratories Inc.) (Amerine *et al.*, 1980).

The fact that bacterial growth and turbidity in bottled vinegar can be prevented by a heat treatment was first noted by Scheele two hundred years ago (Partington, 1962). Like many gram negative organisms, acetic acid bacteria are not particularly heat resistant. Bringing the temperature of the vinegar to 60 °C for a few minutes is sufficient to eliminate the numbers normally encountered. The product is either hot-filled into bottles after treatment or, as in Scheele's original procedure, pasteurised in the bottle.

As an alternative to pasteurisation a chemical preservative such as sulphur dioxide may be used. In the UK cider and wine vinegar may contain up to 200 ppm of SO_2 but for all other types of vinegar 70 ppm is the maximum permitted level.

There is considerable advantage in producing a vinegar containing high levels of acetic acid. It reduces costs of transport and tankage and is more effective in the pickling of high moisture content foods. The maximum concentration of acetic acid that can be produced by fermentation is usually around 10-15 %, although levels up to 18 % have been reported (Kunimatsu *et al.*, 1981). Distillation to concentrate the acetic acid is extremely difficult although a fractional distillation process to produce 20 % acidity vinegar from 10 % has been patented (Buck, 1958). Usually, the principal characteristic of conventionally distilled vinegars is simply their low solids content.

The concentration of acetic acid by freezing out the water in vinegar was noted by Glauber in 1657 and by Stahl some years later (Partington, 1961; Needham, 1971c). A process for freezing vinegar and filtering off the ice crystals was described in a series of patents by Wenzelberger (1951, 1953, 1956) and a process developed by the Chemetron Corp. of Kentucky produces a 20 % acidity vinegar from 12 % by slush freezing and centrifugal separation of the ice (Beverly & Schuhmann, 1968).

An alternative approach that can produce acetic acid concentrations as high as 87 % is to remove water by mixing in a hydrate forming fluid (trichlorofluoromethane) at low temperatures followed by fractional sublimation (Davies, 1980).

9. VINEGAR STANDARDS, COMPOSITION AND ANALYSIS

Sensible food standards, whether legally enforceable or merely recommended guidelines, serve to protect the consumer and the manufacturer from the activities of unscrupulous or inefficient operators. Normally a standard identifies particular qualities associated with a foodstuff, describes the method of analysis to be used and makes some recommendation as to acceptable limits.

Concern over the adulteration of foodstuffs, including vinegar, has been expressed since the earliest times, but as late as 1857 Hassall was able to report that 'some of the vinegars sold at small hucksters' shops, and oyster stalls, consists of little else than diluted sulphuric acid and water coloured with burnt sugar' (Hassall, 1857). Nowadays such instances are less common in the developed world but only as a result of the vigilance of official enforcement agencies, retailers, consumers and the vinegar brewers themselves.

The principal legitimate competitor of vinegar is edible grade synthetic acetic acid, diluted with water and (usually) coloured with caramel. In the UK a series of legal judgements culminating in *Kat* v. *Diment* (1950, IKB 34) found that non-brewed vinegar was a false description of such products. It was held that the secondary components of fermented vinegar conferred a 'smoothness, bouquet and aroma' that was superior, and so the term non-brewed condiment had to be adopted (Food Standards Committee, 1971). Similar restrictions apply to the use of the word vinegar in France, Belgium, Spain and Poland but not in many other countries.

The Codex Alimentarius Commission of the joint FAO/WHO Food Standards Programme is in the process of formulating a recommended European regional standard for vinegar which incorporates the definition:

> '*Vinegar* is a liquid fit for human consumption, produced from a suitable raw material of agricultural origin, containing starch, sugars, or starch and sugars, by the process of double fermentation, alcoholic and acetous, and contains a specified amount of acetic acid.'

The standard then goes on to describe particular vinegars, essential composition and quality criteria, optional ingredients, contaminants, hygiene, weights and measures, labelling, and methods of analysis (Co-ordinating Committee for Europe, 1981). At the time of writing (Feb. 83) this standard is at step 7 in the approval process (out of a total of 8) where the draft is submitted to member governments for comment.

The principal quality criterion of vinegar is the acetic acid content. Where standards exist, the minimum level is usually set at 4 % w/v as in the USA. This level was recommended for the UK by the Food Standards Committee (1971), although many UK bottled vinegars normally contain 5 %. The Codex standard proposes a minimum of 6 % acetic acid in wine vinegars and 5 % for other types. The total acidity of a vinegar is readily determined by titration with standard sodium hydroxide using phenolphthalein as the indicator. The volatile acidity, a truer reflection of the acetic acid content, can be similarly determined either on a steam distillate, or by difference, on the residue left after evaporation.

The determination of acidity cannot, however, distinguish between a true vinegar and diluted acetic acid. A variety of tests have been proposed that will do this, usually based on the fact that fermented vinegars contain numerous minor components other than acetic acid. The simplest, but not the most reliable, is the determination of pH. Non-volatile buffering substances in vinegars give them pH values higher than those observed for equivalent acetic acid solutions. For example, the pH of a 5 % acetic acid solution is around 2·46 whereas values for vinegars of that strength are usually in the range 2·8–3·2 (White, 1971). Spirit and distilled vinegars which have been stripped of most non-volatile materials generally have a pH far closer to that of non-brewed condiments and cannot, therefore, be identified by this method. Similarly, in a blended vinegar, it is not possible to determine whether spirit vinegar or acetic acid has been used on the basis of pH alone.

The classical wet chemical analyses used to distinguish between vinegars and non-brewed condiments are based on the presence, in sample distillates, of compounds such as acetoin (acetylmethylcarbinol), diacetyl, ethanol and various acetate esters. Practical details of these methods can be found in the text of Pearson (Egan *et al.*, 1981).

The oxidation and alkaline oxidation values (OV and AOV) consist largely of the sum of the individual values for acetoin and ethanol. In the AOV, however, acetoin makes a greater contribution to the total since it is oxidised more readily than ethanol under alkaline conditions. The iodine value (IV) is a measure of the acetoin and diacetyl contents. The ester value (EV) is determined by the saponification of a sample of distillate by a known volume of standard alkali followed by back titration. It reflects not only the ester content but also a substantial contribution from other components such as acetoin. Some typical values are presented in Table 5.

Vinegar contains a large number of secondary constituents that contribute to its flavour and aroma. These arise from the particular substrate used and the processes of alcoholic and acetous fermentation. Gas–liquid chromatography has enabled the plethora of volatiles present to be separated and identified. The majority of these would appear to arise at the alcoholic fermentation stage. Of the 16 compounds identified by Jones & Greenshields (1969, 1970a, b, 1971) only propionic acid, isobutyric acid and acetoin increased during acetification. The others, found in the vinegar stock, were all common components in alcoholic beverages. Acetic acid bacteria have been shown to oxidise a range of alcohols to the corresponding acid or ketone (Asai, 1968; Shimizu *et al.*, 1977) and the production of acetoin from acetaldehyde and pyruvate or lactate is well established (Asai, 1968). In an investigation of Spanish wine vinegars, 27 compounds were identified but only the acetates of methanol and butan-2-ol had increased in concentration after acetification (Llaguno, 1977); propionic acid, isobutyric acid and acetoin were not isolated or identified under the procedures used.

TABLE 5
Typical Analysis of Vinegar

Vinegar type	Oxidation value	Alkaline oxidation value	Iodine value	Ester value
Cashew apple[1]	668	—	334	45
Cider[1]	664	—	363	43
Coconut[2]	452–728	—	315–542	19–118
Malt[3]	505–1 770	48–208	180–1 600	72–148
Non-brewed condiment[3]	1–16	0·8–8·0	0–250	0–14
Spirit[4]	90–650	3–20	5–30	0–20
Sugar cane juice[2]	413–811	—	173–552	40–132

[1] Nagarathnamma et al. (1964a).
[2] Nagarathnamma et al. (1964b).
[3] Food Standards Committee (1971).
[4] Egan et al. (1981).

It would appear, therefore, that nearly all the volatiles found in alcoholic beverages, for which there is a prodigious literature, can be expected in vinegars when examined at a sufficiently high sensitivity. The intermediate distillation step in spirit vinegar production will reduce the number and concentration of volatiles, depending on the degree of rectification. Kahn et al. (1972) isolated 27 compounds from spirit vinegar but 35, 49 and 54, respectively, from samples of cider, wine and malt vinegars.

Wine vinegar is an obligatory component of pickles in Spain and a gas chromatographic method to identify the wine fusel alcohols (isobutanol, 2-methylbutanol and 3-methylbutanol) has been proposed for confirmation of its presence (Gil de la Pena et al., 1982).

Some workers have investigated non-volatile components of vinegars such as amino-acids (see, for example, Llaguno, 1977). In view of the small quantities of vinegar consumed at a time, these are probably only important in so far as they contribute to flavour. Some flavour characteristics of Japanese rice vinegars have been attributed to the activity of Acetobacter species and to photochemical reactions (Yamaguchi & Masai, 1975a, b).

Various rapid methods for the differentiation of vinegar from diluted acetic acid have been proposed. The UV absorption spectrum of vinegar distillates was shown to have a maximum between 270 and 285 nm. Non-brewed condiments generally displayed a lower absorbance in this range, but the presence of colourless components in the caramel used for colouring were thought to distil over in some instances and cause equivocal readings (Kearsley & Gibson, 1981). The measurement of osmotic pressure or freezing point depression gave rapid and certain differentiation between non-brewed condiment and vinegars, but it was not possible to distinguish between different vinegars by this method (Kearsley & Gibson, 1981; Kearsley, 1981).

Acetic acid in vinegar has a higher natural content of the radioactive isotope carbon-14 than synthetic material from petroleum. This arises from its more recent biogenesis from atmospheric carbon dioxide. Measurement of the radioactivity contained in the acetic acid has been used as a means for identifying vinegars (Masai *et al.*, 1973; Schmid *et al.*, 1977), although its utility as a method is limited by the fact that it cannot distinguish between vinegar and acetic acid from the destructive distillation of wood or the chemical oxidation of fermentation ethanol.

REFERENCES

ADAMS, M. R. (1978) Small-scale vinegar production from bananas. *Trop. Sci.* **20**, 11–19.

ADAMS, M. R. (1980) The small-scale production of vinegar from bananas. *Rep. Trop. Prod. Inst.* G 132, iv + 15 pp.

ADAMS, M. R. & FLYNN, G. R. (1982) Fermentation ethanol: an industrial profile. *Rep. Trop. Prod. Inst.* G 169, v + 26 pp.

ADAMS, M. R., DOUGAN, J., GLOSSOP, E. J. & TWIDDY, D. R. (1982) Cocoa sweatings—an effluent of potential value. *Agric. Wastes* **4**(3), 225–9.

ADRIANO, F. T. & BANZON, J. (1933) Characteristics of Philippine vinegars. *Philippine J. Agric.* **4**, 229–37.

ALLGEIER, R. J., WISTHOFF, R. T. & HILDEBRANDT, F. M. (1953) Operation of vinegar generators. *Ind. Engng Chem.* (*Ind. edn*) **45**(2), 489–94.

ALLGEIER, R. J., WISTHOFF, R. T. & HILDEBRANDT, F. M. (1954) Packings for vinegar generators. *Ind. Engng Chem.* (*Ind. edn*) **46**(10), 2023–6.

ALLGEIER, R. J. & HILDEBRANDT, F. M. (1960) Newer developments in vinegar manufacture. *Adv. appl. Microbiol.* **11**, 163–82.

AMERINE, M. A., BERG, H. W., KUNKEE, R. E., OUGH, C. S., SINGLETON, V. L. & WEBB, A. D. (1980) *The Technology of Wine Making.* AVI, Westport, Conn.

AMEYAMA, M. & ADACHI, O. (1982a) Alcohol dehydrogenase from acetic acid bacteria, membrane-bound. *Meth. Enzym.* **89**, 450–7.

AMEYAMA, M. & ADACHI, O. (1982b) Aldehyde dehydrogenase from acetic acid bacteria, membrane-bound. *Meth. Enzym.* **89**, 491–7.

ANON. (1971) Coconut vinegar. *Ceylon Ind. Dev. Board, Ind. Prospect Rep.* **25**, 7 pp.

ANON. (1973) Converts pineapple waste to vinegar. *Food Engng* **45**(8), 79.

ARNSTEIN, H. (1923). The manufacture of distilled and molasses vinegar. *The Louisiana Planter and Sugar Manufacturer* **71**(4), 71–2, (5) 91–2.

ASAI, T. (1968) *Acetic Acid Bacteria.* University of Tokyo Press, Tokyo, 343 pp.

BACHMAN, M. R. (1981) Technology appropriate to food preservation in developing countries. In *Developments in Food Preservation*, Vol. 1, S. Thorne, Ed. Applied Science Publishers, London, pp. 1–37.

BAIRD-PARKER, A. C. (1980) Organic acids. In *Microbial Ecology of Foods*, Vol. 1, Academic Press, New York, pp. 126–35.

BEAMAN, R. G. (1969) Vinegar fermentation. In *Microbial Technology*, H. J. Peppler, Ed. Reinhold, New York, 454 pp.

BEAN, M. (1928) Utilisation of whey and casein serum. *Lait* **8**, 388–93.

BEERH, O. P., RAGHURAMAIAH, B., KRISHNAMURTHY, G. V. & GIRIDHAR, N. (1976) Utilisation of mango waste: recovery of juice from waste pulp and peel. *J. Food Sci. Technol.* **13**, 138–41.

BENON, M. (1972) Manufacture of banana wine and vinegar. *French Patent* 2,097,576, 7 April 1972, 6 pp.

BEVERLY, H. W. & SCHUHMANN, L. C. (1968) *US Patent* 3,389,567, 8 pp.

BINSTED, R., DEVEY, J. D. & DAKIN, J. C. (1962) *Pickle and Sauce Making*, 2nd edn. Food Trade Press, London, 274 pp.

BITTING, A. W. (1929) A synopsis of patents pertaining to the manufacture of vinegar. *Fruit Products J. Amer. Vinegar Ind.* **8**(7), 25–7; (8), 16–18; (9), 13–15; (10), 18–20, 27; (11), 16–18; (12), 18–20; **9**, 19–20, 25, 49–51, 86.

BRANNT, A. (1890) *A Practical Treatise on the Manufacture of Vinegar and Acetates, Cider and Fruit Wines.* Henry Carey Baird and Co., Philadelphia, 479 pp.

BROTHWELL, D. R. & BROTHWELL, P. (1969) *Foods in Antiquity.* Thames and Hudson, London, 248 pp.

BROWN, G. D. & RAINBOW, C. (1956) Nutritional patterns in acetic acid bacteria. *J. gen. Microbiol.* **15**, 61–9.

BUCK, R. E. (1958) *US Patent* 3,002,896.

BURROWS, S. (1979) Baker's yeast. In *Microbial Biomass, Economic Microbiology*, Vol. 4, A. H. Rose, Ed. Academic Press, London, pp. 31–64.

CAMPBELL, C. H. (1928) Black vinegar. Its cause and cure. *The Glass Packer* **1**, 15–16.

CAMPBELL, W. A. (1971) *The Chemical Industry.* Longmans, London, p. 108.

CARR, J. G. & PASSMORE, S. M. (1979) Methods for identifying acetic acid bacteria. In *Identification Methods for Microbiologists*, F. A. Skinner & D. W. Lovelock, Eds. Academic Press, London, 315 pp.

CAUDA, A. (1924) Kaki vinegar. *Coltivatore* **70**, 375.

CERASARI, E. & BOTTERI, M. (1953) Possibility of utilisation of banana skin. *Ann. triest. cura univ. Trieste Sez.* **2**, 22–3, 193–206.

CHILD, R. (1964). *Coconuts.* Longmans, London, pp. 186–94.

CHUNG, K. C. & GOEPFERT, J. M. (1970) Growth of *Salmonella* at low pH. *J. Food Sci.* **35**, 326–8.

CONNER, H. A. & ALLGEIER, R. J. (1976) Vinegar: Its history and development. *Adv. appl. Microbiol.* **20**, 81–133.

CO-ORDINATING COMMITTEE FOR EUROPE (1981) *Joint FAO/WHO Food Standards Programme*, Alinorm 81/19.

CORRAN, H. S. (1975) *A History of Brewing*. David and Charles, Newton Abbot, p. 15.

CRUESS, W. V. (1958) *Commercial Fruit and Vegetable Products: a Textbook for Student, Investigator and Manufacturer*, 4th edn. McGraw-Hill, New York, 884 pp.

DAKIN, J. C. (1957) Microbiological keeping quality of pickles and sauces. *BFMIRA Tech. Circ.* 79.

DAKIN, J. C. & DAY, P. M. (1958) Yeasts causing spoilage in acetic acid preserves. *J. appl. Bact.* **21**, 94.

DAKIN, J. C. & RADWELL, J. Y. (1971). Lactobacilli causing the spoilage of acetic acid preserves. *J. appl. Bact.* **34**(3), 541–5.

DAS, B. & SARIN, J. L. (1936) Vinegar from dates. *Ind. Engng Chem. (Ind. edn)* **28**, 314.

DATTA, S. C. & BISWAS, S. C. (1942) Vinegar from sugar cane and fruit juices. *Indian Farming* **3**, 527–30.

DAVIES, J. M. C. (1980) *US Patent*, 4,207,951, 10 pp.

DE LEY, J. & FRATEUR, J. (1974a) The genus *Gluconobacter*. In *Bergey's Manual of Determinative Bacteriology*, 8th edn, R. E. Buchanan and N. E. Gibbons, Eds. The Williams and Wilkins Co., Baltimore.

DE LEY, J. & FRATEUR, J. (1974b) The genus *Acetobacter*. *Ibid.*

DERRY, T. K. & WILLIAMS, T. I. (1960) *A Short History of Technology*. Oxford University Press, London, p. 262.

DESILVA, R. L. & SARAVANAPAVAN, T. Y. (1968) Tea cider—a potential winner. *Tea Quarterly* **39**(3), 37–41.

DESROSIER, N. W. & DESROSIER, J. N. (1977) *The Technology of Food Preservation*, 4th edn. AVI, Westport, Conn., 558 pp.

DIOKNO-PALO, N. & VILELA, L. C. (1967) The possibilities of manufacturing high-grade vinegar from sweetened coconut water. *Sci. Bull. (Philippines)* **12**(1), 52–9.

EBNER, H., POHL, K. & ENENKEL, A. (1967) Self-priming aerator and mechanical defoamer for microbiological processes. *Biotechnol. Bioengng* **9**, 357–64.

EBNER, H. & ENENKEL, A. (1969) Der Frings Alkograph. '*GIT*' *Fachzeitschrift Lab.* **13**(6), 651–4.

EBNER, H. & ENENKEL, A. (1976) *US Patent*, 3,974,068.

EBNER, H. (1982) Vinegar. In *Prescott and Dunn's Industrial Microbiology*, 4th edn, G. Reed, Ed. AVI, Westport, Conn., pp. 802–34.

EGAN, H., KIRK, R. S. & SAWYER, R. (1981) *Pearson's Chemical Analysis of Foods*, 8th edn. Churchill Livingstone, Edinburgh, 591 pp.

EGGEBRECHT, H. (1939) Banana vinegar. *Dtsch. Essigind.* **43**, 145–7.

ENENKEL, A. & EBNER, H. (1970) The effect of improved gas dispersion and gas distribution on gas–liquid transfer. *160th ACS National Meeting, Div. of Microbial Chem.* Chicago, Sept. 1970.

FABIAN, F. W. (1929) Honey vinegar. *Glass Packer* **2**, 511–13.

FLORENZANI, G. & BALLONI, W. (1969) Microbiological study of the alcoholic beverage Tuba and the vinegar Sukang puti prepared from the sap of *Nipa fruticans* in the Philippines. *Ágr. Ital. (Pisa)* **69**(3), 148–457.

FOOD STANDARDS COMMITTEE (1971) *Report on vinegars*, Min. Agric. Fish. and Food. London, HMSO.

FREISE, F. W. (1931) Preparation of vinegar from coffee fruit pulp. *Ind. Engng Chem. (Ind. edn)* **23**, 1108–1109; *Dtsch. Essigind.* **35**, 169–71.

GHOMMIDH, C., NAVARRO, J. M. & DURAND, G. (1981) Acetic acid production by immobilised *Acetobacter* cells. *Biotechnol. Letters* **3**(2), 93–8.

GHOMMIDH, C., NAVARRO, J. M. & DURAND, G. (1982a) A study of acetic acid production by immobilised *Acetobacter* cells: oxygen transfer. *Biotechnol. Bioengng* **24**, 605–17.

GHOMMIDH, C., NAVARRO, J. M. & MESSING, R. A. (1982b) A study of acetic acid production by immobilised *Acetobacter* cells: product inhibition effects. *Biotechnol. Bioengng* **24**, 1991–9.

GIBBS, H. D. (1911) The alcohol industry of the Philippine Islands I. *Philippine J. Sci.* **6**, 99–206.

GIL DE LA PENA, M. L., POLO, C., SANCHEZ, J. J. & LLAGUNO, C. (1982) Deteccion de la presencia de vinaigre de vino en escabeches y encurtidos. II Encutidos. *Rev. Agroquim. Tecnol. Aliment.* **22**(1), 120–32.

GREENSHIELDS, R. N. (1972) *British Patent*, 1,263,059.

GREENSHIELDS, R. N. (1975a) Malt vinegar manufacture I. *Brewer* **61**(729), 295–8.

GREENSHIELDS, R. N. (1975b) Malt vinegar manufacture II. *Brewer* **61**(732), 401–7.

GREENSHIELDS, R. N. (1978) Acetic acid: vinegar. In *Primary Products of Metabolism, Economic Microbiology*, Vol. 2, A. H. Rose, Ed. Academic Press, London, pp. 121–86.

GREENWOOD-BARTON, L. H. (1965) Utilisation of cocoa by-products. *Food Manuf.* **40**(5), 52–6; 109.

GROVE, O. (1914) The amylo process of fermentation. *J. Inst. Brewing* **20**, 248–66.

HADORN, H. & ZURCHER, K. (1973) Manufacture, analysis and evaluation of whey vinegar. *Mitteilungen aus dem Gebiete der Lebensmitteluntersuchung und Hygiene* **64**(4), 480–503.

HALLACK, P. (1921) The use of apples in the manufacture of vinegar. *Deutsches Essigindust.* **25**, 93–4.

HAM, J. (1824) Manufacture of vinegar. *British Patent*, 5,012, 4 pp.

HANSEN, A. E. (1935) Making vinegar by the Frings process. *Food Industries* June, 227, 312.

HANSFORD, C. G. & MARTIN, W. S. (1943) Manufacture of acetic acid on rubber estates for use as a coagulant. *East Afr. Agric. J.* **9**, 153.

HASSACK, P. (1929) Malt vinegar and its manufacture. *Fruit Products J. Amer. Vinegar Ind.* **8**(3), 19–20; (5), 24–6; (7), 30–1, (9), 18–19; and (11), 19–21.

HASSALL, A. H. (1857) *Discovery of Frauds in Food and Medicine*. Longman, Brown, Green, Longmans and Roberts, London, 712 pp.

HOEPPNER, A. (1866) *US Patent*, 68,823, Oct. 16.

HOFFMAN, W. (1926) The production of wine vinegars. *Fruit Products J. Amer. Vinegar Ind.* **5**(10), 14–15.

HROMATKA, O., EBNER, H. & CSOKLICH, C. (1951) Investigations of the vinegar fermentation. IV: About the influence of a total interruption of the aeration. *Enzymologia* **15**, 134–53.

HROMATKA, O. & EBNER, H. (1959) Vinegar by submerged oxidative fermentation. *Ind. Engng Chem. (Ind. edn)* **51**(10), 1279–80.

HROMATKA, O. & EXNER, W. (1962) Investigation of the vinegar fermentation. VIII: Further knowledge on interruption of aeration. *Enzymologia* **25**, 37–51.

HUBER, E. (1927) Der Essig in der altbabylonischen Kultier gesichte. *Dtsch. Essigind*, **31**(1) 12–15, (2) 28–30.

JONES, D. D. & GREENSHIELDS, R. N. (1969) Volatile constituents of vinegar. I: A survey of some commercially available malt vinegars. *J. Inst. Brewing* **75**(5), 457–63.

JONES, D. D. & GREENSHIELDS, R. N. (1970a) Volatile constituents of vinegar. II: Formation of volatiles in a commercial malt vinegar process. *J. Inst. Brewing* **76**(1), 55–60.

JONES, D. D. & GREENSHIELDS, R. N. (1970b) Volatile constituents of vinegar. III: Formation and origin of volatiles in laboratory acetifications. *J. Inst. Brewing* **76**(3), 235–42.

JONES, D. D. & GREENSHIELDS, R. N. (1971) Volatile constituents of vinegar. IV: Formation of volatiles in the Frings process and a continuous process for malt vinegar manufacture. *J. Inst. Brewing* **77**(2), 160–3.

JORGENSEN, A. (1900) *Micro-organisms and Fermentation*, 3rd edn. Macmillan, London, 318 pp.

JUNIOR, O. Z. & AQUARONE, E. (1981) The effect of some variables in the acetification of persimmon wine (Diospyros kaki). *Arq. Biol. Tecnol.* (Brazil) **24**(3), 353–9.

JURITZ, C. F. (1920) The prickly pear (Opuntia). Possibilities of its utilisation. *S. Afr. J. Ind.* **3**, 687–93; 803–14.

KAHN, J. H., NICKOL, G. B. & CONNER, H. A. (1972) Identification of volatile components in vinegars by gas chromatography and mass spectrometry. *Intern. Bottler and Packer* **46**, November, 78–82.

KEARSLEY, M. W. (1974) Concentration of sugars by reverse osmosis. *Food Trade Review*, June 7–11.

KEARSLEY, M. W. & GIBSON, W. J. (1981) Rapid differentiation between vinegars and non-brewed condiments; part I. *J. Assoc. Publ. Analysts* **19**, 83–9.

KEARSLEY, M. W. (1981) Rapid differentiation between vinegars and non-brewed condiments: part II. *J. Assoc. Publ. Analysts* **19**, 121–5.

KEWPIE JOZO KABUSHIKI KAISHA (1973) Process for the continuous production of vinegar by surface fermentation. *British Patent*, 1,205,868, Feb. 7.

KHATTAK, J. N., HANDY, M. K. & POWERS, J. J. (1965a) Utilisation of watermelon juice. Part II. Acetic acid fermentation. *Food Technol.* **19**, 998–1001.

KHATTAK, J. N., HANDY, M. K. & POWERS, J. J. (1965b) Utilisation of watermelon juice. Part I. Alcoholic fermentation. *Food Technol.* **19**, 1284–6.

KIM, M. C., CHO, K. T. & SHIM, K. H. (1980) The manufacture of vinegar from fallen persimmons. *Korean J. Appl. Microbiol. Bioengng.* **8**(2), 103–11.

KING, T. E. & CHELDELIN, V. H. (1954) Oxidations in *Acetobacter suboxydans*. *Biochim. Biophys. Acta* **14**, 108–16.

KING, T. E. & CHELDELIN, V. H. (1956) Oxidation of acetaldehyde by *Acetobacter suboxydans*. *J. Biol. Chem.* **220**, 177–91.

KITTO, H. D. F. (1951) *The Greeks*. Penguin Books, Harmondsworth, p. 93.

KOSIKOWSKI, F. V. (1979) *J. Dairy Sci.* **62**, 1149.

KUNIMATSU, Y., OKUMURA, H., MASAI, H., YAMADA, K. & YAMADA, M. (1981) Production of vinegar with high acetic acid concentration. *US Patent*, 4,282,257.

KUROIWA, T. (1977) *Rice Vinegar: an Oriental Home Remedy*. Kenko Igakusha, Tokyo, 184 pp.

KUTSING, F. T. (1837) *J. Prakt. Chem.*, **2**, 385.

LAMB, A. R. & WILSON, E. (1923) Vinegar fermentation and home production of cider vinegar. *Iowa Agr. Exptl Station Bull.* **218**, 14 pp.

LAWYER, I. B. (1928) Economical vinegar production in a plant of moderate capacity. *Fruit Products J. Amer. Vinegar Ind.* Pt I. **8**(2), 9–11; Pt II. **8**(3), 16–18; Pt III. **8**(4), 20–1.

LEFEVRE, E. (1924) Making vinegar in the home and on the farm. *US Dept. Agric.,* *Farmers Bull.* 1424, 28 pp.

LEIFSON, E. (1954) The flagellation and taxonomy of species of *Acetobacter*. *Antonie van Leeuwenhoek* **27**, 49–62.

LLAGUNO, C. (1971) Spanish wine vinegar. *Process Biochem.* **6**(5), 27–8; 33.

LLAGUNO, C. (1977) Quality of Spanish wine vinegars. *Process Biochem.* **12**(8), 17–19; 44; 46.

LOESECKE, H. W. VON (1929) Preparation of banana vinegar. *Ind. Engng Chem.* (*Ind. edn*) **21**, 175–76.

LOWY, J. (1941) Automatic control improves vinegar manufacture. *Food Industries*, August, 47–8.

LUTWAK-MANN, C. (1938) Alcohol dehydrogenase of animal tissues. *Biochem. J.* **32**, 1364–74.

MALDONADO, O., ROLZ, C. & SCHNEIDER DE CABRERA, S. (1975) Wine and vinegar production from tropical fruits. *J. Food Sci.* **40**, 262–5.

MASAI, H., OIKMORI, S., KANEKO, T. & EBINE, H. (1973) Differentiation of synthetic from biogenic raw materials in various foods with a liquid scintillation counter. I: Acetic acid in foods. *Agric. Biol. Chem.* **37**(6), 1321–5.

MASAI, H. (1980) Recent technical developments on vinegar manufacture in Japan. In Proceedings of the Oriental Fermented Foods, Food Industry Research and Development Institute, Hsinchu, Taiwan, pp. 192–206.

MAYER, E. (1963) Historic and modern aspects of vinegar making (acetic fermentation). *Food Technol.* **17**, 582–4.

MCNARY, R. R. & DOUGHERTY, M. H. (1960) Citrus vinegar. *Univ. Florida, Agric. Exptl Stn (Gainesville) Bull.* 622, 23 pp.

MESSING, W. & SCHMITZ, R. (1976) Citric acid from sucrose—an industrial microbiological process based on molasses. *Chem. Exp. Didakt.* **2**(9), 309–16.

MITCHELL, C. A. (1926) *Vinegar, its Manufacture and Examination*, 2nd edn. Charles Griffin and Co Ltd, London, 211 pp.

MULLER, F. (1978) A modern bioreactor for vinegar production. *Process Biochem.* **13**, 10–11.

MUSPRATT'S Chemistry as applied to the arts and manufactures (1877). Wm MacKenzie, London.

NAGARATHNAMMA, M., DWARAKANATH, C. T. & PRUTHI, J. S. (1964a) Changes in the chemical composition of the raw material during the preparation of vinegar. *Indian Food Packer* **18**(2), 4–7.

NAGARATHNAMMA, M., PRUTHI, J. S. & SIDDAPPA, G. S. (1964b) Variations in the physico-chemical characteristics of commercial vinegars (brewed and synthetic) manufactured in India. *Indian Food Packer* **13**(2), 15–19.

NAKAYAMA, T. (1959) Studies on acetic acid bacteria. I: Biochemical studies on ethanol oxidation. *J. Biochem.* **46**(9), 1217–25.

NAKAYAMA, T. (1960) Studies on acetic acid bacteria. II: Intracellular distribution of enzymes related to acetic acid fermentation, and some properties of a highly purified TPN-dependent aldehyde dehydrogenase. *J. Biochem.* **48**(6), 812–29.

NAKAYAMA, T. (1961a) Studies on acetic acid bacteria. III: Purification and properties of coenzyme independent aldehyde dehydrogenase. *J. Biochem.* **49**(2), 158–63.

NAKAYAMA, T. (1961b) Studies on acetic acid bacteria. IV. Purification and properties of a new type of alcohol dehydrogenase, alcohol-cytochrome-553 reductase. *J. Biochem.* **49**(3), 240–51.

NATHANAEL, W. R. N. (1952a) This history of vinegar production and the use of coconut toddy as a raw material. Part I. Historical introduction. *Ceylon Coconut Q.* **3**, 83–7.

NATHANAEL, W. R. N. (1952b) The history of vinegar production and the use of coconut toddy as a raw material. Part II. Coconut toddy, a raw material for vinegar production. *Ceylon Coconut Q.* **3**, 135–49.

NATHANAEL, W. R. N. (1958) Acetic acid fermentation and the 'generator' process for the manufacture of coconut toddy vinegar. *Coconut Res. Inst. (Ceylon), Bull.* 17, 33 pp.

NEEDHAM, J. (1971a) *Science and Civilisation in China*, Vol. 4 (3), pp. 26, 278, Cambridge University Press, Cambridge.

NEEDHAM, J. (1971b) *Science and Civilisation in China*, Vol. 4 (4), p. 172, Cambridge University Press, Cambridge.

NEEDHAM, J. (1971c) *Science and Civilisation in China*, Vol. 5 (3), Cambridge University Press, Cambridge.

NEUBERG, C. & NORD, F. F. (1919) *Biochem. Z.* **96**, 158 (not seen).

NICKOL, G. B. (1979) Vinegar. In *Microbial Technology*, 2nd edn, Vol. 2, Academic Press, New York, pp. 155–72.

OCHI, T. (1960) *Japanese Patent*, 10,698, 6 August 1960, 8 pp.

OHMORI, S., UOZUMI, T. & BEPPU, T. (1982) Loss of acetic acid resistance and ethanol oxidising ability in an *Acetobacter* strain. *Agric. Biol. Chem.* **46**(2), 381–9.

O'NEAL, R. & CRUESS, W. V. (1951) Clarification of wines and vinegars. *Food Manuf.*, 265.

PAIVOKE, A. E. A., ADAMS, M. R. & PEREMAI, M. (1982) The production of nipa palm vinegar in Papua New Guinea. Rept. No. 4/82, Energy Planning Unit, DME, PNG.

PALMER, G. H. (1980) Malting and mashing. In *An Introduction to Brewing Science and Technology*, Pt I, C. Rainbow & G. E. S. Float, Eds. The Institute of Brewing, London, pp. 10–27.

PARTINGTON, J. R. (1935) *Origins and Development of Applied Chemistry*. Longmans, London, p. 35.

PARTINGTON, J. R. (1961) *A History of Chemistry*, Vol. 2, Macmillan, London, p. 359.

PARTINGTON, J. R. (1962) *A History of Chemistry*, Vol. 1, Macmillan, London, p. 233.

PERSOON, C. H. (1822). *Mycologia Europea*, **1**, 96.

PHILLISKIRK, G. & YATES, H. J. (1978) Method of producing ethyl alcohol. *British Patent*, 1,524,618, 13 Sept.

PIRT, S. J. (1978) Aerobic and anaerobic microbial digestion in waste reclamation. *J. appl. Chem. Biotechnol.* **28**, 232–6.

POORE, H. D. (1920) Orange vinegar—its manufacture and composition. *J. Ind. Engng Chem.* **12**, 1176–9.

POULTNEY, S. V. (1949) *Vinegar Products.* Chapman and Hall, London, 126 pp.

RAINBOW, C. & MITSON, G. W. (1953) Nutritional requirements of acetic acid bacteria. *J. gen. Microbiol.* **9**, 371–5.

RAINBOW, C. (1961) The biochemistry of the *Acetobacter. Progr. Ind. Microbiol.* **3**, 45–70.

RAISTRICK, A. (1973) *Industrial Archaeology.* Paladin, St Albans, p. 37.

RICHARDSON, K. C. (1967) Submerged acetification of a vinegar base produced from waste pineapple juice. *Biotechnol. Bioengng* **9**, 171–86.

ROBERTS, J. M. (1980) *The Pelican History of the World.* Penguin Books, Harmondsworth, 1052 pp.

ROBILLOS, Y. U. (1978) Buri palm and its multi-uses. FOR PRIDECOM Tech. Note (Philippines), No. 188, 2 pp.

ROMBOUTS, F. M. & PILNIK, W. (1980) Pectic enzymes. In *Economic Microbiology Vol. 5. Microbial Enzymes and Bioconversions,* A. H. Rose, Ed. Academic Press, London, 693 pp.

SAMIULLAH, S. & ARA, H. (1969) Studies on date vinegar manufacture. *Pak. J. Sci.* **21**, 126–8.

SCHIERHOLT, J. (1976) Technology and economy of two different fermentation processes from the production of citric acid. In Abstracts of the 5th International Fermentation Symposium, Berlin, p. 49.

SCHMID, E. R., ROGY, I. & KENNDLER, E. (1977) Beitrag zur Unterscheidung von Garungsessig und synthetischem Saureesig durch der Bestimmung der spezifischen C-14 Radioactivitat. *Z. Lebensm. Unters.- Forsch.* **163**, 121–2.

SHIMIZU, H., MIYAI, K., MATSUHISA, H., IWASAKI, E. & JOMOYEDA, M. (1977) Effect of ethanol on acetate oxidation by *Acetobacter aceti. European J. appl. Microbiol.* **3**, 303–11.

SHIMWELL, J. L. (1954) Pure culture vinegar production. *J. Inst. Brewing* **60**(2), 136–41.

SHIMWELL, J. L. (1955) *British Patent,* 727,039.

SIMONIN, R. F. & BERNARD, M. (1958) *British Patent,* 805,698.

SINGER, C., HOLMYARD, E. J., HALL, A. R. & WILLIAMS, T. J. (1956) *A History of Technology,* Vol. 2, Clarendon Press, Oxford, p. 8.

SOLOMONS, G. L. (1969) *Materials and Methods in Fermentation.* Academic Press, New York, 331 pp.

SOYER, A. (1853) *The Pantropheon or History of Food and its Preparation.* Simpkin, Marshall and Co., London, 474 pp.

SPURGIN, M. M. (1964) Vinegar base production from waste pineapple juice. *Queensland J. Agric. Sci.* **21**, 213–32.

STOIK, A. C. & DAKIN, J. C. (1966) *Moniliella,* a new genus of *Moniliales. Antonia van Leeuwenhoek* **32**, 399.

TANNAHILL, R. (1973) *Food in History.* Stein and Day, New York, 448 pp.

TSUKAHARA, T. & NAKAMURA, Z. (1946) Preparation of vinegar from sweet potatoes with black rot. IV: Addition of yeast and mother vinegar. *J. Soc. Brewing, Japan* **43**, 75–8.

TSUKAHARA, T. & NAKAMURA, Z. (1950) Preparation of vinegar from sweet potatoes with black rot. V: Time of filtering and composition of residue. *J. Soc. Brewing, Japan* **44**, 1–2.

VALLERY-RADOT, R. (1937) *The Life of Pasteur*. Constable and Co., London, 484 pp.

VANDECAVEYE, S. C. (1926) Improved method for making cider vinegar. *Washington Agric. Exptl Station Bull.* **202**, 5–26.

VARMA, U. P. (1959) Vinegar from palm juice. *Bihar Agric. Coll. Mag.* **10**, 35–42.

VAUGHN, R. H. (1942) The acetic acid bacteria. *Wallerstein Labs. Commun.* **5**, 5–26.

VAUGHN, R. H. (1954) Acetic acid: Vinegar. In *Industrial Fermentations*, Vol. 1, L. A. Underkofler and R. J. Hickey, Eds., Chemical Publishing Co. Inc., New York, pp. 498–535.

VIRMANI, R. S. (1950) *Indian Food Packer* **4**(1), 13.

WAHID, M. A. & CHUGHTAI, M. I. D. (1969) Studies in the chemical activities of microorganisms. VII: Acetic acid (Vinegar) from indigenous raw materials. *Pak. J. Scientific Res.* **21** (3 and 4), 88–93.

WEAST, R. C. (1975) *Handbook of Chemistry and Physics*, 55th edn. CRC Press, Cleveland, Ohio.

WENZELBERGER, E. P. (1951) *US Patent*, 2,559,204.

WENZELBERGER, E. P. (1953) *US Patent*, 2,647,059.

WENZELBERGER, E. P. (1956). *US Patent*, 2,657,555.

WHITE, J. (1970) Malt vinegar manufacture. *Process Biochem.* **5**(10), 54–6.

WHITE, J. (1971). Vinegar quality—legal and commercial standards. *Process Biochem* **6**(5), 21–5; 50.

WILSON, C. A. (1976) *Food and Drink in Britain*. Penguin Books, Harmondsworth, 425 pp.

WUSTENFELD, H. (1923) Raw spirit or rectified spirit (in vinegar generation). *Dtsch. Essigind.* **27**, 414.

WYANT, Z. N. (1919) Vinegar. *Michigan Agr. College Exptl Station Spec. Bull.*, No. 98, 27 pp.

YAMAGUCHI, G. & MASAI, H. (1975a) Sunstruck flavour of rice vinegar. *Agric. Biol. Chem.* **39**(10), 1903–5.

YAMAGUCHI, G. & MASAI, H. (1975b) Peroxidized flavour and acidic fraction of rice vinegar. *Agric. Biol. Chem.* **39**(10), 1907–11.

ZALKAN, R. C. & FABIAN, F. W. (1953) The influence of vinegar eels (*Anguillula aceti*) on vinegar production. *Food Technol.*, 453–5.

Chapter 2

The Microbiology of Vegetable Fermentations

REESE H. VAUGHN

Department of Food Science and Technology,
University of California, Davis, USA

1. INTRODUCTION

The knowledge of the art of pickling vegetables (fermentation) is a process of preservation of foods that is lost in antiquity. It may have been developed in the Orient as suggested by Pederson (1960) but until more evidence is available, its origin will remain obscure. In any event, this method of food conservation has been used for many centuries and is one of the important methods of food preservation still in use for vegetables and fruits where production by canning, drying or freezing is not the method of choice.

Most, if not all vegetables, may be pickled (fermented) in brine. The most important products produced in whole or in part by fermentation (lactic acid) are pickles, sauerkraut and olives. Lesser quantities of other vegetables including carrots, cauliflower, celery, okra, onions, sweet and hot peppers and green tomatoes are also fermented, to be used in mixed pickles or as specialty items (cocktail onions, various peppers and green tomatoes). A more complete array of fermented vegetables is listed by Fleming (1982).

The relative importance of sauerkraut, pickles and olives in the food industry of the United States is shown by production data arranged in Tables 1, 2 and 3. The apparent *per capita* consumptions of these three commodities are shown in Table 4.

Cucumbers comprise the largest single crop grown for pickling. The major portion of this production is from three states: Michigan, Wisconsin

Reese H. Vaughn

TABLE 1
Production of Cabbage for Sauerkraut in the United States

| Year | Amount harvested | | Production | | Yield | | Value | | |
	ha	acres	MT	Tons	Per ha (MT)	Per acre (tons)	Dollars (average) Per MT	Per ton	Total dollars (thousands)
1966	4 304	10 760	161 604	179 560	37·55	16·69	22·00	20·00	3 596
1967	5 712	14 280	246 060	273 400	43·09	19·15	18·70	17·00	4 653
1968	5 024	12 560	208 665	231 850	41·54	18·46	19·80	18·00	4 179
1969	5 112	12 780	200 250	222 500	39·17	17·41	20·90	19·00	4 237
1970	5 192	12 980	239 490	266 100	46·12	20·50	19·47	17·70	4 707
1971	4 584	11 460	211 455	234 950	46·12	20·50	19·25	17·50	4 111
1972	4 320	10 800	178 290	198 100	41·26	18·34	23·54	21·40	4 245
1973	5 216	13 040	197 235	219 150	37·82	16·81	27·28	24·80	5 424
1974	5 564	13 910	253 305	281 450	45·52	20·23	34·10	31·00	8 720
1975	4 724	11 810	215 775	239 750	45·67	20·30	34·54	31·40	7 525
1976	4 588	11 470	208 845	232 050	45·51	20·23	34·32	31·20	7 235
1977	4 212	10 530	211 275	234 750	50·16	22·29	33·90	30·50	7 166
1978	4 228	10 570	196 011	217 790	46·36	20·60	35·00	31·50	6 857
1979	3 920	9 800	214 038	237 820	54·60	24·27	35·20	31·60	7 525
1980	3 636	9 090	187 992	208 880	51·70	22·98	37·80	34·10	7 122
1981	4 080	10 200	221 481	246 090	54·30	24·20	40·82	36·80	9 045

Source: US Dep. Agric. (1982); *The Almanac of the Canning, Freezing, Preserving Industries* (1982).

TABLE 2
Production of Cucumbers for Pickles in the United States

| Year | Amount harvested | | Production | | Yield | | Value | | Total dollars (thousands) |
	ha	acres	MT	Tons	Per ha (MT)	Per acre (tons)	Dollars (average) Per MT	Per ton	
1966	52 408	131 020	484 020	537 800	9·22	4·10	89·76	81·60	43 866
1967	62 480	156 200	539 415	599 350	8·64	3·84	100·32	91·20	54 662
1968	59 328	148 320	508 014	564 460	8·57	3·81	101·31	92·10	52 003
1969	54 008	135 020	465 300	517 000	8·62	3·83	101·09	91·90	47 534
1970	53 432	133 580	529 920	588 800	9·92	4·41	103·51	94·10	55 391
1971	51 040	127 600	506 790	563 100	9·92	4·41	102·52	93·20	52 461
1972	51 532	128 830	514 035	571 150	9·97	4·43	103·40	94·00	53 660
1973	50 372	125 930	538 920	598 800	10·71	4·76	109·23	99·30	59 448
1974	52 804	132 010	537 300	597 000	10·17	4·52	144·10	131·00	77 954
1975	56 068	140 170	606 825	674 250	10·96	4·87	141·90	129·00	86 730
1976	51 352	128 380	570 477	633 800	11·12	4·94	138·60	126·00	79 751
1977	49 516	123 790	561 465	623 850	11·34	5·04	140·00	126·00	78 651
1978	53 776	134 440	616 950	685 450	11·47	5·10	144·00	130·00	88 814
1979	52 672	131 680	602 073	668 970	11·43	5·08	161·00	145·00	97 186
1980	46 504	116 260	548 253	609 170	11·79	5·24	185·00	166·00	101 264
1981	39 000	97 500	517 842	575 380	13·28	5·90	194·00	175·00	100 629

Source: US Dep. Agric. (1982); The Almanac of the Canning, Freezing, Preserving Industries (1982).

TABLE 3
Production of California Olives

Year	Bearing		Production		Per ha (MT)	Per acre (tons)	Value		Total dollars (thousands)
	Hectarage	Acreage	MT	Tons			Dollars (average) Per MT	Per ton	
1966	10 642	26 604	56 700	63 000	5·33	2·37	265·10	241·00	15 183
1967	10 816	27 041	12 600	14 000	1·17	0·52	421·30	383·00	5 362
1968	10 800	26 999	77 400	86 000	7·18	3·19	404·80	368·00	31 648
1969	10 932	27 330	63 000	70 000	5·76	2·56	360·80	328·00	22 960
1970	11 035	27 588	46 800	52 000	4·23	1·88	271·70	247·00	12 844
1971	11 072	27 681	49 500	55 000	4·48	1·99	162·80	148·00	8 140
1972	11 327	28 317	21 780	24 200	1·91	0·85	456·50	415·00	10 043
1973	11 424	28 560	63 000	70 000	5·51	2·45	438·90	399·00	27 930
1974	11 396	28 491	52 650	58 500	4·61	2·05	477·40	434·00	25 389
1975	11 632	29 080	60 300	67 000	5·31	2·36	369·60	336·00	22 512
1976	12 314	30 784	72 000	80 000	5·85	2·60	363·00	330·00	26 400
1977	13 634	33 076	38 700	43 000	3·21	1·30	447·80	403·00	17 329
1978	15 066	37 213	113 400	126 000	8·37	3·39	336·70	303·00	38 178
1979	14 945	36 912	55 800	62 000	4·15	1·68	453·30	408·00	25 296
1980	14 633	36 144	98 100	109 000	4·76	3·02	408·90	368·00	40 112
*1981			40 410	44 900			772·60	695·00	31 222
1982			131 400	146 000			532·20	479·00	69 934

Source: Olive Admin. Comm. (1977–1981); US Dep. Agric. (1982); *The Almanac of the Canning, Freezing, Preserving Industries* (1983).
* Acreage estimates discontinued.

TABLE 4

Per Capita Consumption of Pickles, Sauerkraut and Olives (Processed Weight)

Year	Apparent consumption per person					
	Pickles		Sauerkraut		Olives	
	kg	lb	kg	lb	kg	lb
1920	0·54	1·2	0·32	0·8		0·3
1930	0·82	1·8	1·04	2·3		0·5
1940	1·00	2·2	0·95	2·1		0·7
1950	1·50	3·3	0·86	1·9		0·8
1960	2·04	4·5	0·68	1·5	0·36 (0·13)[1]	0·8 (0·36)[1]
1966	3·00	6·6	0·64	1·4	0·36 (0·17)	0·8 (0·40)
1968	3·50	7·7	0·72	1·6	0·32 (0·10)	0·7 (0·25)
1969	3·50	7·7	0·64	1·4	0·54 (0·14)	1·2 (0·36)
1971	3·45	7·6	0·72	1·6	0·41 (0·16)	0·9 (0·41)
1972	3·54	7·8	0·64	1·4	0·32 (0·17)	0·7 (0.44)
1973	3·63	8·0	0·64	1·4	0·32 (0·13)	0·7 (0·33)
1974	3·58	7·9	0·68	1·5	0·41 (0·16)	0·9 (0·43)
1975	3·54	7·8	0·59	1·3	0·36 (0·15)	0·8 (0·40)
1976	3·82	8·4	0·64	1·4	0·45 (0·22)	1·0 (0·48)
1977	3·63	8·0	0·64	1·4	0·45 (0·23)	1·0 (0·50)
1978	3·78	8·4	0·59	1·3	0·36 (0·12)	0·8 (0·55)
1979	3·87	8·6	0·59	1·3	0·54 (0·11)	1·2 (0·49)
1980	3·54	7·8	0·59	1·3	0·41 (0·12)	0·8 (0·55)
1981	3·33	7·4	0·31	0·7	0·45	1·0

Source: US Dep. Agric. (1968, 1977, 1982).
[1] Figures in ( ) represent California canned ripe olives, taken from data of Olive Admin. Comm. (1977–1980).

and California. However, cucumbers for pickling are grown in other states where the climatic conditions are favourable and there is a constant demand for them by the picklers.

Sauerkraut is the only product other than pickles fermented in large quantity. Cabbage production for kraut is localised in the states bordering the Great Lakes, including New York, Pennsylvania, Ohio, Michigan, Indiana, Wisconsin, and Illinois and in the west where the climate is favourable and there is an established demand as in Colorado, Oregon, and Washington.

Commercial olive production is confined almost entirely to the Sacramento and San Joaquin valleys of central California. The only other producing areas in North America are Arizona and Baja California,

Mexico where comparatively small quantities are grown. Olives will grow very well in other parts of the United States and Mexico but climatic conditions are not suitable for the economical setting of fruit. The olive tree to be commercially productive must have winter-chilling but at the same time is very susceptible to freezing.

2. SAUERKRAUT PRODUCTION

The historical evolution of the production of the product we know as sauerkraut is amply discussed by Pederson (1960, 1979) and Pederson & Albury (1969). It is sufficient to recognise that cabbage (*Brassica oleracea*) has been known and commonly used for at least 4000 years.

Sauerkraut, the product resulting from the natural lactic acid fermentation of salted, shredded cabbage is literally acid (sour) cabbage. The antecedents of sauerkraut differed considerably from that produced at present. At first the cabbage leaves were dressed with sour wine or vinegar. Later the cabbage was broken or cut into pieces, packed into containers and covered with verjuice,* sour wine or vinegar. Just when the acid liquids were replaced by salt and a spontaneous fermentation resulted is not known. The author has speculated that the method used today developed during the period AD 1550 to 1750 (Vaughn, 1982).

For at least 150 years sauerkraut has been made in the home as a means of 'saving' fresh cabbage which otherwise would spoil before it could be used. In the interim the production of sauerkraut has become an important food industry. Even so, a significant quantity is still produced in the home where vegetable gardens still exist.

Cabbage varieties (cultivars) best suited for use in the major production areas are used. Early, midseason and late types normally are grown. Cultivars formerly used have been replaced in part by those bred to be well-adapted to mechanical harvesting and at the same time have higher soluble solids and less water, thus reducing the generation of liquid wastes (Stamer, 1975). Mild-flavoured, sweet, solid, white-headed cabbage is sought because it makes a superior product.

2.1. Preparation for Fermentation

Mature, sound heads of cabbage are trimmed to remove the outer green, broken, or dirty leaves. Then the cores are cut by a reversing corer that

---

* Verjuice is the acid juice from green (unripe) grapes or other sour fruit according to the Shorter Oxford English Dictionary [Ed.].

leaves the cut core in the head. The head of cabbage is then sliced by adjustable, rotary knives into shreds as fine as about 0.16–0.08 cm ($\frac{1}{16}$–$\frac{1}{32}$ in.). The preference is for long, finely cut shreds, but the thickness is determined by the judgement of the manufacturer and the inherent limitations of the slicing machines and the cabbage used. The cut cabbage (also known as slaw) is then transported by belts or carts to the vats or tanks. The salting procedure varies. In some factories the shreds are weighed on conveyor belts and the correct amount of salt is sprinkled on the slaw by a proportioner as the mass moves along the belt to the vat. In other plants where hand carts are used the cabbage may be weighed in each cart or the slaw in carts may be weighed occasionally to check the amount being delivered to the vat. An attempt is made to make a uniform distribution of salt as the tank is filled. A concentration in the range of 2.25–2.5% salt is used. Forks are used to uniformly distribute the shreds dumped into the vat.

Brine begins to form as soon as the slaw is salted. Once the tank has been filled to the proper level it is closed. Within a few hours the brine has formed and the fermentation has started. At the time of filling to the desired level the shreds are covered with a sheet of plastic large enough to cover much more than the area in the top of the tank. The plastic sheeting is placed against the top of the slaw with the edges draped over the sides of the vat to form an open bag. Then water or preferably salt brine is placed in the bag so that the weight of the added solution forces the shredded cabbage down into the brine until the uppermost shreds are covered. It is mandatory that the slaw be completely immersed to prevent undesirable darkening and flavour changes in the shreds. This method of weighting the cover provides nearly anaerobic conditions once carbon dioxide begins to be formed by fermentation. The use of the plastic cover has eliminated the problem of oxidative yeast growth on the brine surface as well as the loss of acidity and production of a yeasty flavour in the kraut.

2.2. Microbiology of the Sauerkraut Fermentation

Once brine has covered the salted, weighted slaw a bacterial fermentation has started in a sequence of species responsible for the lactic acid fermentation. Although the lactic fermentation was described by Pasteur in 1858 and it was studied extensively in the intervening years, it was not until 1930 that a definite sequence of lactic acid bacterial species was found by Pederson to be responsible for the fermentation of sauerkraut. Pederson found that the fermentation was initiated by the heterofermentative species *Leuconostoc mesenteroides* and was followed by heterofermentative rods and finally by homofermentative rods and cocci. Additional studies by Pederson & Albury (1954, 1969) firmly established that *Leuconostoc mesenteroides* initiated the lactic fermentation of sauerkraut. They also more closely identified the species and sequence of the other bacteria involved. It is now accepted that the kraut fermentation is initiated by *Leuconostoc mesenteroides*, a gas-forming species whose initiation of growth is more rapid than other lactic bacteria and is active over a wide range of temperatures and salt concentrations. It produces lactic and acetic acids and carbon dioxide that quickly lower the pH, thus limiting the activity of undesirable micro-organisms and enzymes that might soften the cabbage shreds. The carbon dioxide replaces air and creates an anaerobic atmosphere conducive to prevention of oxidation of ascorbic acid and darkening the natural colour of the cut cabbage. Carbon dioxide also stimulates the growth of many lactic acid bacteria. Also *L. mesenteroides* may provide growth factors needed by the more fastidious species found in the fermentation.

During the early stages of the fermentation when *L. mesenteroides* is multiplying rapidly the natural contaminants of the slaw may develop temporarily. However, these incidental bacteria, largely gram-negative coliform and pseudomonad types generally are undetectable by growth in a day or two. At the same time that these contaminants are disappearing the heterofermentative *Lactobacillus brevis* and the homofermentative *Lactobacillus plantarum* and sometimes *Pediococcus cerevisiae* begin to increase rapidly and add their contributions to the major end products including lactic and acetic acids, carbon dioxide and ethanol.

Minor end products also appear. A variety of additional volatile compounds are produced by the fermenting bacteria or by auto-chemical reactions or by the intrinsic enzymes of the fermenting cabbage itself. Diacetyl and acetaldehyde were reported by Hrdlicka *et al.* (1967) as the primary carbonyls produced during kraut fermentation. Volatile sulphur compounds are major flavour components of fresh cabbage and also of sauerkraut according to Bailey *et al.* (1961) and Clapp *et al.* (1959). On the other hand, according to Lee *et al.* (1976), the major amount of the volatiles in sauerkraut is accounted for by acetal, isoamyl alcohol, n-hexanol, ethyl lactate, cis-hex-3-ene-1-ol, and allyl isothiocyanate. Only the two latter compounds have been identified as major constituents of fresh cabbage. Lee and associates (1976) concluded that although these two compounds define the character of sauerkraut, they do not contribute significantly to its quality. Instead they believe that the fresh, fruity aroma of such compounds as ethyl butyrate, isoamyl acetate, n-hexyl acetate and mesityl oxide probably are more important in determining the acceptability of sauerkraut.

2.3. Control of Temperature of Fermentation

The important controlling factor in the sauerkraut fermentation at a salt concentration of around 2·25 % is the temperature. Now it is quite clear that a temperature of about 65 °F is optimum for the fermentation. This was first recorded by Parmele *et al.* (1927), Marten *et al.* (1929) and others. The detailed study of Pederson and Albury reported in 1969 clearly showed that a temperature of about 18 °C (65 °F) with a salt concentration of 2·25 % should be considered normal in the kraut-producing areas of the United States. At, or near, this temperature the desirable sequence of lactic acid bacteria is initiated. As a result a final total acidity of 1·7–2·3 % acid (calculated as lactic acid) is produced and the ratio of volatile to non-volatile acid (acetic/lactic) is about 1:4. The fermentation is completed in 1–2 months, depending upon the amount of fermentable materials, fluctuation in salt concentration and temperature. As would be expected, they found that the rate of acid production was faster at higher temperatures. As the temperature was increased they observed a change in the sequence of lactic acid bacteria found as well as a marked change in rate of acid formation. First, the growth of *Leuconostoc mesenteroides* was retarded and *Lactobacillus brevis* and *Lactobacillus plantarum* dominated the fermentation. At a temperature of 32 °C (89·6 °F) and above the fermentation became essentially a homofermentation dominated by *Lactobacillus plantarum* and *Pediococcus cerevisiae*. The flavour and aroma of the kraut deteriorated and became reminiscent of acidified cabbage because of the preponderance of lactic acid formed by the two homofermentative species. It was also found that sauerkraut fermented at the higher temperatures darkened readily and therefore should be canned as quickly as possible after the fermentation was determined to be complete.

Perhaps the most important observation Pederson and Albury made was that sauerkraut could be successfully fermented even when started at the low temperature of 7·5 °C (45·5 °F). *Leuconostoc mesenteroides* grows at lower temperatures than the other lactic acid bacteria involved in a normal fermentation. Consequently, at the low temperature a total acidity of 0·4 % calculated as lactic is produced in about 10 days and 0·8–0·9 % in less than a month. This acidity together with the saturation of the mass of shredded cabbage and brine with carbon dioxide produced by the bacterium is sufficient to provide conditions necessary for preservation and later completion of the fermentation provided that anaerobic conditions are maintained throughout the period of dormancy in the winter months. When the mass of sauerkraut warms sufficiently in the spring, the fermentation is completed by the two species of *Lactobacillus* and the *Pediococcus* known to grow very poorly or not at all at the low temperature. This manoeuvre may require 6 months or more before the fermentation is completed. Kraut held over the winter in this fashion is generally of superior quality because it remains cool and is not subjected to excessive temperature during fermentation. This variation in fermentation practice enables the processor to have a supply of new, completely fermented kraut throughout most of the year without resorting to expensive incubation procedures.

2.4. Defects and Spoilage of Sauerkraut

Most of the problems involving discoloration (autochemical oxidation), loss of acidity, off-flavour and odours (mouldy, yeasty and rancid), slimy, softened kraut and pink-coloured kraut, all caused by aerobic growth of moulds and/or yeasts, can all be eliminated by providing anaerobiosis as done when the fermenting cabbage has been covered with a plastic sheet weighted with water or preferably brine (Pedersen & Albury, 1969).

Whether the induction of the red colour in white cabbage juice by *Lactobacillus brevis* described by Stamer *et al.* (1973) will be observed in industrial fermentations remains to be seen.

Slimy or ropy kraut has been recognised as a defect for many years. It generally is the result of dextran formation caused by *Leuconostoc mesenteroides* and is a transitory problem. This species prefers to ferment fructose rather than glucose so in the fermentation of sucrose, the fructose is decomposed but leaves the glucose to form dextrans which vary from gelatinous to a ropy slime surrounding the bacterial cells. The fermenting sauerkraut may become quite slimy during the intermediate stage of fermentation. With more time the dextrans are utilised by the other lactic acid bacteria. This condition certainly should not be considered a defect but rather a normal step in the sequence of fermentation. Slimy kraut caused by pectinolytic activity is permanent in effect.

3. THE PREPARATION OF PICKLES

The cucumber (*Cucumis sativus*) is one of the oldest vegetables cultivated continuously by man. It is thought to have had its origin in India more than 3000 years ago. It is utilised both as a fresh vegetable and as various pickled products and is grown widely. However, care must be taken to protect the plants against frost and drought and to control their insect pests and microbial parasites.

Cucumbers for pickling must be grown from varieties known to have regular form, firm texture and overall good pickling characteristics. Formerly the common pickling cucumber varieties recommended by various authorities included the Chicago pickling, Boston pickling, Jersey pickling, National pickling, Heinz pickling, Snow's perfection and various other strains of lesser importance. These varieties, all open-pollinated (monoecious) plants which bear both male and female blossoms, have been largely replaced by hybrids developed to be used with once-over mechanical harvesters. The new varieties have a preponderance of female flowers and for this reason are called gynoecious but are not 100 % female. Now, however, most gynoecious seed must have some open-pollinated seed added to ensure a good crop. These new cultivars often are more uniform in size and shape and have greater growth vigour than the open-pollinated ones grown previously. Also some of the hybrids are early maturing so they can be used advantageously in prolonging the harvest period.

The hybrids developed for once-over mechanical harvest have the same desirable criteria valid for hand harvested cucumbers. At present, Michigan is the only state to have gone heavily to machine harvesting of cucumbers, having gathered over 95 % of its crop by machine in recent times.

Pickling cucumbers are harvested while still immature. Fully ripened ones are unfit for pickling because they become too large, change colour and shape, are full of mature seeds, and are too soft for most commercial uses. Whether hand or machine harvested, care must be taken in picking and transporting the cucumbers to avoid undue bruising and crushing. As with all fresh produce to be processed rather than sold in the fresh market, it should be mandatory to deliver the harvested cucumbers to the salting station or factory as soon as possible to prevent possible deterioration. A long holding time prior to brining allows the cucumbers to 'sweat' thus promoting the growth of undesirable softening organisms which may cause spoilage early in the brine fermentation before an inhibitory pH has developed which will tend to control the pectinolytic or cellulolytic microbes nearly always found to be present on the cucumbers at harvest.

Sorting to remove all crushed or broken, defective and distorted cucumbers (wilt, rot, crooks, nubbins, etc.) should be done before brining to minimise spoilage during the fermentation. Sorting is followed by size grading unless the cucumbers are to be fermented field run. Mechanical graders separate the cucumbers into various sizes. Final sizing and sorting is done after fermentation.

Three kinds of cucumber pickles are produced. They include fresh pack (also known as fresh cure, home style and by other names) which, at most, are held in salt brine for up to 2 days, then packed in tin cans or glass jars and pasteurised; salt stock pickles from which a variety of processed products are produced; and fermented dill pickles. The fresh pack pickles undergo a marginal fermentation (consult Pederson, 1979) whereas the two others undergo a complete lactic acid fermentation.

It has been variously estimated that up to 50 % of the annual harvest of pickling cucumbers is made directly into fresh pack, pasteurised products including whole dills, dill spears (wedges), dill slices, chips, sweet slices, etc., and the remainder of the crop is converted into fermented salt stock pickles or fermented dill pickles by lactic acid fermentation. The finished salt stock is desalted and processed into various staple products including sweet and sour pickles, mixed pickles, processed dills, sliced pickles, relishes, etc.

3.1. Brining Techniques for Pickles

In the brining industry the concentration of salt is determined by hydrometry in most control situations. The salt present in a brine is expressed in degrees Salometer which is percent saturation of NaCl by weight. A saturated solution of pure sodium chloride (100° Salometer) contains 26·359 g per 100 ml at 60 °F (15·5 °C). Thus, a Salometer reading of 10° is equal to 2·64 % salt by weight (rounded to the nearest tenth). Salt hydrometers generally are calibrated so that the readings (either in degrees Salometer or percent salt by weight) cover several ranges of salt: low, medium or high. There are two general methods for preparing produce for fermentation: dry salting and brining.

3.1.1. Dry Salting

The dry salting method for brining is not used very much for cucumbers at present. However, the method is used for other produce, especially cauliflower, red bell and pimento peppers and sometimes other vegetables including carrots, celery, okra and salt-cured ripe olives and is the method of choice for sauerkraut.

Many fresh vegetables have a specific gravity of less than one, and therefore tend to float when placed in salt solutions that have specific gravities above one. Because of the buoyancy, headboards are mounted inside the tops of brine tanks and held in place by timbers, to keep the vegetables submerged in the brine. The buoyancy of the brined vegetables can cause physical damage to those in the top layers. The buoyancy problem occurs with cucumbers and is very much of a problem with peppers because they are hollow. This requires placement of false heads (baffles) at 3–4 ft intervals in deep tanks to prevent crushing the peppers at the top of the tank.

Dry salting of cucumbers is done by adding dry salt at the rate of about 50 pounds for every 1000 lb of small cucumbers and 65 pounds per 1000 pounds of large cucumbers. (A cushion of brine 12–24 in. is added before the cucumbers are placed in the tank. This prevents bruising, breaking or crushing the fresh cucumbers when they are dumped.) Salting varies according to the vegetable but those used as mixed pickles with cucumber pickles generally are kept in quite high salt brines. For example, cauliflower and celery are kept at 60° Salometer or higher.

When full the tank is covered with a circular, slatted, wooden head so there is room for about 6 in. of brine above the cover which is then secured with heavy timbers held at the ends with clamps. For convenience in handling, the slatted cover is generally constructed so that there are two or three semi-circular pieces for large tanks. If the brine formed by osmosis does not submerge the cucumbers and top cover when the tank is closed, 40° Salometer brine is added to the desired level. A day or two after the tank is filled and closed the brine should be recirculated in order to help equalise the concentration of salt throughout the mass.

3.1.2. Brine Salting

Most picklers use the brine salting method for fermenting cucumbers rather than the dry salting technique just described. The brine varies from 20° to 40° or more Salometer. The low brine generally varies from 20° to 30° Salometer and is used for the start of fermentation. The 40° Salometer brine generally is used during storage of fermented salt stock or to start curing of other vegetables used with cucumbers in making the mixed pickle product. If wooden tanks are used the cucumbers are filled into tanks and are headed in the manner already described.

In recent years, moulded plastic and fibreglass tanks have been favoured for replacement of the wood or concrete containers lost by attrition. These plastic or fibreglass tanks have some distinct advantages. They are inert to biological degradation or corrosion as are wood and concrete, respectively; they do not have to be maintained during the off season, as do wood tanks, to keep them from drying out and developing leaks which may require extensive coopering to repair. Metal corrosion and resultant contamination of the cucumbers with copper and iron is eliminated because the drain valves are plastic (polyvinyl chloride) as is all other pertinent piping. The most significant advantage of these newer containers, however, is that, if properly designed, they have closures that are nearly completely airtight so that growth of aerobic yeasts and the problems of loss of acidity and of softening are greatly minimised or eliminated. Polyethylene sheet plastic may be used in the same manner as described above with sauerkraut or as done with cucumbers and olives held in open wood tanks in California. In this latter case, the plastic is floated on the surface of the brine and secured to the inside of the tank with pliable wooden slats nailed so that the plastic is held in place at the surface of the brine. This placement will provide nearly anaerobic conditions unless the plastic has perforations or the slats are improperly spaced so that air can contact the brine. 'Sealtight', a wax used in the wine industry can be used to seal the plastic cover to the sides of the tank if necessary.

3.2. Microbiology of the Cucumber Fermentation

Once the cucumbers have been brined and the tank closed, there is a rapid development of micro-organisms in the brine. In most cases no attempt is made to control the micro-organisms in the brines so the cucumbers undergo a 'spontaneous' fermentation. The natural controls which affect the microbial populations of the fermenting cucumbers include the concentration of salt and temperature of the brine, the availability of fermentable materials, and the numbers and types of micro-organisms present at the start of fermentation. The rapidity of the fermentation is correlated with the concentration of salt in the brine and its temperature.

The initial brine strength is variable according to the choice of the individual pickler. Formerly, higher concentrations of salt were used in the initial brine because high levels of salt were thought to retard spoilage. Now cucumbers are generally fermented in brines in the range of 20°–30° Salometer salt (about 5–8 % NaCl). At this concentration of salt, the sequence of species of lactic acid bacteria approximate the succession already described for the fermentation of sauerkraut. However, with cucumbers *Leuconostoc* types never predominate the initial stages of the fermentation, even at 5 % salt. At 8 % salt these bacteria may not be detected at all. The other species of lactic acid bacteria, *Pediococcus cerevisiae*, *Lactobacillus brevis* and *Lactobacillus plantarum* occur in most, if not all fermentations made of 20°–30° Salometer brines. *Pediococcus cerevisiae* and *Lactobacillus brevis* are less resistant to salt than is *Lactobacillus plantarum* so sometimes they are absent in the higher concentration (30° Salometer) brine. *Lactobacillus plantarum* is the most salt resistant species but it is severely retarded at salt concentrations of 40° Salometer and above and little, if any, growth occurs at above 45° Salometer.

During the primary fermentation, a great number of unrelated bacteria, yeasts, and moulds have been isolated. All are widely distributed in nature and, at the start of the fermentation, are much more abundant than the desirable lactic acid bacteria in spontaneous fermentations. Therefore, the primary stage of fermentation is the most important part of the pickling process. If during this period the fermentation does not proceed normally, any of the unessential micro-organisms may dominate the fermentation and cause spoilage. The primary stage normally lasts 2 or 3 days and exceptionally as long as 7 or more days. During this time, the lactic acid bacteria and fermenting and oxidising yeasts increase rapidly, and the undesirable forms diminish and may disappear entirely as a result of the rapid increase in total acidity and drop in the pH value of the brine.

In fermenting cucumber brine stabilised at about 20° Salometer salt, a mixture of the low- and high-acid-tolerant lactic bacteria predominate during the intermediate stage of fermentation. If the fermentation is normal, the extraneous and undesirable bacteria will have all disappeared in 10–14 days, although yeasts are still present in significant numbers, specifically if the fermentation is aerobic because this enables the oxidative yeasts to survive and grow along with the other micro-organisms.

The final stage of fermentation is completed by the species *Lactobacillus brevis*, *Lactobacillus plantarum* and *Pediococcus cerevisiae* and these are responsible for the build-up of lactic acid in uncontrolled fermentations in salt brines of 20°–30° Salometer. All three species are found when the cucumbers are fermented at about 30° Salometer but the activity of *Pediococcus cerevisiae* is much restricted at this concentration, and it does not proliferate once the pH falls to about 3·7. This leaves the two lactobacilli species to complete the fermentation (Etchells *et al.*, 1975). At completion, the total acidity may be as high as 0·9% calculated as lactic acid and have a pH value as low as 3·3 if oxidative yeasts have been kept inactive.

The data of Etchells & Jones (1943) shown in Fig. 1 demonstrate the changes in the populations of coliform bacteria, acid-forming microbes, and yeasts formed in natural fermentations of brined cucumbers in salt concentrations of 20°, 40°, and 60° Salometer, respectively. It is obvious that the coliform bacteria are readily inhibited in brine fermentations with 40° Salometer or less because of the rapid development of acid by the lactic acid bacteria. However, in the 60° Salometer brines, the lactic acid bacteria and the salt-resistant coliform bacteria (see dotted line in Fig. 1) and yeasts

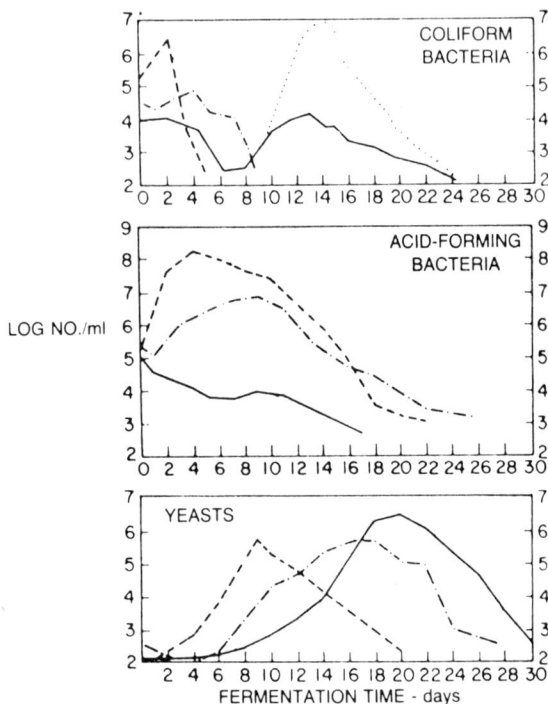

Fig. 1. Effects of brine strength on the predominating microbial groups in natural fermentations of brined cucumbers. (– – – –) 20° Salometer; (– · – · –) 40° Salometer; (———) 60° Salometer. (From Etchells & Jones, 1943.)

compete for the fermentable materials and may produce large quantities of CO_2 and H_2 gas and cause a large number of hollow cucumbers (bloaters). This is one of the major reasons for picklers using low salt brine for fermentation today. As will be discussed below, gas purging of the fermentation also has a major role in elimination of bloaters.

3.3. Fermented Dill Pickles
Genuine dill pickles differ from the other well known dill pickles (fresh cure and processed dills) because they are the product of a lactic acid fermentation in a dill weed flavoured, spiced salt brine of about 20° Salometer which gives them the distinctive flavour and aroma of the genuine dill pickles.

All commercial sizes of cucumbers may be used but the larger sizes generally are made into fermented dills. They are generally fermented in a low-salt brine of 20° Salometer or less but some choose to ferment the cucumbers at about 30° Salometer. It is a common practice to add vinegar to the brine to decrease the pH value to prevent the growth of undesirable spoilage micro-organisms.

The fermentation is usually active for 3 weeks to a month and an additional curing period is considered to be essential because during the period (up to 2 months after start of the fermentation) the flesh of the cucumbers becomes entirely translucent. The optimum temperature for the fermentation is between 70° and 80°F unless they are held at a constant room temperature inside.

The fermented brines contain from 0·5 to 1·2 % total acidity calculated as lactic acid. In addition a small amount of acetic acid, ethanol, and other minor products is produced by the lactic acid bacteria and yeasts during the fermentation. The pH values range from about 3·3 to 3·5 if the pickles have been held in nearly anaerobic containers. Otherwise, if oxidative yeasts are present, the pH values will be higher because of the loss of acid devoured by them.

Formerly, most picklers used 50 gallon barrels for fermentation of dill pickles, although a few did use small tanks. However, bulk fermentation must now be considered the chief mode of fermentation. Increased understanding of the need for anaerobic fermentations has contributed to bulk fermentations in wood tanks filled with a plastic film and plastic and fibreglass containers designed to furnish anaerobiosis.

'Overnight', 'Icebox' or Refrigerated dill pickles are similar to dills except that they are stored and fermented at 38°–45°F where a slow lactic acid fermentation produces a total acidity (calculated as lactic) of only about 0·3–0·6 % at the end of 6 months. These refrigerated pickles retain more or less of the fresh cucumber flavour and are highly prized as a food by many people. However, because of their perishability, they have to be kept under refrigeration until sold for consumption. Their availability, generally at delicatessens, is not widespread.

At the start of either type of dill fermentation, a mixture of many unrelated bacteria, yeasts, and moulds, all widely distributed in nature, far outnumber the lactic acid bacteria when the pickles are brined. However, if the fermentation is normal, the lactic acid bacteria soon predominate and proceed in the sequence already described for the salt stock fermentations. However, because of the lower salt concentration and the lower temperature in the case of the refrigerated dill pickles, *Leuconostoc mesenteroides* is more active and plays a more important role than with the salt stock pickles. The studies described by Pederson & Ward (1949) and

Pederson & Albury (1950) verify the initiation of the fermentation by *Leuconostoc mesenteroides* at lower temperatures and salt concentrations.

3.4. Deterioration of Pickles

Most of the spoilage of cucumbers during fermentation, curing, and storage is caused by the activity of micro-organisms, either by the elaboration of spoilage enzymes (softening of pectin and cellulose) or as the result of undesirable production of gaseous end products (CO_2 and H_2) which cause excessive gas pressure and distortion of the flesh resulting in internal cavities. Tissue destruction and loss of texture or firmness caused by cellulolytic and pectinolytic enzymes generally means nearly total economic loss. The defect known as 'bloater' or 'floater' spoilage caused by excessive gas pressure is another common microbial spoilage which results in the production of internal cavities or distorted stock (see Fig. 2).

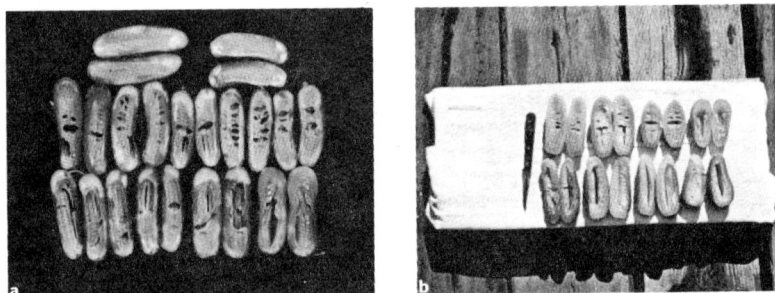

Fig. 2. Gaseous spoilage of pickles. (a) Severe lens and balloon bloaters in partially cured brine-stock pickles; (b) bloaters in small sized brine-stock pickles (about 1 in or less in diameter). (From Etchells *et al.*, 1973; courtesy H. P. Fleming.)

Affected cucumbers may have lens-shaped internal cavities or the locules may be slightly separated. When gas production is really severe the locules become completely separated and the flesh in each locule is compressed so that the interior becomes hollow and the shape then reminds one of a balloon. Cucumbers damaged by destructive gas pressure can be salvaged in part by diverting them to relish type products. At the present time bloater spoilage of dill pickles may mean a loss because dill relish is not an item of importance.

3.5. Softening

Softening is the result of pectinolytic or cellulolytic enzyme activity produced by micro-organisms capable of growing under the conditions of acidity, salinity, etc., found in pickle brines. Softening is a progressive spoilage. It occurs most frequently soon after the cucumbers are brined. The first manifestation of softening is alteration of the skin of the cucumber. Usually the blossom end is attacked first but, in a short time, the entire skin may be affected, becoming slippery and easily sloughed from the pickles. This slipperiness has given rise to the descriptive terms 'slips' or 'slippery' pickles in the industry. 'Mushy' pickles result when the softening enzymes penetrate into the deeper layers of cells and more and more pectic materials are attacked. Surprisingly, the form of the pickle may appear to be normal, but if pressure is applied, it turns mushy.

Bacteria, moulds, and yeasts all produce pectinolytic enzymes of which three different ones are recognised. Pectin methylesterase (pectinesterase) splits off methyl groups from the pectin molecule leaving pectic acid. Polygalacturonase degrades pectic acid leaving saturated digalacturonic acid or higher oligouronides. Polygalacturonic acid *trans*-eliminase attacks pectic acid leaving unsaturated digalacturonic acid or higher oligouronides as the major end products.

Pectic enzymes produced by a variety of bacteria have been studied and well described by Vaughn and his associates. The Gram-positive bacilli have been studied in detail. These include *Bacillus subtilis, B. pumilus, B. polymyxa, B. macerans* and *B. stearothermophilus* (see Nortji & Vaughn, 1953; Nagel & Vaughn, 1961; Davé & Vaughn, 1971; and Karbassi & Vaughn, 1980). The Gram-negative types, including the genera *Achromobacter, Aerobacter, Aeromonas, Escherichia, Erwinia* and *Paracolobactrum* also have strains producing pectinolytic activity (see King & Vaughn, 1961; Hsu & Vaughn, 1969; and Vaughn *et al.*, 1969b).

All of the bacteria mentioned above have been shown to degrade pickles, making them slippery and then mushy in texture when tested *in vitro* with pure cultures and sterilised cucumbers when in a 20° Salometer brine with a pH value of 5·5 or above. It is concluded that species of bacteria can cause softening of cucumbers if the pectinolytic bacteria come to predominate the microbial populations of the pickles through mishandling of the harvested cucumbers so that they are held too long and can undergo sweating before they are brined or if, for some reason, the lactic acid fermentation is retarded or arrested so that the pH values of the brined cucumbers remain relatively high for several days.

Different moulds and yeasts also have the ability to degrade pectinous material. A variety of moulds produce softening enzymes including both cellulolytic and pectinolytic types. The moulds may produce pectinesterase, polygalacturonase and pectin-*trans*-eliminase. These enzymes have been carefully described by Phaff (1947) with *Penicillium chrysogenum* and by Edstrom & Phaff (1964) who used *Aspergillus fonsecaeus* to describe the purification and properties of pectin-*trans*-eliminase.

The softening fungi include representatives of the genera *Alternaria*, *Aspergillus*, *Cladosporium*, *Dematium*, *Fusarium*, *Geotrichum*, *Mucor*, *Myrothecium*, *Paecilomyces*, *Penicillium*, *Phoma* and *Trichoderma*. Etchells *et al.* (1955) showed that moulds grow and secrete softening enzymes into the cucumber flowers. Then, the introduction of the enzyme laden fresh or dried flowers adhering to the cucumbers on which they have developed, provides the causal factor for spoilage when the cucumbers are brined. Tanks filled with small cucumbers retaining a high percentage of flowers or with experimentally added detached flowers possess great enzyme activity, and the cucumbers generally become soft or have developed inferior firmness. Losses caused by contaminated flowers can be greatly reduced or made negligible by simply removing the original cover brine and replacing it with new brine (Etchells *et al.*, 1958).

Draining the cover brine from tanks of small cucumbers about 36 h after brining or washing the cucumbers prior to brining as is done in the controlled fermentation process (Etchells *et al.*, 1973) effectively lowers the level of softening enzymes. Softening enzymes are inhibited by the tannin-like compounds found in grape leaves (Bell & Etchells, 1958) and other plants (Bell *et al.*, 1962, 1965a, b) but, unfortunately, no official government approval for use of the inhibitor under commercial conditions has been granted. Recent state and federal regulations concerning the disposal of salt brines in the pickling industries have prompted a rush of studies designed to reclaim the brines for recycling. Many investigations have been made but despite many efforts the problem is still acute and demands severe restriction of salt usage in brining. The simplest method for reclaiming the brine would be the use of heat to inactivate enzymes and micro-organisms, followed by precipitation, flocculation and filtration procedures commonly used for water purification. If the acid is undesirable it can be easily removed by the use of oxidative yeasts in a system purging the brine with air. The concentration of salt brine obviously can be done by incineration or reverse osmosis but is most impractical from the economic standpoint.

3.6. Gaseous Spoilage

Gas-producing micro-organisms known to cause gaseous deterioration of pickles represent a variety of yeasts and bacteria. The first strong evidence that gaseous spoilage was caused by micro-organisms was presented by

Veldhuis and Etchells in 1939. They reported that hydrogen was produced in significant quantities in cucumber fermentations at 60° Salometer brine and in some, but not all, fermentations at lower salt concentrations. They also isolated, but did not identify, a bacterium that produced significant quantities of hydrogen, probably an *Aerobacter* (see Etchells *et al.*, 1945). In 1941 Jones *et al.* and Etchells and Jones suggested that gas production by unidentified yeasts was the cause of 'floater' spoilage.

Activity of yeasts in natural pickle fermentations is undesirable, either because they cause copious gas production and increase the propensity for bloater spoilage or because they utilise lactic acid and, unless controlled, cause an increase in pH value to where spoilage bacteria can renew activities. The fermenting yeasts have been found to be members of the genera *Brettanomyces*, *Hansenula*, *Saccharomyces* and *Torulopsis* by Etchells *et al.* (1961). The oxidative yeasts were identified as belonging to the genera *Candida*, *Endomycopsis*, *Debaryomyces* and *Zygosaccharomyces* to be responsible for film formation on salt stock pickles. (*Brettanomyces* is now *Torulopsis*. *Endomycopsis* is now *Pichia*. *Zygosaccharomyces* is now *Saccharomyces*.)

It has been apparent for some years that the lactic acid bacteria might be involved in floater formation. Etchells & Bell (1956) showed that *Lactobacillus brevis*, one of the gas-forming lactic acid bacteria, caused floater formation *in vitro*. More recently most of the unknown factors in the complete explanation of 'bloater' spoilage have been uncovered by Etchells and his associates. They first observed that when unheated large-sized cucumbers were brined, serious bloating occurred even when *Lactobacillus plantarum* was the fermenting species (Etchells *et al.*, 1973). This phenomenon was explained when it was found that the brined unheated cucumbers respired enough carbon dioxide into the brine so that when combined with the small amount produced by *L. plantarum* it was enough to cause floater damage (Fleming *et al.*, 1973b).

Besides the coliform organisms, other gas-forming bacteria found in the initial stage of the pickle fermentation are known to cause *in vitro* spoilage in pasteurised, brined cucumbers. These include the gas-forming pseudomonad, *Aeromonas liquefaciens*, and the *Bacillus polymyxa-macerans* aerobic bacilli (Vaughn, 1953). Thus, it is seen that all of the gas-forming micro-organisms found in pickle brines, yeasts or bacteria, desirable or undesirable, may at one time or another be responsible for producing enough carbon dioxide and/or hydrogen to cause floater spoilage if helped along by the cucumbers themselves.

Fortunately, technical information now available may eliminate gaseous spoilage of cucumbers if picklers use the knowledge now available. This entails simple purging of the brine with nitrogen gas to sweep carbon dioxide from the brine until the fermentation is completed (Etchells *et al.*, 1973; Fleming *et al.*, 1973*b*, 1975).

A method for controlled fermentation of salt stock pickles was developed by Etchells *et al.*, 1973, 1975) and has been in commercial use for several years. This method has been developed to favour the growth of the starter culture (*Lactobacillus plantarum* alone or in a mixture with *Pediococcus cerevisiae*) rather than the initial natural population. Although the entire controlled fermentation is in limited use, the nitrogen purging of brines of carbon dioxide has been almost universally adopted and has had a significant impact on the industry through increased yields and improved quality of salt-stock pickles (see Fleming *et al.*, 1975; Fleming, 1979; Costilow *et al.*, 1977). In any event, there has been a dramatic decrease in floater spoilage and a most welcome increase in salt stock quality as the result of this development. The damaging effect of too much gas pressure on the timbers of a headed tank of brined salt stock is shown in Fig. 3.

Air purging of commercial salt-stock pickle fermentations has been studied by Costilow *et al.* (1981) during two brining seasons. They

Fig. 3.   Damage caused by excessive gas pressure on the timbers of a headed tank of brine salt stock. (Courtesy H. P. Fleming.)

concluded that air-purging was as efficient as nitrogen in preventing formation of bloater pickles and that there were no significant effects of the various treatments they studied. However, softening did occur in two tanks but no reasons(s) for the occurrence of softening was found. Laboratory fermentations done by Gates & Costilow (1981) were designed to study factors influencing softening and treatments which might prevent softening of salt-stock pickles. The cucumbers were softened much more rapidly and extensively when purged at 100 ml air/min than at 20 ml air/min and softening could not be prevented by initial acidification or by use of 35° Salometer brine. Softening was not found when air-purged lots were treated with controlled fermentation process; with added 0·035% potassium sorbate; nitrogen purging for the first 2 days and then air-purging; or use of blanched cucumbers inoculated by use of cover brine which had washed unblanched cucumbers. Apparently softening of air-purged pickles is caused by the growth of oxygen-dependent, sorbic acid-sensitive organisms growing in or on the cucumbers.

3.7. Unusual Deterioration

The production of black pickles was first investigated in detail by Rahn (1913) who reported that the black colour resulted from the production of iron sulphide caused by bacterial reduction of sulphate in gypsum ($CaSO_4$) to hydrogen sulphide which then reacted with the iron in the brine to produce the black iron sulphide. Fabian *et al.* (1932) confirmed the work of Rahn and extended it to include consideration of the possible liberation of hydrogen sulphide during the course of bacterial decomposition of protein. The bacteria possibly responsible for hydrogen sulphide production were not identified. An additional source of blackening was found by Fabian & Nienhuis (1934) to result from the production of a black, water-soluble pigment by *Bacillus nigrificans*. According to Fabian and associates blackening can be prevented by elimination of iron and sulphate contamination and by controlled fermentation of the brine.

Black brine in pickle fermentations, instead of always involving bacterial reduction of sulphate or protein sulphur compounds, in all probability frequently is caused by the reaction of iron with polyphenolic compounds to form complex iron 'tannates' which are black, bluish-black or greenish-black in colour. Iron must be oxidised to the ferric state to start the reaction and enough oxygen must be available to keep it going. This reaction starts at the surface of the brine and extends downward as the oxygen penetrates.

Although sulphate reducing micro-organisms have not, to the author's knowledge, been recovered from pickle brines the possibility exists that they might be in the future. Sulphate reducing bacteria have been recovered from salt brines used in storage of olives (Levin & Vaughn, 1966).

3.8. Controlled Fermentation of Pickles

Pure culture fermentation of brined cucumbers was reported by Etchells *et al.* (1964). This study led to the concept of 'In Container' or 'Ready to Eat' of a variety of kinds of pickles. The processes for production of the ready to eat dill pickles and other products were described in a public service patent by Etchells *et al.* (1968). The process required heat-shocking and aseptic packing of the pickles into sanitised containers, followed by covering with a pasteurised brine (heated to 170 °F and cooled to 40 °F) and inoculation of the brine with pure cultures of lactic acid bacteria to give a controlled fermentation. However, an attempt to adapt the pure culture technique to tanks was unsuccessful because of unresolved economic problems. Instead, a bulk fermentation procedure has been described (Etchells *et al.*, 1973, 1975) which is economically practical, especially if the essential steps are followed, and will eliminate most losses by spoilage organisms.

Some of the steps prepared by Etchells and associates are new; others have been practised in the industry for over 50 years. However, together the procedural steps greatly advance the art, science and technology of pickle fermentation.

Because it was impractical to eliminate the contaminating microorganisms with heat as was done with the pure culture process, thorough washing and in-container chlorination of the 25 ° Salometer cover brine (about 80 ppm of chlorine) were employed. The brine is acidified with acetic acid (food grade) or with vinegar concentrate to an initial pH value of about 2·8, which results in a concentration of about 0·16 % acetic acid when the equilibration is complete. The cover brine was rechlorinated about a half day after the cucumbers were brined.

Now that the process is in extensive commercial use it has been determined that chlorination is not necessary, so it is no longer a step in the controlled fermentation process. Thorough washing to remove dirt and lower the concentrations of undesirable micro-organisms and softening enzymes, together with acidification, holds the natural microflora in check prior to addition of buffer and the starter culture (see Fleming, 1982).

Salt is added to the cover brine to maintain the original brine strength which otherwise would be diluted because of the water content of the cucumbers (approximately 95 %). The amount of dry salt added over the next few days will depend upon the size of the cucumbers being brined. The added salt on equilibration maintains the brine strength at or near that of the original cover brine.

After the first salt addition has reached equilibrium but before the second salt addition and 3–4 h before the addition of the starter culture(s), sodium acetate is added to buffer the acidified cover brine whose pH value is raised from below 4·0 to about 4·6 (Etchells *et al.*, 1973). The buffering is done to ensure that all of the fermentable sugars will have been utilised during the active lactic acid fermentation. Obviously, addition of sodium hydroxide to increase the pH of the brine will, if properly done, have the same effect for the alkali will react with the acetic acid to form sodium acetate and thus buffer the brine. Commercial picklers commonly use this method of buffering the brine. Sodium hydroxide is added, preferably as pellets contained in plastic bags. The bags are punctured to allow gradual dissolution and release of the hydroxide into the stream of acidified brine continuously discharging from the side-arm of the purger.

The starter culture may be made with the two species of homofermentative lactic acid bacteria: *Lactobacillus plantarum* and *Pediococcus cerevisiae* or *L. plantarum* alone. The requirements are that the cultures selected be able to produce maximum performance under the conditions supposed to be optimum for fermentation. They must grow at their best at 75°–85°F, not be retarded by 6–8 % salt, and produce a minimum amount of carbon dioxide. If cultures of both genera are used, neither strain must inhibit the growth of the other.

Fig. 4. Tank of fermentation salt stock pickles undergoing nitrogen purging (note frothy effluent exiting from purger side-arm). (Courtesy H. P. Fleming.)

Nitrogen purging is started as soon as the cucumbers have been brined. It is continued during the entire fermentation, which is completed within 7–12 days under optimum conditions of temperature (Fig. 4).

4. THE FERMENTATION OF OLIVES

Our knowledge of the origin of table olive fermentation is lost in antiquity. Fortunately, however, the history of the table olive industry in California has been fairly well documented. According to LeLong (1890) the first olive trees in the state were seedlings grown from seed said to have been planted at the Mission San Diego in 1769. The seeds were brought from San Blas, Mexico by Don Jose de Galvez during an expedition to rediscover the port of Monterey. The seedling trees thus obtained, after careful selection became the source of the present mission variety of *Olea europaea*.

Although olives were used for oil production in the California missions as early as 1780, olive oil production did not occur outside the missions until 1871. The olive was not planted extensively until about 1860, but by 1870 was showing promise of being important to California agriculture. Between 1870 and 1900 many varieties of olives had been imported from the Mediterranean area and much effort had been made in testing them, principally for oil producing qualities, since at that time oil was the major product of the industry.

Olive pickling for table use, practised as an art in the missions, on the ranches, and in the homes for many years, was not of much commercial importance until about 1900. (The early agricultural literature of California contains directions for pickling ripe and green olives.)

For some unknown reason, the art of pickling 'ripe' olives was studied more extensively than that of 'green' olives. Cruess (1958) reported that about 1900 it was independently discovered by Professor Bioletti of the University of California and Mrs Freda Ehmann, a commercial olive packer, that ripe olives, after a preliminary treatment with lye (sodium hydroxide solution) to destroy the bitter glucoside oleuropein, could be canned and preserved by heat in much the same way as other foods. This development, together with application of science and technology have, over the years, combined to make the California canned ripe olive the major product in the industry.

Olive oil, which was a major product of the developing commercial industry, still accounted for the utilisation of an appreciable quantity of fruit each year until about 1960. Then, because of increased harvest costs and competitive factors from abroad, oil production became and remains largely a salvage operation and tons of olives used for oil approximate those used for fermenting Spanish-type green olives, another salvage operation.

The disposition of California olives for products in approximate order of importance include black-ripe and green-ripe canned olives (whole and pitted), Spanish-style, Sicilian-type, Greek-type including brined and salt-cured fruits and oil. Canned ripe olives are the major products of the industry and may account for more than 70 % of all of the olives harvested. Green-ripe canned olives have to be processed and canned at harvest time. Fresh or direct cure black olives also are processed and canned throughout the harvest period of up to 2·5 months from September through November in high yield crop years.

Of necessity, because of lack of processing space, the remainder of the olives destined for processing have to be stored in salt brine prior to making them into canned ripe olives. Olives in brine undergo a lactic acid fermentation. Thus there are four brine fermentations including 'storage', Sicilian-type, Spanish-type and Greek-type brined olives.

The 'storage' and Sicilian-type fermentations may be considered to be identical, for the fruits are placed directly in brine with no prior lye treatment whereas the Spanish-type olives are lye treated to destroy most of the bitterness, washed to remove some of the alkali, and then brined. The brined Greek-type olives are placed in a high salt brine, which, on equilibration, may be too strong for the lactic acid bacteria to ferment the olives. An acetic fermentation caused by acid-forming, salt-tolerant yeasts generally results if the concentration of salt stays at 40° or more Salometer. Salt-cured Greek-type olives are cured with dry rock salt and become desiccated rather than undergoing a fermentation, so they will not be considered further.

4.1. Commercial Varieties

There are five main major varieties of olives growing in bearing acreage in California. The Mission olive, formerly the main variety of the industry has, during the past quarter century, declined to last place in importance because of its tendency to produce small fruits and its late maturity which endangered the crop to frosting. The main varieties, in commercial importance, grown now are the Manzanilla, Sevillano and Ascolano in the order named. Lesser varieties also are grown, especially the Barouni, which is seldom used for canned ripe olives, but it is utilised in all sizes for Spanish-type olive production. It is also sold on the fresh-produce market for home pickling as are some of the Northern California Sevillano fruits and other varieties, at the discretion of the fresh-market shippers. All varieties except the Mission are of foreign origin: the Manzanilla and Sevillano came from Spain, the Ascolano from Italy and the Barouni from Tunisia.

Each variety is of distinctive size, shape and general usefulness. The Sevillano olives are the largest in size, followed in order by the Ascolano, Barouni, Manzanilla and Mission varieties. The Manzanilla most nearly approaches the requirements of an all-purpose olive because it may easily be used for the production of California ripe olives, green fermented olives, or olive oil. The characteristics of the other varieties limit their usefulness in one way or another.

4.2. Harvesting

Olives to be used for making canned ripe olives are harvested starting around the middle or latter part of September and, if there is a large crop, ending about Thanksgiving time in late November. The time to start will depend on the variety of fruit, the locality where grown, the growing season, climatic conditions and other factors. A sharp frost causing partial freezing of the fruit is enough to terminate the picking of olives for processing. Frosted olives are generally salvaged for oil production. It is desirable to remove all, or nearly all of the olives produced in a season to foster a good set of fruit the next year. The olive tree is a notorious alternate bearer and if the fruits are not removed each year the tree tends to produce a significant crop in alternate years.

Harvesting practices favour the selection of fruit most desirable for the production of ripe and green olives because they are the major products of the industry. Therefore, when the majority of the fruit in a grove has reached the desired maturity, the harvest is started and continued, unless interrupted by rain, until the crop is gathered.

Mature olives, at the time of picking, are at the colour turning stage, from green to straw yellow or, at most, cherry red. More highly coloured fruit, deep red to dark purple, may be overripe. This very highly coloured fruit generally deteriorates during the lye treatments, and consequently is diverted to oil production, or if the flesh is still firm may be used for preparation of the brine-cured or salt-cured olive specialities of the Greek-type.

California canned-black ripe olives, generally uniformly black in colour after canning, are made from fruit ranging in colour from green to cherry red at harvest. The California green-ripe or 'home-cured' olives having a yellowish-green to light greenish-brown, frequently mottled colour after canning are made from fresh olives having a green to cherry red colour. California fermented Sicilian- and Spanish-type olives are made from fruits ranging in colour from green to straw yellow.

Machine harvesting is slowly making inroads in the traditional hand harvesting of olives. Machine tree-shakers are being used in newer groves where the trees have been pruned in a manner to promote removal by shaking. In the foreseeable future some hand harvesting will have to be done because in old groves the trees were pruned so that machine removal was impractical because it did not remove enough fruit or the trees were infirm and limb breakage caused much damage. Studies also have been made with chemical spray treatment to facilitate machine harvest of the olives (see Fridley *et al.*, 1971 and Hartmann & Opitz, 1977 for more details on mechanical harvesting).

Unfortunately, fresh olives are quite easily bruised and the amount of bruising is increased when the fruits are harvested by machine. However, the bruises do not affect the appearance of the canned black-ripe olives or the brined Greek-type olives but the bruises do persist in the canned green-ripe and the fermented green Sicilian- and Spanish-type olives.

Hand labour is reduced as much as possible to ensure economy of operation. Harvested fruit, whether hand- or machine-harvested, is placed in bulk bins for transportation to the processing plants by truck or other mechanised equipment. These bins, widely used in the food industry, are designed to be handled by fork lift trucks. They are about 4 ft square and 2 ft deep, have a two-part pallet entry and if filled completely, hold 1000 lb or more of olives.

Sweating of the fruits held for too long a time in bins can become a problem in avoidable spoilage. To avoid possible fruit damage, the olives should be run through the various plant operations in as short a time as possible. It is preferable that all bins of olives should be handled in not more than 24 h including delivery, dumping onto the transfer lines, running through the destemmer and trash remover, sorting and size grading. In the next few hours the olives should be started in process either as direct cure, placed in brine storage for Sicilian-type or for later processing or lye treated and brined.

In years when there is an exceptionally large yield, some packers store olives under refrigeration for varying lengths of time. The olives are cold-susceptible so they should not be stored below 45 °F in order to avoid an undesirable taste in the processed fruit. Freshly harvested olives can be held under refrigeration for up to 2 weeks if the refrigerated storage is properly operated and the stacks of bins are ventilated. On longer holding, moulding develops in the centre of the mass of olives, and the loss increases with increase in storage time.

A better method for refrigerated storage involves covering the olives with a 20° Salometer brine and making the containers anaerobic. With this method the olives can be held for at least 6 months without loss caused by spoilage organisms.

4.3. The Fermentation of Storage and Sicilian-type Olives

These fermentations are considered identical because the fruits are brined without any lye treatment to eliminate bitterness. If there are no cherry red olives in a tank the fruit can be used for Sicilian-type olives, or the fruit can be processed into canned black-ripe olives, according to consumer demand.

Fig. 5. Some of the plastic bottles that replaced the wooden barrels for fermentation of Spanish-type olives.

The open fermentation tanks are filled, headed and brined in much the same way already described for cucumbers. The newer plastic bottles (Fig. 5) and fibreglass tanks (Fig. 6) are filled with olives, brined, and the cover locked in place to keep the olives submerged in the brine. False heads are not required.

The salt concentration of the brine in the tank will vary with the variety of olives and the final disposition of the fruit. Ascolano and Sevillano olives are subject to salt shrivel so a lower concentration of brine (16°–20° Salometer salt) will be used if either variety is to be sold as Sicilian-type fruit. Otherwise the salt strength will range up to 32° Salometer salt because, in the processing of black-ripe olives, shrivel is reduced to a minimum by use of a needling device to pierce the skin of the olives. This

Fig. 6. Tops of a battery of 10 000 gallon fibreglass tanks used for storage of olives for future processing.

practice facilitates osmotic exchange between the needled olives and the processing solutions which include 0·9 % lye, plain water, acidified water, and 10°–12° Salometer salt. This manipulation markedly reduces or eliminates the shrivel.

The brined olives undergo a lactic acid fermentation. The amount of acidity produced is quite variable but usually will range between 0·2 % and 0·7 % calculated as grams lactic acid per 100 ml of brine. The development of acid in the storage brines shows much variation because of several factors. Sevillano olives do not 'fresh cure' well, so the majority of processors hold this variety in salt brine for a minimum of 30 days before starting the black-ripe canned olive process. This holding period does not favour an abundant development of acidity, for the olives ferment slowly at the ambient temperatures found in the brines, especially during the latter part of the harvest season. If held in open tanks, there may be a loss in acidity because of the activity of oxidative yeasts. This has been an important factor when open tanks of holding solution olives are kept in shaded or covered areas during the colder months when the undesirable yeasts and moulds are more active than the desirable lactic acid bacteria. The practice now is to provide anaerobiosis for all fermenting olives to prevent loss of acidity once it is formed. This is done by use of plastic film to cover the brine surface in open tanks or by providing either polyethylene or fibreglass containers with covers designed to minimise the access of air to the fruit.

The changes in the microbial populations observed in these fermentations may be considered to be identical if both types are held at the same salt concentration. The lactic acid bacteria found in these fermentations are of the same kinds as those already described for the sauerkraut and pickle fermentations.

In contrast to the sauerkraut and pickle fermentations which are carried out in the presence of less salt, many of the olives, including the Manzanilla and Mission varieties, are fermented in the presence of comparatively high concentrations of salt. The higher concentrations further restrict the sequence of lactic acid bacteria so that the only species still persisting is *Lactobacillus plantarum*. After the salt reaches a concentration of 40° Salometer or more, if acid is produced, it is acetic acid formed by fermenting yeasts still able to function well in the elevated concentration of NaCl (Vaughn *et al.*, 1976).

The initial population of extraneous organisms, consisting mainly of coliform bacteria and bacilli disappear slowly in normal fermentations as compared to the cabbage and cucumber fermentations where they all go within a few days if the acid production is normal (sauerkraut) or the fermentation is controlled as with the cucumbers. The extraneous population in holding solution olives disappears in about 10–14 days but, if the fermentation is not normal they can, and have, caused spoilage.

The spoilage problems of these and the other olive fermentations will be discussed in detail below.

4.4. The Fermentation of Spanish-type Olives

The experimental study of the green olive fermentation was first reported by Cruess (1930) and until this time was of no particular interest to the industry, although according to Dunn (1866–1867) the Spanish Queen or Sevillano olive was introduced to the state prior to 1866. The work of Professor Cruess stimulated interest in the production of Spanish-type green olives and the industry showed a slow increase in production until the Spanish Civil War nearly eliminated such olives from the US. Then the industry began to increase production, There was a gradual increase in the quantity of Spanish-type green olives fermented until about 1955. All sizes of fruits of all varieties except the Ascolano were fermented. However, the adoption of the industry-wide marketing agreement limiting the sizes of each variety that could be canned and substantial increases in production costs made it unprofitable to continue making Spanish-type olives from all sizes. The Barouni olives were exempt because of their unsuitability for canning. At present the production of Spanish-type green olives is strictly a salvage operation, and the small non-canning sizes of all varieties, including the Ascolano, are utilised.

Also for economic reasons, the use of the traditional 50 gal oak barrel has been discontinued since commercial development of rigid plastic, bottle-shaped containers of 400 gal capacity made with polyethylene and drain fitting of polyvinyl chloride became available to the industry. These plastic bottles have a number of advantages. They hold the equivalent of 8 barrels of olives, and are mobile with the aid of fork-lift trucks, even when filled with olives and brine. The use of bottles permits lye treatment, washing (leaching) and brining in the same container as was done by Ball *et al.* (1950), who used large redwood tanks holding the equivalent of about 55 barrels (50 gal/barrel). Also a considerable saving is realised because no expensive coopering is involved and the bottles require no maintenance when not in use.

The bottled olives are covered with a lye solution which varies between 0·9 % and 1·25 % NaOH as used in California. More concentrated lye solutions must be used with care, for they frequently cause softening and blistering, as well as undesirable skin sloughing. All varieties are susceptible to lye damage. Fruit lye-treated during early harvest (15 September to 15 October) is prone to develop blisters when gaseous fermentation starts as the skin has been separated from the flesh because the lye solution was too warm. If the skin remains intact, gas formation accumulated underneath causes a blister to form. This has been commonly known as 'fish-eye' spoilage in the industry.

Cooling of the lye solution and also the olives is used to combat this problem. The practice has been to use block ice or a heat-exchanger to cool the lye solutions during that part of the season when the weather is warm and ambient temperatures remain high during daylight.

The lye is allowed to penetrate about $\frac{1}{2}$ to $\frac{3}{4}$ of the way to the pits of all varieties treated with the exception of the Barouni which must be treated to the pit to avoid a discoloration problem. Unless the flesh of the latter variety is completely 'cut' with lye, it will become an undesirable reddish purple colour in the area not exposed. The colour will intensify as the acidity of the brine increases. It is thought that a leuco-anthocyanin present in the fruit is responsible for the colour change.

The time necessary to obtain the desired lye penetration will vary according to the concentration and temperature of the solution and the variety, size, maturity and temperature of the olives. An attempt is made to maintain a schedule which provides for the desired penetration in 12–14 h at the most.

During the development of the Spanish-type olive segment of the industry, the removal of residual lye by washing and leaching with water extended for 24 h before the olives were brined. The leaching water was changed every 3–6 h during the day. The night interval, unless a night crew was available, might reach 10 h between changes. By 1943 the trend was to shorten the washing-leaching period in order to reduce the greying of the colour of the olives. Now, the olives are quite alkaline when brined because the number of changes of water have been reduced to 3 or 4 in 24 h (Vaughn *et al.*, 1943).

At the start, the industry used two different salt concentrations when brining olives for the Spanish-type fermentation. Since the Sevillano variety is susceptible to salt shrivel the processors started this variety at salt concentrations of 15°–20° Salometer and slowly increased the concentration to about 30°–32° Salometer. Since the Manzanilla variety did not shrivel it was brined in 40° Salometer brine which equilibrated at 30°–32° Salometer making it unnecessary to keep adding salt to the brine.

At the present time, the majority of all varieties used in the industry are brined with about 40° Salometer salt which is acidified with lactic acid to neutralise the residual alkalinity remaining at the time of brining. Most processors add enough excess acid to lower the pH value of the stabilised olive and brine to between 4·5 and 5·0.

Glucose (crystalline corn sugar) may be added at the time of brining or after salt stabilisation. The sugar is added at the rate of approximately 1 lb per 50 gal of olives and brine. The use of the less rigorous washing and leaching prior to brining has largely eliminated the need for much added sugar because of limitation on loss from the olives.

In normal fermentation of Spanish-type green olives the initial stage of the process is the most important from the standpoint of potential spoilage if the brines are not acidified. Acidification eliminates the original contaminating population of dangerous Gram-negative and Gram-positive spoilage bacteria and, at the same time provides an optimum pH for activity of the lactic acid bacteria (Fornachon *et al.*, 1940).

In the early studies on the bacteriology of Spanish-type green olive fermentations it was found that there was a difference in the species and their sequence in Sevillano fermentations conducted in low salt concentrations as compared with the higher salt brine fermentation of the Manzanilla variety. As shown by Vaughn *et al.* (1943) *Leuconostoc mesenteroides* and Streptococci were found in low salt fermentations of the Sevillano variety. *L. mesenteroides*, which dominated the latter part of the secondary stage of fermentation, disappeared from the population within 3 or 4 weeks. The non-gas-forming species *Lactobacillus plantarum* dominated the last part of the intermediate and all of the final stage of fermentation. The gas-forming species *Lactobacillus brevis* was found during the final stage of fermentation but never approached the population levels created by *L. plantarum*. Furthermore, *L. brevis* was never found in the higher salt fermentations of the Manzanilla variety. Table 5 summarises some of the predominating population trends described, and gives the accompanying changes in total acidity and pH values found.

Pediococci were not found in any of the fermentations made by Vaughn *et al.* (1943). However, in later studies (Ball *et al.*, 1950; Vaughn & Martin, 1971) *Pediococcus cerevisiae* was isolated from Spanish-type brines in the last part of the initial stage of fermentation and the first phases of the intermediate stage of fermentation, then it declined rapidly. Not all of the Spanish-type olive brines contain *P. cerevisiae*. Now that all varieties of olives are started in 40° Salometer salt brines the gas-forming *L. brevis* also may not be found in the fermentations. The only species of lactic acid bacterium sure to be found in all fermentations of the Spanish-type is *L. plantarum*.

4.5. Control of Spanish-type Fermentations

The olive fermentation goes very slowly as compared to either the sauerkraut or pickle fermentations. Data in the literature show that either the cabbage or cucumber fermentations will have produced maximum total acidity before the olive fermentation has passed entirely through the initial stage of fermentation (see Etchells *et al.*, 1975; Pederson, 1979; Vaughn *et al.*, 1943). Olives for Spanish-type fermentations brined in late September and early October produce more total acidity because of the more favourable ambient temperatures. The olives brined from the middle of October until the end of the season ferment more slowly and may become dormant soon after the fermentation starts because of the drop in temperature at the approach of winter. Therefore, it should be obvious that to prevent dormancy it is necessary to practise temperature control.

The fermentation of all varieties of Spanish-type olives brined in California can be accelerated by proper incubation temperatures. In commercial scale experiments made in 1930 by Cruess it was indicated that an average temperature of 70°–75°F was useful for increasing acid production without impairing the organoleptic qualities of the fermented olives. Studies by Vaughn *et al.* (1943) showed that the optimum temperatures for maximum acid production of pure cultures of *L. mesenteroides* and *L. plantarum* was 86°F and for *L. brevis* was 93·2°F.

A temperature in the range of 75°–86°F, first recommended by Cruess, is commonly used for incubation at present, but generally only to the extent

TABLE 5

Gross Floral and Chemical Changes in Brine from a Sevillano Fermentation

Time in days	Approximate numbers of micro-organisms per ml of brine		Total acidity, grams lactic acid per 100 ml brine	pH	Grams NaCl per 100 ml brine	Most abundant bacteria or yeasts isolated during the stages of fermentation
	Gram-positive	Gram-negative				
				Primary stage		
0	43	254	0·0	8·20	6·25	Gram-negative bacteria *Aerobacter* and *Pseudomonas*
1	1 500	3 050	0·014	6·80	—	
2	6 890 000	—	0·037	6·35	—	
3	120 500 000	13 500 000	0·054	5·75	3·04	Gram-positive bacteria *Streptococcus* and *Leuconostoc*
5	390 000 000	228 500 000	0·108	5·20	—	
7	237 000 000	27 600 000	0·153	5·00	—	A few yeasts
				Intermediate stage		
9	707 000 000	22 000 000	0·153	4·65	—	Gram-negative bacteria *Aerobacter*
11	—	—	0·234	4·30	—	
12	410 000 000	2 950 000	0·198	4·50	3·28	Gram-positive bacteria *Leuconostoc* and *Lactobacillus*
15	34 000 000	0	0·243	4·35	3·33	
18	126 000 000	0	0·297	4·40	3·51	
21	140 000 000	0	0·333	4·35	3·63	No yeasts
				Final stage		
28	—	0	0·423	4·22	3·69	Gram-positive bacteria *Lactobacillus plantarum*
35	14 000 000	0	0·405	4·20	3·69	*Lactobacillus brevis*
42	3 500 000	0	0·414	4·05	3·86	
56	4 500 000	0	0·445	4·20	3·91	No Gram-negative bacteria or yeasts
77	1 500 000	0	0·432	4·20	3·83	—
196	700 000	0	0·414	4·10	4·09	—
365	2 650 000	0	0·514	4·50	4·09	—

Source: Vaughn et al. (1943).

that fermented Spanish-type olives are required for early delivery to the trade.

Fermenting olives should not be incubated until the potential spoilage bacteria have been eliminated in the uncontrolled fermentations. In this case the time required for disappearance of the undesirable bacteria varies from 1 to 3 weeks, depending upon the activity of the lactic acid bacteria and other factors as availability of fermentable material and brine temperature. The processors who acidify the initial cover brine can, if necessary, start incubation as soon as the fermentation is initiated.

Fermentation of Spanish-type olives also can be accelerated by use of 'starter' cultures and the addition of fermentable sugar. In 1930 Cruess recommended the use of starters of normal brine. Later (1937), Cruess suggested the use of pure cultures of lactic acid bacteria to ensure the start of fermentation. Pure culture starter inoculations were made extensively in California from 1937 until about 1955, particularly with the Manzanilla variety. *Lactobacillus plantarum* was always used for starter culture preparation. Details for preparation and use of starters have been described by Vaughn *et al.* (1943). Although pure culture starters are available from commercial culture laboratories, when inoculation is indicated, normal brine is used to reseed the abnormal fermentation because of economic reasons.

The need for addition of fermentable sugar to replace that lost through washing and leaching after lye treatment was first recognised by Cruess (1930). He recommended that corn sugar (glucose) be added to obtain satisfactory acid development in Manzanilla and Sevillano olives which otherwise did not develop enough acidity. Supplementary sugar is used extensively with the Barouni, Manzanilla, and Mission varieties. A 1–3 week wait before adding sugar is practised if a natural unacidified fermentation is used. Otherwise, sugar is added along with the acid at the time of brining. For the best results and superior olives the fermentations are controlled to a pH value of at least 4·0 and, preferably, 3·8 to avoid malodorous Zapatera spoilage.

Acidification of the brine also was first suggested by Cruess (1930) as a means of preventing potential loss of fruit. It was reported by Fornachon *et al.* (1940) that *Lactobacillus brevis* and other gas-forming species of lactobacilli had optimum pH values in the range of 5·0–6·0 for growth and decomposition of different substrates. This latter study was believed to be good evidence for the probable need to acidify all olive brines destined to undergo a lactic acid fermentation. Therefore, studies, for the most part under commercial conditions, were made by Vaughn *et al.* (1943). It was found that when brines acidified with either acetic or lactic acid also received a starter culture of *Lactobacillus plantarum* and added glucose, satisfactory fermentations always were obtained. Acidification apparently helps spark the activity of the lactic fermentation as well as eliminating the undesirable spoilage organisms.

Perhaps the most important control for protecting olives in fermentation, whether storage, Sicilian-, or Spanish-type brines, is the maintenance of anaerobic conditions. Control of the oxidative moulds and yeasts is mandatory to prevent destruction of desired acidity, but only recently has become recognised as a problem by the industry as a whole (see Balatsouras & Vaughn, 1958; Mrak *et al.*, 1956; Vaughn *et al.*, 1969a).

The introduction of plastic film and moulded plastic containers in the 1960s was responsible for improvement in the fermentation of all brined green olives in California. For the first time the use of pliable plastic film to cover the brined olives in the open bulk fermentation tanks (redwood) permitted an airtight closure that, once in place, needed little maintenance and provided prevention of growth of film-forming moulds and yeasts.

The first attempt to restrict the brine surface exposure to air in 50-gal barrels was by the use of cellar bungs commonly used in the wine industry. These bungs did not prevent spillage caused by diurnal expansion and contraction of the brines. Therefore, it was still necessary to add fresh brine to the barrels daily if the film-producing organisms were to be held to a minimum.

Expansion bungs were designed to minimise spillage. The first such

Fig. 7.   A barrel yard full of barrels of Spanish-type green olives. Note the plastic fermentation bungs.

bungs were improvised by cutting the bottoms out of 1 qt size carbonated beverage or whisky bottles and inserting the necks in rubber stoppers of a size to fit the size openings of the barrels. This improvised device controlled expansion and contraction of the brines without spillage. Nonetheless, breakage was a problem. Finally a plastic bung was developed (Fig. 7). This safer and more durable bung, 6 in (15 cm) in diameter and 8–10 in (20–25 cm) long, provided a constant air surface to total volume ratio of 28.3 in^2 (183 cm^2) to 50 US gal. (182 litres) of olives and brine. The bungs were fitted with a hinged lid to protect the brine from insects, an important concession to sanitation to prevent insect contamination.

The centre opening in the removable tops of the plastic bottles (Figs 5, 8) used for fermentation of Spanish-type green olives has the same diameter as that of the plastic bung just described. The advantage of the plastic bottles

Fig. 8. Lid for a 600 gallon plastic bottle. Note the 6 in diameter opening which has been maintained in all sizes of tank, plastic or fibreglass.

over the 50-gal barrels is very obvious—28.3 in^2 (183 cm^2) exposed air surface to 400 gal (1455 litres) of olives and brine. The surface area of brine exposed to the air can be reduced further by floating a circular disc of slightly less diameter on the surface of the brine in the top opening. Air exposure can be entirely eliminated by floating a 1 in (2·5 cm) layer of paraffin, microcrystalline wax, or 'vaspar' (a 1 to 1 mixture of paraffin and vaseline) on the brine surface in the top opening. Data reported by Vaughn & Martin (1971) have shown a significant increase in acid production of olives fermented in the plastic bottles as compared with those fermented in 50 US gal. (182 litres) barrels or in 200 US gal. (730 litres) plastic liners held in wooden shells which also have been used for Spanish-type fermentations. This difference is the direct result of better air control in the 400 US gal. (1455 litres) plastic bottles.

It is possible and also practical to complete the Spanish-type olive fermentation in from 3 to about 9 weeks under ideal commercial conditions by use of good control measures. These control measures require use of an acidified brine; adjustment of the salt concentration of the brine to $20°$–$30°$ Salometer; maintenance of a brine temperature of $75°$–$85°F$ by incubation; to ensure the presence of desirable lactic acid bacteria in the brine by use of starter if indicated; and the addition of supplementary sugar to the brine to provide for the production of at least 0.8% total acidity (calculated as grams lactic acid per 100 ml of brine). It is mandatory that anaerobic conditions must be maintained (see Ball *et al.*, 1950; Vaughn & Martin, 1971).

The fermentation data shown in Fig. 9 emphasise the possibility of rapid

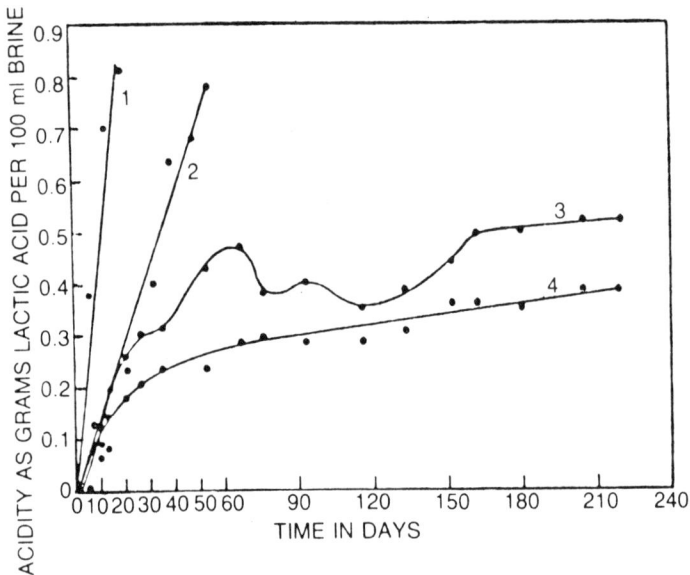

Fig. 9. Manzanilla olive fermentations: difference in acid production in controlled bulk fermentations compared with conventional barrel fermentations. (1, 2) Bulk, 2730 gallons; (3, 4) barrel, 50 gallons. Zero time: 20 October 1948. (From Ball *et al.*, 1950.)

fermentation with controlled bulk fermentations where the ideal conditions are met as indicated above.

4.6. Spoilage Problems

All olives that are fermented or processed may be subject to microbiological spoilage. The commonest and best-known spoilage types caused by micro-organisms are gassy deterioration, malodorous fermentations, and tissue softening. Gassy fermentation and softening occur most frequently and under the widest kinds of conditions in all stages of the lactic acid fermentation, as well as in olives undergoing processing for canning.

4.6.1. Gassy, 'Floater' or 'Fish-eye' Spoilage

This deterioration is characterised by the development of blisters which result from the accumulation of gases which cause the separation of the skin from the flesh of the olives and by the formation of gas-pockets which may extend to the pits of the fruit as shown in Fig. 10. Gas pockets are not observed when blisters are caused by too concentrated or too warm lye treatment solutions, so this chemical spoilage should not be confused with bacterial gas spoilage.

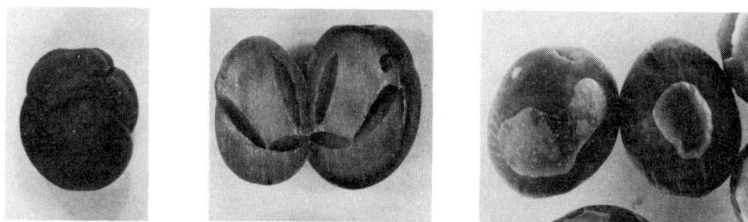

Fig. 10. Gas pocket formation in olives. (From West *et al.*, 1974.)

It is well established that the coliform bacteria are responsible for most of the blister and gas pocket formation. This has been amply verified by the studies of Cruess & Guthier (1923), Alvarez (1926), Tracy (1934), and Vaughn and his students (Foda & Vaughn, 1950; Gililland & Vaughn, 1943; Vaughn *et al.*, 1943; and West *et al.*, 1941). All of the species of coliform bacteria have been implicated as agents of gassy spoilage except *Escherichia coli* (see Foda & Vaughn, 1950).

The species *Bacillus polymyxa* and *B. macerans* also cause gassy spoilage in olives (Gililland & Vaughn, 1943; Vaughn, 1954). These species can also cause softening of olives. *Aeromonas liquefaciens*, the gas-forming pseudomonad may form gas pockets in olives and, like the bacilli, is equally important as a cause of softening (Vaughn *et al.*, 1969b). As shown by Gililland & Vaughn (1943) saccharolytic species of the anaerobic genus *Clostridium* also cause violent gassy deterioration in olives. These anaerobic species may also be involved in the softening of olives but are probably more important for the malodorous fermentations they create (butyric fermentation and zapatera spoilage).

Formerly, it was the contention of the author that only hydrogen-producing bacteria were dangerous. There always are biological exceptions. In 1972 Vaughn *et al.* associated yeasts of the genera *Saccharomyces* and *Hansenula* with gassy fermentation and softening of olives. These yeasts produced typical gas blisters but no fissure formation was observed. Two of the species, *Saccharomyces kluyveri* and *S. oleaginosus*, also caused severe softening but the cultures of *Hansenula* were not pectinolytic.

Control measures for gassy deterioration for the most part include sanitation, regulated control of the fermentation by acidification, and, in the case of processed olives for black-ripe or green-ripe canning, use of pasteurisation during washing (see Vaughn (1954) for more detail).

4.6.2. Malodorous Fermentations

There are three extremely malodorous bacterial fermentations which develop in olives. They are the butyric acid fermentation, hydrogen sulphide fermentation, and zapatera spoilage.

The butyric acid fermentation has been associated with olives since Hayne & Colby (1895) first recorded olive spoilage by the 'butyric ferment' in California. This abnormality is characterised by its butyric acid or rancid butter odour during the initial stages of the development of the fermentation. As the spoilage progresses the odour intensifies and finally becomes objectionably odoriferous.

Gililland & Vaughn (1943) were the first to isolate pure cultures of anaerobic, spore-forming butyric acid bacteria from olive brines spoiled by butyric fermentation. All of the cultures were found to be saccharolytic, non-proteolytic types of the genus *Clostridium*. Most of the cultures were very closely related to or identical with the species *Clostridium butyricum*. Sevillano olives were prone to developing butyric spoilage because the salt concentrations were kept low to avoid salt shrivel. If the salt concentration is kept in the range of 28°–32° Salometer, the strength now used by the industry, butyric fermentation cannot develop. The spoilage always was observed during the initial stage of fermentation in storage, Sicilian- and Spanish-type olives. The Sevillano variety was frequently affected, but the other varieties as well, if the salt was in the range of 20° Salometer and the pH value was above 4·5. Now, olives affected by the butyric fermentation are rare in the industry.

Hydrogen sulphide fermentation in olives is characterised by the typical identifying odour of H_2S gas. At first the odour may be slight, but as the fermentation progresses the odour becomes more intense and reminds one of rotten eggs. Black brines may occur in this abnormality if sufficient contaminating ferrous iron is present to react to cause the black iron sulphide. Black brines have been observed by the author in both storage and Sicilian-type olive brines. Chalky white brines also have been observed in Spanish-type olives when contaminating zinc from galvanised pipelines, buckets, and barrel hoops got into the brine and the whitish zinc sulphide was formed. The majority of hydrogen sulphide fermentation brines, although odoriferous, are clear or exhibit a slight microbial turbidity.

Early published reports on the occurrence of hydrogen sulphide spoilage in brined olives is lacking, and there is no authenticated record of the first hydrogen sulphide fermentations occurring in California olives. The author first observed and recognised the hydrogen sulphide fermentations as such during the 1937 harvest season in the upper Sacramento valley. In all probability this fermentation has occurred for as long as olives have been brined anywhere in the world.

From 1937 on, serious attempts were made to isolate sulphate reducing bacteria from affected sulphuretted brines. Autotrophic enrichments could be maintained for several transfers but after three or four such transfers the enrichments then failed to grow. It was not until 1966 that the studies made by Levin and Vaughn showed that the autotrophic 'mineral' media used in the earlier studies lacked essential nutrients necessary for perpetuating the growth of most, if not all cultures of sulphate-reducing vibrios belonging to the genus *Desulfovibrio*.

The halophilic species *Desulfovibrio aestuarii* was associated with the hydrogen sulphide fermentation of many samples fermenting storage and Sicilian-type olives of the Sevillano variety. Control of the sulphate-reducing *D. aestuarii* is accomplished by control of the pH value of the brine to below 5·5 by acidification or control of the fermentation otherwise. Salt concentrations have no effect because strains of the bacteria grow at 50°–60° Salometer.

Hydrogen sulphide fermentation can be avoided if the brines in open tanks of olives are pumped over to recirculate the brine after every heavy rain to ensure that the pH values in the upper layers are inhibitory.

Salvage of sulphuretted olives is possible by replacing the brine and then applying violent aeration to oxidise the remaining hydrogen sulphide. More than one change of brine plus more aeration may be necessary. Once the sulphuretted odour is depleted the brine must have the pH value adjusted to a safe level below 5·5.

'Zapatera' spoilage, another malodorous fermentation of brined olives, apparently was first described by Cruess (1924) who had observed the abnormal olives while on a visit to Spain. This abnormality occurs in all types of olives and, to the author's knowledge, is found in all of the olive growing areas of the world where olives undergo a lactic acid fermentation. The zapatera off-odour is first described as 'cheesy' or 'sagey' but as the spoilage progresses the 'cheesy' odour disappears and, as the odour intensifies, it develops into an unmistakably foul, faecal-like, stench.

Under the conditions that prevail in California, zapatera, unlike the butyric fermentation, develops when the desirable lactic acid fermentation stops before the pH value of the brine has dropped to around 4·5. At the start, the pH value of the infected brine increases as the total acidity decreases. There is a continuous loss in acidity as the spoilage progresses (Ball, 1938; Cruess, 1941; Vaughn *et al.*, 1943).

At first the cause of zapatera was confused. Smyth (1927), apparently the first to investigate the cause of the spoilage, concluded that it was the result of the activity of one or more of a group of spore-forming, proteolytic, facultative rods normally found in the soils of Andalusia, an olive and grape growing area in Spain. In Argentina, Soriano & Soriano (1946) and Soriano (1955) claimed that zapatera spoilage was caused by the sulphate-reducing *Desulfovibrio desulfuricans*. However, the odour of hydrogen sulphide is either not detectable or is not very pronounced in the case of zapatera either in California olives or those from the various olive growing regions. It is therefore doubtful that the Sorianos had isolated the causal organism.

The previous failure to isolate bacteria capable of causing zapatera prompted the author and his associates to make a study of the acidic constituents of normal and zapatera affected olives. It was found that normal fermented olives contained acetic, lactic and some succinic acid, whereas zapatera brines also contained formic, propionic, butyric, valeric, isovaleric, caproic and caprylic acids (see Delmouzos *et al.*, 1953). This information suggested that species of *Clostridium* were associated with zapatera spoilage, because previous studies by Bhat & Barker (1947) and Tabachnick & Vaughn (1948) had demonstrated that lactate utilisation was accentuated when acetate was present. Additional study by Kawatomari & Vaughn (1956) associated a number of species of *Clostridium* with the spoilage. *Clostridium befermentans* and *C. sporogenes* predominated among the bacteria studied.

However, this association of *Clostridium* with zapatera did not give a complete explanation of the cause of the spoilage. Propionic acid was one of the acids found in the spoiled brines. *Clostridium propionicum* was not found in the investigation made by Kawatomari and Vaughn. Therefore, an additional search was made to determine if species of *Propionibacterium* might be associated with the abnormality. Plastourgos & Vaughn (1957) found isolates representative of *P. pentosaceum* and *P. zeae* to be abundant in zapatera brines. All produced propionic acid from lactate in culture media and in olive brines. It was certain therefore that the propionic bacteria caused the development of the 'cheesy' odour described above. It was determined that the spoilage was caused by the participation of two genera of bacteria, *Propionibacterium* and *Clostridium*. It is one manifestation of nature's attempt to mineralise the olives.

Control to prevent zapatera development involves directing the lactic fermentation until the pH value is at least 4·0. It is preferable that the value be 3·8 or below. Olives affected with zapatera really are not salvageable because, once the spoilage becomes apparent the odours cannot be removed. Nonetheless, zapatera olives are still found in commercial channels throughout the world where olives are consumed. Some people accept them because they have no conception of what good olives are or because their olfactory senses are impaired.

4.7. Softening Spoilage

The softening of olives in process or in brines is most generally caused by the activity of pectinolytic micro-organisms. Bacteria, moulds, and yeasts all are known to cause the softening of olives. However, because the form and texture of fresh olives can be changed by using too concentrated lye solutions, by frosting or by heating, it is not always easy to determine whether the softening is of chemical or physical origin or is caused by microbes.

Softening causes up to three characteristic changes in the appearance of the olives. The very descriptive terms 'soft stem end', 'nail head', and 'sloughing' are used in the industry to indicate the type of spoilage under consideration. These different manifestations of softening have been observed in all kinds of pickled olives and in all varieties grown in California.

Soft stem end spoilage (Fig. 11) is caused by various bacteria, moulds, and yeasts capable of producing pectinolytic enzymes. Olives are destemmed

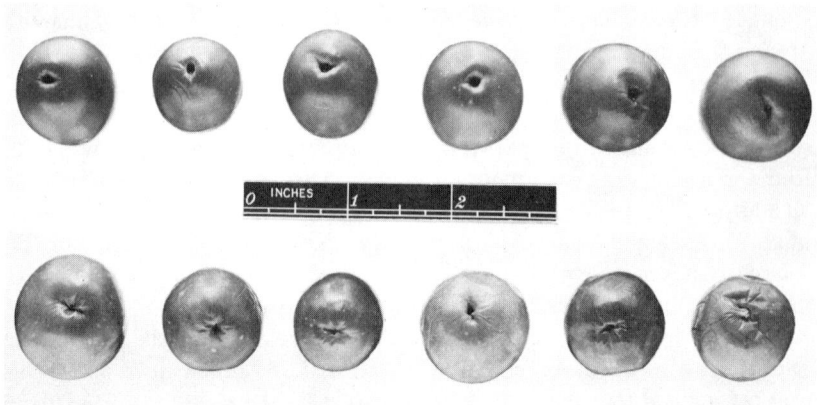

Fig. 11. Stem-end shrivel of Sevillano olives from storage brines. Top row, controls; bottom row, stem-end shrivel. (From Nortje & Vaughn, 1953.)

by machine on arrival at the processing plant or in the field at harvest when gathered from the trees. Destemming generally exposes and leaves interior tissues unprotected by stem tissues, so pectinolytic enzymes enter through the unprotected stem area and cause splitting of the pectic materials into much smaller fragments; so softening of the affected tissue results and the softening causes a puckering of the stem end. As more tissue is attacked, the softened area may expand to the entire flesh and the whole olives become soft and, often, of very mushy texture.

The bacteria found to be involved in soft stem end spoilage include species of *Bacillus* (Nortje & Vaughn, 1953), *Clostridium* (Vaughn, 1953) and various genera of Gram-negative bacteria (Vaughn *et al.*, 1969b).

Moulds found by Balatsouras and Vaughn (1958) to cause soft stem end spoilage included species of *Aspergillus*, *Fusarium*, *Geotrichum*, *Paecilomyces*, and *Penicillium*.

Yeasts found to be involved in soft stem end spoilage included oxidative, pink yeasts of the genus *Rhodotorula* (Vaughn *et al.*, 1969a) and fermenting yeasts belonging to the genus *Saccharomyces* (Vaughn *et al.*, 1972).

Pectinolytic enzymes produced by the bacteria are active at a pH range from about 5·5 to 10·0 and have an optimum pH for maximum softening at values from about 8·0 to 8·5. It should be obvious that the bacterial enzymes cannot be much of a factor in softening unless, for some reason, the brine fermentation is retarded. On the other hand, they can be very damaging in the preparation of olives to be canned by causing trouble during the final stages of washing prior to canning. The soft stem end caused by bacteria is controlled by brine acidification and/or control of the lactic fermentation and in the case of the ripe olive process by pasteurisation.

The mould and yeast enzymes are active at pH values in the range commonly found in the brines of storage, Sicilian- and Spanish-type olives (down to at least 3·8) and are still active at neutrality. One may conclude that moulds and yeasts cause the softening of olives in brine from pH 5·5 to the lowest pH values observed.

The bacteria generally all produce two pectinolytic enzymes: pectin methyl esterase which degrades the pectin molecule to pectic acid by de-methylation, and either endo- or exo-polygalacturonic acid *trans*-eliminase, which causes degradation of the pectate (polygalacturonic acid) to either unsaturated digalacturonic acid or unsaturated trigalacturonic acid.

The yeasts known to degrade pectin produce polygalacturonase which yields saturated digalacturonic acid. Most of the moulds produce polygalacturonase which produces monogalacturonic acid as the main end product. However, the mould *Aspergillus fonsecaeus*, studied by Edstrom & Phaff (1964) produces pectin *trans*-eliminase, and the major end products of pectin splitting are unsaturated and methylated galacturonates.

Strictly oxidative micro-organisms belonging to the yeasts and/or moulds are best controlled by creation of anaerobiosis. The control of fermenting yeasts is not so simple. It is felt that the best preventative measure is to direct the lactic acid fermentation, thus exhausting the supply of fermentable food for such yeasts. Pectinolytic yeasts do not occur very frequently in brined olives. The episode described by Vaughn *et al.* (1972) was the first encounter with fermenting, pectinolytic yeasts in 35 years of experience with olives by the author.

Nail head spoilage (Fig. 12) is characterised by the formation of a concave depression under the skin of the olives which causes the skin to depress into the concave area generally nearly devoid of tissue. The depressions vary from about $\frac{1}{8}$ to $\frac{1}{4}$ in (0·3 to 0·6 cm) in diameter. The spoilage is of infrequent occurrence and the cause is imperfectly known. The author has reproduced a kind of nail head spoilage by using a rounded blunt punch to bruise but not penetrate the skin of fresh olives, then fermenting them in brine and finally making them into canned black-ripe olives. The resultant abnormality was identical to that observed with commercial samples (Vaughn, 1956). It may be that nail head spoilage is a defect due to a combination of bruising and physiological decomposition of the bruised area under the skin.

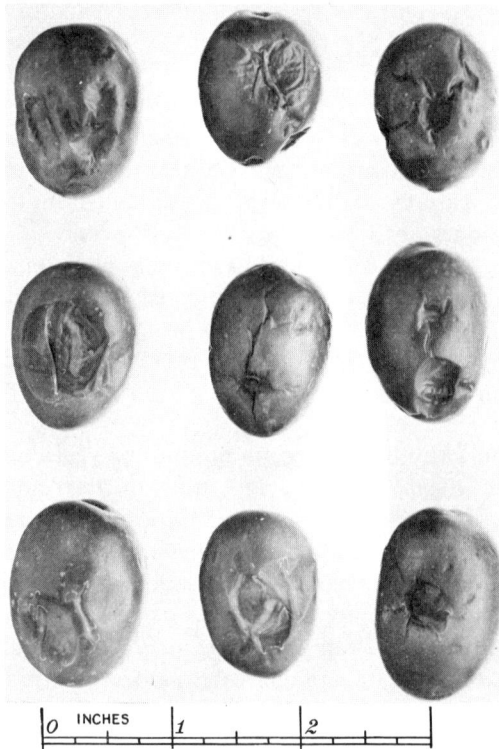

Fig. 12.   Stages of nail head spoilage of Sevillano olives from storage brine.

Sloughing spoilage (Fig. 13) occurs with olives being processed for black-ripe canned olives (Vaughn *et al.*, 1969b). However, the Gram-negative pectinolytic bacteria described in 1969 did not cause rupture of the skin and sloughing of the flesh, although the olives became soft and mushy. It was thought that skin rupture might be caused by cellulolytic micro-organisms. A search was made for cellulase-producing organisms from olives undergoing sloughing spoilage. Cellulolytic bacteria were found which were able to cause skin rupture and sloughing of sterile olives to a greater or lesser degree. The most active cellulolytic bacterium was identified as *Cellulomonas flavigena* by Patel & Vaughn (1973).

Control is very simple. Pasteurisation may be used during the washing period or the washing cycle may be reduced from 4 to 3 days.

Fusarium species isolated from storage and Sicilian-type brines by

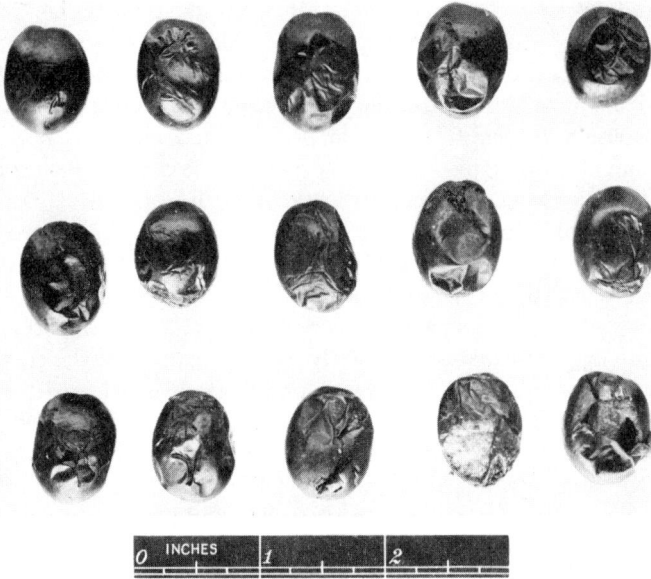

Fig. 13. Various stages in sloughing spoilage of ripe olives (Manzanilla variety) during the pickling process. (From Vaughn *et al.*, 1969b; see also Patel & Vaughn, 1973.)

Balatsouras & Vaughn (1958) had been found to be cellulolytic as well as pectinolytic. Although not tested *in vitro* it is conceivable that these species might cause some sloughing which would occur in storage olives during black processing. These micro-organisms would be controlled by involving strict anaerobiosis in the storage fermentation.

4.8. Other Abnormalities

Two other biological abnormalities occur in olives. They are 'yeast spot' formation on green olives and refermentation of bottled green olives. Yeast spot formation is a very common defect associated with fermented green olives in California and other olive growing regions of the world. This abnormality is characterised by the development of raised white spots (pimples or pustules) directly below the pores (stomata) in the skin of the olive. A colony of micro-organisms forms between the epidermis and the underlying flesh. The Sevillano variety is prone to develop this defect and it is found in all kinds of green fermented olives. It is not confined to California alone but also is observed in other countries where olives are grown and fermented. 'Yeast spots' also may be observed in pickled cucumbers and fermented green tomatoes. Although commonly called 'yeast spots' throughout the California industry, it was found by Vaughn *et al.* (1953) that most, if not all, of the pustules contained lactic acid bacteria. These bacteria were identified as *Lactobacillus plantarum* and *L. brevis* and other strains closely related to the latter species. The cause of such colonial development is not known, and no method of control is available.

The affected olives are perfectly healthy and normal in other respects, but some loss of value of the fermented olives occurs because such olives are considered unsightly by the olive brokers.

Refermentation of glass packed olives (generally stuffed) can occur with accompanying gas formation, unsightly sediment caused by the growth of micro-organisms and spewing of gas-propelled brine which leaves damaged labels and salt deposits when the brine dries. The cause is a reservoir of fermentable materials still remaining in the olive tissue, or the unwitting addition of sugar contained in pimento and almond stuffing for pitted olives, or other spices and flavouring constituents added when the olives are packed in glass jars.

Most refermentation is caused by lactic acid bacteria and, sometimes, a mixture of the lactobacilli and yeasts. To effectively control refermentation it must be determined that the fermentable materials in the olives and other added spices, etc., have been decomposed. The practice of refermenting pitted olives stuffed with pimento or nuts for at least a month before finally packing the olives in glass is the common method for avoidance of this defect. Heating of the glass packed olives in brine to a centre temperature of 185°–190°F has been used. Some packers use sorbic acid (potassium sorbate) as a preservative, and vacuum seals are preferred.

Refermented olives can be reclaimed without problems but the cost of packing and then repacking is doubled because adequate control was not used when the olives were first packed.

4.9. Later Developments
Studies during the past 18 years have been directed toward ways to increase the rate of fermentation of Spanish-type olives, especially with the Manzanilla variety. Attention has been given to studies on the use of temperature and the antibacterial compounds found in olives.

Heat received the first attention by Samish *et al.* (1966) who reported a very significant increase in the rate of the lactic acid fermentation of green olives following a short, prebrining treatment, which, in effect, caused lye peeling of the fruits. With this method the rate of fermentation was increased when the concentration and the temperature of the alkali solution was increased (Samish *et al.* 1968).

Etchells *et al.* (1966) reported that a prebrining heat treatment in water, after lye treatment to reduce the bitterness of the olives, increased the fermentability of the heated olives more than those receiving only lye treatment. As a result, they concluded that the fermentability of the various varieties of olives depended more on their inhibitory content than any other property they might have. Similar results were reported by Borbolla y Alcala *et al.* (1971).

The possibility of a microbial inhibitor in olives had been suggested in 1954 by Vaughn who speculated that oleuropein could eventually be found to inhibit the lactic acid bacteria. There was no scientific evidence that such inhibitors might be present in olives until Fleming & Etchells (1967) reported finding an inhibitor for lactic bacteria in green olives. They reported the inhibitor to be soluble in water and ethanol, heat stable in water at boiling, and was destroyed in alkaline conditions. Unfortunately, the results reported had been done with frozen olives which are never pickled in California because freezing adversely affects the texture.

A year later, Juven *et al.* (1968a, b) reported that the bitter glucoside of green olives inhibited the growth of lactic acid bacteria. The following year, 1969, Fleming *et al.* described an inhibitor that was a phenolic compound without acid-hydrolysable reducing sugar but having a bitter taste. In 1970 Juven and Henis identified the main inhibitory components of green olives as the glucoside oleuropein and its aglycone. It appears from examination of the literature that the compounds studied by the Israeli and United States' workers probably were identical. This assumption is supported by the detailed work of Fleming *et al.* (1973a) which showed that the two hydrolysis products of the glucoside, the aglycone and elenoic acid, inhibited the lactic acid bacteria but oleuropein had no effect.

Although the two hydrolysis products of oleuropein appear to be inhibitory to the lactic acid bacteria *in vitro*, there has to be some reservation concerning their inhibitory role in Spanish-type fermentations. The stability of the antimicrobial entity in alkali is poor as reported by Fleming & Etchells (1967); Juven & Henis (1970); and Juven *et al.* (1968b). It sometimes is the practice in California to leach lye-treated green olives with 3 or 4 changes of water in a 24-h period and then use an unacidified brine. When so treated the olives are generally quite alkaline and remain so for some time. Under these conditions it is believed that the inhibitory aglycone remaining would be subject to further degradation.

Also there is a difference of opinion concerning the inhibition caused by oleuropein. Juven *et al.* (1968a) reported that it caused inhibition of various bacteria, including *Lactobacillus plantarum* and *Leuconostoc mesenteroides*. Fleming *et al.* (1973a) reported no such inhibition by the glucoside. More recently Garrido-Fernandez & Vaughn (1978) made an *in vitro* study to determine the possible utilisation of oleuropein as a major source of carbon by various micro-organisms found in the fermentation of green olives. They reported that both the desirable lactic acid bacteria and the spoilage organisms used oleuropein as a source of carbon, many without showing a significant growth delay. An increase in oleuropein from 0·2 % to 0·4 % (w/v) had little or no effect on the spoilage organisms but delayed somewhat but did not prevent the eventual regrowth of the lactics tested.

Another disconcerting factor is that the skin (epidermis) of fresh olives is known to have a low permeability for water and gases as reported by Duran & Tamayo (1964). The permeability of the skin is greatly increased by being subjected to a hot lye treatment, by heat shocking the olives after regular lye treatment or freezing the olives. These chemical–physical methods all have the same valid criticism—they may adversely affect the texture of the fruit.

4.10. Elimination of Fermentation in Green Olive Processing

A method for salt-free storage of olives that combined acidulated water (lactic and/or acetic acids), the preservative sodium benzoate and anaerobiosis was described by Vaughn *et al.* (1969c). This method is used throughout the industry to store olives for black-ripe processing formerly held in brine storage. The use of salt-free storage has eliminated the problem of salt-shrivel with the Ascolano and Sevillano olives and has markedly improved the texture and flavour of Sevillano olives stored in the acidulated solution. For some unknown reason the Mission olives do not store well in this solution for extended time (up to 6 months) but become softened and grainy in texture after 1 or 2 months of storage.

The salt-free method was developed to overcome the problems of disposal of salt brines, resulting from legislation for environmental protection. The salt-free solutions can be disposed of by biological deterioration. An additional bonus exists. Vaughn & Martin (1967–1968) observed that green olives lost much of their bitterness when stored for several months in the salt-free environment. The olives, when repacked with the correct salt brine to balance the acidity of the fruits, have very good organoleptic properties and, on the basis of 'blind' tastings have passed as green fermented olives.

5. FERMENTATION OF OTHER VEGETABLES

The fermentation of vegetable tissues other than those already considered above includes a wide variety of types. It has been speculated that in the past probably most vegetables have been preserved by brining and fermentation. The vegetables mentioned in the literature include beets, brussels sprouts, carrots, cauliflower, celery, chard, citron, corn, green beans, unshelled green peas, green tomatoes, lettuce, unshelled lima beans, mustard leaves, okra, onions, peppers, pepper mash, radishes, and turnips (see Etchells *et al.*, 1947; Fleming, 1982; and Pederson, 1979). Some of these are available for purchase at the retail level such as green tomatoes, onions and peppers; others are produced in this country to be used only in commercial mixed pickle preparations such as cauliflower, carrots and celery; still others are produced only in the home or also made for regional consumption or as ingredients for other foods such as okra and mustard greens.

Brining or dry salting are used to start preservation of various vegetables. The salt concentrations reported vary from about 10° Salometer to 60° Salometer or more. In the case of the products being made in salt concentrations up to 40° Salometer there is a lactic acid fermentation but at the higher concentrations of 60° Salometer there is no appreciable lactic acid formation but, if acid-forming yeasts are present, some acetic acid may be detected. Generally leafy vegetables are dry salted to start preservation much as in the making of sauerkraut or they may be brined.

Vegetables other than cabbage and cucumbers have not received too much attention by scientists interested in pickling. Notable exceptions are the work of Etchells *et al.* (1947), who investigated the brining and dry-salting of a variety of vegetables; Orillo *et al.* (1969), who investigated the fermentation of Philippine vegetable blends; and Pederson (1979).

The vegetables under consideration here may be fermented at 12·5° to 20° Salometer salt. If so, the microbial sequence of lactic acid bacteria generally follows the classical sauerkraut fermentation described by Pederson (1930). At higher salt levels up to about 40° Salometer the sequence is skewed to development of a homofermentation dominated by *Lactobacillus plantarum*. At the highest concentrations of salt (about 60° Salometer) the lactic fermentation ceases to function and if any acid is detected during brine storage it is acetic acid, presumably produced by acid-forming yeasts which are still active at this concentration of salt.

Some vegetables are not fermented at all but are packed fresh in vinegar as is done with many varieties of sweet and hot peppers, including the popular Italian green peperoncini imported into the USA, generally packed in white wine vinegar.

Onions and cauliflower are two vegetables nearly always added to the mixed pickle products of the retail trade. According to Cruess (1958), cauliflower may be preserved by holding in brine at 60° Salometer salt to prevent fermentation or cured in a 40° Salometer salt where the homolactic fermentation takes place. In either case, if browning becomes a problem, potassium metabisulphite (up to 100–200 ppm) is added to restore the white colour. When used for mixed pickles, the warm water leaching removes the bisulphite along with the salt.

Onions also are one of the more important pickled vegetables produced in the United States to be used as an ingredient in mixed pickles. According to Cruess (1958), prepared onions are either placed in about 60° Salometer brine to prevent fermentation, or fermented in brine in up to 40° Salometer salt, prior to finishing as ingredients for mixed pickles. Besides the popular mixed pickles, onions also are used as ingredients for various table foods, consumed alone or in cocktails. These onions generally are smaller and are produced in Holland, largely as a 'cottage industry' product. In any event, Rol & Gersons (1965) have indicated that the silverskin or Holland onions after fermentation are able to be stored in brine for one or two years without significant loss of quality if the onion brine after fermentation was fortified with lactic acid, rather than acetic acid.

REFERENCES

ALVAREZ, R. S. (1926) A causative factor of 'floaters' during the curing of olives. *J. Bacteriol.* **12**, 359–65.

BAILEY, S. D., BAZINET, M. L., DRISCOLL, J. L. & McCARTHY, A. I. (1961) The volatile sulfur components of cabbage. *J. Food Sci.* **26**, 163–70.

BALATSOURAS, G. D. & VAUGHN, R. H. (1958) Some fungi that might cause softening of storage olives. *Food Res.* **23**, 235–43.

BALL, R. N. (1938) Seventeenth Annual Technical Conference, California Olive Assoc. Proc. mimeograph, p. 30.

BALL, R. N., VAN DELLEN, E., JAQUITH, J. B., VAUGHN, R. H., TABACHNICK, J. & WEDDING, G. T. (1950) Experimental bulk fermentation of California green olives. *Food Technol.* **4**, 30–2.

BELL, T. A. & ETCHELLS, J. L. (1958) Pectinase inhibitor in grape leaves. *Bot. Gaz.* **119**, 192–6.

BELL, T. A., ETCHELLS, J. L., SINGLETON, J. L. & SMART, W. W. G., JR. (1965a) Inhibition of pectinolytic and cellulolytic enzymes in cucumber fermentations by sericea. *J. Food Sci.* **30**, 233–9.

BELL, T. A., ETCHELLS, J. L. & SMART, W. W. G., JR. (1965b) Pectinase and cellulase enzyme inhibitor from sericea and certain other plants. *Bot. Gaz.* **126**, 40–5.

BELL, T. A., ETCHELLS, J. L., WILLIAMS, C. F. & PORTER, W. L. (1962) Inhibition of pectinase and cellulase by certain plants. *Bot. Gaz.* **123**, 220–3.

BHAT, J. V. & BARKER, H. A. (1947) *Clostridium lacto-acetophilum* nov. spec; and the role of acetic acid in the butyric fermentation of lactate. *J. Bacteriol.* **54**, 381–91.

BORBOLLA Y ALCALA, J. J. DE LA, GONZALEZ-CANCHO, F. & GONZALEZ-PELLISO, F. (1971) Aceitunas verdes y de color cambiante en salmuera. *T. Grasas y Aceites* **22**, 455–60.

CLAPP, R. C., LONG, L., JR., DATES, G. P., BISSETT, F. H. & HASSELSTROM, T. (1959). The volatile isothio-cyanates in fresh cabbage. *J. Am. Chem. Soc.* **81**, 6278–81.

COSTILOW, R. N., BEDFORD, C. L., MINGUS, D. & BLACK, D. (1977) Purging of natural salt-stock pickle fermentations to reduce bloater damage. *J. Food Sci.* **42**, 234–40.

COSTILOW, R. N., GATES, K. & BEDFORD, C. L. (1981) Air purging of commercial salt-stock pickle fermentations. *J. Food Sci.* **46**, 278–82.

CRUESS, W. V. (1924) Olive pickling in Mediterranean countries. California State Agr. Exptl Sta. Cir. 278, 1–33.

CRUESS, W. V. (1930) Pickling green olives. California State Agr. Exptl Sta. Bull. 498, 1–42.

CRUESS, W. V. (1937) Use of starters for green olive fermentations. *Fruit Prod. J.* **17**(1), 1–12.

CRUESS, W. V. (1941) Olive products. *Ind. Engng Chem.* **33**, 300–3.

CRUESS, W. V. (1958) *Commercial Fruit and Vegetable Products*, 4th edn. McGraw-Hill, New York.

CRUESS, W. V. & DOUGLAS, H. C. (1936) An interesting spoilage of Sicilian olives. *Fruit Prod. J.* **15**, 334.

CRUESS, W. V. & GUTHIER, E. H. (1923) Bacterial decomposition of olives during pickling. California State Agr. Exptl Sta. Bull. 368.

DAVÉ, B. A. & VAUGHN, R. H. (1971) Purification and properties of a polygalacturonic acid *trans*-eliminase produced by *Bacillus pumilus*. *J. Bacteriol.* **108**, 166–74.

DELMOUZOS, J. G., STADTMAN, F. H. & VAUGHN, R. H. (1953) Malodorous fermentation acidic constituents of zapatera olives. *J. Agr. Food Chem.* **1**, 333–4.

DUNN, H. D. (1866–1867) California—Her Agricultural Resources. *Trans. Calif. State Agr. Soc.* 507–42.

DURAN, G. M. & TAMAYO, A. I. (1964) Estudio sobre la estructura histologica del fruito de *Olea europea* L. *Grasas y Aceites*, **15**, 72.

EDSTROM, R. D. & PHAFF, H. J. (1964) Purification and certain properties of pectin *trans*-eliminase from *Aspergillus fonsecaeus*. *J. Biol. Chem.* **239**, 2403–8.

ETCHELLS, J. L. & BELL, T. A. (1950) Film yeasts on commercial cucumber brines. *Food Technol.* **4**, 77–83.

ETCHELLS, J. L. & BELL, T. A. (1956) Bloater formation by gas-forming lactic acid bacteria in cucumber fermentations. *Bact. Proc.* 28.

ETCHELLS, J. L., BELL, T. A. & COSTILOW, R. N. (1968) Pure culture fermentation process for pickled cucumbers. U.S. Patent No. 3,403,032.

ETCHELLS, J. L., BELL, T. A., FLEMING, H. P., KELLING, R. E. & THOMPSON, R. L. (1973) Suggested procedure for the controlled fermentation of commercially brined pickling cucumbers—the use of starter cultures and reduction of carbon dioxide accumulation. *Pickle Pak. Sci.* **3**, 4–14.

ETCHELLS, J. L., BELL, T. A. & JONES, I. D. (1955) Cucumber blossoms in salt stock mean soft pickles. N. Carolina Agr. Exptl Sta. Progr. Rept.

ETCHELLS, J. L., BELL, T. A., MONROE, R. J., MASLEY, P. M. & DEMAIN, A. L. (1958) Populations of softening enzyme activity of filamentous fungi on flowers, ovaries, and fruit of pickling cucumbers. *Appl. Microbiol.* **6**, 427–40.

ETCHELLS, J. L., BORG, A. F. & BELL, T. A. (1961) Influence of sorbic acid on populations and species of yeasts occurring in cucumber fermentations. *Appl. Microbiol.* **9**, 145–9.

ETCHELLS, J. L., BORG, A. F. & BELL, T. A. (1968) Bloater formation by gas-forming lactic acid bacteria in cucumber fermentations. *Appl. Microbiol.* **16**, 1029–35.

ETCHELLS, J. L., BORG, A. F., KITTEL, I. D., BELL, T. A. & FLEMING, H. P. (1966) Pure culture fermentation of green olives. *Appl. Microbiol.* **14**, 1027–41.

ETCHELLS, J. L., COSTILOW, R. N., ANDERSON, T. E. & BELL, T. A. (1964) Pure culture fermentation of brined cucumbers. *Appl. Microbiol.* **12**, 523–35.

ETCHELLS, J. L., FABIAN, F. W. & JONES, I. D. (1945) The *Aerobacter* fermentation of cucumbers during salting. Michigan State Agr. Exptl Sta. Tech. Bull. 200.

ETCHELLS, J. L., FLEMING, H. P. & BELL, T. A. (1975) Factors influencing the growth of lactic acid bacteria during the fermentation of brined cucumbers. In *Lactic Acid Bacteria in Beverages and Food*, J. G. Carr, C. V. Cutting & G. C. Whiting, Eds. Academic Press, London, New York, San Francisco.

ETCHELLS, J. L. & JONES, I. D. (1941) An occurrence of bloaters during the finishing of sweet pickles. *Fruit Prod. J.* **20**, 370, 381.

ETCHELLS, J. L. & JONES, I. D. (1943) Bacteriological changes in cucumber fermentation. *Food Ind.* **15**, 54–6.

ETCHELLS, J. L., JONES, I. D. & LEWIS, W. M. (1947) Bacteriological changes during the fermentation of certain brined and salted vegetables. United States Department of Agriculture Technical Bulletin, 947.

FABIAN, F. W. & BRYAN, C. S. (1932) Experimental work on cucumber fermentation. I. The influence of sodium chloride on the biochemical and bacterial activities in cucumber fermentations. Michigan State Agr. Exptl Sta. Tech. Bull. 126.

FABIAN, F. W., BRYAN, C. S. and ETCHELLS, J. L. (1932) Experimental work on cucumber fermentation. V. Studies on cucumber pickle blackening. Michigan State Agr. Exptl Sta. Tech. Bull. 126.

FABIAN, F. W. & NIENHUIS, A. L. (1934) Experimental work on cucumber fermentation. VII. *Bacillus nigrificans* n.sp. as a cause of pickle blackening. Michigan State Agr. Exptl Sta. Tech. Bull. 140.

FABIAN, F. W. & WICKERHAM, L. J. (1935) Experimental work on cucumber fermentation. VIII. Genuine dill pickles—a biochemical and bacteriological study of the curing process. Michigan State Agr. Exptl. Sta. Bull. 146.

FLEMING, H. P. (1979) Purging carbon dioxide from cucumber brines to prevent bloater damage—a review. *Pickle Pak. Sci.* **6**, 8–22.

FLEMING, H. P. (1982) Fermented vegetables. In *Economic Microbiology*, Vol. 7, *Fermented Foods*. A. H. Rose, Ed. Academic Press, London, pp. 227–58.

FLEMING, H. P. & ETCHELLS, J. L. (1967) Occurrence of an inhibitor of lactic acid bacteria in green olives. *Appl. Microbiol.* **15**, 1178–84.

FLEMING, H. P., ETCHELLS, J. L., THOMPSON, R. L. & BELL, T. A. (1975) Purging of CO_2 from cucumber brines to reduce bloater damage. *J. Food Sci.* **40**, 1304–10.

FLEMING, H. P., THOMPSON, R. L., ETCHELLS, J. L., KELLING, R. E. & BELL, T. A. (1973b) Bloater formation in brined cucumbers fermented by *Lactobacillus plantarum*. *J. Food Sci.* **38**, 499–503.

FLEMING, H. P., THOMPSON, R. L., ETCHELLS, J. L., KELLING, R. E. & BELL, T. A. (1973c) Carbon dioxide production in the fermentation of brined cucumbers. *J. Food Sci.* **38**, 504–6.

FLEMING, H. P., WALTER, W. M. JR. & ETCHELLS, J. L. (1969) Isolation of a bacterial inhibitor from green olives. *Appl. Microbiol.* **18**, 856–60.

FLEMING, H. P., WALTER, W. M. JR. & ETCHELLS, J. L. (1973a) Antimicrobial properties of oleuropein and products of its hydrolysis from green olives. *Appl. Microbiol.* **26**, 777–82.

FODA, I. O. & VAUGHN, R. H. (1950) Salt tolerance in the genus *Aerobacter*. *Food Technol.* **4**, 182–8.

FORNACHON, J. C. M., DOUGLAS, H. C. & VAUGHN, R. H. (1940) The pH requirements of some heterofermentative species of *Lactobacillus*. *J. Bacteriol.* **40**, 649–55.

FRED, E. B. & PETERSON, W. H. (1922) The production of pink sauerkraut by yeasts. *J. Bacteriol.* **7**, 257–69.

FRIDLEY, R. B., HARTMANN, H. T., MEKLSCHAU, J. J., CHEN, P. & WHISLER, J. (1971) Olive harvest mechanization in California. California State Agr. Exptl Sta. Bull. 885, 1–26.

GARRIDO-FERNANDEZ, A. & VAUGHN, R. H. (1978) Utilization of oleuropein by microorganisms associated with olive fermentations. *Canadian J. Microbiol.* **24**, 680–4.

GATES, K. & COSTILOW, R. N. (1981) Factors influencing softening of salt-stock pickles in air-purged fermentations. *J. Food Sci.* **46**, 274–7.

GILILLAND, J. R. & VAUGHN, R. H. (1943) Characteristics of butyric acid bacteria from olives. *J. Bacteriol.* **46**, 315–22.

HARTMANN, H. T. & OPITZ, K. W. (1977) Olive production in California. University of California Div. Agr. Sci. Leaflet 2474, 1–64.

HAYNE, A. P. & COLBY, G. E. (1895) Olives. California Agr. Exptl Sta. Reports, 1895, 1–37 (Appendix to report for 1894–95).

HRDLICKA, J., CURDA, D. & PAVELKA, J. (1967) Volatile carbonyl compounds during fermentation of cabbage. Sb. vys. Sk. Chem.-technol. Praze, Potraviny. E15-51. (Original not seen—cited by Lee *et al.*, 1974.)

HSU, E. J. & VAUGHN, R. H. (1969) Production and catabolite repression of the constitutive polygalacturonic acid *trans*-eliminase of *Aeromonas liquefaciens*. *J. Bacteriol.* **98**, 172–81.

JONES, I. D. & ETCHELLS, J. L. (1943) Physical and chemical changes in cucumber fermentations. *Food Ind.* **15**, 62–4.

JONES, I. D., ETCHELLS, J. L., VELDHUIS, M. K. & VEERHOFF, O. (1941) Pasteurization of genuine dill pickles. *Fruit Prod. J.* **20**, No. 10, 304–5, 316, 325.

JUVEN, B. & HENIS, Y. (1970) Studies on the antimicrobial activity of olive phenolic compounds. *J. appl. Bacteriol.* **33**, 721–32.

JUVEN, B., SAMISH, Z. & HENIS, Y. (1968a) Identification of oleuropein as a natural inhibitor of lactic fermentation of green olives. *Israel J. Agr. Res.* **18**, 137–8.

JUVEN, B., SAMISH, Z., HENIS, Y. & JACOBY, B. (1968b) Mechanism of enhancement of lactic acid fermentation of green olives by alkali and heat treatments. *J. appl. Bacteriol.* **31**, 200–7.

KARBASSI, A. & VAUGHN, R. H. (1980) Purification and properties of polygalacturonic acid *trans*-eliminase from *Bacillus stearothermophilus*. *Can. J. Microbiol.* **26**, 377–84.

KAWATOMARI, T. & VAUGHN, R. H. (1956) Species of *Clostridium* associated with zapatera spoilage of olives. *Food Res.* **21**, 481–90.

KING, A. D., JR. & VAUGHN, R. H. (1961) Media for detecting pectolytic gram-negative bacteria associated with the softening of cucumbers, olives, and other plant tissues. *J. Food Sci.* **26**, 635–43.

LEE, C. Y., ACREE, T. E., BUTTS, R. M. & STAMER, J. R. (1976) Flavor constituents of fermented cabbage. *Proc. IV Int. Congress Food Sci. and Technol.* **1**, 175–8.

LELONG, B. M. (1890) The Mission olive. California State Bd. Hort. Ann. Rpt 1890, 185–9.

LEVIN, R. E. & VAUGHN, R. H. (1966) *Desulfovibrio aestuarii*, the causative agent of hydrogen sulfide spoilage of fermenting olive brines. *J. Food Sci.* **31**, 768–72.

LUH, B. S. & PHAFF, H. J. (1951) Studies on polygalacturonase of certain yeasts. *Arch. Biochem. Biophys.* **33**, 212–27.

MARTEN, E. A., PETERSON, W. H., FRED, E. B. & VAUGHN, W. E. (1929) Relation of temperature of fermentation to quality of sauerkraut. *J. Agric. Res.* **39**, 285–92.

MRAK, E. M. & BONAR, L. (1939) Film yeasts from pickle brines. *Zentr. Bakteriol. Parasitenk. Abt. II* **100**, 289–94.

MRAK, E. M., VAUGHN, R. H., MILLER, M. W. & PHAFF, H. J. (1956) Yeasts occurring in brines during the fermentation and storage of green olives. *Food Technol.* **10**, 416–19.

NAGEL, C. W. & VAUGHN, R. H. (1961) The characteristics of a polygalacturonase produced by *Bacillus polymyxa*. *Arch. Biochem. Biophys.* **93**, 344–52.

NORTJE, B. K. & VAUGHN, R. H. (1953) The pectinolytic activity of species of the genus *Bacillus*: Qualitative studies with *Bacillus subtilis* and *Bacillus pumilus* in relation to softening of olives and pickles. *Food Res.* **18**, 57–69.

ORILLO, C. A., SISON, E. C., LUIS, M. & PEDERSON, C. S. (1969) Fermentation of Philippine vegetable blends. *Appl. Microbiol.* **17**, 10–13.

PARMELE, H. B., FRED, E. B., PETERSON, W. H., McCONKIE, J. E. & VAUGHN, W. E. (1927) Relation of temperature to rate and type of fermentation and to quality of commercial sauerkraut. *J. Agric. Res.* **35**, 1021–38.

PASTEUR, L. (1858) Memoire sur la fermentation appelee lactique. *Mem. Soc. Imp. Sci. Agr. Lille Ser. 2* **5**, 13–26.

PATEL, I. B. & VAUGHN, R. H. (1973) Cellulolytic bacteria associated with sloughing spoilage of California ripe olives. *Appl. Microbiol.* **25**, 62–9.

PEDERSON, C. S. (1930) Floral changes in the fermentation of sauerkraut. New York (Geneva) Agr. Exptl Sta. Tech. Bull. 168, 1–37.

PEDERSON, C. S. (1960) Sauerkraut. In *Advances in Food Research, Vol. 10*, C. O. Chichester, E. M. Mrak and G. F. Stewart, Eds. Academic Press, New York.

PEDERSON, C. S. (1975) Pickles and sauerkraut. In *Commercial Vegetable Processing*, B. S. Luh and J. G. Woodruff, Eds. Avi Publishing Co., Westport, Conn.

PEDERSON, C. S. (1979) *Microbiology of Food Fermentations*, 2nd edn. Avi Publishing Co., Westport, Conn.

PEDERSON, C. S. & ALBURY, M. N. (1950) The effect of temperature upon bacteriological and chemical changes in fermenting cucumbers. New York State Agr. Exptl Sta. Bull. 744.

PEDERSON, C. S. & ALBURY, M. N. (1954) The influence of salt and temperature on the microflora of sauerkraut fermentation. *Food Technol.* **8**, 1–5.

PEDERSON, C. S. & ALBURY, M. N. (1969) The sauerkraut fermentation. New York State Agr. Exptl Sta. Bull. 824.

PEDERSON, C. S. & KELLY, C. D. (1938) Development of pink color in sauerkraut. *Food Res.* **3**, 583–8.

PEDERSON, C. S. & WARD, L. (1949) The effect of salt upon the bacteriological and chemical changes in fermenting cucumbers. New York State Agr. Exptl Sta. Bull. 273.

PETERSON, W. H. & FRED, E. B. (1923) An abnormal fermentation of sauerkraut. *Zentr. Bakteriol. Parasitenk. Abt. II* **58**, 199–204.

PHAFF, H. J. (1947) The production of exocellular pectic enzymes by *Penicillium chrysogenum* I. On the formation and adaptive nature of polygalacturonase and pectinesterase. *Arch. Biochem.* **13**, 67–81.

PLASTOURGOS, S. & VAUGHN, R. H. (1957) Species of *Propionibacterium* associated with Zapatera spoilage of olives. *Appl. Microbiol.* **5**, 267–71.

RAHN, O. (1913) Bacteriological studies on brine pickles. *The Canner and Dried Fruit Packer* **37**, No. 20, 44; No. 21, 43.

ROELOFSEN, P. A. (1936) Protopektinase vormende gisten. Verslag 16e vergadering Verenig. Proefstation Personeel Djember, October.

ROELOFSEN, P. A. (1953) Polygalacturonase activity in yeast, *Neurospora* and tomato extract. *Biochim. Biophys. Acta* **10**, 410–13.

ROL, W. & GERSONS, L. (1965) The addition of lactic acid during the brining of silverskin onions. *Food Processing and Marketing* **33**, 13–14.

SAMISH, Z., COHEN, S. & LUDIN, A. (1966) Method for the preservation of olives. Israeli Patent Application No. 24907.

SAMISH, Z., COHEN, S. & LUDIN, A. (1968) Progress of lactic acid fermentations of green olives as affected by peel. *Food Technol.* **22**, 1009–12.

SEATON, H. L., HUTSON, R. & MUNCIE, J. H. (1936) The production of cucumbers for pickling purposes. Mich. Agr. Exptl Sta. Special Bull. 273.

SIMS, W. L. & ZAHARA, M. B. (1978) Growing pickling cucumbers for mechanical harvesting. Coop. Extension Serv. Univ. of Calif., Leaflet 2677, 1–14.

SMYTH, H. F. (1927) A bacteriologic study of the Spanish green olive. *J. Bacteriol.* **13**, 56.

SORIANO, S. (1955) La bacteria causante de la aceituna 'zapatera' y su control. Primera conferencia nacional de Olivcultura. Ministerio de Agricultura y Canaderia, Buenos Aires, Argentina, pp. 397–401.

SORIANO, S. & SORIANO, A. M. DE (1946) Estudio microbiologico de una alteracion de aceitunas conservadaes en salmuera. *Rev. asoc. Argentina dietol.* **4**(13), 132.

SPAIN, 1956. Consejo Superior de Investigaciones Cientificas. Patronato Juan de la Cierva Cordoriri. El aderezo de aceitunas verdes. Madrid.

STAMER, J. R. (1975) Recent developments in the fermentations of sauerkraut. In *Lactic Acid Bacteria in Beverages and Food*, Vol. 1, J. G. Carr, C. V. Cutting and G. C. Whiting, Eds. Academic Press, London, New York, San Francisco.

STAMER, J. R., HRAZDINA, G. & STOYLA, B. O. (1973) Induction of red color formation in cabbage juice by *Lactobacillus brevis* and its relationship to pink sauerkraut. *Appl. Microbiol.* **26**, 161–6.

TABACHNICK, J. & VAUGHN, R. H. (1948) Characteristics of tartarate-fermenting species of *Clostridium*. *J. Bacteriol.* **56**, 435–43.

TRACY, R. L. (1934). Spoilage of olives by colon bacilli. *J. Bacteriol.* **28**, 249–65.

VAUGHN, R. H. (1953) Unpublished data. Davis, Calif.

VAUGHN, R. H. (1954) Lactic acid fermentation of cucumbers, sauerkraut and olives. In *Industrial Fermentations*, L. A. Underkofler and R. J. Hickey, Eds. Chemical Publishing Co., New York.

VAUGHN, R. H. (1956) Unpublished data. Davis, Calif.

VAUGHN, R. H. (1982) Lactic acid fermentation of cabbage, cucumbers, olives and other produce. In *Prescott and Dunn's Industrial Microbiology 4th edn*, Gerald Reid, Ed. Avi Publishing Co., Westport, Conn.

VAUGHN, R. H., DOUGLAS, H. C. & GILILLAND, J. R. (1943) Production of Spanish-type green olives. California State Agr. Exptl Sta. Bull. 678, 1–82.

VAUGHN, R. H., JAKUBCZYK, T., MACMILLAN, J. D., HIGGINS, T. E., DAVÉ, B. A. & CRAMPTON, V. M. (1969a) Some pink yeasts associated with softening of olives. *Appl. Microbiol.* **18**, 771–5.

VAUGHN, R. H., JOE, T., CRAMPTON, V. M., LIEB, B. & PATEL, I. B. (1976) Acid forming yeasts and fermentation of olives. Abstracts of the Annual Meeting of the American Society for Microbiology, 188.

VAUGHN, R. H., KING, A. D., JR., NAGEL, C. W., NG, H., LEVIN, R. E., MACMILLAN, J. D. & YORK, G. K. II. (1969b) Gram negative bacteria associated with sloughing, a softening of California ripe olives. *J. Food Sci.* **34**, 224–7.

VAUGHN, R. H., LEVINSON, J. H., NAGEL, C. W. & KRUMPERMAN, P. H. (1954) Sources and types of aerobic microorganisms associated with the softening of fermenting cucumbers. *Food Res.* **19**, 494–502.

VAUGHN, R. H. & MARTIN, M. H. (1967–1968) Unpublished data. Madera, Calif.

VAUGHN, R. H. & MARTIN, M. H. (1971) Fermentation en masse des olives vertes style Espagnol en Californie. Informations Oleicoles Internationales, Madrid, No. 56–57, Oct–Dec. 1971, pp. 209–17.

VAUGHN, R. H., MARTIN, M. H., STEVENSON, K. E., JOHNSON, M. G. & CRAMPTON, V. M. (1969c) Salt-free storage of olives and other produce for future processing. *Food Technol.* **23**, 124–6.

VAUGHN, R. H., STEVENSON, K. E., DAVÉ, B. A. & PARK, H. C. (1972) Fermenting yeasts associated with softening and gas-pocket formation in olives. *Appl. Microbiol.* **23**, 316–20.

VAUGHN, R. H., WON, W. D., SPENCER, F. B., PAPPAGIANIS, D., FODA, I. O. & KRUMPERMAN, P. H. (1953) *Lactobacillus plantarum* the cause of 'yeast spots' on olives. *Appl. Microbiol.* **1**, 82–5.

VELDHUIS, M. K. & ETCHELLS, J. L. (1939) Gaseous products of cucumber fermentations. *Food Res.* **4**, 621–30.
WEST, N. S., GILILLAND, J. R. & VAUGHN, R. H. (1941) Characteristics of coliform bacteria from olives. *J. Bacteriol.* **41**, 341–52.

Chapter 3

Cheese Fermentations

J. H. GALLOWAY and R. J. M. CRAWFORD

*The West of Scotland Agricultural College,
Auchincruive, Ayr, Scotland, UK*

1. INTRODUCTION

Cheese and cheese products derived from the fermentation of milk are of major nutritional and commercial importance throughout the world. These foods range from simple cheese of variable characteristics and quality, made by empirical methods in the home in countries where conditions are generally unsuitable for milk production, to consistent high quality international varieties made in the primary dairying countries by highly industrialised modern practices.

Cheese is a wholesome and interesting foodstuff which can provide a large part of the human's requirements of protein, fat—a good source of energy—calcium and minerals (Table 1).

The variety of cheese types is seen in the fact that one authoritative book *Cheese Varieties and Descriptions* (USDA, 1978) gives an index of 800 cheese names and contains descriptions for more than four hundred. The same source gives the following means of classifying cheese.

1. Very hard (grating):
   (a) Ripened by bacteria: Asiago old, Parmesan, Romano, Sapsago, Spalen.
2. Hard:
   (a) Ripened by bacteria, without eyes: Cheddar, Granular or Stirred-curd, and Caciocavallo.
   (b) Ripened by bacteria, with eyes: Swiss, Emmentaler and Gruyère.

TABLE 1

Composition of Cheese of Various Types (per 100 g)

	Hard Cheddar	Semi-hard Edam	Blue-veined Roquefort	Soft Camembert	Cottage cheese
Water (g)	35	43	40	51	79
Fat (g)	33	24	31	23	0·4
Protein (g)	26	26	21	19	16·9
Calcium (g)	0·83	0·76	0·32	0·38	0·09
Vitamin A (retinol equivalents, μg)	380	250	300	240	3
Thiamin (μg)	50	60	30	50	30
Riboflavin (mg)	0·50	0·35	0·70	0·45	0·28
Energy content					
(kJ)	1 670	1 330	1 500	1 180	340
(kcal)	400	320	360	280	82

Source: Porter, 1975.

3.　Semi-soft:
   (a) Ripened principally by bacteria: Brick and Munster.
   (b) Ripened by bacteria and surface micro-organisms: Limburger, Port du Salut, and Trappist.
   (c) Ripened principally by blue mould in the interior: Roquefort, Gorgonzola, Blue Stilton and Blue Wensleydale.
4.　Soft:
   (a) Ripened: Brie, Butter, Camembert, Cooked, Hand and Neufchâtel (as made in France).
   (b) Unripened: Cottage, Pot, Bakers', Cream, Neufchâtel (as made in the United States), Mysost, Primost and fresh Ricotta (USDA, 1978).

More recently the International Dairy Federation (IDF, 1981) has produced a catalogue of cheeses based on the following characteristics: raw material; type of consistency; interior; exterior. The IDF method of grouping cheese (Table 2) is based on the sequence of characteristics in terms of their recognition by the consumer. The type of milk which is subjected to a process of fermentation and ripening influences the flavour of the cheese and is given top priority in the listing. Thereafter comes consistency and internal appearance, external features and then fat and moisture contents which are important but less vital to the consumer, unless very detailed information is required, than to regulatory or marketing agencies.

TABLE 2
IDF Method of Cheese Grouping

Raw material	Cow's milk
	Sheep's milk
	Goat's milk
	Buffalo's milk
	Casein
	Albumin and globulin
Type of consistency	Hard cheese
	Semi-hard and semi-soft cheese
	Soft cheese
	Fresh cheese
	Acid curd cheese
Interior	Large round openings
	Medium-sized round openings
	Small round openings
	Irregular openings
	No openings
	Blue-green mould veins
	White mould veins
	Addition of spices
	Addition of herbs
Exterior	Hard, dry rind
	Hard rind with smeary surface
	Soft, dry rind
	Soft rind with smeary surface
	Soft rind with white mould
	Soft rind with green mould
	Soft rind with paraffin wax
	No rind
Fat in dry matter	Cheese made from skim milk
	Cheese made from whole milk
Moisture content	Trade standards
	Statutory standards
	Mean values

Source: IDF (1981).

World cheese output rose by 3·1 % in 1982 to a level just over 11 million kg (FAO, 1982). This increase was similar to that of the previous two years. The most rapid increases occurred in Oceania where the estimated growth was 12 %. In the EEC and other Western European countries, cheese production increased by about 2–3 % (IDF, 1984).

Cheese consumption varies dramatically between consumers in different countries. In 1981, the latest year for which complete figures are available, the consumption of cheese varied to the extent shown in Table 3.

TABLE 3
Cheese Consumption in Certain
Countries in 1981 per Head
(kg of all types)

Greece	21·6
France	18·9
Italy	14·3
Federal Germany	14·1
Sweden	13·9
Netherlands	13·4
Denmark	10·9
USA	9·8
New Zealand	8·5
United Kingdom	6·4
USSR	4·6
Republic of Ireland	3·6
Japan	0·7

Source: Churcher, 1984.

As may be seen from these statistics the British consumer is well down the world league for cheese consumers.

2.   THE USE OF PURE CULTURES—HISTORICAL

It would be inappropriate in this chapter to attempt to trace the origins of a number of cheese varieties and their related fermentations. However, it is relevant to mention a few of the important developments in the early history of the use of starters in the production of Cheddar cheese as an example of developments in fermentation technology which are similar for several important international varieties.

The village of Cheddar, situated at the southern foot of the Mendip Hills in the county of Somerset, has given its name to a variety of cheese prized for its full flavour, smooth texture and long-keeping character. Reference to Cheddar cheese in early times was made by Sheldon (1911) who stated that the variety was popular during the reign of Queen Elizabeth I (1558–1603) and could be traced back to three centuries earlier. In 1655, Samuel Hartlib (Simon, 1956) described Cheddar cheese as the best in England. In his book on cheese, Burdett (1935) quotes a letter written in the early 17th century by Viscount Conway to Lord Poulett in which the writer described the scarcity of supplies of this variety which resulted in the cheeses being ordered before they were made.

Cheesemaking was practised in Scotland in the same period but in this case a variety was made in which there was very little fermentation. The main dairying area in Scotland at that time and until the early 19th century was the County of Ayr. Aiton (1811) recording the state of the agricultural industry in Ayrshire in the early 19th century described two types of cheese, one the native variety Dunlop or Ayrshire, a 'sweet-milk cheese', and English cheese which he described as being more pronounced in flavour than Dunlop—he was probably referring to the Cheddar variety.

The secret of making Cheddar cheese was held solely by the makers in Somerset for many centuries. With the interchange of knowledge which took place during the 19th century, cheesemakers outside the county of Somerset began to practise the method and were very successful. In Scotland by this time—the early 19th century—the farmers of the counties of Wigtown and Kirkcudbrightshire were becoming aware of the profit to be made from making cheese and they were enthusiastic about the Cheddar variety because of its superior keeping characteristic. At this time the popularity of the Dunlop variety began to decline; the cheese was very perishable and it is probable that considerable quantities of the cheese deteriorated rapidly due to the very 'sweet' condition of the curd (insufficient acidity to restrict spoilage bacteria).

In the mid-19th century Harding of Marksbury in Gloucestershire, an expert in cheese production, declared his abounding confidence in the Cheddar system of manufacture but his ideas on the merits and fundamental principles involved were very vague as indeed were those of other cheesemakers at that time (Macdonald, 1908). It was appreciated that the salient feature of the system was the development of acid in the curd formed on the addition of the rennin enzyme extracted from the fourth stomach of milk-fed calves to milk impregnated with sour whey retained from the previous day's cheesemaking. Harding and his contemporaries did not know why it was that acid whey played such a vital part in the process. From our present knowledge we can explain the action by the fact that the whey abounded in bacteria capable of producing lactic acid and when added to the fresh milk hastened the formation of the curd and cheese. Pasteur (1857) had proved an earlier theory that the formation of acid in milk was a biological process, and was indeed caused by a special micro-organism which he named 'levure lactique'. Lister (1878) isolated an organism from milk to which he gave the name *Bacterium lactis*.

Until the middle of the 19th century, cheesemaking was a relatively simple practice carried out on a small scale on individual farms. In 1851 (Fussell, 1955) the first cheese factory was established in Oneida County,

USA, and proved so successful that within a few years several factories had been established in the area. In 1870 the first British factory was opened in Derbyshire (Fussell, 1955). During the next ten years there was considerable expansion and numerous small co-operative factories were established. This movement was only partially successful. Much cheese of inferior quality was produced due to lack of expert knowledge on how to deal with the larger volumes of milk. Two developments during the late years of the century were to prove of great value in raising the standard of the finished cheese by the more effective control of the fermentation.

In the year 1890 the Danish scientist Storch (1890) used a selected strain of bacteria in souring cream for buttermaking. This—the first scientific work on the subject of bacterial fermentations used in the dairy industry— was to prove of great importance. Although the first pure culture was used in the manufacture of butter, the knowledge gained therefrom was soon to find application in the cheesemaking industry. It should be recorded that in the same year similar reports of the use of selected bacterial cultures were published in Germany (Weigmann, 1890) and the USA (Conn, 1889).

Prior to, and for some considerable time after Storch's discovery various methods were used to bring about the required amount of souring essential for success in the cheesemaking process. These were threefold:

(a) Natural souring caused by the growth and acid production of the natural bacterial flora of the milk and chiefly controlled by adjustments in the temperature of the milk (Fream, 1892).

(b) Addition to the milk of sour whey or buttermilk. Many of the more shrewd cheesemakers followed the practice of obtaining whey from a neighbouring farm enjoying a successful period of cheese manufacture (Macdonald, 1908).

(c) Addition of a home-made 'starter'. It was common practice to allow a portion of milk to coagulate and then use the clotted milk as a means of promoting souring in the milk used for cheesemaking (Stevenson, 1911).

The second development of great value to the cheesemaker was the introduction of a method of determining the amount of souring in the preparation of cheese.

Lloyd (1891, 1899) established a test by means of which the amount of acid present in milk or other material could be measured, thereby putting the process of souring on a scientific basis for the first time. By his work over the last decade of the 19th century, Lloyd contributed greatly to the knowledge and practice of cheesemaking. The test which he introduced remains to this day one of the most important aids in the manufacture of first quality cheese.

Discoveries are not always accepted and put into practice immediately. However, the practice of using pure strains of bacteria in cheese manufacture was adopted by many cheesemakers within a few years of the original work of Storch (1890). Culture starters were first used in cheese manufacture in south-west Scotland following an investigation (Campbell, 1898) begun in 1895 into the cause of a discoloration common to much of the cheese made in the area at that time. A committee set up to investigate the fault reached the conclusion that the proliferation of the contaminating organisms causing the defect should be inhibited by (a) thorough cooling of the evening milk and (b) the use of a vigorous pure culture to start the fermentation in the mixed milk in the morning when cheesemaking was commenced. The success which followed extensive trials carried out in the area did much to establish the practice of using pure culture starters.

The change in the scale and knowledge of cheesemaking since the early years of this century has resulted in the care of starters changing from simple largely uncontrolled methods employing little equipment to laboratory controlled techniques involving specially designed apparatus. This change has been one of necessity since from the economic viewpoint the cheesemaking process must be of the shortest possible duration consistent with the production of a high quality product and this is only possible if the fermentation process is of uniform speed from vat to vat and from day to day.

In the past twenty years or so there has been almost universal adoption of the practice of pasteurising the milk used for the manufacture of cheese. While not required by law, pasteurisation is recognised by cheesemaking companies as essential to uniform product quality. Pasteurisation of milk, performed by heating to temperatures in the region of 70–72 °C destroys bacteria capable of producing acid during the cheesemaking process. When milk is drawn from a healthy udder it contains few bacteria but after it has been exposed to contamination from the atmosphere of the byre and equipment used in the dairy it is liable to contain a greatly increased number of bacteria, some of which are harmful to cheese manufacture, others capable of producing lactic acid. The adoption of pasteurisation as a pre-manufacturing treatment coincided with a stricter control of the bacteriological quality of milk and the introduction of refrigerated storage of milk on the farm from the mid-1950s in the United Kingdom. Great emphasis is now placed on the production of milk containing few bacteria and the success of the milk marketing boards in achieving high quality standards is shown in the fact that in 1983 more than half of the milk supplies in the area of the main milk marketing board in Scotland had an average total bacteria count of less than 15 000/ml (SMMB, 1983).

With the elimination of the naturally-occurring souring bacteria of milk either due to the hygienic and cooling measures adopted on farms or because of the heat treatment to which milk is subjected in the cheese factory the role of the lactic acid bacteria used during cheese manufacture has become more decisive.

A fascinating account of the developments of starters for the cultured dairy products industry has been prepared recently by Lundstedt (1983).

3. ISOLATION AND SELECTION OF LACTIC ACID CULTURES FOR CHEESEMAKING

Culture collections of academic and research institutions together with laboratories of dairy industry organisations and specialist commercial firms maintain by various methods the lactic acid bacteria isolated and used in cheesemaking in many countries. Some of these starter cultures have been used for 50 years or more and their exact origin is frequently difficult to determine with accuracy. Sometimes there is further confusion because the identity of the culture is primarily the task of the individual culture collection and there is no international coding arrangement. It is not infrequent for the same culture to be given different codes by different collections. This serves to confuse, especially when mixtures of strains of lactic acid bacteria are prepared and an overall code for the mixture is created.

The lactic streptococci were originally isolated from sour milk and cream by Lister (1878) and Orla-Jensen (1919) respectively. Sandine and his co-workers (1972) have reviewed the ecology of the lactic streptococci and conclude that the natural habitat of *Strep. lactis*, which is used in cheese fermentations, is plant material. Strains of *Strep. lactis* are easily isolated from souring milk, especially if thallium acetate is added to the milk (1:2000). This chemical inhibits many common organisms of milk but has less effect on the streptococci (Nichols & Hoyle, 1948).

A simple procedure for isolating *Strep. lactis* is as follows. Add thallium acetate (0·05 g) to 100 ml of several fresh raw milks from individual farm supplies. Incubate at 20–22 °C until the milks coagulate. Select those soured milks which have the most attractive clean acid smell. Discard those soured milks which have a malty or burnt smell since this indicates that

TABLE 4
Differentiating Characteristics of Lactic Streptococci

	Strep. lactis	*Strep. diacetylactis*	*Strep. cremoris*	*Strep. thermophilus*
Growth at 39·5 °C	+	+	−	+
Growth at 50 °C	−	−	−	+
NH_3 from arginine	+	+	−	−
Acid from maltose	+	+	−	−
CO_2 and diacetyl produced from citrate	−	+	−	−
% NaCl inhibiting growth	4·0–6·5	4·0–6·5	2·0–4·0	<2·0
Group N antigen	+	+	+	−

+ Growth or positive reaction; − no growth or negative reaction. Source: Law & Sharpe, 1978a.

Strep. lactis var *maltigenes* is predominant. Sub-culture the selected soured milks by adding 1 % of the soured milk to sterile skim milk. Incubate at 22 °C until coagulation takes place. Select several of the 'wild' cultures which have acidified the milk in the shortest time. Prepare surface stroke plates using yeast dextrose agar* and incubate at 30 °C until well isolated colonies are formed in 48–72 h. Pick off a number of well-isolated colonies into sterile milk and incubate at 20–22 °C until the milk coagulates. Sub-culture each isolate by adding 1 % to sterile milk and incubate at 20–22 °C. Those isolates which coagulate the milk in 24 h at 22 °C have potential for further purification and identification for use as starters. When the most active isolates have been obtained—an activity test is described below (IDF, 1980)—identification of a few promising strains should be made. This is based on the fact that serological group N streptococci consist of *Strep. cremoris*, *Strep. lactis*, *Strep. diacetylactis* and *Strep. thermophilus*.

Further identification is based on the well-established set of growth and biochemical characteristics noted in Table 4.

By the procedure given above it is unlikely that the isolates will prove to be *Strep. cremoris*. While reports exist which indicate that *Strep. cremoris* has been isolated from raw milk, this is rare and the normal source is fermented milk products. It is probable that isolates of *Strep. cremoris* from fermented milk products, even where the products are obtained from

* Peptone 2 %, lemco 1 %, dextrose 0·5 %, NaCl 0·5 %, Yeastrel 0·3 %, Agar 2 %, pH 7.

small scale raw milk operations, are derived originally from pure cultures supplied as starters.

Further stages in the isolation and selection of streptococci for cheesemaking include further purification of promising isolates, checks on the isolates to determine whether or not they produce carbon dioxide e.g. *Strep. diacetylactis* (Crawford, 1960) and determination of phage relationships.

The property of the culture to produce carbon dioxide is of importance to the cheesemaker because while CO_2 is required to produce small holes in Dutch cheese it is liable to cause open texture faults in Cheddar cheese.

Knowledge of the phage relationship of the new isolate is essential to the starter supply laboratory since this information is vital to fitting it into rotations of phage-unrelated strains in the cheese factory. The information on its phage relationship is obtained by determining the effect, after 6–8 h incubation at 30 °C, of different seitz-filtered phage preparations spotted on a lawn of the isolate on dried M17 agar (Terzaghi & Sandine, 1975).

West (1983) discusses various approaches to minimising the incidence and extent of starter culture inhibition due to bacteriophage infection. In relation to starters he comments on the development of phage-resistant cultures. Naturally occurring phage-resistant strains are those that, without any genetic modification in the laboratory, are resistant to a large number of phages. It is estimated that generally around 30% of lactic strains are naturally phage resistant, but as West points out, this may be misleading because many of the isolates are actually the same strain. The second type of phage-resistant strain is the phage-resistant mutant obtained by selecting the surviving cells from challenging a phage-sensitive strain with phages in the laboratory. Many phage-sensitive strains with good cheesemaking characteristics can be made phage-resistant by laboratory techniques. Heap and Lawrence (1977) have described a test simulating Cheddar cheesemaking for selecting phage-resistant starter strains.

The further testing of the isolate includes trial cheesemaking using the isolate on its own as a single-strain culture or blended with one or more non-gas-producing strains in a multi-strain starter, or in mixtures with one or more strains which produce acid, aromatic compounds such as diacetyl and carbon dioxide.

It is essential for small scale cheesemaking trials to be undertaken using well established starter cultures for comparison. These trials are intended to confirm acid production properties of the isolate, determined by activity testing, and also to check on the sensory qualities of cheese made by it.

Mention has already been made of the strains of *Strep. lactis* which produce malty odour in milk and malty off-flavour (the primary flavour compound is 3-methylbutanol) in Cheddar cheese (Sheldon *et al.*, 1971). Some strains of starter bacteria have been associated with bitter flavour in Cheddar cheese (Lowrie & Lawrence, 1972), through the formation of excessive amounts of proteolytic enzymes and the resulting production from casein of bitter peptides in concentrations beyond their flavour threshold. The report (Anon., 1982) of the work of Richardson and co-workers at Utah State University suggests that the use of strongly proteinase positive (Prt+) strains in cheesemaking leads to bitterness in Cheddar cheese. Other off-flavours produced in cheese by lactic streptococci are associated with the formation of fruity flavoured esters in cheese where some strains of *Strep. lactis* and *Strep. diacetylactis* survive in high numbers in the curd. The formation of the off-flavours in this case is associated with the production of ethanol, from acetaldehyde, and its combination with butyric and hexanoic acids (Bills *et al.*, 1965) to form ethyl butyrate or ethyl hexanoate.

Other criteria for the selection process are highlighted in recent reports from the USA. Richardson (Anon., 1982) points out that the ability of a culture to coagulate milk in 24 h at 22 °C depends on the organism's properties of breaking down casein to produce soluble compounds for the protein building requirements of the organism during growth. Normal milk has sufficient soluble nitrogenous compounds for only about 20 % of the growth capability of the organism. The isolates which coagulate milk in this simple screening procedure described above, and used for many years, are those which have the ability to cause breakdown of the casein. This property is dependent on the presence of a proteinase enzyme associated with the cell wall (Prt+); isolates which tend to be discarded do not have this property (Prt−). He also comments that if a culture is propagated by daily transfer for a long time there will be a build-up of Prt− variants which are produced as cells divide and lose the DNA plasmid associated with the cell wall proteolytic activity.

The role of proteinases, peptidases and peptide transport in the growth of the lactic streptococci in milk is shown in Fig. 1.

The views of Richardson (Anon., 1982) and reports from New Zealand on the properties of proteinase-negative and proteinase-positive starter strains provide very important information which should, in future, be taken into account in the isolation and selection of starter bacteria and on their preparation as starters, and finally in their use in cheese manufacture and role in cheese quality.

As an alternative to the isolation of 'new' strains of lactic streptococci suitable for cheese production from raw milk and other sources, several laboratories are now actively involved in research using genetic engineering techniques to make existing strains phage resistant and otherwise more suitable for cheese production through change in some of their characteristics. West (1983) lists three approaches to the production of cellular phage resistance. One of these is membrane non-adsorption which is based on the concept of the ability of a phage to 'recognise' a particular site on the bacterial cell wall for its attachment prior to DNA injection.

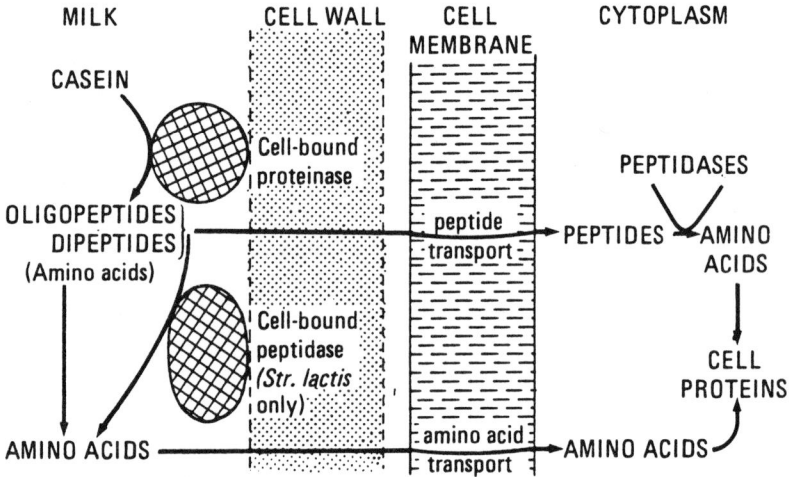

Fig. 1. Role of proteinases, peptidases and peptide transport in the growth of group N streptococci in milk. (From Law & Sharpe, 1978a, p. 267; reproduced by permission of *J. Appl. Bacteriol.*)

Cellular mutation, which may bring about fundamental changes to the cell wall, may be accomplished by gene alteration. If the specific site on the cell membrane changes, the phage which is able to attack the unaltered parent cell wall is unable to recognise the new site and is not able to adsorb. Other possibilities through the development of new genetic approaches include the creation of immunity by lysogeny and restriction/modification influences. Details of the regulation of lactose metabolism in dairy streptococci and approaches in genetic alteration are given by McKay (1982).

4. LACTOSE UTILISATION AND ACID PRODUCTION BY LACTIC STREPTOCOCCI AND FORMS OF STARTER AVAILABLE TO THE CHEESEMAKER

Lactic acid bacteria possess the enzyme lactate dehydrogenase which is essential for the production of lactic acid in cheese and fermented milks. The simplified scheme for the conversion of lactose to lactic acid is shown below.

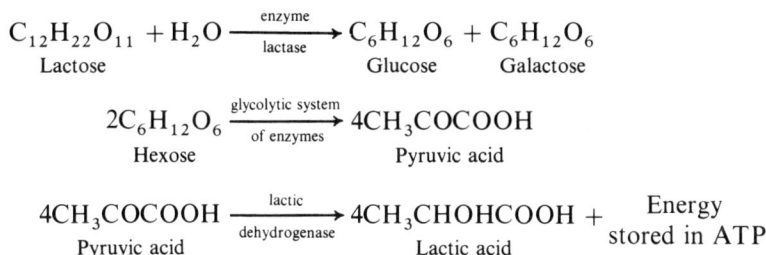

$$C_{12}H_{22}O_{11} + H_2O \xrightarrow[\text{lactase}]{\text{enzyme}} C_6H_{12}O_6 + C_6H_{12}O_6$$

Lactose   Glucose   Galactose

$$2C_6H_{12}O_6 \xrightarrow[\text{of enzymes}]{\text{glycolytic system}} 4CH_3COCOOH$$

Hexose   Pyruvic acid

$$4CH_3COCOOH \xrightarrow[\text{dehydrogenase}]{\text{lactic}} 4CH_3CHOHCOOH + \begin{array}{l}\text{Energy} \\ \text{stored in ATP}\end{array}$$

Pyruvic acid   Lactic acid

Lactic acid produced by the biochemical action of the starter bacteria differs in the structural configuration and optical rotation.

$$
\begin{array}{cc}
\text{COOH} & \text{COOH} \\
| & | \\
\text{HO—C—H} & \text{H—C—OH} \\
| & | \\
\text{CH}_3 & \text{CH}_3 \\
\text{L(+) Lactic acid} & \text{D(−) Lactic acid}
\end{array}
$$

The amount of levo- and dextro-rotatory lactic acid produced in cheese and fermented milk depends on the enzymatic specificity.

Amer & Lammerding (1983) have demonstrated the differences which exist between starters of lactic acid bacteria in the proportions of levo- and dextro-rotatory lactic acids produced in cultured dairy products.

Recent advances in knowledge of the pathways for lactose utilisation by the lactic streptococci are reviewed by McKay (1982). The review includes comment on the possible reasons for the relative instability of lactose utilising ability in a proportion of streptococcal cells within a culture.

The products of lactose utilisation have different roles in different cheeses and various fermented milk products. During the manufacturing process the development of lactic acid is essential to the process. The rennet action is aided by the development of acid. The various stages of the process for many cheese types are linked with the development of acidity and corresponding properties of the curd in terms of firmness brought about by

TABLE 5

Starters—Forms Available to the Cheesemaker

Form of starter	Produced/ supplied by	Action required in cheese factory	Comments advantages/disadvantages
A. Liquid			
(i) Mother cultures	Commercial firms, culture collections	Daily transfer and build-up through intermediate stages to bulk starter for addition to cheese vat. For Cheddar cheese making, around 1–2% (v/v) of the quantity of cheesemilk is required as inoculum of bulk starter. 0·5–1% (v/v) inoculum is required for transfer stages	Initial cost low but substantial costs incurred in laboratory and production labour and facilities. Needs full control at all stages to ensure phage-free pure cultures being added to cheese vat. Acid production and other starter characteristics liable to alter after a period of daily transfer. Requires a few days from receipt to develop normal activity. Several days required to build up sufficient quantity for vat inoculation

Some suppliers may inoculate sterile starter medium and immediately freeze before dispatch. Thawing of the medium is completed on receipt at the cheese factory and incubation provided until the culture milk medium has clotted. Propagation is then made by daily or frequent transfer.

(ii) Bulk starters	Cheesemaking factories	Direct addition to vat	Where a number of small to medium-size cheese factories operate within one company and transport facilities are suitable it may be desirable to undertake the production of all bulk starter requirements at one unit for dispatch daily to the individual locations

B. *Frozen* (Fig. 2)

(i)	Unconcentrated mother cultures	Commercial firms	Thawing and all transfer operations from laboratory stages to bulk starter	Generally as for A(i) above. The cheese factory can maintain its own starter collection under proper conditions. Liquid N_2 and alternative means of storage expensive and the former may not be readily available
(ii)	Unconcentrated feeder starters	Central starter laboratories of cheese companies. Commercial starter supply firms	Inoculation bulk starter medium. Store at $-18°C$ for up to 3 months from date of manufacture	Limits the starter production requirements (laboratory and labour) at the cheese factory. Allows a large company to rationalise starter production at one centre which should be completely isolated from cheese production operations. The staff at such a centre should not engage in phage testing of suspect materials. The equipment and methods used at the starter production centre must be completely reliable. The equipment and procedures used at the cheese factory must ensure phage-free, pure, active bulk starter for cheesemaking. Dispatch and transport arrangements from production centre must ensure that cultures remain in frozen condition until received at cheese factory. The starter production centre can use techniques which ensure that only starters of known activity and identity are supplied for cheesemaking

(*continued*)

TABLE 5—contd.

	Form of starter	Produced/supplied by	Action required in cheese factory	Comments advantages/disadvantages
(iii)	Concentrated (starter production)	Commercial firms	Thawing and addition to bulk starter medium. The storage conditions suggested by commercial firms to maintain the activity of their cultures vary. The following is given as a guide: $-45\,^{\circ}\mathrm{C}$ up to 1 month. $-80\,^{\circ}\mathrm{C}$ up to 4 months. $-196\,^{\circ}\mathrm{C}$ (above liquid N_2) several months	Advantages generally as for B(ii) above. Storage facilities more expensive. Provides the cheese factory with access to a wide range of starters of different activity and phage relationships. Allows the factory to concentrate its efforts on protecting the bulk starter by suitable equipment and procedures
(iv)	Concentrated (cheese production)	Commercial firms	Direct addition to cheese vat. Storage conditions of $-45\,^{\circ}\mathrm{C}$ or lower to maintain activity for periods of around 1 month	Completely eliminates all starter preparation at the cheese factory. Economics of use depend on many factors. Some modifications to cheese production methods may be required because of differences in acid production characteristics compared to fresh cultures. Quality of starter completely dependent on commercial supplier.

C. Freeze-dried

		Recovery and full transfer to bulk starter stage	
(i) Unconcentrated	Culture collections. Commercial firms	Recovery and full transfer to bulk starter stage	Can be stored in cool conditions for several months thus allowing the cheese factory to maintain its own starter collection.
			Full starter propagation and handling required at the cheese factory. Generally as for A(i) and B(i) above
(ii) Concentrated (starter production)	Commercial firms	Inoculation of bulk starter medium. The storage conditions suggested by commercial firms to maintain the activity of their cultures vary. The following is given as a guide: $-20\,°C$ for up to several months	As with B(ii) and B(iii) above, their use allows the cheese factory to eliminate laboratory transfer of starters.
			Full precautions still required in preparing bulk starter.
			The chances of infection with phage are reduced but depend entirely on the mechanical protection of the bulk starter medium and aseptic techniques during inoculation.
			Storage of freeze-dried cultures is less costly than those in the frozen state
(iii) Concentrated (cheese production)	Commercial firms	Direct addition to cheese vat. One company indicates that its starters will maintain full activity for at least 3 months if stored below $10\,°C$	Completely eliminates all starter preparation at the cheese factory. Reduces chances of 'phage infection. Economics of use depend on many factors.
			Some modifications may be necessary in cheese production methods because of altered rates of acid production by this type of starter.
			Starter quality dependent on commercial supplier. Generally as B(iv) above

the expulsion of whey from the curd. Control of the amount of acid developed is critical to the production of the required characteristics of the final cheese. Cheese varieties such as Cheshire and Lancashire are more acid (around pH 4·8 when several weeks old) than Cheddar (pH around 5·0 at the same age), this being brought about by retaining more lactose in the curd at the end of the process to allow acid production to continue in the early stages of ripening. When Cheddar cheese is graded the presence of crumbly body and texture indicates the tendency of the cheese to be over acid. This means that it will require to be marketed earlier than normal. It is well established that the lactic acid produced in cheese is an inhibitor of spoilage bacteria and also of pathogens such as *Staphylococcus aureus*. The role and significance of the products of the fermentation in cheesemaking vary with the individual variety. Reiter *et al.* (1967) produced Cheddar

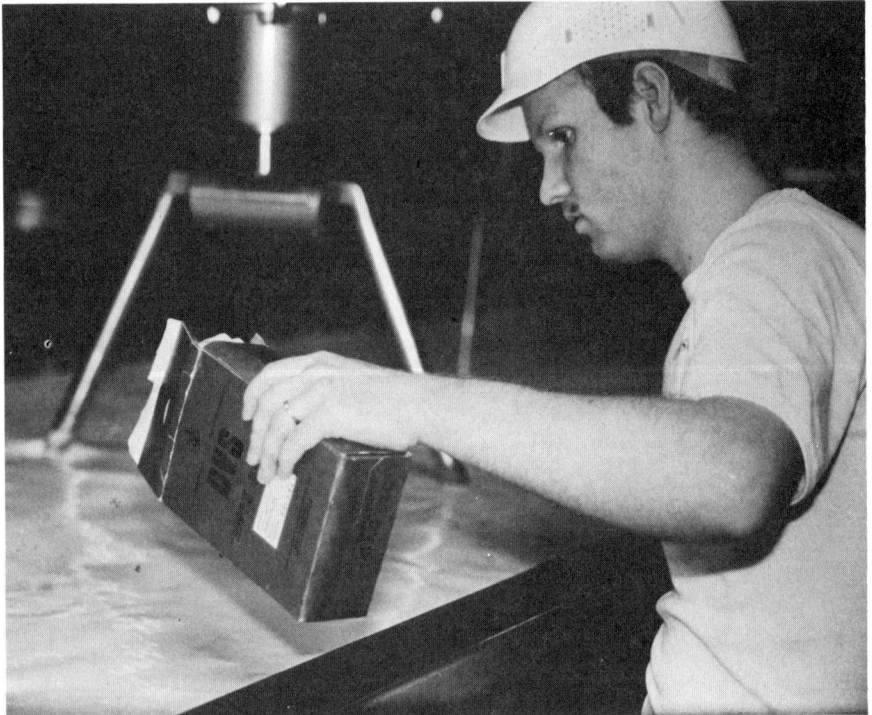

Fig. 2.   Frozen starter 'pellets' being added direct to cheesemilk in vat (courtesy of Chr. Hansen's Laboratorium A/S, Denmark).

cheese under aseptic conditions and demonstrated that the starter streptococci were able to produce cheese with typical flavour. But Law *et al.* (1976a) reported that there is no relationship between the amounts of enzymes of starter streptococci in Cheddar cheese and the rate of development of typical Cheddar flavour. The enzymes of the starter cells remain active in the cheese after most of the bacteria have died out in the first month of ripening (Law *et al.*, 1974). Law *et al.* (1976b) demonstrated that the non-starter microflora in cheese had very little effect on the development of typical flavour.

Kristofferson (1967) was of the opinion that a negative redox potential was necessary for balanced flavour development in Cheddar cheese.

Law & Sharpe (1978a) suggest that the role of the lactic streptococci in cheese ripening is that of creating the correct environment of pH and redox potential and supplying flavour precursors which are then transferred by non-enzymic reactions to flavour compounds. One of the flavour precursors is likely to be methionine which is converted into methanethiol (not produced in significant amounts by lactic streptococci (Law & Sharpe, 1978b)) which along with H_2S are important in the characteristic flavour of Cheddar cheese (Manning *et al.*, 1976; Manning, 1974).

At the present time the cheesemaker can choose from various forms of starter culture depending on the size and complexity of this cheesemaking operation. The possibilities are presented in Table 5.

5. STARTERS—FACTORS AFFECTING ACTIVITY

Cheesemakers recognise the need to be able to predict the rate and extent of acid production in cheese production. It is particularly important in modern cheese production systems capable of making milk into cheese at the rate of 50 000 litres per hour that the starter activity is uniform from vat to vat and is predictable.

5.1. Individuality of Starter Strains
One of the most important factors is the properties and fermentation characteristics of the individual starter culture. Strains of starter bacteria possess characteristics which are hereditary and are normally retained when the culture is propagated but it is well recognised that in the case of single-strain starters daily transfer may lead to the development in the culture of a proportion of slow acid mutants which, when they reach a

significant proportion of the culture, cause a lowering of the overall starter activity compared to the original level. In starters composed of more than one strain or species of lactic streptococcus it is well known that a shift in the amounts of components of a mixture may occur and result in change in the rate of acidity production by the starter used by the cheesemaker.

Many cheese technologists recommend that the bulk starters to be used for cheesemaking should be subjected to an activity test before use. Activity testing may also be applied to pre-bulk stages of starter production especially if new cultures of unknown activity are introduced. The IDF (1980) points out that there are many published methods for activity testing. It reviews the most important factors which affect the results of activity tests, for example: the conditions of holding the sample of starter; the degree of heating of the milk used in the test; the type and composition of the milk used; whether rennet is added to the milk used in the test; the temperature and time of incubation before the acidity is measured; the accuracy and standardisation of addition of starter inoculum; titration methods. Three different procedures are described (IDF, 1980) for activity testing—one of these being a method known as the 'vitality test' which simulates cheesemaking (Cox & Lewis, 1972). This test measures the amount of acid produced by a 2 % starter inoculum in milk over 6 h at 30 °C.

The advent of 'direct-to-vat' concentrated cultures—the cheesemaker inoculates the vat of cheesemilk directly with concentrated starter prepared by a starter supply organisation rather than with bulk starter prepared in the cheese factory—may well eliminate the need for activity testing especially when the cheesemaker has confidence in the supplier and its products. It is possible to carry out an activity test on a commercial concentrated starter but great care must be taken in weighing out the required amount of inoculum since the starter is highly concentrated and inaccurate weighing will result in variable inocula of cells.

The acid production activity of thermophilic starters used in the production of Emmental and Gruyère cheeses may be determined either at a constant temperature, chosen between 38 and 45 °C, or at temperatures which match the temperature curve in cheesemaking operations (IDF, 1980).

5.2. Stimulation or Inhibition of Growth (and Related Acid Production) of Starter Bacteria

Substances which are stimulatory or inhibitory to starter bacteria vary in their presence in milk. IDF (1980) summarises the combinations and systems in milk which affect the degree of acid formation as follows:

Natural retarding substances: the H_2O_2–CNS-lactoperoxidase system; immunoglobulins; oxygen

Added retarding substances: residual antibiotics in milk; disinfectants; detergents

Stimulants: carbonic acid; thermolabile substances (SH-compounds with a low molecular weight); heat resistant stimulants; stimulants produced during heating of milk

5.3. The Effect of Cheese Process Conditions on Starter Bacteria

In cheese production the process conditions which affect the rates and extent of acid development include the amount of inoculum added and the temperatures used. The cooking stage to which the curd is subjected to remove whey and firm the curd is an important factor in view of the relationship between bacterial growth and temperature.

5.4. The Influence of Infection of the Starter Bacteria with Bacteriophage

Bacteriophage remains the most serious single cause of inhibition of mesophilic starter bacteria used in cheesemaking. The role of bacteriophage in slow acid production in cheesemaking was recognised by Whitehead & Cox (1932) and various aspects of the problem have been

Fig. 3. Modern installation for starter preparation (courtesy of Alfa Laval).

investigated since then. The phages which affect the lactic acid bacteria are all of the DNA type with either prolate, polyhedral or isometric heads and usually non-contractile tails. Infection of starter bacteria involves adsorption, digestion of the cell wall and injection of phage DNA.

One possibility of limiting bacteriophage proliferation in cheese factories is to use rotations of cultures which are phage-insensitive. This action, along with other phage-related criteria for starter selection and preparation, plus complete avoidance of infection of the culture from the atmosphere and scrupulous sterilisation of cheesemaking vats and equipment, allow the cheesemaker to proceed with cheesemaking with confidence but also caution, bearing in mind the financial losses associated with severe cases of starter inhibition by bacteriophage.

6.   ENSURING DESIRED ACID PRODUCTION IN CHEESEMAKING

The following guidelines should be adopted in cheesemaking:

6.1. Factory Design and Environmental Measures

1.   Design, construct and equip the factory to make cleaning and sanitising easy and effective.
2.   Ensure that the curd production and other cheesemaking areas are effectively ventilated so that there is frequent air change to restrict the build-up of bacteriophage.
3.   Wherever possible install air filtration to protect starter production areas and if possible curd production from airborne bacteriophage.
4.   Ensure that whey utilisation takes place as far away from the starter production unit as possible because of the dangers of airborne bacteriophage.
5.   Consider all whey residues as potential sources of contamination and practice good sanitation at all stages of whey utilisation and disposal.

6.2. Starter Selection Measures

6.   Choose active starters in relation to the quantity used (i.e. in theory the concentration of starter cells in milk at the beginning and end of cheesemaking). In practice the cheesemaker bases his starter addition on a percentage (w/w or v/v) to the milk in the vat and judges the end of the process by titratable acidity and/or pH.
7.   Decide on starter rotation or alternative (Lawrence, 1978).

8. Select any skimmed milk powder used to prepare the starter growth medium on the basis of freedom from antibiotics and low thermoduric counts.

9. Where possible select starters whose 'phages do not contaminate the atmosphere quickly, i.e. starters with long latent period and low burst size (Douglas, 1975).

6.3. Process Methods

10. Ensure that starter production methods are adequate to avoid bacteriophage infection (Cox & Stanley, 1978).

11. Equipment must protect liquid starter medium against airborne infection.

12. If in doubt about adequacy of equipment to protect starter milk from airborne 'phage, use a special starter medium which prevents 'phage multiplication (Cox & Stanley, 1978; Sandine, 1979).

13. Practise strict and effective sterilisation of cheesemaking equipment, especially vats, so as to avoid phage infection from equipment surfaces (Sandine, 1979).

14. When mixing the milk used for cheesemaking avoid using compressed air unless it is certain that phage in the air is filtered out, since the phage can withstand milk pasteurisation temperatures.

15. Use short ripening times between starter addition and rennet addition to restrict phage infection from atmosphere.

16. Avoid overheating of curds and whey and have regard to any information on the effect of scald temperatures on specific starters. Information may be obtained from starter supply companies.

6.4. Quality Assurance Measures

17. Test all tanker supplies of milk for antibiotic residues. Do not use milk containing antibiotics above 0·02–0·04 i.u. penicillin/ml where mesophilic starters are used for cheese production. *Strep. thermophilus* starters used for some cheese varieties are more sensitive and are seriously inhibited at this level of residual antibiotics.

18. Practise regular and frequent checks for starter activity (IDF, 1980) and purity.

19. Make daily tests for bacteriophage (IDF, 1980; Anderson & Meanwell, 1942) in whey samples and take care to heat-sterilise all infected whey and test materials. Do not carry out the tests in or near the starter laboratory.

20. Check thermometers on receipt and regularly while in use against a master thermometer of known accuracy to ensure that the cheesemaker does not inadvertently cook the curds and whey above the chosen maximum scald for the particular cheese type.

21. The laboratory must ensure that all solutions used in acidity titrations and buffers and pH standard solutions for pH measurements are of the correct strength. Electrodes and pH meters must be checked for accurate working on a regular and frequent basis.

22. Because of the risk of transferring bacteriophage from whey to starter and cheese ensure that staff employed in whey disposal and utilisation do not have access to starter production and cheesemaking operations until they have made a complete change of all protective clothing.

7. INVESTIGATING ABNORMALITIES IN STARTER ACTIVITY IN CHEESE PRODUCTION

It has been pointed out earlier that there are a variety of factors which affect the multiplication of starter bacteria in milk and related acid production in cheesemaking.

The cheesemaker controls the rate of acid production in the production stages according to the requirement for the particular variety. He adjusts the quantity of starter added to the cheesemilk to give him the required production or 'make' times and he has to take into account variations in the rate of growth and acid production of different cultures. Failure by the cheesemaker to control the rate of acid production within the cheese-making process may lead to cheese of inferior quality, e.g. over acid, short or crumbly body. Given reliable information from the laboratory on any proposed changes in the starters to be used, e.g. starters X and Y to be brought into a rotation are more active than starters R and S which they are replacing, the able cheesemaker will be able to cope by reducing the amount of starter used and perhaps by some slight adjustments to the production process.

The cheesemaker's biggest worry is of inhibitory rather than stimulatory influences in his cheesemilk. 'Slowness' or slow acid production leads to extended production times which increase production costs and alter the operational schedules of the factory. Staff confidence is also affected.

Inferior quality cheese may also result especially if the final pH of the cheese remains above the accustomed level and bacterial contaminants are not inhibited.

The guidelines referred to above for ensuring the desired acid production in cheesemaking indicate some preventative measures and the existence of an efficient and harmonious link between the laboratory and the cheese production team should do much to avoid slowness.

There may be occasions when extra investigations are required and these should be carefully planned. In the authors' experience one of the most unnecessary limitations to successful and prompt investigational work on slow cheesemaking during a period of variable acid production is the lack of samples, e.g. bulk starters, cheesemilk or whey (first and last vats). It is good practice to take a minimum of appropriate samples and hold them untested in the refrigerator overnight until the results of the previous day's cheese production are clear. If there has been slowness or reduced acid production, the laboratory staff or investigational team have materials to examine. If cheesemaking has been normal then no additional testing is necessary and the samples are discarded. The cost of taking the samples is very small compared to the value of cheese quality lost through not being able to investigate and rectify the cause of slowness through lack of sample materials from the faulty fermentation.

Tests additional to those given in the guidelines above may be needed and some possibilities are indicated below.

7.1. Milk Supply

1. Check for residual antibiotics with more than one method since the test organisms used in different procedures are not inhibited to the same extent by various antibiotics (Haverbeck *et al.*, 1983; Thorogood & Ray, 1984).
2. Examine milks for residual sanitising agents.

7.2. Starters

3. If the production is based on factory-based preparation from mother culture and intermediate to bulk starter, test samples from each stage for activity and phage infection.
4. If in doubt, check with the suppliers the 'phage relationships and blending possibilities to help limit 'phage build-up and avoid mixing cultures which are incompatible. Remember that some starter bacteria produce antibiotics which are inhibitory to other starter bacteria.

7.3. Equipment

5. Examine starter making equipment and ancillaries for defects which would allow unsterile air containing phage to be drawn into the starter medium during cooling of the starter medium, i.e. when the starter vessel is under partial vacuum.

7.4. Cheese Production

6. Discuss with the cheeseroom staff the various parameters: cleaning and sterilisation of equipment; amounts of starter used; accuracy of measuring amounts of starter required for each vat; scald temperatures; cooking times; overall make times.
7. Inconsistency of operations should be noted and discussed with the cheesemaker.
8. Establish whether or not there is any pattern to the slowness, e.g. the slow acid production is more severe in the later vats in the day.
9. Test additional swabs of vats and whey samples to examine possible causes of failure.

7.5. Environment

10. Sample the air of key areas, e.g. starter room, vat area of cheeseroom and around equipment used for dewheying operations, and examine for phage active against the starter available. An alternative to mechanical air sampling is the exposure of individual agar plates seeded with starters in regular use in the areas mentioned above followed by incubation and examination for plaques—evidence of lytic phage.
11. Check that if air filtration is used, both Pre and High Efficiency Particulate Air (HEPA) filters have been replaced in accordance with the supplier's instructions and are working efficiently.
12. Inspect, sample and test to ensure that all parts of the equipment and environment are cleaned and sanitised in a methodical and effective way. This applies to starter and cheesemaking equipment; the air in starter rooms and cheese production area, whey disposal and storage equipment, and building surfaces in production areas.

8.   MILK—SUBSTRATE FOR FERMENTATIONS IN CHEESE PRODUCTION

The composition of milk varies for a variety of reasons: type and breed of animal, feeding, stage of lactation, disease, etc., but the following percentages (w/v) may be considered representative (Table 6).

TABLE 6

	Cow	Goat	Sheep	Buffalo
Fat	3·5–4·0	3·5–5·5	5·5–7·0	6·8–7·5
Lactose	4·7–5·2	4·0–5·0	4·3–5·0	4·8–5·0
Casein	2·7–3·0	3·0–3·2	4·5–5·0	3·2–3·4
Albumin and globulin	0·4–0·5	0·5–0·7	0·8–1·0	0·7–0·9
Ash	0·9–0·95	0·7–0·9	0·9–1·0	1·0–1·05

Source: Veisseyre, 1979.

A more extensive list of the constituents and composition of cows' milk is given by Scott (1981) and is shown in Table 7.

8.1. Lactose

From a fermentation point of view lactose is the most important constituent of milk. Other sugars are present in milk but only in small amounts. Lactose, which is in solution in the milk, is composed of one molecule of one of the isomers α or β-glucose linked to one molecule of β-galactose.

Lactose is peculiar to mammals, the amount contained in the milk varying according to the mammal concerned, e.g. the lactose content of cows' milk varies between 4·7 and 5·2 %, goats' milk from 4·0 to 5·0 %, ewes' milk from 4·3 to 5·0 %, mares' milk from 6·0 to 6·5 % and human milk from 6·5 to 7·0 % (Veisseyre, 1979).

Lactose can be hydrolysed by reaction with strong acids such as hydrochloric and sulphuric according to the amount of acid used and the temperature at which the reaction takes place. However, lactose hydrolysis can also take place due to enzymic action which is particularly important in the cheesemaking process. For example, microbes such as some yeasts, moulds and bacteria are able to produce the enzyme lactase, which reacts with the lactose, producing enzymic hydrolysis. Even more important, since it is the natural method of the breakdown of lactose, is the action of bacteria which ferment the lactose to lactic acid and, at the same time, may be responsible for the production of other substances such as acetylmethylcarbinol and diacetyl which are responsible for flavour production. Other by-products of the fermentation process include carbon dioxide and, with the aid of certain bacteria, the production of propionic acid which is especially important in the manufacture of Emmental or Gruyère de Comté cheese characterised by the presence of 'eyes' or holes in the cheese due to the action of the propionibacteria which ferment the cheese to produce

TABLE 7

Composition of Cow's Milk as a Raw Material for Cheese

Macro component	Approximate percentage composition	Micro components
Fat	3·75	Some diglycerides but mainly triglycerides (C_4–C_{18}, C_{18-1}, C_{18-2}, C_{20-2} and C_{20-3})
Lipids	0·05	Lecithin, cephalin, sphingomylin
Proteins	3·38	Caseins, 2·78 %
		α casein, 1·67 %
		β casein, 0·62 %
		γ casein, 0·12 %
		κ casein, 0·37 %
		Whey proteins, 0·60 %
		α lactalbumin, 0·13 %
		β lactoglobulin, 0·35 %
		immunoglobulin, 0·08 %
		serum albumin, 0·04 %
		Traces of other nitrogenous substances
Lactose	5·0	Milk sugar
Salts (minerals)	0·9	Calcium, magnesium, sodium, potassium, phosphates, citrates, chlorides, sulphates, etc. (iron, manganese, copper, cobalt, etc.).
Water	87	

Minor constituents

Pigments	Carotene, riboflavin, xanthophyll
Enzymes	Lipases, proteases, reductases, phosphatases, lactoperoxidases, catalase, oxidases, etc.
Vitamins	Fat soluble D, E and K
	Water soluble C and the B group
Gases	Oxygen, nitrogen, carbon dioxide (as carbonic acid), ammonia, sulphuretted hydrogen, etc.
Volatiles	Extraneous volatiles—petrol, paraffins, etc.
Cellular matter	Epithelial cells, leucocytes
Micro-organisms	Bacteria (normal udder flora), contaminants (i.e. bacteria, yeasts, moulds, etc.)
Contaminants	Seeds, straw, leaves, disinfectants, manure, urea, soils and even fuel oils. (Note that the presence of the contaminants is a result of carelessness during milk production.)

Source: Scott, 1981.

propionic acid and CO_2 which accumulates and forms holes in the cheese. Other bacteria can produce butyric acid which is responsible for flavour and texture defects in cheese.

While the amount of lactose present in milk varies, it is seldom a limiting factor in the fermentations used in cheesemaking. The craft of the cheesemaker is to control acid production and this is done by limiting the amount of fermentable sugar present in the curd. The whey expelled during cheese production contains most of the lactose.

8.2. Nitrogenous Substances

On average, the amount of nitrogenous substances found in milk is around 3·48 % and is comprised of the following fractions (Veisseyre, 1979).

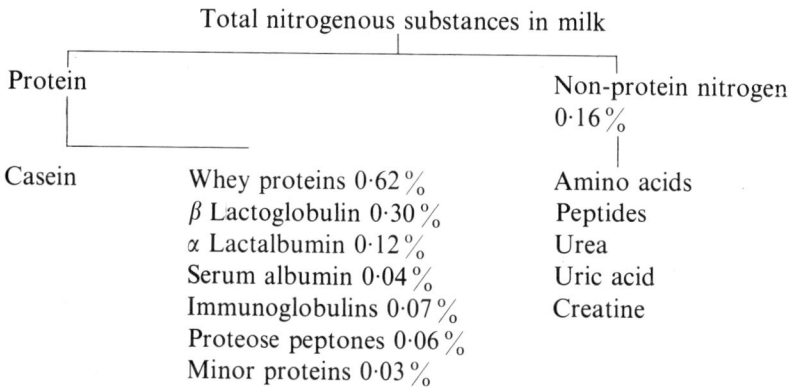

Total nitrogenous substances in milk

Protein		Non-protein nitrogen 0·16 %
Casein	Whey proteins 0·62 %	Amino acids
	β Lactoglobulin 0·30 %	Peptides
	α Lactalbumin 0·12 %	Urea
	Serum albumin 0·04 %	Uric acid
	Immunoglobulins 0·07 %	Creatine
	Proteose peptones 0·06 %	
	Minor proteins 0·03 %	

8.2.1. Casein

This amounts to approximately 2·7 % (w/w) of milk (around 80 % of the total nitrogenous material found in the milk) (Aschaffenburg & Drewry, 1959), is peculiar to milk and is mainly present in micelles (colloidal-sized aggregates of molecules). The protein molecules contain amino groups, which have basic properties, and carboxylic groups, which have acidic properties. Ionisation of these groups is affected by the hydrogen ion concentration (pH) of the solution and is at a minimum at the iso-electric point. Solubility of proteins is also at a minimum at the iso-electric point and caseins will be precipitated at pH levels around 4·6. This precipitation can be caused by the falling pH due to lactic acid production when milk is fermented.

The structure of the casein micelle is complex, containing a number of different casein molecules. Alpha-s-casein contributes about 45–50 %, 25–30 % is beta-casein, 8–15 % is kappa-casein and 3–7 % gamma-casein. It is now believed that the kappa-casein occurs mainly on the outer surface of the micelle and is an important influence in stabilising the micelle and keeping it in suspension (Payens, 1981).

When rennet acts on milk it is the kappa-casein which is split first, yielding para-kappa-casein and a glycomacropeptide. This split occurs at a particular point in the molecule between two specific amino acids which give a structure susceptible to the enzyme action. The action reduces the stability of the micelle and makes it possible for the micelles to link together to form a coagulum.

The casein complex also contains calcium phosphates and citrates which are particularly important in cheesemaking. According to Scott (1981) only 30–35 % of the calcium in the milk is in the ionic or reactive state with 50 % bound to the citrates and only 10 % to the phosphates. Temperature, pH and the amount of each salt present affect the distribution of the salts in the milk. Although a relatively small proportion of the calcium is bound to the phosphate in the milk, this is significant. When milk is heat treated, some of the calcium phosphate alters from the soluble state to become colloidal with the casein. On the other hand, cooling the milk has exactly the opposite effect when more of the calcium becomes soluble.

The enzyme chymosin which is contained in the commercial product, rennet, relies on the divalent calcium ion in order to coagulate milk. Much of the milk in continental Europe is heat treated to 80 °C for 30 s and cooled prior to cheesemaking. Since this high temperature reduces the speed of rennet action resulting in a weaker curd due to partial precipitation of the soluble calcium salts, calcium chloride is added to the milk at a rate of 0·01–0·03 % in order to restore the calcium balance. If an excess of calcium is added a bitter taste may be formed in the finished cheese.

8.2.2. Whey Proteins

As can be seen from Table 7, the whey proteins amount to 0·62 % (w/w) of the milk. The milk serum contains the whey protein which is composed mainly of albumins, incorporating α-lactalbumin, β-lactoglobulin and serum albumin, which constitute 15 % of the total protein in addition to the immunoglobulins, proteose peptones and minor proteins. Unlike casein, the whey proteins are not precipitated when the milk reaches a pH of 4·6. They are enclosed in the curd mass during the coagulation period but a large proportion is released into the whey when the curd is broken since they are water soluble. The small amount remaining in the curd is contained eventually in the body of the cheese, and since they are composed of amino acids, they eventually affect the flavour of the cheese. The serum proteins also play a part in the metabolic processes involved in bacterial growth during cheese ripening.

The minor proteins account for about 5 % of the whey protein material and are difficult to classify. They comprise lactotransferrine or the red protein, which contains cysteine and iron, the latter being responsible for the red colour, lactolline which is adsorbed on to the precipitated casein and the membrane proteins of the fat globules.

Whey solids precipitated by techniques of acidification and heating are used in some countries for the production of cheese, e.g. Ricotta (Italy) and Gjetost (Norway).

8.3. Fat

Milk fat is a very important constituent of milk from the point of view of cheesemaking, not so much from the point of view of the actual fermentation but more from the fact that the fat content of cheese determines many aspects of the consistency, mouth-feel, taste and smell of the cheese as well as its nutritive value. The fat content of cheese ranges from less than 4 % for creamed Cottage cheese to over 65 % for Double Cream cheese. The amount of cheese produced is closely related to the amount of fat in the milk. In many sections of the cheese industry the ratio of casein to fat is standardised to obtain consistent quality of cheese.

From the point of cheese quality the fat fraction is very important. In cheese like Cheddar, any enzyme activity which affects the fat and causes rancidity is likely to result in the cheese being downgraded. Some time ago the authors investigated an instance of downgrading of Cheddar cheese at a commercial cheese factory and were able to demonstrate that contamination of the cheese from water containing large numbers of *Pseudomonas* spp. which released lipases was the cause of the defect. Al-Darwash (1983) has shown that there is a close relationship between numbers of psychrotrophic lipase-producing bacteria in milk during storage prior to cheesemaking and cheese quality. The temperature of storage of milk prior to cheesemaking is very important from the point of view of growth of psychrotrophic bacteria and cheese quality.

On the other hand in certain cheese varieties such as blue-veined types and the Italian varieties, alterations to the fat fraction, which result in rancid by-products, are encouraged by processing. Some manufacturers of blue-veined types homogenise the milk to break the fat globules into smaller units which, being free of their protective membrane, are more subject to the action of lipase enzymes which produce typical rancid flavours and odours.

Lipolysis affects some of the fat content of the cheese. The free fatty acids and the resultant components, although only in small quantities have a considerable effect on the organoleptic qualities of the ripened cheese (Veisseyre, 1979). For instance the degree of lipolysis varies with the type of cheese, e.g. a Saint Paulin type cheese contains 2–3·5 g of free fatty acids per kg of ripened cheese, Camembert 20–50 g, Blue-veined cheese 30–60 g per kg of ripened cheese and Emmental 8–10 g. However, the types of fatty acids liberated vary according to the type of cheese involved. Blue-veined cheeses have a higher proportion of palmitic and oleic acids while the Camembert has a significant amount of oleic acid which is probably liberated due to the action of the lipase enzymes produced by the mould cultures. On the other hand, free fatty acids can undergo subsequent changes giving rise to the formation of secondary products which play an important role in the flavour of the cheese. This is particularly so in the case of the blue-veined cheese where the dehydrogenases secreted by the mould cultures *Penicillium glaucum* give rise to saturated fatty acids which produce β ketones (R—CO—CH$_2$—COOH) which, due to decarboxylation produce methylketones (R—CO—CH$_3$) giving the cheese a piquant flavour.

In the case of some Italian varieties, lipase preparations are added to bring about the development of flavour, much of it derived from the fat fraction. Rennet which is especially rich in lipase or a lipase preparation may be added to the milk. The resultant effect is that the added lipases hydrolyse the fat to fatty acids and thereby increase the rancidity.

Milk fat has physical properties which point to the fact that it is a mixture. For example, the colour varies, it melts and sets over a temperature range, the specific gravity varies according to the temperature of the milk, and it is soluble in fat solvents such as petroleum and ether. These physical properties depend on the nature and proportions of the constituents since, chemically, milk fat consists of a mixture of true fats, i.e. glycerides or glycerine esters of fatty acid which, in turn, hold a number of substances, in solution or by adsorption, such as lecithin, cholesterol, carotene and the fat soluble vitamins A, D and E. Esters are derivatives of acids obtained by the exchange of the replaceable hydrogen for alkyl radicals.

Milk fat contains at least sixteen fatty acids, only some of which are water soluble. Some are odourless and tasteless while others have a strong odour and can produce a bitter flavour in dairy products, e.g. butyric acid. The fatty acids are composed of straight chains of carbon atoms joined together by single bonds to form saturated fatty acids or by double bonds to form unsaturated fatty acids. The lower members of the series are liquids which have pungent odour and corrosive action and are water soluble; the intermediate members are oily liquids which have an unpleasant smell and are slightly soluble in water while the higher members from C_{10}, capric, upwards, are mainly solids which are insoluble in water, but soluble in ethanol. The saturated acids found in cows' milk which have a single bond between each of the carbon atoms are butyric, caproic, caprylic, capric, lauric, myristic, palmitic, stearic and arachidic while the unsaturated ones are decenoic, dodecenoic, tetradecenoic, and oleic (all of which have one double bond), linoleic which has two double bonds and linolenic which has three.

The fatty acids present in milk vary from one mammal to another, e.g. the amount of caproic, caprylic and capric fatty acids is considerably higher in goats' milk than in cows' milk which, in turn, produces a piquant peppery flavour in goats' milk cheese which is not found normally in cheese made from cows' milk. Ewes' milk has a much higher content of capric acid than cows' milk and this gives rise to a slight peppery flavour in the cured cheese.

It is also possible to vary the fatty acid content of the milk by altering the type of food given to the cow. If cows are given a diet composed of oil-containing foods which increase the content of the unsaturated fatty acids such as linoleic (Scott, 1981), this gives rise to rapid oxidation causing a rancid flavour.

8.4. Enzymes

Enzymes are protein substances produced by living cells which act as biological catalysts capable of bringing about chemical reactions usually in aqueous solutions. They have the very important property of specificity which is lacking in many chemical catalysts. Enzymes are present in milk, either naturally in the milk secretion, from micro-organisms present in the milk on production and from organisms present in milk as contaminants.

The principal enzymes found in milk are lipase, phosphatase and protease, which react to hydrolysis, while xanthine oxidase and lacto-peroxidase cause an oxidation/reduction type of reaction.

Lipase is present in milk in two forms: the plasma lipases or those associated with the milk serum, some of which become attached to the casein micelles. The membrane lipases are adsorbed irreversibly onto the fat globules, especially immediately after milking when it is cooled. The lipase enzyme adsorbed on the fat globule membrane causes rancidity due to the release of short chain fatty acids. Milk lipase is activated by heat, agitation and homogenisation. Milk for some continental varieties of cheese is homogenised so as to affect the cheese flavour by producing increased lipase reaction. Lipase is light sensitive and also sensitive to metal, e.g. copper and sodium and magnesium chloride. Some micro-organisms found in milk can produce lipase which is resistant to 80 °C.

Phosphatase is extremely important in milk as it is destroyed by pasteurisation temperature and therefore acts as an indicator to decide whether or not milk has been heat treated to a specific temperature.

Protease is the enzyme responsible for splitting the amino acid bonds in the protein chains to produce peptides and amino acids. Proteases may be formed in milk before cheesemaking. The temperatures at which the proteases are inactivated are above those normally used in cheese production.

Lysozyme is an enzyme which originates in milk from leucocytes and has an important bactericidal effect on Gram-positive bacteria. Lysozyme is now being used industrially for the prevention of blowing of some types of cheese.

Lactoperoxidase is present in milk and may be of importance in cheesemaking in relation to starter activity. The antibacterial activity of the lactoperoxidase/thiocyanate/hydrogen peroxide system ($LP/SCN^-/H_2O_2$) is well established. Some starter strains are sensitive to this system. The role of the lactoperoxidase is to act as a catalyst in a reaction in which non-inhibitory levels of hydrogen peroxide in milk oxidise thiocyanate to an unknown inhibitor (Reiter, 1978). Lactoperoxidase is not destroyed by the normal heat treatment of milk for cheesemaking. It is destroyed when milk is heated to over 70 °C for 20 min.

8.5. Minerals or Salts

The amount of salts in milk varies with the species, the breed, stage of lactation, condition of the animal and season of the year. Several are of fundamental importance in cheesemaking.

The most important salts found in milk are potassium, citric acid, calcium, chloride, phosphorus, sodium and magnesium. Others which vary greatly according to the animal's diet are iron, copper, aluminium, bromine, zinc and manganese. Many of the latter are bound to the proteins in the milk, or in the case of the iron and copper to the protein membrane of the fat globule.

Citric acid is present in the form of citrates and is very important in varieties of cheese which have small gas holes as a feature of their texture. The citrate in milk is the material from which diacetyl and carbon dioxide are formed by some starter bacteria. In some varieties where a completely close texture is required citrate is not beneficial to cheese quality.

The mineral salts are present in the milk in solution or in a colloidal form associated with the casein micelles present in the milk. The chlorides of potassium and sodium are in true solution whereas the phosphates and citrates of calcium and magnesium are partly in the colloidal state (where the particle size varies from that of true 'molecular' solutions to that of coarse suspensions) and partly in the soluble state (Verma & Sommer, 1957).

A proportion of the phosphorus in the milk is in the organic state, and gives rise to phospholipids and phosphoric esters (i.e. acid derivatives obtained by the exchange of the replaceable hydrogen for alkyl radicals; many esters have a fruity smell), and part of this is in the colloidal state and combined in the casein. The other portion is in the inorganic form, of which the greater quantity is in the soluble state, giving rise to phosphates, and the remainder in the colloidal state producing tri-calcium phosphate.

The calcium is also present in the organic form as a colloid bound to the casein and in the inorganic form, part of which is non-ionised salts, part ionised calcium and the remainder in the colloidal state, giving rise to tri-calcium phosphate associated with calcium caseinate bound to the casein micelles.

There is a natural balance between the ionised calcium and magnesium on the one hand and the calcium and magnesium complexes present in the milk. For example, an increase in the calcium ions is advantageous to rennet action.

Mineral salts contained in milk and transferred into cheese are important from a nutritional point of view.

8.6. Vitamins

These organic substances are present in milk as trace elements but, nevertheless, are important as they have a direct effect on the growth, maintenance and function of micro-organisms. A wide variety of vitamins are present in milk. Vitamins can be divided into two groups—those which are fat soluble, e.g. Vitamins A, D, E and K and those which are water soluble, i.e. the Vitamin B complex and C. So far as cheese is concerned, the vitamins present in milk have an effect on the micro-organisms used in the manufacture of cheese, in particular their growth factors.

Some vitamins are of more importance in cheese than others.

A number of related tocopherols show Vitamin E activity. The most active is α tocopherol which is found on the surface of the fat globules. Scott

(1981) suggests that since this vitamin has antioxidant properties it probably has an effect on cheese flavour in conjunction with the fat in ripened cheese.

Vitamin B_2, riboflavin, is responsible for the yellow-green pigment in whey. It is resistant to pasteurisation temperature. The amount in cheese can be increased due to the action of certain organisms known as the smear bacteria which are responsible for surface ripening of some continental varieties of soft cheese, e.g. Livarot.

Nicotinic acid, which is also part of this vitamin complex, forms an essential part of various oxidising enzymes. Pantothenic acid is active in the ripening of cheese.

Vitamin B_6 is found in milk in the form of pyridoxal which can withstand pasteurisation temperature and is necessary for the metabolic processes of micro-organisms, especially in regard to the proteins and lipids. It plays an important part in the reaction of enzymes with regard to amino acids which in turn are the eventual breakdown products formed in ripened cheese and responsible for flavour compounds.

Vitamin B_{12} is responsible for protein and methionine synthesis and the metabolism of the propionibacteria which produce propionic acid and carbon dioxide in the ripening of Swiss and similar cheeses. About 10 % of this vitamin is destroyed by pasteurisation temperature. The growth of lactic acid-producing bacteria and certain moulds are responsible for a decrease in the amount of this vitamin. Milk is a source of this vitamin and animals fed on pasture rich in cobalt, produce milk with an increased amount of this vitamin which is bound to the milk protein.

9. TYPES OF MILK COAGULUM FORMED IN CHEESEMAKING

Veisseyre (1979) suggested that the different cheese types may be broadly classified on the basis of the coagulation:

(a)   lactic;
(b)   rennet;
(c)   mixed and rennet.

He describes these broad coagulation types as follows:

'*Lactic*' *coagulation* is due to the fermentation of the lactose to lactic acid by lactic acid-producing bacteria. This action means that, in turn, the pH of the milk is lowered which causes an alteration in the casein micelles formed from the union of many molecules of casein. Acidification causes progressive demineralisation of the casein micelles. Eventually, when the pH is lowered to 5·2 at 20 °C the micelles become unstable and clump together to form a gel. Demineralisation continues until the pH reaches 4·6 which is the iso-electric point of casein. The protein is then precipitated in the form of floccules of casein.

There are two important aspects of a lactic coagulum. One is the temperature of the milk, which should be about 20 °C to destabilise the micelles. The other is the method of acidifying the milk. This must be done carefully with the aid of a bacterial culture so that the acid forms slowly to give a uniform curd. To attain a good lactic coagulum it is essential that the milk supply is of good hygienic quality and that the temperature is correct so that the bacteria are able to react under favourable conditions.

Only very small amounts of rennet are used in the production of this type of coagulation.

There are two main types of cheese produced by the action which takes place in a lactic type of coagulation. These are:

(i) Fresh lactic curd cheese, e.g. Scottish Crowdie, the French type collectively known as 'Fromage frais' or 'Pâtes fraîches', of which there are many different varieties, and the Quarg or Quark which is made in Germany.

(ii) American type Cottage cheese.

Both types of cheese involve the use of active mesophilic starter cultures.

The fermentation involved may be either homofermentative or heterofermentative depending on the type of culture used, but consideration must be given to the by-products of the fermentation in relation to their effect on the characteristics of the cheese.

In the production of the fresh lactic curd type it is normal to use a starter culture which produces lactic acid and also utilises the citrate of the milk to produce aroma compounds such as diacetyl. Production of this compound is dependent on the starter containing *Strep. diacetylactis* or *Leuconostoc* spp.

It is better to avoid these two organisms in cultures for the production of American type Cottage cheese curd since one of the products of the fermentation is carbon dioxide which may cause textural defects in the product. However, use is made of these bacteria in preparation of the soured cream dressing which is normally added to the bland cottage cheese curd prior to packaging. Some mixed-strain cultures, i.e. those containing acid and aroma-forming bacteria may only produce small quantities of carbon dioxide and may be used for Cottage cheese. Advice should be taken from the supplier of the culture as to its gas-producing properties.

Direct acidification has been used as an alternative to fermentation by starter cultures and progress has been reviewed by Fox (1978).

'*Rennet*' *coagulation* is the most common type of coagulation and is dependent on the action of the proteolytic enzyme chymosin E.C. 3.4.23.4 (Anon., 1979) or alternative coagulants.

Chymosin acts on the kappa-casein which loses the stabilising property of the α_{s1} and β casein in the presence of calcium. The casein micelles become floccular and fibrous and form a network which retains the moisture and the fat globules. The firmness of this gel depends on calcium phosphate and the casein is transformed into calcium phosphate paracaseinate. The type of curd formed is dependent on this reaction which in turn influences the quality of the finished cheese.

Factors which affect rennet action are the strength of the commercial rennet, the temperature, the pH, the calcium content of the milk, the colloidal calcium phosphate, the size of the casein micelles and the soluble protein content, especially the β-lactoglobulin. Indirectly, the health and food of the animal together with the stage of lactation also play a part in rennet coagulation.

Rennet coagulation is the basis of the manufacture of hard varieties of cheese such as many of the traditional British varieties, e.g. Cheddar, Cheshire, Derby, Gloucester, Dunlop, and Leicester, the French Cantal, Gruyère de Comté and Beaufort, the Italian Parmesan, Grana, Provolone, Mozzarella, and many others.

Basically, the cheese milk is inoculated either with homofermentative or heterofermentative starter cultures and, depending on the cheese variety, other organisms may be added to the milk.

So far as the British varieties are concerned the cultures are of lactic streptococci and may be either single-strain, multi-strain or mixed-strain starter cultures of strains of *Strep. cremoris, Strep. lactis* and, in addition for the mixed-strain starter cultures, *Leuconostoc* spp. with or without *Strep. diacetylactis.*

The Cantal cheese, made in the Auvergne region of France, is somewhat similar to Cheddar cheese. Mixed-strain starter cultures of homofermentative types used in the manufacture of the traditional British varieties are also used to make the Cantal cheese.

On the other hand, the Gruyère de Comté cheese, made in the Jura area of France utilises mixed-strain starter cultures of homofermentative and heterofermentative lactobacilli. The homofermentative lactobacilli include such organisms as *Lact. acidophilus, Lact. bulgaricus, Lact. lactis* and

Lact. helveticus and the heterofermentative cultures are *Lact. fermenti, Lact. brevis, Lact. casei* and *Lact. plantarum*. The latter two organisms produce flavour and aroma since they are both lipolytic and proteolytic. In addition, propionic acid bacteria are also part of the culture used to make this cheese.

The Beaufort is the mountain equivalent of the Gruyère and is manufactured in Haute Savoie. Only slits appear in the cheese as compared with the 'eye' structure or holes found in the Gruyère cheese. The Beaufort cheese lacks the influence of the propionic acid bacteria responsible for the 'eyes' in Gruyère.

The Italian Grana cheeses, of which Parmesan is the most famous, are made using a starter culture consisting of *Strep. thermophilus* and *Lact. bulgaricus*. In addition to the bacterial activity, lipase enzyme may be used and is mixed with the rennet so that the fermentation, which is mainly due to the rennet action on the milk protein, is enhanced by the lipase.

The Italian *pasta filata* cheeses such as Provolone and Mozzarella are made by a process of stretching the curd in hot water after fermentation and before brining. The cultures used are of thermoduric organisms, e.g. *Strep. thermophilus, Strep. durans, Lact. lactis, Lact. thermophilus* and *Micrococcus freudenreichii*.

A '*mixed' acid and rennet coagulation* is formed by the combined action of the rennet and lactic acid produced by fermentation. The temperature of the cheese milk is adjusted to 32 °C and this temperature is maintained during the manufacturing period on the day of making the cheese. The temperature of 32 °C is favourable both to the production of acid by the lactic acid-producing starter bacteria and also to the action of the rennet or other coagulating enzymes.

Many of the continental varieties of soft and semi-hard cheese are made on the basis of a mixed coagulum. These types of cheese can be subdivided into two main groups (Veisseyre, 1979):

(a) Those which in traditional form have a rind. Examples of this group are: Gouda, Saint Paulin, Pont-l-Évêque and Scottish Carrick. It should be appreciated that many cheeses are now produced in rindless form by the use of packaging soon after production.

(b) Those which are ripened with the aid of moulds, e.g. Brie, Coulommiers, Camembert, Carré de l'Est, Bresse Bleu, Bleu d'Auvergne, Roquefort, Gorgonzola, Danish Blue, the English Stilton and Scottish Caledonian Blue.

The starter cultures used to produce the first group are mixed-strain cultures of lactic acid-producing organisms, e.g. *Strep. cremoris* and/or *Strep. lactis* plus the *Leuconostoc* organisms and *Strep. diacetylactis*. The leuconostocs and other citrate-utilising bacteria have an important role in producing small gas holes in Dutch type cheese. This is a characteristic required by the cheesemaker and expected as typical of this type by the consumer. This group contains varieties in which the fermentation is controlled by reducing the lactose content of the curd and whey by the addition of water during the process. In addition, cultures of the smear bacteria, e.g. *Bacterium linens* are also used in the manufacture of Pont-l'Évêque and Livarot among others. The smear culture may be added direct to the cheese milk or added to the brine solution used to salt the cheese. Yeasts may also have a role in the ripening of these two cheeses.

The surface mould-ripened varieties are produced with the aid of the white mould species—*Penicillium candidum* and *Penicillium caseicolum* for the Brie and Camembert type of cheese. In addition, *Geotrichum candidum* plays a part in the ripening of the white mould-ripened varieties.

The most important species of blue mould culture is *Penicillium glaucum*. Some strains of this mould give a blue colour and others produce a green mould. The strain, *Penicillium roqueforti* is found naturally in the caves where the Roquefort cheese is ripened. Often yeasts are in symbiotic growth with the mould cultures on the surface of many mould-ripened varieties of cheese, for example, *Saccharomyces* and *Torula* spp. grow along with strains of lactobacilli, e.g. *Lact. casei.*

10.   SUMMARISED TECHNOLOGY OF SELECTED CHEESE TYPES

10.1. Stages in the Production of Cheddar Cheese
Modern Cheddar cheesemaking operations are outlined in Table 8.

10.2. Camembert and Other White Mould-ripened Soft Cheese (Pâtes Molles)
Soft cheese characterised by the surface growth of white *Penicillium* spp. makes up the main cheese type in France. Many studies have been made on the surface flora of white mould cheese and on the interrelationship between the components of the surface flora. For many years the starter bacteria used in France for cheese of the Camembert type comprised *Strep. lactis, Strep. cremoris, Strep. diacetylactis* and/or *Leuconostoc cremoris*. Changes have taken place in recent years in the methodology for these

TABLE 8

Stages in the Production of Cheddar Cheese

	Time (hours min)	Temp. (°C)	
Milk heat treatment			While there is no legal requirement in the United Kingdom to heat treat milk for cheesemaking, almost all cheese is made from pasteurised milk (72°C/15 s)
Addition of starter	0·00 (Titratable acidity 0·15% lactic acid) (pH 6·7)	30–32	1–2% (v/v) of mesophilic starter, e.g. single-strain *Strep. cremoris* or *Strep. lactis* or combination of these acid producers. Some cheesemakers prefer to use mixed-strain cultures despite the possibility of open texture due to CO_2 production
Addition of rennet	0·15	30–32	Calf rennet preferred by many. Because of cost some cheesemakers use bovine rennet, i.e. from older animals or coagulants from microbial sources
Curd formation			Curd starts to form around 6 min after rennet addition. Allowed to firm until ready for cutting in 40–45 min
Cutting of curd	0·55	30–32	Curd gently cut into cubes about $8 \times 8 \times 8$ mm. Care taken to avoid fat and casein losses in whey
Scalding of curd/whey mixture	1·55	39–40	Gentle raising of temperature of curd and whey mixture. Whey is now being expelled from curd particles which become firmer

(continued)

TABLE 8—contd.

	Time (hours min)	Temp. (°C)	
Drainage of whey	3·00	<39	Whey is removed when the acidity of the whey pressed from a handful of curd reaches around 0·22–0·25 % lactic acid. This is a critical stage of the process and the cheesemaker will decide what action to take on the basis of how the starters have performed in previous cheesemaking
Cheddaring			The traditional process to achieve fusion of the curd consists of piling and turning the blocks of curd for around $1\frac{1}{2}$–$1\frac{3}{4}$ h until the texture resembles the breast meat of the chicken. Modern industrial methods mechanise this stage
Milling of curd	4·45 (TA 0·65 % lactic acid) (pH 5·2)		The cheddared curd is milled into 'chips' about 50 mm × 15 mm × 15 mm
Salting of curd	4·50		Salt is added in amounts suitable to provide 1·5–1·8 % (w/w) in the finished cheese
Hooping of curd	5·00		The salted curd is added to individual 19 kg capacity or other moulds made of metal or plastics. One mechanised commercial system includes pressing around 1 tonne of cheese in a large hoop followed by cutting of the pressed curd into 19–20 kg rectangular blocks

Pressing	For up to 18 h pH 5·1	A new alternative to hooping and pressing is the continuous block forming of cheese whereby 19–20 kg rectangular cheeses are formed by fusing salted curd under vacuum in about 30 min without pressing of curd in individual moulds (Anon., 1977)
Wrapping the film		A very high proportion of Cheddar cheese is now made in rindless form by sealing the cheese after pressing or forming in an O_2 impermeable film or laminate. The packaging material prevents dehydration of the cheese surface—thereby increasing cheese yield and preventing mould formation provided all seals have been properly formed and no O_2 is within the pack
Curing	Primary curing for 2 months	Temperature of 10 °C
Grading	Normally after 2 months from production	Sensory evaluation of firmness (body). flavour and odour, texture, colour and finish by subjective methods
Further curing storage and distribution	3–12 months from production	The period of curing may vary from 3 months for mild Cheddars with high moisture content, e.g. around 38 % to 9–12 months for mature Cheddars with lower moisture content. The cheese merchant will select cheese suitable for particular markets

cheeses and also in the organisms selected for their manufacture. Sponcet (1983) discusses these developments and compares the production methods.

The most important characteristics of mixed-strain cultures of the composition given below is to produce lactic acid, aroma compounds, some carbon dioxide and initiate enzyme action during ripening of the cheese. The mesophilic starters used for soft cheese develop acidity more slowly than those required for Cheddar cheese—1 % inoculum of a suitable Camembert starter will bring about an acidity of 0·6–0·7 % lactic acid at 32 °C in 6 h compared to 0·75–0·85 % lactic acid for a Cheddar cheese starter under the same conditions. Recent trends in France for consumers to prefer cheese with a mild taste have led to the development of so-called 'stabilised paste' cheese. These products have the characteristics of the pâtes molles in dry matter, size and general appearance but the pH after salting is much higher, the fat content is higher and the shelf-life is longer (Sponcet, 1983). The production of this type of cheese is dependent on the use of a thermophilic culture. In the early stages of this development part of the mesophilic starter was replaced by *Streptococcus thermophilus* which became dominant. Sponcet (1983) reports that starters of *Strep. thermophilus* are used on their own for the production of pâtes molles cheese—see Table 9.

10.3. Gruyère de Comté

Gruyère de Comté cheese, made in Jura, Doubs and Haute Savoie, differs from the Swiss Emmental cheese in the size of the 'eyes' or holes in the cheese which are smaller in Gruyère de Comté. The holes are formed due to propionic acid fermentation and the production of CO_2 from the action of the propionibacteria used in addition to the normal starter culture bacteria in the manufacture of the cheese.

Gruyère de Comté, like Emmental and Beaufort, is of the hard pressed variety with good keeping quality and is easily transported over long distances. The dry matter content of the cheese is high and it has a firm rind. Today the manufacture of Gruyère de Comté cheese accounts for almost a quarter of the total French cheese production and exceeds 160 000 metric tons per annum (Veisseyre, 1979).

10.3.1. Summary of Production
The cheese is made from evening milk held at 15 °C which has been partially skimmed the following morning together with the morning milk which is

TABLE 9
Soft Cheeses: Comparison of Production Methods

	Camembert (old fashion)	Traditional soft cheese (modern technology)	Stabilised pastes
Preparation of milk	Raw milk	Storage on farm 24–36 h Fat—standardisation Pasteurisation 72 °C 20 s Prematuration 0·1–0·5 % Mesophilic starter	Storage on farm 0·2 % Mesophilic starter
		12–13 °C overnight Thermisation (a form of heat treatment)	
Starter	No or 1 %, 30 °C Milk acidity 25 °D	1·5–2 % Mesophilic starter 30–35 °C pH 6·4–6·45	2 % Thermophilic starter 35–38 °C 30–40 min
Coagulation	15–20 ml/100 litres 520 mg chymosin/litre	25 ml/100 litres 520 mg chymosin/litre	25 ml/100 litres 520 mg chymosin/litre
Coag. time	15 min	8–10 min	8–10 min
Total coag. time	60 min	3 × coag. time	3 × coag. time
Cutting	No	Small or large according to type	Yes
Particle size			1·5 × 1·5 × 1·5 cm
Stirring	No	Small in amount according to type	3 times
Total time	—	50–60 min	45 min
Moulding	With ladle	Multi-block moulds	Multi-block moulds
Drainage	2 turns over 16 h at 28–29 °C Cooling at 18–20 °C pH 4·6	Variable per type for some hours at 28 °C Cooling at 20 °C pH 4·7–4·9	5 turns, 3 times at 28 °C Cooling at 20 °C pH 5·0–5·4
Salting	Dry	Brine 30–50 min, 10–13 °C	Brine 30–50 min, 10–13 °C
Curing	12–14 days, 13–15 °C	9 days, 12–13 °C	9 days, 11–12 °C

Source: Sponcet (1983).

naturally of lower fat content. The cheese is produced in small factories called 'fruitières' staffed by possibly only one man and a boy. About 300–500 litres of milk makes one Gruyère de Comté cheese in a chaudière or copper vat.

The temperature of the raw milk is raised to 32–34 °C then a rennet preparation called the 'présure naturelle' made from dried vells, i.e. the dried fourth stomach of the suckling calf, is added to the milk. This 'présure naturelle' is prepared by macerating the dried vells in whey at 30–35 °C in the 'recuite', the term given to a portion of the previous day's whey which has been acidified and boiled in order to precipitate the denatured protein and thereafter cooled. The acidification is due to an acid liquid, the 'aisy'. The 'aisy' is the result of the induced ripening of part of the 'recuite' (Veisseyre, 1979) which forms a culture of thermophilic lactic-acid-producing organisms such as *Streptococcus thermophilus*, *Lactobacillus helveticus* and *Lactobacillus lactis*. The 'présure naturelle' therefore is a mixture of the coagulating enzyme and the acid-producing bacteria. Pure cultures of thermophilic lactic-acid-producing bacteria are also added to the cheese milk. These bacteria help to retard the growth of putrefactive bacteria present on the dried vells. Therefore, a good 'présure naturelle' which has an acidity of 0·80–1·0 % lactic acid is responsible for multiplication of the thermophilic lactic bacteria and also coagulation of the milk.

After coagulation of the milk in the vat the surface curd is turned over to prevent it becoming too cold, then the curd is cut with a traditional harp knife until the pieces of curd are about the size of a wheat grain. The curd is settled for a few minutes then stirred for 15–20 min. The temperature is then raised in 30–35 min to 52–53 °C stirring continuously. The whey is drained off about 45–60 min after maximum scald.

The curd is collected into a cloth in the whey in the vat and then transferred into the cheese mould. It is then pressed for 20–24 h. The cheese is turned several times during this period and the cheese cloth changed. The temperature in the interior of the cheese remains at 35 °C or higher.

After pressing, the cheese is salted by wiping the cheese surface with fine salt and then put in a curing room for 2–3 weeks at 10–12 °C. During this time it is salted, wiped and turned daily. The proteolytic action of the lactobacilli ripens the cheese and breaks down the casein. Finally, the propionibacteria, which are responsible for the 'eyes' or holes in the cheese, begin to develop. The cheese is transferred to a curing room at 16–17 °C to encourage the growth of these organisms. It is seldom necessary to use pure cultures of these organisms since they are frequently present in the raw milk and withstand the scalding process. These bacteria produce propionic and acetic acid which contribute to the flavour and aroma of the cheese and finally carbon dioxide which causes the 'eye' formation. The cheese is stored in the curing room for 2–3 months to permit the action of these organisms.

10.4. Fresh Cheese

This description covers several types of cheese including Cottage cheese, Quarg and various forms of French Pâtes fraîches.

The cheese is ready for consumption immediately after the fermentation is complete and there is no period for curing or ripening between production and consumption.

Fresh cheese is frequently used in salad dishes and may be mixed by the cheesemaker or by the consumer with savoury materials such as herbs and garlic or with sweet materials, jams, etc.

The following outline production method (Table 10) is for lactic curd cheese made from separated milk which normally contains around 0.05–0.1% milk fat. A product of this type may be consumed on its own in salads or spread on bread, etc. On the other hand the low fat curd base may be mixed with cream to produce different types of product with or without added flavouring materials. It can be used for cheese cake.

10.5. Blue-veined Cheese

Blue-veined cheeses are among the most popular types in many countries, for example Stilton in England, Roquefort and Bresse Bleu in France, Gorgonzola in Italy, Danablu in Denmark, to mention only a few.

These varieties are made by different methods which confer particular characteristics but all require certain common factors for their successful production. In all cases selected moulds are used to produce the visible characteristics of blue/green veining. The moulds are aerobic and require a plentiful supply of oxygen for their development. This means that production methods for blue-veined cheese all depend on creating open texture aerobic conditions within the cheese to allow mould growth. In addition to conferring visible characteristics on the cheese the moulds contribute the enzymic means for fat and protein alteration during curing.

10.6. Caledonian Blue

The method of production (Table 11) of this cheese is a modification of the procedure used for Bleu d'Auvergne from the Massif Central region of France. The production method for Bleu d'Auvergne is similar to that for the world famous Roquefort which is made from sheep's milk.

TABLE 10
Fresh Cheese: Outline of Production

Milk separation	
Heat treatment	Heating to 72 °C for 15 s, cooling to 18–20 °C
Starter addition	0·5 % (v/v) of a mesophilic mixed-strain starter producing lactic acid and diacetyl
Rennet addition	3 ml/100 litres of milk
Incubation period	16–18 h at 18–20 °C until the acidity of the coagulating milk is 0·50 % lactic acid (pH 4·6–4·7)
Drainage of curd	The coagulated curd is poured into fine pure nylon bags which are then pressed for 4–5 h to remove some of the whey from the curd

Standardisation of curd base	The moisture content of the drained curd is standardised to conform to legal requirements for skimmed milk soft cheese. At this time pasteurised cream may be added to raise the milk fat level to that required for other categories of soft cheese
Salt and antimycotic addition	Up to 1 % (w/w) of salt may be added, and a permitted antimycotic, such as potassium sorbate, to prevent mould spoilage. These materials should be thoroughly mixed with the curd
Homogenisation	This step, which greatly improves the texture of lactic curd cheese, consists of passing the standardised curd through a curd homogeniser
Addition of flavouring materials	Some materials such as flavouring salts which dissolve in the soft curd may be added to the curd before homogenisation. Other flavouring materials such as herbs, comminuted vegetables, e.g. peppers and fruits, should be thoroughly mixed into the base curd
Packaging	Single-service plastics pots are normally used and can be attractively printed
Storage and distribution	It is normal practice to distribute the packaged product cold at 4–5 °C for immediate sale. Cheese made under hygienic conditions and containing antimycotic has a shelf life of 4–5 weeks

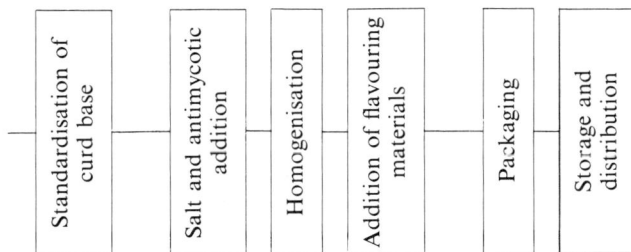

TABLE 11

Caledonian Blue: Outline of Production

	Time (hours min)	Temp. (°C)	
Milk treatment			Standardisation of fat to 3·5 % (w/w). Heating to 72 °C for 15 s. Cooling to 32 °C
Starter addition	0·00	32	1·5 % (w/w) mesophilic mixed-strain starter
Mould addition	Within a few minutes		A culture of *Penicillium glaucum* is added according to the supplier's recommendations
Rennet addition	0·15	32	30 ml for 100 litres of milk
Coagulation period			Curd starts to form in around 35–40 min and becomes firmer as time elapses
Cutting of the curd	1·30	32	The cheesemaker cuts the curd into $\frac{5}{8}$ in cubes, carefully avoiding damage which would cause excessive loss of curd fines and fat

Curd treatment	1·40	The soft cubes of curd are left undisturbed for 15–20 min and then gently mixed for 10 min
Curd settling	1·50	The stirring of the curds and whey is stopped. The whey continues to drain from the curds and accumulate at the top of the vat
Drainage	2·00	Whey is removed and the curds are piled in a tray made of perforated stainless steel to allow firming and further whey drainage
Moulding (hooping)	2·15	Perforated moulds are filled with curd and placed on a draining table
Turning and acid development	until 08.00 Air temp. 16–18°C, humidity 90–95% RH	The moulds are turned at $1\frac{1}{2}$h intervals four or five times and then left undisturbed overnight during which time the fermentation continues
Brine salting	Morning of 2nd day repeated on 3rd and 4th day after start of production	Wash in brine solution Baumé 20°; pH 5·2, temp. 16–18°C. Between brining retain in clean moulds on trays. Room should be at 16–18°C and 90–95% RH

(continued)

TABLE 11—contd.

	Time (hours min)	Temp. (°C)	
Dry salting	4th day after start of production		Transfer to room at 8–10 °C and 90–95 % RH. Rub the surface of the cheese with salt and leave a small quantity of salt (about 25 g) on the top surface of each cheese (2½ kg)
	6th day after start of production		Dry salt as above for 2nd time
1st skewering	8th day after start of production		Stainless steel needles are used to make channels into the centre of the cheese to allow air to penetrate for the developing moulds
Wrapping	One month after start of production		Wrap in aluminium foil
2nd skewering	Immediately after wrapping		Repeat skewering of cheese to further encourage mould growth
Further curing	For up to 3 months from start of production		Cut a cheese to determine maturity. The blue/green veins should be developed through the cheese. The taste should be pleasant acid but not bitter. The curing room conditions are usually 8–10 °C; 95 % RH for total of 2 months from start of production followed by holding at 2–3 °C until distribution and consumption. The use of lower temperatures for the earlier curing period will slow the ripening processes

11. CONCLUSION

It is evident from the above information that the fermentation process is an extremely complicated one. It is dependent on many different factors inclusive of bacteria, moulds and yeasts and the optimum growth factors necessary for these micro-organisms, i.e. the correct balance of the milk constituents and, in addition, temperature, humidity, air and balance of salt and pH. Apart from these, the other factors, which are the result of the action of the micro-organisms, produce and continue the initial fermentation process through to the final curing of the cheese, depending on the type being manufactured.

REFERENCES

AITON, W. (1811) *General View of the Agriculture of the County of Ayr*. A. Napier, Glasgow.

AL-DARWASH, A. K. A. (1983) Ph.D. Thesis, Glasgow University.

AMER, M. A. & LAMMERDING, A. M. (1983) *Cultured Dairy Products J.* **18**(2), 6.

ANDERSON, E. B. & MEANWELL, L. J. (1942) *J. Dairy Res.* **13**, 58.

ANON. (1977) *Dairy Industries International* **42**(11), 4.

ANON. (1979) In *Enzyme Nomenclature—The International Union of Biochemistry*. Academic Press, London.

ANON. (1982) *The Cheese Reporter*, September 17th, 7.

ASCHAFFENBURG, R. & DREWRY, J. (1959) Proc. XV International Dairy Congress, Vol. 3, 1631.

BILLS, D. D., MORGAN, M. E., LIBBEY, L. M. & DAY, E. A. (1965) *J. Bacteriol.* **117**, 318.

BURDETT, O. (1935) *A Little Book of Cheese*. Gerald Howe Ltd, London.

CAMPBELL, J. R. (1898) *Trans. Highland and Agricultural Soc. of Scotland*, 10.

CHURCHER, E. H. (1984) *Dairy Mirror*, Feb., 4–5.

CONN, H. W., 1889–1900, Conn. Agr. exptl Sta., Ann. Rpts; Knudsen, S. (1931) *J. Dairy Res.* **2**, 137.

COX, W. A. & LEWIS, J. E. (1972) In *Safety in Microbiology*, D. A. Shapton & R. G. Board Eds. Academic Press, London.

COX, W. A. & STANLEY, G. (1978) In *Streptococci*, F. A. Skinner & L. B. Quesnel Eds. Academic Press, London, p. 279.

CRAWFORD, R. J. M. (1960) Ph.D. Thesis, University of Glasgow.

DOUGLAS, J. (1975) *Bacteriophages*. Chapman and Hall Ltd, London.

FAO (1982) *Production Yearbook 1981*, Vol. 35, 234.

FOX, P. F. (1978) In International Dairy Federation Doc. 108. IDF Publications, Brussels.

FREAM, W. (1892) *Elements of Agriculture*, 4th edn. Murray, London.

FUSSELL, G. E. (1955) *Dairy Engng* **72**(2), 53.

HAVERBECK, J., MULLAN, W. M. A. & WALKER, A. L. (1983) *J. Soc. Dairy Technol.* **36**(2), 36.

HEAP, H. A. & LAWRENCE, R. C. (1977) *N.Z. J. Dairy Sci. Technol.* **11**(1), 16.

INTERNATIONAL DAIRY FEDERATION (1980) *Starters in the Manufacture of Cheese*, Doc. 129. IDF Publications, Brussels.

INTERNATIONAL DAIRY FEDERATION (1981) *IDF Catalogue of Cheeses*, Doc. 141. IDF Publications, Brussels.

INTERNATIONAL DAIRY FEDERATION (1984) *Annual Memento*, 14.

KRISTOFFERSEN, T. (1967) *J. Dairy Sci.* **50**, 279.

LAW, B. A., CASTANON, M. & SHARPE, M. E. (1976a) *J. Dairy Res.* **43**(2), 301.

LAW, B. A., CASTANON, M. & SHARPE, M. E. (1976b) *J. Dairy Res.* **43**(1), 117.

LAW, B. A. & SHARPE, M. E. (1978a) In *Streptococci*, F. A. Skinner & L. B. Quesnel Eds. Academic Press, London, p. 263.

LAW, B. A. & SHARPE, M. E. (1978b) *J. Dairy Res.* **45**, 267.

LAW, B. A., SHARPE, M. E. & REITER, B. (1974) *J. Dairy Res.* **41**(1), 137.

LAWRENCE, R. C. (1978) Proceedings XX International Dairy Congress, 2ST.

LISTER, J. (1878) *Q. J. Micro. Sci.* **18**, 177. (Breed, R. S., Murray, E. G. D. & Hitchens, A. P. (1948) *Bergey's Manual of Determinative Bacteriology*, 6th edn. Baillière, Tindall & Cox, London.)

LLOYD, F. J. (1891) *J. Bath and West of England Soc.* **2** (Moir, G. M. (1942) *New Zealand Department of Agriculture Bulletin*, 162).

LLOYD, F. J. (1899) *Report on Cheese Making*. H.M. Stationery Office, London.

LOWRIE, R. J. & LAWRENCE, R. C. (1972) *N.Z. J. Dairy Sci. Technol.* **7**, 51.

LUNDSTEDT, E. (1983) *Cultured Dairy Products J.* **18**, 10.

MACDONALD, J. (1908) *Stephen's Book on the Farm*, 5th edn. Blackwood, Edinburgh and London.

MCKAY, L. L. (1982) In *Developments in Food Microbiology—1*, Ch. 5. Applied Science Publishers, London, pp. 153–82.

MANNING, D. J. (1974) *J. Dairy Res.* **41**(1), 81.

MANNING, D. J., CHAPMAN, H. R. & HOSKING, Z. D. (1976) *J. Dairy Res.* **43**(2), 313.

NICHOLS, A. A. & HOYLE, M. (1948) *J. Dairy Res.* **15**(2), 374.

ORLA-JENSEN, S. (1919) *The Lactic Acid Bacteria*. Ejner Munksgaard, Copenhagen.

PASTEUR, L. (1857) *C.r. Acad. Sci.* **45**, 915. (Hammer, B. W. *Dairy Bacteriology*, 3rd edn. John Wiley, New York.)

PAYENS, T. A. (1981) In *Proceedings from the Second Biennial Marschall International Cheese Conference*, Madison, USA: Miles Laboratories Inc., Madison, USA, pp. 122–37.

PORTER, J. W. G. (1975) *Milk and Dairy Foods*. Oxford University Press, Oxford.

REITER, B. (1978) *J. Dairy Res.* **45**(1), 131.

REITER, B., FRYER, T. F., PICKERING, A., CHAPMAN, H. R., LAWRENCE, R. C. & SHARPE, M. E. (1967) *J. Dairy Res.* **34**, 257.

SANDINE, W. E. (1979) *Lactic Starter Culture Technology*. Pfizer Inc., New York.

SANDINE, W. E., RADICH, P. C. & ELLIKER, P. R. (1972) *J. Milk Food Technol.* **35**, 176.

SCOTT, R. (1981) *Cheesemaking Practice*. Applied Science Publishers Ltd, London.

SCOTTISH MILK MARKETING BOARD (1983) *Milk Bulletin*, October.

SHELDON, J. P. (1911) In *The Standard Cyclopedia of Modern Agriculture and Rural Economy*. The Gresham Publishing Company, London.
SHELDON, R. M., LINDSAY, R. C., LIBBEY, L. M. & MORGAN, M. E. (1971) *Appl. Microbiol.* **22**, 263.
SIMON, A. L. (1956) *Cheeses of the World*, 1st edn. Faber and Faber, London.
SPONCET, M. (1983) *Dairy Industries International* **48**(8), 10.
STEVENSON, W. (1911) In *The Standard Cyclopedia of Modern Agriculture and Rural Economy*. The Gresham Publishing Company, London.
STORCH, V. (1890) *Nogle Undersøgelser over Flødens, Syrning*, 18 Beretn. fra Forsøglab. (Knudsen, S. (1931) *J. Dairy Res.* **2**, 137.)
TERZAGHI, B. E. & SANDINE, W. E. (1975) *Appl. Microbiol.* **29**, 807.
THOROGOOD, S. A. & RAY, A. (1984) *J. Soc. Dairy Technol.* **37**(2), 38.
UNITED STATES DEPARTMENT OF AGRICULTURE (1978) *Cheese Varieties and Descriptions*. USDA, Washington, D.C.
VEISSEYRE, R. (1979) *Technologie du Lait*, 3rd edn. La Maison Rustique, Paris.
VERMA, I. S. & SOMMER, H. H. (1957) *J. Dairy Sci.* **40**, 331.
WEIGMANN, H. (1890) (Knudsen, S. (1931) *J. Dairy Res.* **2**, 137).
WEST, R. A. (1983) *Dairy Industries International* **48**(6), 21.
WHITEHEAD, H. R. & COX, G. A. (1932) *N.Z. J. Sci. Technol.* **13**, 304.

Chapter 4

Fermented Milks

HELENA OBERMAN

*Institute of Fermentation Technology and Microbiology,
Technical University, Łódź, Poland*

1. INTRODUCTION

According to FIL-IDF (1969) fermented milks are: 'products prepared from milks—whole, partially or fully skimmed, concentrated milk or milk substituted from partially or fully skimmed dried milk homogenized or not, pasteurized or sterilized and fermented by means of specific micro-organisms'. The origin of the cultured dairy products is obscure; they date back to the dawn of civilisation, although it is difficult to be precise about the date when they were first made.

In Europe, Asia and Africa, from time out of mind sour milk was known as being more stable and advantageous than fresh. It preserved the high quality nutrients present in milks in a relatively more stable form.

Mention of cultured dairy products is found in some of the earliest writings of civilised man: e.g. the Bible, the sacred books of Hinduism. An old legend tells that an angel brought down the pot which contained the first yoghurt or leben. Another claims that ancient Turks, who were Buddhists, used to offer yoghurt to the angels and stars who protected them (cit. after Rašić & Kurmann, 1978).

In the bibliography of the Roman Emperor Elagabatum (AD 218–222) (l.c. 1978) two recipes of soured milk preparations are mentioned: 'opus lactarum' composed from soured milk, honey, flour and fruits, and 'oxygala' made from sour milk, vegetables and some spices. Known scientists of early ages, such as Hippocrates, Avicenna, Galen and others, considered milk not only a food product but a medicine as well. They prescribed sour milks for curing disorders of the stomach, intestines and other troubles. There are good reasons to believe that milk could be a very effective means of preventing arteriosclerosis in particular. Sour milks were used also as cosmetics and preservants of food against spoilage.

In the early part of the 20th century Metchnikoff (1845–1916) claimed that owing to lactic acid and other products present in sour milks fermented by lactic acid bacteria, the growth and toxicity of anaerobic, spore-forming bacteria in the large intestine are inhibited. Lactic acid is biologically active and capable of suppressing harmful micro-organisms especially putrefactive ones and so has a favourable effect on human vital activities.

Metchnikoff's theory of longevity considerably influenced the spread of fermented milk products to many countries, particularly to Europe. He promoted also extensive studies concerning biochemical and physiological properties of fermented milks.

The consumption of fermented milks per person in a year depends on the world region and on the local acceptability of these products.

According to data published by FIL-IDF (1981) the leading user in 1979 with 38·9 kg was Finland, followed by Sweden (33·5 kg) and Denmark (26·4 kg). In the UK consumption did not exceed 8·9 kg per person, per year, in USA 3·2 kg, in USSR 6·5 kg and in Poland 2·5 kg. The consumption of yoghurt is highest in Bulgaria with 31·5 kg per person per year (in UK 1·7 kg, in USA 3·2 kg).

Currently about 2·3 % of the total dairy products market is in the form of cultured dairy products and they have a tendency to a marked increase in sales (Manus, 1979). Very helpful here is the use of pure cultures, together with programmes for their improvement, progress in technology and particularly the increased understanding of their beneficial effects on nutrition and on physiology of humans.

The great popularity of fermented milks is attributed also to their attractive taste as well as to their extended shelf-life obtained at low temperatures at which the survival of pathogenic microflora is greatly diminished, particularly at low pH. The vital factor and health value of milk food results from the optimal balance of its components.

2. COMPOSITION AND DIETARY VALUE OF FERMENTED MILK PRODUCTS

The composition of fermented milk products depends on that of initial milks and on the specific metabolism of growing cultures. Modern processes effect milk fermentation under predictable, controllable and precise conditions to yield fermented products of high and standardised nutritional value.

The typical composition of fermented milks is given below (FIL-IDF, 1982):

Dry matter	ca. 14–18 %
Protein	4–6 %
Fat	0·1–10 %
Lactose	2–3 %
Lactic acid	0·6–1·3 %
Carbohydrates	
(including added fruits)	5–25 %
pH	3·8–4·6
Degree of acidity (°SH)	40–70 (in special cases, higher)
Alcohol content: in kefir	0·5–2 % (in both products with
in koumiss	2–3 % considerable volumes of CO_2)

(plus natural aromatic compounds, complex and specific for the particular milk product).

Because of the great latitude which the legal provision in general allows, the composition can vary over a wide range.

The earliest information concerning chemical and microbiological composition of fermented milk products was given at the end of the 19th century. Early investigations showed the presence of mixed micro-organisms. Metchnikoff (1904) pointed out the presence of *Bacillus bulgaricus*, cocci and yeasts in yoghurt. Grigoroff in 1905, isolated rod-shaped bacteria called *Bacillus A* from Bulgarian milk (Rašić & Kurmann, 1978). Other investigators have shown in fermented milks the presence of lactobacilli, including *Lactobacillus longus* plus *Bacillus lebensis*, *Bacillus* exhibiting and not exhibiting granules, *Streptobacillus*, Yoghurt bacillus and many other strains. Rašić & Kurmann (1978) present in their book a review on the original microflora of fermented milks as reported in early investigations.

A contribution to the nomenclature and identification of microflora of sour milk products was given by Orla-Jensen (1943) and by Rogosa & Sharpe (1959). Today it is evident that of all lactobacilli found in the sour milk products *Lactobacillus bulgaricus* is the most essential in the production of many milk foods.

The streptococci were reported in early researches under different names: *Micrococcus*, *Streptococcus lebenis*, *Diplostreptococcus*. Makrinov (1909) found in prostokvasha and matzoni strains similar to *Streptococcus hollandicus* designated by Orla-Jensen as *Streptococcus thermophilus.*

The presence of yeasts in many milk products was also reported. They were found in yoghurt, kefir, koumiss, hooslanka, zhentitsa, in symbiotic relation to lactic acid bacteria, responsible for the specificity of fermented product, though according to Nikolov (1962) and Katrandzijev (1961, 1962) milk yeasts and moulds encountered in Bulgarian yoghurt belong to the secondary contaminating microflora.

Summing up all findings concerning the microflora of original fermented milks it is evident that original microflora consisted mainly of different types of Lactobacilli and of Streptococci and of minor proportions of yeasts and of milk moulds, being in associated growth and showing mutual symbiotic relationships.

Lactic acid bacteria require a sugar such as lactose for growth and a wide range of amino acids, vitamins and other growth factors. Milk is a satisfactory medium except that amino acids and low molecular weight peptides are present at low concentrations. Therefore rapid growth of micro-organisms in milk, and acid production, requires a proteinase system and a lactose metabolising system.

'Homofermentative' lactic acid streptococci and lactobacilli ferment lactose (or glucose) almost exclusively to lactic acid forming only small amounts of formate, acetate and ethanol. 'Heterolactic' fermentation may occur by galactose metabolism in the presence of oxygen and at low temperatures or from loss of either lactose-phospho-transferase system (Demko *et al.*, 1972) or lactate dehydrogenase (McKay & Baldwin, 1974a, b). Thus lactic acid bacteria useful in milk fermentation, homolactic when grown anaerobically in the presence of an excess of fermentable sugars, have a latent potential for the alternative metabolism of pyruvate. Only little is known about the regulatory activities of these alternative pathways (Lawrence & Thomas, 1979).

For the details concerning the enzymic and genetic mechanisms for carbohydrate metabolism in some lactic acid bacteria the publications of McKay *et al.* (1970), McKay (1978), and Kempler & McKay (1979) may be recommended.

One of the very important factors determining the specific identity of fermented milk products is the flavouring compounds. In buttermilk, cream products and in some other sour milks the compounds of particular importance are diacetyl and acetoin, produced by *Streptococcus lactis* subsp. *diacetylactis* (Matuszewski *et al.*, 1936) or *Leuconostoc* strains producing them from lactose, or by some bacteria from citrate. Diacetyl is responsible for the characteristic 'buttery' nut-meat aroma in milks. Concentration of diacetyl in fermented milks is rather low (ca. 4–5 $\mu g/ml$), in contrast to acetoin concentration, often found up to 300–500 $\mu g/ml$ (Lawrence & Thomas, 1979).

A major area of discussion among the researchers relates to the mechanism of the formation of the aroma compounds. Early work showed that diacetyl is obtained by oxidative decarboxylation of α-acetolactate (DeMan, 1956; Pette, 1949; Seitz *et al.*, 1963a, b). Speckman & Collins (1968) reported that this compound is an intermediate in acetoin production resulting from the reaction between the acetaldehyde-thiamine-pyrophosphate complex and acetyl-CoA. Bruhn & Collins (1970) have found that diacetyl and acetoin formation are regulated by the supply of acetyl-CoA available.

The physiological significance of the diacetyl accumulation in lactic acid fermentation is suggested by Harvey & Collins (1963). Diacetyl could probably be the neutral, non-toxic product accumulated in the medium in the excess of pyruvate pool, produced both from lactose and from citrate metabolism of lactic acid bacteria (Coventry *et al.*, 1978).

In some strains of lactic acid bacteria and in some contaminated milk products the microflora diacetyl reductase, the enzyme responsible for the loss of flavour in fermented milks, is widely distributed. Bacteria with low diacetyl-reductase activity or mutants lacking diacetyl reductase are of great value for dairy purposes.

The lack of a desirable flavour may be due also to changes in chemical composition of milk. Probable causes include the lowered citrate level in the milk, insufficient culture incubation time, pH level and some other important physico-chemical and physiological factors (Oberman *et al.*, 1982).

Another very important carbonyl flavouring compound produced by lactic acid bacteria in fermented milks is acetaldehyde. It is undesirable in excess in buttermilk and in cream products; however it is thought to be the principal flavour component in natural yoghurt. It may result from lactose metabolism although it may result also from the metabolism of nitrogen containing substances (Lees & Jago, 1978a, b). *Streptococcus thermophilus* and particularly *Lactobacillus bulgaricus* possess the enzyme reducing acetyl-CoA to acetaldehyde, and in most strains no further conversion of acetaldehyde is effected, which causes the accumulation of acetaldehyde in yoghurt cultures.

A variety of other neutral and of acidic compounds may also contribute to the flavour and aroma of fermented milks. Ethanol is produced in small amounts by *Leuconostoc* spp., which possess active alcohol dehydrogenase and it is also the metabolic product of lactose fermenting yeasts present in kefir, koumiss and other similar products. Important acids are: formic, acetic, propionic, caproic, caprylic, capric, butyric and iso-valeric acids, provided by lactic acid fermentation and enzymatic transformation of amino acids. Carbon dioxide produces carbonation of certain products. All of the above compounds are necessary to bring out the total flavour of fermented milk products. Even the minor metabolic products, being in trace concentrations, may have an important role in balancing the desirable flavour in milk. The role of starter cultures is of particular value here (Sharpe, 1979; Stanley, 1980). The majority of flavouring compounds are produced from lactose but some of them may be derived from the metabolism of other milk constituents.

In fermented milk products there also occurs a significant change in free amino acid content, amounting to several times as much as in ordinary milk. In yoghurt, the free amino acid content amounts to about 1 % of the total proteins.

There is also a liberation of a significant amount of peptides during milk fermentation. Their concentration is variable, depending on the bacterial strain being used and on changes occurring during the manufacture of milk.

The lipase activity of some lactic acid bacteria influences the changes in fatty acid pattern and free fatty acids pool. Their amounts are different in milks of different origin.

The biological activities of lactic acid bacteria result also in changes in the vitamin level in fermented milks. There is a decrease at about 50 % in the vitamin B_6 and B_{12} content and in the ascorbic acid level. On the other hand folic acid, folinic acid and choline contents increase by more than 100 %. Only small changes are registered for other vitamins (vitamins A, B_1, B_2, niacin) (Rašić & Kurmann, 1978).

Summarising the above it is evident that the fermented milk products are improved in their basic nutritive value by their increasing digestibility in comparison with ordinary milk. The lactose content is reduced, the β-galactosidase present in lactic acid organisms influences tolerance of the product in lactase-deficient people. Lactic acid, in addition to its nutritive value, represents a physiological advantage, particularly the $L(+)$ form often produced by lactic acid strains.

The balanced content of several vitamins, regulation of cholesterol metabolism, increase in the digestibility of proteins and fat and improved utilisation of some cations all make fermented milk products among the most valuable natural products recommended for human nutrition.

3. TRADITIONAL FERMENTED MILK PRODUCTS

The oldest traditional methods applied to the production of fermented milks depended on climatic and regional circumstances in which the people lived. They were also influenced by the old customs transmitted from generation to generation.

The most popular traditional names of original fermented milk products are given in Table 1. Originally, fermented milks were prepared from the milk of sheep and buffalo and to a lesser extent from that of goat, cow or mare.

The fermentation was carried out in cloth or skin bags or in vessels of wood or pottery.

Propagation of natural microflora was initiated with a small quantity of the previously coagulated milk to seed the fresh portion of milk. Also milk was acidified with a small piece of lamb's or calf's stomach or with a portion of dried sour milk (Koroleva & Kondratenko, 1978).

In Bulgaria 'podkvasa', a kind of natural leaven produced by shepherds from sheep's milk, contained the best composition of naturally occurring souring strains used as a starter for souring milk.

In all countries where traditional lactic acid fermentation of milk exists at present, the original microflora acts as a mixed, naturally stabilised population of undefined or only partially defined composition. As is reported in many investigations, the original fermented milk samples showed the presence of various lactic acid bacteria, yeasts and milk moulds with *Streptococcus thermophilus* and *Lactobacillus bulgaricus* predominating. Taxonomy of the above strains is given by Accolas (1982) but there still remains open the question of their identification and precise evaluation for dairy purposes. The vast amount of different fermented milks produced with similar bacterial species yet which differ very much from each other, confirm the large spectrum of metabolic activity and specificity of the strains used, even though they belong to the same species.

3.1. Yoghurt

The origin of yoghurt is not very clear. According to some sources it originated in Asia where the ancient Turks lived as nomads. Still other authors are of the opinion that yoghurt originates from the Balkans. The inhabitants of Thrace used to make soured milk called 'prokish' which later became yoghurt. The Slavs adopted the procedure of yoghurt preparation and yoghurt became their traditional food (Chomakov, 1973). According to Koroleva & Kondratenko (1978) probably koumiss preceded yoghurt

TABLE 1
Fermented Milk Products*

Traditional name	Country of origin	Milk types, conditions	Microflora
Prokish Prostokvasha	Asia, Africa, Europe Middle Asia, Balkans	Fermentation in a cloth bag Fermentation in clay vats	Mixed lactic-acid, unknown *Str. thermophilus*, often with *L. bulgaricus*
Yoghurt (yaghurt)	Middle Asia, Balkans	Cows', sheep's, goats' or mixed milk	*Str. thermophilus, L. bulgaricus, Micrococci*, other lactic acid cocci, yeasts, moulds
Bulgarian milk	Bulgaria	Cows', sheep's, goats' or mixed milk	*L. bulgaricus*, also with *Str. thermophilus*
Kefir	Caucasus	Sheep's, cows', goats' or mixed milk, fermentation in skin bag or in wooden barrels	*Str. lactis, Leuconostoc* spp., *L. caucasicus, Saccharomyces kefir, Torula kefir, Micrococci*, spore-forming *Bacilli*
Koumiss	Asiatic steppes	Mares', camels' or asses' milk, fermentation in skin bag	*L. bulgaricus, L. acidophilus, Torula koumiss, Saccharomyces lactis, Micrococci*, spore-forming *Bacilli*
Brano	Bulgaria	Sheep's and cows' milk	*L. bulgaricus, Str. thermophilus*, lactose-fermenting yeasts
Hooslanka	East Carpathian Mountains	Sheep's, cows' or mixed milk, fermentation in wooden vats ('berbenitza')	*Str. lactis, Str. thermophilus, L. bulgaricus*, lactose-fermenting yeasts
Zhentitsa	East Carpathian Mountains	Sheep's milk, fermentation in mountain pastures	Mixed lactic-acid microflora, yeasts
Riazhenka	Ukraine-USSR	Baked cows' milk, earthenware vessel	*Str. thermophilus* often with *L. bulgaricus*
Varenets	USSR	Cows' milk, earthenware vessel	

Product	Region	Milk	Microflora
Vilia (Filia)	Finland	Cows' milk	*Str. lactis, Str. cremoris, Geotrichum candidum*
Taet-mjölk	Scandinavia	Cows' milk	Mixed lactic-acid microflora (mesophilic strains)
Kjaddermilk	Scandinavia	Cows' milk	*L. bulgaricus, Str. thermophilus, L. casei*
Skyr	Iceland	Cows' milk, rennin addition, draining out of whey	
Søs-tej	Hungary	Sheep's milk, rennin addition, partial draining out of whey	Mixed, not defined, lactic acid microflora
Leben, labneh	Lebanon and some Arab countries	Goats' or sheep's milk, fermentation in skin bag or in earthenware vessel	*Str. lactis, Str. thermophilus, L. bulgaricus*, often lactose-fermenting yeasts
Dahi (dadhi)	India, Persia	Cows', buffaloes' milk	*Str. lactis, Str. thermophilus, L. bulgaricus, L. plantarum*, lactose-fermenting yeasts
Matzun, matzoni	Caucasus, Armenia	Sheep's, goats', buffaloes' or mixed milk	*Str. thermophilus*
Airan	Caucasus, Bulgaria	Cows', sheep's or mixed milk	*Str. thermophilus* often with *L. bulgaricus*
Gioddu	Italy, Corsica, Sardinia	Cows', sheep's milk	*Str. thermophilus, L. bulgaricus*
Syuzma Tan (than)	Azerbaijan Armenia	Cows' milk Goats', sheep's or mixed milk, fermentation in cloth bag	'Bulgarian rods'
Tulum, torba, kurut	Turkey and Asia	Goats', sheep's or cows' milk, fermentation in cloth bag	Mixed microflora similar to yoghurt producing organisms, specific for region of milk fermentation
Gruzovina	Yugoslavia	Sheep's, cows' or mixed milk, fermentation in cloth bag	

* acc. to: Chomakov *et al.* (1973), Koroleva & Kondratenko (1978), Matuszewski & Supińska-Jakubowska (1949), Pijanowski (1971), Rašić & Kurmann (1978), Tamime & Robinson (1978).

preparation. The nomads, who in the 5th century lived along the Danube and around the Black Sea (Pra-Bulgars) introduced the procedure for koumiss preparation of yoghurt production from sheep's milk instead of mares' milk.

Original yoghurt is prepared in Bulgaria from goats' or cows' boiled, high solids milk, inoculated at 40–45 °C with a portion of previously soured milk. To keep the temperature constant the pot containing inoculated milk is thoroughly wrapped in furs and placed for 8–10 h in the oven (Matuszewski & Supińska-Jakubowska, 1949). until a smooth, relatively highly viscous, firm and cohesive curd with very little wheying off is formed.

There are controversial data concerning the original microflora of yoghurt. The presence of various physiological groups of micro-organisms was reported in early investigations on original products but these reports also pointed out that the predominant role in production of yoghurt lay with *Lactobacillus bulgaricus* and *Streptococcus thermophilus* (Koroleva & Kondratenko, 1978; Rašić & Kurmann, 1978). Widely distributed yeasts (*Candida mycoderma, Candida krusei, Candida tropicalis*) were regarded as spoilage micro-organisms. Other bacterial strains, *Streptococcus lactis, Streptococcus lactis* subsp. *diacetylactis, Leuconostoc* spp., *Streptococcus lactis* var. *taette* (slime producer), were regarded as supplementary microflora (Teplý, 1970).

In original Bulgarian and Yugoslavian yoghurts *Geotrichum candidum* was also found.

Rašić & Kurmann (1978), summarising the findings concerning the original yoghurt microflora, divided it into three groups:

(a) Essential microflora—consisting of *Streptococcus thermophilus* and *Lactobacillus bulgaricus.*

(b) Non-essential—represented by homofermentative lactic acid strains other than in group (a) and by heterofermentative lactic acid bacteria. Some of them may be used beneficially for supplementing the original microflora: for example, *Lactobacillus acidophilus, Bifidobacterium bifidum, Propionibacterium shermanii, Streptococcus lactis* subsp. *diacetylactis.*

(c) Contaminants: yeasts, moulds, coliforms and other undesirable micro-organisms.

The metabolic activity of yoghurt bacteria results in a considerable increase in cell numbers. The total count of viable yoghurt bacteria ranges between 200 and 1000 million per ml of fresh yoghurt, but decreases during subsequent storage.

Finished yoghurt is thus the end product of a symbiotic culture of

Streptococcus thermophilus and of *Lactobacillus bulgaricus* growing at temperatures in the range 40–45 °C.

A proportion of 1:1 of the 'rods' and 'cocci' forms is considered to be optimum for flavour and texture production (Chandan *et al.*, 1969; Vedamuthu, 1982) but 1:5 or 1:10 or 2·1:1·2 are also favourable (Rašić & Kurmann, 1978; Koroleva & Kondratenko, 1978).

Faster growth of streptococci at the beginning of fermentation brings about accumulation of moderate amounts of lactic and acetic acids, acetaldehyde, diacetyl and formic acid. Availability of formate and the changes in the oxidation–reduction potential in the medium stimulate the growth of *Lactobacillus bulgaricus*. Yoghurt is finished at pH 4·2–4·3.

Lactobacillus bulgaricus demonstrates a much stronger proteolytic activity than does *Streptococcus thermophilus*. By liberating from milk proteins a number of amino acids, stimulation of growth of *Streptococcus thermophilus* occurs. The content of liberated amino acids is considerably higher than is necessary to meet the nitrogen requirement of *Streptococcus thermophilus*, and hence a considerable increase occurs in the free amino acids content of finished yoghurts. Of the individual amino acids glutamic acid and proline are present in the highest amounts.

Yoghurt bacteria, particularly *Streptococcus thermophilus* exhibit a marked sensitivity to antibiotics and other inhibitory substances present in milk. Their destruction may be also caused by bacteriophage.

Yoghurt, as a product, is relatively highly viscous, firm and cohesive. Its body characteristics are greatly influenced by the careful regulation of production conditions. Top quality yoghurt is smooth, without grittiness or granules and without effervescence. It is a highly acid product.

The quality of strains used in starters is of particular importance. The characteristic flavour is contributed mainly by lactobacilli producing lactic acid and acetaldehyde. But the complexity of flavour is secured by the balanced level of many by-products represented by other carbonyl compounds as well as by the amino acids released into the milk. Details concerning the amino acid level, protein decomposition, changes in fatty acids and vitamins may be found in the books of Rašić & Kurmann (1978) and of Koroleva & Kondratenko (1978).

Yoghurts exhibit an antagonistic effect against a number of pathogenic and saprophytic organisms but this effect shows many variations depending on the bacterial strains used, and on their particular antagonistic properties.

Among the various cultured dairy products yoghurt has gained tremendous popularity and now finds many different applications.

Detailed descriptions of certain aspects of the manufacture of yoghurt and yoghurt-like products and of their wide application for different purposes, and of their microbiology, may be found in the large monographs of Rašić & Kurmann (1978), Tamime & Greig (1979), Vedamuthu (1979) and Schulz (1966).

3.2. Bulgarian Milk

Bulgarian milk is undoubtedly one of the yoghurt family of foods. Katrandzijev (1962) supposes that it originates from Trak's tradition, i.e. from the tradition of the sheep breeders who came from Asia to Bulgaria in 5th century bringing the tradition of sour milk preparation, currently existing in Bulgaria. Bulgarian milk is an extremely sour milk prepared from boiled goats' or cows' milk inoculated with a portion of a previous fermented milk. The ripening is carried out at 40–45 °C near to or in the oven, in the same manner as yoghurt is prepared.

At present the commercial production of Bulgarian milk uses as the starter *Lactobacillus bulgaricus* as a monoculture or mixed with *Streptococcus thermophilus*. Incubation takes place at 37 °C. The level of milk acidity is at least 1·4 % but in some cases attains as much as 4 %. Soured milk is stored at 7 °C.

The fermented product lacks flavour and aroma. Some companies produce 'Bulgarian buttermilk' with the cultures of *Lactobacillus bulgaricus* and starters for cultured buttermilks (Manus, 1979).

3.3. Leben, Dahi and Related Products

Leben is one of the oldest fermented milks produced in the Middle East. It is a concentrated yoghurt-like or kefir-like product. The condensation is accomplished by hanging the fermented curd in a cloth bag which allows the whey to drain out. In Turkey a goats' or sheep's skin bag is used; in Egypt instead of a bag an earthenware, porous vat enabling the removal of moisture is used. In certain areas it is rolled in balls and sun-dried to produce a curd mass (Tamime & Robinson, 1978).

There is a mixed microflora acting in Leben production, consisting of *Streptococcus lactis*, *Streptococcus thermophilus*, *Lactobacillus bulgaricus* and lactose-fermenting yeasts.

The related fermented milks are known under different names: labneh (or lebneh)—Lebanon and some Arab countries; tan (or than)—Armenia; torba, kurut, tulum—Turkey; gioddu—Italy; matzun—USSR. In some rural communities of the Middle East, concentrated fermented milks produced from the surplus of summer milk are essential as foodstuff for winter.

Dahi (dadhi) is the Indian equivalent of yoghurt produced from boiled cows', buffaloes', or mixed milk. Inoculated milk is kept overnight close to the oven. Dahi made from buffaloes' milk has a higher curd content. Dahi is fermented with *Streptococcus lactis*, *Streptococcus thermophilus*, *Lactobacillus bulgaricus*, *Lactobacillus plantarum* and by lactose-utilising yeasts (Vedamuthu, 1982).

The diet of Middle Eastern communities also includes: stirred yoghurt, smoked yoghurt, kishk (yoghurt mixed with cracked wheat), chanklich (yoghurt mixed with herbs and spices (thyme)), labneh-anbaris (covered with oil) (Tamime & Robinson, 1978).

3.4. Kefir

Kefir belongs to the class of acid and alcoholic fermented milks. Traditional kefir was prepared by the inhabitants of the Caucasus Mountains in Russia, in leather bags or in oak vats. The fermentation was initiated by the white to yellow grains, resembling cooked rice, insoluble in water, gelatinous, of irregular size, distributed on the inner surface of the vat or bag. Original kefir grains cannot be precisely reconstructed, they are recovered from sour milk and used repeatedly. When added to milk they swell and turn white forming a slimy, jelly-like product. The composition of kefir grain microflora is still a matter for debate. The grains contain lactobacilli, streptococci, micrococci, and also yeasts in a specific symbiotic relationship to the bacteria. The kefir granules are held together by a polysaccharide called kefiran. Two species of yeasts have been identified: *Saccharomyces kefir* and *Torula kefir*; certain lactobacilli: *Lactobacillus caucasicus* and *Lactobacillus casei*; and cocci: *Leuconostoc* spp. As spoiling micro-organisms were found: micrococci, spore-forming bacilli and coliforms (Koroleva & Kondratenko, 1978; Kosikowski, 1977; Matuszewski & Supińska-Jakubowska, 1949).

Traditional kefir contains 70 % of lactobacilli, 20 % of streptococci and 5 % of yeasts (Pijanowski, 1971). It is prepared by adding kefir grains to boiled cows' milk. Incubation is carried out at 23–25 °C overnight until acidity attains 30–40 °SH. The major end products of the fermentation are: lactic acid *ca.* 0·8 %, ethanol and CO_2 *ca.* 1 %; traces of acetaldehyde, diacetyl and acetoin plus other minor components influence the flavour of kefir. Of the total nitrogen, 7 % is in the form of peptones and 2 % as amino acids. There is a slight increase in the content of vitamins B_1 and B_2 and in folic acid during the fermentation. In the presence of *Propionibacterium* strains a marked increase in vitamin B_{12} level is noted. Kefir flavour is mildly alcoholic and yeast-sour. When agitated kefir foams and fizzes. For recovery the kefir grains are washed with clean, cold water and stored in water at 4 °C for up to 8–10 days. They may be also stored in a dried state showing activity for 12–18 months. Vayssier (1978) found in two specimens of kefir grains differing proportions of *Streptococcus lactis, Streptococcus lactis* subsp. *diacetylactis, Leuconostoc mesenteroides, Lactobacillus casei alactosus, Lactobacillus cellobiosus, Saccharomyces florentinus* and in kefir beverages also other streptococci were found depending on the origin of starter. Summarizing the results Vayssier proposes to prepare kefir with a constant proportion of: *Streptococcus lactis, Streptococcus lactis* subsp. *diacetylactis, Leuconostoc mesenteroides, Lactobacillus brevis/cellobiosus, Lactobacillus casei var. alactosus* and of *Saccharomyces florentinus* (5×10^6 per g). According to Koroleva & Kondratenko (1978) kefir grains also contain acetic acid bacteria.

3.5. Koumiss

Original koumiss is made from mares' milk, which contains about 7 % of lactose. Its name derives from a tribe called Kumanes who lived along the river Kumane in the Asiatic steppes. In earlier days, to accelerate the fermentation of koumiss, pieces of horse flesh or tendon or some vegetable matter were added to the mares' milk placed into bags made from the skin of lamb, presumably to provide microflora needed for fermentation. Mares' milk does not coagulate at the isoelectric point of casein and hence koumiss is not a curdled product. The major end products in koumiss are: 0·7–1·8 % (0·7–0·9 %) of lactic acid, 1·3 % of ethanol (according to USSR standard 0·6–2·5 %) and 0·5–0·88 % of CO_2 (Matuszewski & Supińska-Jakubowska, 1949; Pijanowski, 1971). Milk proteins are hydrolysed in koumiss. Still there is no exact information concerning the detailed characteristics of koumiss.

The microflora content in original koumiss is very variable. The main microflora is represented by *Lactobacillus/Bacterium orienburgii, Lactobacillus bulgaricus, Lactobacillus acidophilus,* and by lactose fermenting yeasts, *Torula koumiss, Saccharomyces lactis.* Also it is possible to find in it, lactic acid streptococci, coliforms and some spore-forming bacilli. Finished koumiss is of sourish-alcoholic flavour and fizzy appearance.

The original procedure for koumiss preparation is as follows: fresh mares' milk (3–10 parts by volume) is mixed with a finished previous koumiss (1 part). The mixture is placed in an appropriate skin bag (used only for koumiss preparation). Every 1–2 h the milk is agitated with a special apparatus and when strong foam and the specific sourish flavour appears (after 3–8 h) young koumiss is finished and ready for consumption.

The temperature of incubation varies from 20 to 22 °C, sometimes from 25 to 32 °C. Further ripening proceeds at low temperatures. Middle koumiss is obtained after 24 h and strong after 2–4 days of maturation.

The principles of modern koumiss manufacture are similar to the traditional ones: fresh mares' milk is inoculated with 30 % of specially prepared starter. Incubation is carried out at 28 °C, with agitation from time to time (every 1 or 2 h), until the desirable acidity (0·7–0·8 %) is obtained. Then the milk is cooled to 20 °C, bottled, capped and stored for 24 h at 4–5 °C. The starter is prepared from 1 part of *Lactobacillus bulgaricus* incubated at 37 °C for 7 h and 2 parts of *Torula* spp. incubated at 30 °C for 15 h. To the prepared mixture of strains, mares' milk is added, according to a special procedure, until acidity reaches 1·4 % (Chandan *et al.*, 1969).

Shigayeva & Ospanova (1982) proposed new starters for koumiss, the preparation consisting of *Streptococcus lactis*, *Lactobacillus bulgaricus* and *Saccharomyces lactis* (koumiss yeasts) and including also *Acetobacter aceti* (0·02 %) to improve the specific aroma. For the use of above starter new technology was developed and the storage of koumiss was extended until 14 days. Stoyanova *et al.* (1982), considering the antibiotic properties of koumiss, stated that the original koumiss as well as freeze-dried preparations possessed high antibiotic activity particularly when strong koumiss was tested. In comparison with the young koumiss, the strong preparation showed 51 % higher activity. After testing, standardised koumiss was found to contain: acidity 40 °SH, alcohol content 1·5 %, count of viable cells $4·97 \times 10^7$/ml and $1·43 \times 10^7$/ml of bacteria and of yeasts respectively.

Koumiss is considered to be a therapeutic drink. In the USSR it is used for the treatment of pulmonary tuberculosis. A wide range of topics including the significance of the therapeutic effect of koumiss and expediency of its use in various diseases, comparisons of medicinal properties of natural and reconstituted koumiss (heat dried and freeze-dried), physical and chemical properties of it, composition and prospects for horse farming for milk are given by Anashima (1979).

Koumiss-like beverages are prepared from cows' milk. Czuzova (1958) describes 'kurunga', a Mongolian koumiss-like product produced with a bacterial and yeast starter of unknown composition.

3.6. Other Specific Traditional Products

3.6.1. Airan

This is a sour milk prepared from cows' milk containing 1 % of fat. Milk is inoculated with *Lactobacillus bulgaricus*. After acidification the fermented product is stirred, cooled to 5 °C and bottled. Acidity does not exceed 52 °SH. Airan is a very refreshing Bulgarian beverage, particularly pleasant when consumed in summer (Koroleva & Kondratenko, 1978).

3.6.2. Riazhenka, Prostokvasha, Varenets

Riazhenka is widely distributed in USSR. It is a sour milk, similar to yoghurt. It is prepared with 'Metchnikoff's' starter, 1–5 % being added. The starter contains *Lactobacillus bulgaricus* and *Streptococcus thermophilus* strains with specific growth and acidification rates. Acidity of riazhenka is near 48 °SH. The product is very notable for its pure sour-acid flavour (Koroleva & Melnikova, 1973).

Prostokvasha is another fermented milk very popular in the USSR, again it is similar to yoghurt. It is prepared from pasteurised milk containing 6 % fat. The starter consists of *Lactobacillus bulgaricus* and *Streptococcus thermophilus*.

Varenets is boiled milk inoculated with *Lactobacillus bulgaricus* and *Streptococcus thermophilus*, and is also very popular in the USSR.

3.6.3. Snezhanka

Snezhanka is soured milk prepared in Bulgaria from cows' and buffaloes' milk in the ratio 80:20 or from cows' and sheep's milk in the ratio 70:30. The fat content in the mixed milk must not be lower than 4·9 %. Milk is supplemented by addition of 6 % of sugar and is manufactured according to procedures used for yoghurt production. Fermentation proceeds at 42–45 °C until acidity reaches 36–38 °SH. The product can be stored at 8–10 °C for 20–48 h (Koroleva & Kondratenko, 1978).

3.6.4. 'Brano' Milk

'Brano' milk is produced in Bulgaria. There are three methods for its preparation:

(a)   Sheep's milk is boiled and at 30–35 °C is treated with a special starter. After the milk has curdled, the product is stored overnight in a cold place and then is placed into a wooden barrel to which every day a new portion of boiled, fresh milk is added.

(b)   The same as the above procedure except at the last step—instead of fresh milk a new portion of soured milk is added.

(c)   Sour milk is drained through a cloth bag (similar to dahi preparation) and milk solids are collected and put into the wooden barrel. The resulting product is often called 'drained milk'.

Main 'brano' microflora consists of *Lactobacillus bulgaricus* and of *Streptococcus thermophilus*, but the number of viable cells decreases during storage of fermented milk. Supplementary micro-organisms belong to the lactose-fermenting yeasts, responsible for the specific sharp sour-alcoholic flavour of 'brano' (Koroleva & Kondratenko, 1978).

3.6.5. Hooslanka and Zhentitsa

Similar to 'brano' is the hooslanka produced in eastern parts of the Carpathian Mountains. The traditional product is prepared from sheep's or cows' milk evaporated to 25 % of the initial volume (high solid medium). At 40–45 °C milk is placed into an elongated wooden vat called a 'berbenitza', the inner surface of which is covered with the portion of earlier prepared hooslanka. After 24 h of fermentation the vat is firmly closed.

Much hooslanka is consumed. It may be stored over several years. The lactic acid content of hooslanka is nearly 2 %, alcohol level *ca.* 0·5 % and slight saturation with CO_2. Supińska & Pijanowski (1937) found that in several months old hooslanka *Lactobacillus bulgaricus* and lactose-fermenting yeasts were viable while *Streptococcus* cells were not active.

Zhentitsa is another specific fermented milk product from the region of East Carpathian Mountains. It is prepared from sheep's milk and fermented at 35–40 °C. The maturation of zhentitsa is carried out at low temperatures in the mountain pastures, which favours the microbial purity of fermented milk. Preparation of zhentitsa is similar to that of 'brano' described above (Matuszewski & Supińska-Jakubowska, 1949).

3.6.6. Vilia, Taetmjölk, Kjaddermilk

Vilia is a fermented milk originating in Finland. It is made from cows' milk. The product has a stringy or ropy texture, a pleasant sharp taste and a good diacetyl flavour. Vilia is inoculated with a culture containing variants of *Lactobacillus bulgaricus* and of capsule-producing strains of *Streptococcus lactis*, *Streptococcus cremoris*, also of *Streptococcus lactis* subsp. *diacetylactis*, *Leuconostoc citrovorum* and of *Geotrichum candidum*. The acidity of vilia is about 42–43 °SH. The presence of *Geotrichum candidum* lowers the acidity of the product. In Finland vilia is consumed daily in large quantities. It is the most popular cultured milk and is used at breakfast and as a snack with several additives (Vedamuthu, 1982; Manus, 1979). Taetmjölk and kjaddermilk are fermented products specific to Scandinavian countries. Their shelf-life is near 10 months. Taetmjölk contains *ca.* 1 % of lactic acid, 0·3–0·5 % of alcohol and traces of acetic acid. It is also saturated with CO_2. Original taetmjölk is inoculated with the leaves of *Pinguicola vulgaris*. Inoculum is cultivated at 35 °C during 12–20 h and 1 % of it is added to the milk. Maturation is continued over 2–3 days (Matuszewski & Supińska-Jakubowska, 1949).

3.6.7. *Skyr and Søs-tej*

Skyr is a fermented milk product in Iceland. It is prepared from skimmed, boiled milk treated at 40 °C with rennin and simultaneously inoculated with a starter derived from previously fermented milk. After 16–24 h of incubation the whey is drained out through a cloth bag. Before consuming it, skyr is mixed with whole fresh milk or with cream and sugar (Matuszewski & Supińska-Jakubowska, 1949).

Skyr contains *Lactobacillus bulgaricus* and *Streptococcus thermophilus* and also mesophilic lactobacilli. Yeasts, although often present in it, are there as contaminants rather than as part of the essential microflora.

Søs-tej is a Hungarian beverage prepared from rennin treated sheep's milk. The product is concentrated by partial draining of the whey (Pijanowski, 1971).

4. DIETARY FERMENTED MILKS

4.1. Acidophilus Milk

Acidophilus milk is produced by fermentation of milk with *Lactobacillus acidophilus*. This bacterium forms part of the normal intestinal microflora and is able to survive the severe conditions in the intestinal tract of man or animal. Milk containing viable *Lactobacillus acidophilus* cells is of great therapeutic importance, particularly in controlling intestinal disorders.

Lactobacillus acidophilus produces a very sour milk product with only traces of by-products. The milk needs first to be heated at 120 °C for 15 min to denature and release some of the peptides from milk proteins. At 37–38 °C milk is treated with 5 % of milk starter and incubated for 18–24 h. The product is finished after acidity reaches 1 % then it is cooled and bottled. Acidic conditions produced by *Lactobacillus acidophilus* in the intestinal tract of man discourage the growth and proliferation of gas-forming putrefactive bacteria in the gut. For effective intestinal therapy the use of *Lactobacillus* strains originally isolated from healthy humans is suggested (Chandan *et al.* 1969; Rašić & Kurmann, 1978).

4.2. Bioghurt (Acidophilus Yoghurt) and Biogarde

Bioghurt is milk fermented with *Lactobacillus acidophilus* and *Streptococcus lactis* (non-symbiotic strain) moderated in acidity. In some preparations *Lactobacillus bulgaricus* is added to enhance acidification. Preparation is similar to yoghurt production with the modification of cultural conditions according to the starter which is being used.

Biogarde is produced using *Lactobacillus acidophilus*, *Streptococcus thermophilus* and *Bifidobacterium bifidum* strains. The last strain plays a beneficial role in maintaining balanced intestinal flora as it accounts for about 40% of the faecal flora in the large intestine. Lactocidin and acidophilin antibiotics produced by *Lactobacillus acidophilus* and the antiviral activity of *Bifidobacterium bifidus* contribute to the healing effect of milk fermented products containing the above strains (Rašić & Kurmann, 1978).

4.3. Yakult
This is another new processed milk product marketed in Japan. It contains a *Lactobacillus casei* strain isolated from the human intestinal tract. Yakult is prepared from skim-milk with the addition of glucose and Chlorella extract dissolved in hot water, filtered and sterilised. As a starter, *Lactobacillus casei* (Shirota strain) is added. Fermentation proceeds for 4 days at 37 °C until acidity reaches *ca.* 2·7%. Milk is bottled after addition of flavours. The culturing produces small amounts of citric, succinic, malic and acetic acids and acetaldehyde, diacetyl and acetoin. Consumption of Yakult was shown to increase *Lactobacillus casei* in human faeces and to decrease *Escherichia coli*. Additionally Yakult was shown to be effective against various intestinal diseases of the enteric system (Speck, 1978).

4.4. Aerin and Smetanka
These are new fermented milk products produced in USSR with viscous lactic acid streptococci belonging to *Streptococcus* and *Leuconostoc* spp. isolated from original fermented sour milks taken from different parts of the USSR.

Leuconostoc lactis, *Leuconostoc dextranicus*, *Leuconostoc cremoris*, *Streptococcus lactis* and *Streptococcus cremoris* were introduced into low-fat milk in various ratios. In the process of long-term cultivation some starters acquired a symbiotic character with synergy. Such starters were named 'Dnepryanski'. Into some varieties of these starters *Lactobacillus casei* and *Acetobacter aceti* were introduced (Romanskaya *et al.*, 1982). Aerin is of slightly viscous consistency, and a homogeneous, good flavoured product. Smetanka is produced from 10% fat cream, is acidified until 28 °SH and also has a viscous consistency and good balanced flavour.

4.5. Other Specific Dietary Products

4.5.1. Ymer

This is a cultured milk product of Danish origin with minimum 3·5% fat, 6% of milk protein, 11% non-fat solids or slightly higher. It is prepared by a classical process combined with a newer one, reverse osmosis, to concentrate skim milk (Samuelson & Ulrich, 1982).

4.5.2. Vitana

A Swiss yoghurt, this contains no less than 9 vitamins. It is prepared from partly skimmed milk and is available in several flavours (Anon., 1976).

Possibilities of biological enrichment of vitamins in fermented milk beverages by supplying the starter microflora with *Propionibacterium* strains were presented also by Černa & Hrabova (1982) and Wachol-Drewek & Roczniak (1982).

4.5.3. Syuzma

This is a national dietetic cultured milk product of Azerbaijan made from cows' milk, standardised to 3·3% fat content. As a starter, thermophilic strains of *Streptococcus* sp. and of 'Bulgarian' bacillus (1:1) are used. Fermentation proceeds at 40–45°C until the acidity reaches 32–35°SH. The resulting thick curd is cut and after 10 min partial separation of whey is obtained. Syuzma is pressed and distributed into briquettes. In the product the fat content is not less than 15%, moisture *ca.* 70%, acidity *ca.* 80°SH. The product is pure in taste, homogeneous, dense and of spreadable consistency (Azimov, 1982).

4.5.4. Progurt

This is produced in Chile with a mixture (1:1) of *Streptococcus cremoris* and of *Streptococcus lactis* subsp. *diacetylactis* at 26–27°C. After 12 h, when acidity reaches 0·8–0·9%, it is warmed to 40–44°C and the fat level is standardised to 5%, the pH is 4·4–4·5. Sometimes a mixed culture of *Lactobacillus acidophilus* and of Bifidobacteria may be added before homogenisation (Vedamuthu, 1977).

5. CULTURED BUTTERMILK

Cultured buttermilk is made from fresh skim-milk or from partially skimmed pasteurised milk fermented commonly with one or more selected strains of *Streptococcus lactis, Streptococcus cremoris* and one or more species of citric acid fermenting streptococci, *Leuconostoc cremoris*, sometimes *Streptococcus lactis* subsp. *diacetylactis*. These strains are good acid producers at 21–24 °C, with pleasant lactic acid flavour, coexisting with the aroma-producing strains. Buttermilk is produced at 21–24 °C to retain the balanced growth of both types of strains. At temperatures higher than 24 °C usually insufficient growth of aroma-bacteria occurs and the product lacks the specific diacetyl flavour. The quality of milk used for buttermilk production should be of the highest value from physico-chemical and microbiological points of view (Kosikowski, 1977; Foster *et al.*, 1957).

6. SOUR CREAM

Cultured sour cream is manufactured in a similar manner to buttermilk. It differs only in the milk fat content which should be not less than 18 %. With flavourings added, the milk fat level should be not less than 14·4 %. The characteristic flavour arises as a result of the fermentation products formed by the starters acting in the milk. For souring the cream the same strains are recommended as for buttermilk production. The proper balance between the acid and aroma producers is necessary. This balance is influenced by the medium in which starter is propagated, the method of storage and the temperature of culturing. Starter cultures for buttermilk and sour cream and also for cream-cheese should have a good balanced flavour and should be able to grow actively at the processing temperature (often 21–22 °C), to produce optimal acidity and flavour in the processing time (12–14 h). Using *Streptococcus lactis* subsp. *diacetylactis* strains it is necessary to select strains producing smaller amounts of acetaldehyde but greater amounts of diacetyl. The desirable ratio of diacetyl to acetaldehyde is greater than 3:1 but less than 4·5:1 (Lindsay *et al.*, 1965; Kosikowski, 1977; Gordon & Shapton, 1977; Oberman *et al.*, 1981; Vedamuthu, 1982).

7. STARTERS FOR FERMENTED MILK PRODUCTION

The micro-organisms which bring about the required fermentation changes in fermented milks are widely distributed in natural environments. They can be isolated from raw milks as well as from many plants and related sources and hence these media form a natural habitat of lactic-acid-producing strains and a natural basis for the development over the centuries of the fermented products currently available.

In traditional processes the practice was to hold over a portion of fermented milk as a starter for the fresh milk. The basis for starter technology was created by the works of Orla-Jensen (1943). The developments in isolation, identification and stabilisation of cultures led to advances in their handling.

Natural cultures, represented by a small quantity of fermented milks of desired quality, are still used in domestic manufactures, for example in Bulgaria 'podkvasa' is the best source of original strains (Koroleva & Kondratenko, 1978).

Pure cultures isolated from natural habitats followed original starters. Being improved with genetic methods and screened with specific methods they enabled the large developments in the fermented milks to take place (Koroleva & Pyatnitsyna, 1982; Piatkiewicz *et al.*, 1981).

Commercial starters can be divided into those whose composition is variable and unknown in terms of species identity (in some cases) and in terms of phage sensitivity, and those which are made from pure, defined cultures, reproducible at will.

The great development of microbiology as a science and the transition of domestic manufacture of fermented milks to industrial production, increased knowledge about the microflora producing the expected changes in milk and so influenced starter technology. Commercial firms began to supply the starter cultures about 80 years ago, basing their products on the experience of milk specialists who recognised by the smell and taste the best sour milk to use as starter. Much of the fermented milks are still made with the descendants of the early cultures.

The most modern practice is based however on the banks of proven cultures maintained in deep freezers, liquid nitrogen or in a freeze-dried state, also in concentrated form. The strains are distributed to creameries where one or two sub-culturing stages precede the production procedure. In the case of concentrates, cultures may be added directly to the fermentation vat (Chuzkova *et al.*, 1982; Bouillaune *et al.*, 1982; Priidak & Bannikova, 1982; Kringelum, 1982; Libudzisz *et al.*, 1982).

Pure strains sub-cultured in the laboratory or in industrial conditions may contain a mixture of variant cells. They accumulate in the population depending on the strain and on the sub-culturing medium. The strains vary in the ease with which they lose plasmids which are considered to carry part or all the genes controlling *lac* (lactose utilisation) and *prt* (proteolytic activity) (Limsowtin *et al.*, 1978). If the genetic information for the restriction or modification system in lactic acid bacteria such as lactic streptococci, is carried on plasmids, the diversity of strains that can be identified on the basis of sensitivity to 'phage will be very evident. Some restriction in this diversity, but to a limited extent, may be attained with the optimisation of cultural conditions (Oberman & Libudzisz, 1980; Oberman *et al.*, 1981). Also the development of continuous yoghurt production suggests that some strains of *Streptococcus thermophilus* and of *Lactobacillus bulgaricus* are stable (Lawrence & Thomas, 1979).

Thus in all starters it is of the utmost importance to maintain the culture in a form which will prevent the decrease in cell viability and in activity through the accumulation in the population of undesirable variants of cells.

Particular variations may be noted using mixed, undefined strains and using multiple starters, composed of selected strains. Imbalance among the strains used may be brought about by differences in culturing conditions, presence of antibiotics in milk and the action of 'phages (Lawrence & Thomas, 1979; Oberman & Libudzisz, 1978, 1980).

To overcome problems of deterioration in single strains and in mixed cultures, sub-culturing, traditionally applied in the dairy industry, should be reduced to a minimum. Helpful here are ready-to-use cultures, exhibiting the required characteristics (Jakubowska *et al.*, 1980; Oberman *et al.*, 1981; Jakubowska *et al.*, 1978; Piatkiewicz *et al.*, 1977). Liquid nitrogen or a low temperature deep-freezer ($-40\,°C$ or below) are particularly suitable for culture storage. Conventional deep freezers ($-18\,°C$ to $-20\,°C$) may be less satisfactory to prevent the deterioration of starters.

Much interest is being shown in the use of lyophilised culture concentrates to avoid the cost involved in transporting frozen cultures. Cell numbers in concentrates range usually from 10^{10} to 10^{11} cells per g.

One important factor common to all starters is quality control, ensuring that the strain used is of the best quality. During the rotation of starter in the processing of fermented milks in the creameries the secondary, often not wanted, selection of starters occurs. Only thorough training and understanding of the persons in charge, responsible in creameries for the starters can be effective in identifying and correcting deviations in the activity of the starters. The monitoring of the cultures' activities plus 'phage detection tests should constitute a regular part of the quality control programme.

8. PHYSIOLOGICAL AND NUTRITIONAL ASPECTS OF FERMENTED MILKS

The beneficial effect of fermented milk products in human nutrition results not only from their high nutritional value related to the great variety of the components in milk. It is also dependent on the content of many metabolic products resulting from biochemical activities of lactic acid bacteria. Lactic acid, the main chemical compound, shows bacteriostatic and in some cases bactericidal effects against putrefactive micro-organisms which are sensitive to its action. Particularly sensitive are spore-forming bacilli and coliforms.

Other organic acids (acetic, propionic, formic), although produced in small quantities may even exert much stronger antimicrobial effects than lactic acid (Metchnikoff, 1904; Chung & Goepfert 1970; Daly *et al.*, 1970).

Several other antibacterial substances have also been demonstrated and identified. Nisin, produced by some *Streptococcus lactis* strains, is active against Gram-positive bacteria, especially against spore-forming anaerobic bacilli. Diplococcine, formed by *Streptococcus cremoris*, is active only against *Streptococcus lactis* (Hirsch *et al.*, 1951; Hirsch, 1952).

Pseudomonas species are inhibited by citrate-utilising cocci. This activity is greater in *Leuconostoc citrovorum* than in *Streptococcus lactis* subsp. *diacetylactis* (cit. after Rašić & Kurmann, 1978). Also *Lactobacillus bulgaricus* exerts an inhibiting effect against *Pseudomonas* species and some other undesirable organisms (Bielecka *et al.*, 1982a, b).

In lactobacilli the antagonistic effect is associated, in addition to lactic acid, with hydrogen peroxide (Wheater *et al.*, 1952; Dahiya & Speck, 1968), with lactolin, an antibiotic produced by *Lactobacillus plantarum* (Kodama, 1952) and with lactocilin and acidophilin, antibiotics found in *Lactobacillus acidophilus* (Vincent *et al.*, 1959; Vakil & Shahani, 1965). Another antibiotic called 'bulgarican' was isolated from *Lactobacillus bulgaricus*. It is active in acidic pH only against various Gram-positive and Gram-negative bacteria (Reddy & Shahani, 1971).

Other types of antibacterial substances cannot be excluded. Antimicrobial activity of many fermented milks is still being confirmed in recent work. For example Zubkova & Mytnik (1982) reported strong antibacterial activity in kefir which had been stored 4 weeks. Also Abou-Donia (1982) found the inhibition of *Salmonella* species by many lactic acid bacteria.

Thus antimicrobial effects of fermented milks can be attributed to organic acids, antibiotic factors, volatile acids, hydrogen peroxide and to other still unidentified substances present in fermented products. Cultured milks provide also living cells able to proliferate in human intestine and discourage the growth of harmful organisms. The presence of a large number of living micro-organisms of a special metabolic function, when milks are consumed regularly, may contribute to the development and maintenance of non-specific immunological reactions in the human body.

Fermented milk is also a valuable component which can be used in special dietary situations. It may be helpful in the secretion of gastric and intestinal juices. In lactase-deficiency there is a better tolerance of fermented milks. Nutrients in fermented milks are much more easily assimilated and they very often eliminate putrefactive processes. Products with reduced fat content may be recommended for weight-reducing diets and with sorbose or sorbitol for sugar free diets.

The beneficial effect of fermented milks in treating gastric diseases is not only attributable to the content of easily digested proteins but also to the high buffer capacity. Yoghurt has been proposed to cure sub-normal acidity, hyperacidity, gastritis, and ulcerous diseases.

In countries along the Mediterranean Sea and the Balkans yoghurt has long been used as a remedy. Shepherds in Near and Middle East used to drink yoghurt with water in order to protect themselves against some intestinal diseases. The beneficial effect of fermented milks on the metabolism of blood lipids was also indicated (Rašić & Kurmann, 1978).

According to Mann & Spoerry (1974) Maasai tribesmen in Africa consuming large quantities of yoghurt-like products lowered the level of blood cholesterol, probably because yoghurt contains certain constituents impairing the cholesterol synthesis. Kondratenko *et al.* (1982a, b) investigated nutritive, dietetic and curative effects of a product fermented with 'Bulgarian' rods. The liquid and dry products were recommended as wholesome foods for breast-fed children. Fermented milks favourably affected alterations in the mouth cavity, normalised leucocyte count and stimulated haematopoiesis. Serum cholesterol dropped to 22%. Also aerin and kefir improved metabolic processes of pre-school children (Mostovaya *et al.* 1982). Considerable increase occurred in the balance and retention of nitrogen and in the absorption of fat, as well as in the balanced vitamin supply. In Rašić and Kurmann's monograph concerning yoghurt (1978) also external uses of yoghurt are described: in skin injury, eczema and oral infections and in the treatment of large ulcers or skin excoriations in cancer.

Fermented milks are also known as healing cosmetics (Piatkiewicz & Libudzisz, 1982).

The dietetic and prophylactic properties of yoghurt and yoghurt-like products, and their healing effects in certain conditions were recognised by many peoples, in different world regions. It resulted in the wide application of fermented milk products and their manufacture on a large scale. Today they have an extremely important role to play in improving nutrition, promoting health, lengthening humans' life and maintaining their work capacity.

REFERENCES

ABOU-DONIA, S. A. (1982) XXI Int. Dairy Congress, Moscow, Brief Communications, Vol. 1, book 2, p. 144.

ACCOLAS, J. P. (1982) Bulletin FIL-IDF, Document 145, p. 3.

ANASHIMA, N. (1979) *Konievodstvo i Konnyj Sport*, **2**, 32.

ANON. (1976) *Schweiz. Milchztg.* **102**(94), 636.

ANON. (1979) *Deutsche Milchwirtschaft*, **30**(21), 790.

AZIMOV, A. M. (1982) XXI Int. Dairy Congress, Moscow, Brief communications, Vol. 1, book 2, p. 619.

BHATTACHARYA, D. C. (1979) *Indian J. Dairy Sci.* **32**(2), 168.

BIELECKA, M., MELAN, K. & RUSZKIEWICZ, A. (1982a) XXI Int. Dairy Congress, Moscow, Brief Communications, Vol. 1, book 2, p. 281.

BIELECKA, M., RUSZKIEWICZ, A. & MELAN, K. (1982b) XXI Int. Dairy Congress, Moscow, Brief Communications, Vol. 1, book 2, p. 283.

BOUILLAUNE, C., LANDON, M., FOURIER, M. & DESMAZEAUD, M. (1982) XXI Int. Dairy Congress, Moscow, Brief Communications, Vol. 1, book 2, p. 485.

BRUHN, J. C. & COLLINS, E. B. (1970) *J. Dairy Sci.* **53**, 857.

ČERNA, J. & HRABOVA, H. (1982) XXI Int. Dairy Congress, Moscow, Brief Communications, Vol. 1, book 1, p. 278.

CHANDAN, R. C., GORDON, J. F. & WALKER, D. A. (1969) *Process Biochem.*, February, 3.

CHOMAKOV, H. (1973) *The Dairy Industry in the Peoples Republic of Bulgaria*, Booklet. Agricultural Academy, Bulgaria.

CHUNG, K. C. & GOEPFERT, J. M. (1970) *J. Food Sci.* **35**, 326.

CHUZKOVA, S. P., BELOVA, G. A., SIDOROVA, E. A., KORNELYUK, A. N. & KLIMKOVA, L. J. (1982) XXI Int. Dairy Congress, Moscow, Brief Communications, Vol. 1, book 2, p. 528.

Consumption Statistics for Milk and Milk Products (1979), (1981) Bulletin FIL-IDF, Document 131.

COVENTRY, M. J., HILLIER, A. J. & JAGO, G. R. (1978) *Austr. J. Dairy Technol.* **33**, 148.

CZUŻOVA, Z. (1958) *Mołocznaja Promyszl.* **34**, 19, 6.

DAHIYA, R. S. & SPECK, M. L. (1968) *J. Dairy Sci.* **51**, 1568.

Dairy Industry of the USSR (1982) XXI International Dairy Congress, Moscow.

DALY, C., SANDINE, W. E. & ELLIKER, P. R. (1970) *J. Dairy Sci.* **53**, 637.

DEMAN, J. C. (1956) *Netherlands Dairy Milk J.* **10**, 38.

DEMKO, G. M., BLANTON, S. J. B. & BENOIT, R. E. (1972) *J. Bacteriol.* **112**, 1335.

FIL-IDF (1969) International Standard 47.

FIL-IDF (1981) Consumption statistics for milk and milk products, 1979. IDF Document 131, p. 17.

FLÜCKIGER, E. (1982) FIL-IDF Bulletin, Document 143, p. 93.

FOSTER, E. M., NELSON, F. F., SPECK, M. L., DOETSCH, R. N. & OLSON, J. C., JR (1957) *Dairy Microbiology*. Prentice-Hall Inc., Englewood Cliffs, N.J.

GORDON, J. F. & SHAPTON, N. (1977) *J. Soc. Dairy Technol.*, **30**, 1, 15.

HARVEY, R. J. & COLLINS, E. B. (1963) *J. Bacteriol.* **86**, 1301.

HIRSCH, A. (1952) *J. Dairy Res.* **19**, 290.

HIRSCH, A., GRINSTED, E., CHAPMAN, H. R. & MATTICK, A. T. R. (1951) *J. Dairy Res.* **18**, 205.

JAKUBOWSKA, J., LIBUDZISZ, Z. & PIATKIEWICZ, A. (1980) *Acta Microbiol. Pol.*, **29**, 2, 135.

JAKUBOWSKA, J., PIATKIEWICZ, A. & LIBUDZISZ, Z. (1978) *Acta Alim. Pol.*, **IV**, 2, 191.

KATRANDŻIJEV, K. (1961) Blgarsko kiselo mljako. Izd. na BAN, Sofia, 211.

KATRANDŻIJEV, K. (1961) Blgarsko kiselo mljako. Mikrobiologični i dietični kačestva. BAN, Sofia, Bulgaria.

KEMPLER, G. M. & MCKAY, L. L. (1979) *Appl. Environ. Microbiol.* **37**, 1041.

KODAMA, R. (1952) *J. Antibiot.* **5**, 72.

KONDRATENKO, M. C., CHRISTOVA, A. L., KONDAREVA, C. Z., TODOROV, K., KOZAREVA, M. & SPASOV, S. (1982a) XXI Int. Dairy Congress, Moscow, Brief Communications, Vol. 1, book 1, p. 297.

KONDRATENKO, M. S., SPASOV, S., STEFANOVA, Y., KOCHKOVA, V. & KONDAREVA, S. Z. (1982b) XXI Int. Dairy Congress, Moscow, Brief Communications, Vol. 1, book 1, p. 298.

KOROLEVA, N. S. & KONDRATENKO, M. S. (1978) Simbioticzeskije zakwaski termofilnych bakterii w proizwodstvie kisłomołocznych produktov. Piszczevaja Promyszlennost, Moskwa. Technika, Sofia.

KOROLEVA, N. S. & MELNIKOVA, E. V. (1973) Mołocznaja Promyszlennost **10**, 4.

KOROLEVA, N. S. & PYATNITSYNA, I. N. (1982) XXI Int. Dairy Congress, Moscow, Brief Communications, Vol. 1, book 2, p. 536.

KOSIKOWSKI, F. V. (1977) *Cheese and Fermented Milk Foods.* 2nd edn. Edwards Bros. Inc., Ann Arbor, Michigan.

KRINGELUM, B. W. (1982) XXI Int. Dairy Congress, Moscow, Brief Communications, Vol. 1, book 2, p. 326.

LAWRENCE, R. C. & THOMAS, T. D. (1979) In *Microbial Technology*, A. T. Bull, D. C. Elwood and C. Ratledge, Eds. Cambridge University Press, London-New York-Melbourne, p. 187.

LEES, G. J. & JAGO, G. R. (1978a) *J. Dairy Sci.* **61**, 1205.

LEES, A. G. & JAGO, G. R. (1978b) *J. Dairy Sci.* **61**, 1216.

LIBUDZISZ, Z., PIATKIEWICZ, A. & OBERMAN, H. (1982) XXI Int. Dairy Congress, Moscow, Brief Communications, Vol. 1, book 2, p. 540.

LIMSOWTIN, G. K. J., HEAP, H. A. & LAWRENCE, R. C. (1978) *N.Z. J. Dairy Sci. Technol.* **13**, 1.

LINDSAY, R. C., DAY, E. A. & SANDINE, W. E. (1965) *J. Dairy Sci.* **48**, 863.

MCKAY, L. L. (1978) *Food Technol.* **32**, 181.

MCKAY, L. L. & BALDWIN, K. A. (1974a) *Appl. Microbiol.* **28**, 342.

MCKAY, L. L. & BALDWIN, K. A. (1974b) *J. Dairy Sci.* **57**, 181.

MCKAY, L. L., MILLER, A., SANDINE, W. E. & ELLIKER, P. R. (1970) *J. Bacteriol.* **102**, 804.

MAKRINOV, I. A. (1909) *Wiestnik Bakteriolo-Agronomiczeskoj Stancji* **15**, 17.

MANN, E. J. (1978) *Dairy Industries International*, December, 19.

MANN, G. V. & SPOERRY, A. (1974) *Am. J. Clin. Nutrit.* **27**, 464.

MANUS, L. J. (1979) *Cultured Dairy Prod. J.* **14**, 2, 9.

MATUSZEWSKI, T. & SUPIŃSKA-JAKUBOWSKA, J. (1949) *Mikrobiologia Mleczarska.* PIWR, Warszawa.

MATUSZEWSKI, T., PIJANOWSKI, E. & SUPIŃSKA, J. (1936) *Polish Agricultural and Forest Annual*, **XXI**, 2.

METCHNIKOFF, E. (1904) *Revue Scientifique*, Vol. II (cit. after Rašić & Kurmann, 1978).

MOLSKA, I., MONIUSZKO, I., KOMOROWSKA, M. & MERILAINEN, V. (1982) XXI Int. Dairy Congress, Moscow, Brief Communications, Vol. 1, book 1, p. 305.

MOSTOVAYA, L. A., KULTCHITSKAYA, V. P., ROMANSKAYA, N. N. & KOCHUBEY, S. I. (1982) XXI Int. Dairy Congress, Moscow, Brief Communications, Vol. 1, book 1, p. 300.

NIKOLOV, N. (1962) *Blgarsko kiselo mljako i drugi mlečnokiseli produkti.* Zemizdat, Sofia.

OBERMAN, H. & LIBUDZISZ, Z. (1978) *Acta Alim. Pol.*, **IV**, 201.

OBERMAN, H. & LIBUDZISZ, Z. (1980) Proc. VII cont. Culture Symp., Prague, p. 619.

OBERMAN, H., LIBUDZISZ, Z. & PIATKIEWICZ, A. (1981) IVth Intern. Conf. on Culture Collection, Brno, Abstracts, T-18.

OBERMAN, H., PIATKIEWICZ, A. & LIBUDZISZ, Z. (1982) *Die Nahrung.* **26**, 615.

ORLA-JENSEN, S. (1943) *The Lactic Acid Bacteria.* Ergänzungsband, Ejnar Munksgaard, Copenhagen.

PETTE, J. W. (1949) Proc. 12th Int. Dairy Congress, Vol. 2, p. 572.

PIATKIEWICZ, A., LIBUDZISZ, Z. & JAKUBOWSKA, J. (1977) *Acta Microbiol. Pol.* **26**, 407.

PIATKIEWICZ, A. & LIBUDZISZ, Z. (1982) *Bull. Pollena.* **XXVI** (4–5), 77.

PIATKIEWICZ, A., LIBUDZISZ, Z. & OBERMAN, H. (1981) *Adv. Biotechnol.* **II**, 491.

PIJANOWSKI, E. (1971) *Zarys Chemii i Technologii Mleczarstwa.* PWR i L. Warszawa, Vol. I.

PRIIDAK, T. A. & BANNIKOVA, L. A. (1982) XXI Int. Dairy Congress, Brief Communications, Vol. 1, book 2, p. 357.

PURMAN, J. (1976) *Prumysl Potravin* **27**, 697.

RANGAPPA, K. S. & ACHAYA, K. T. (1975) Indian Dairy Products (cit. after E. R. Vedamuthu (1982) In: *Economic Microbiology*, Vol. 7. A. H. Rose, Ed. Academic Press, London).

RAŠIĆ, J. Lj. & KURMANN, J. A. (1978) *Yoghurt. Scientific Grounds, Technology, Manufacture and Preparations.* Technical Dairy Publishing House, Copenhagen.

RAŠIĆ, J. Lj. & MITIC, S. (1962) *Prehr. Ind.* **12**, 158.

REDDY, G. V. & SHAHANI, K. M. (1971) *J. Dairy Sci.* **54**, 748.

ROGOSA, M. & SHARPE, E. (1959) *J. Appl. Bacteriol.* **22**, 329.

ROMANSKAYA, N. N., BASHKIROVA, R. S., DYMENT, G. S., TOVKACHEVSKAYA, L. D. & KOCHUBEY, S. I. (1982) XXI Int. Dairy Congress, Moscow, Brief Communications, Vol. 1, book 1, p. 306.

ROSI, J. (1978) *Sci. Tec. Latt.-Casearia* **29**, 59.

ROZHKOVA, I. V., BAVINA, N. A. & PADARYAN, I. M. (1982) XXI Int. Dairy Congress, Moscow, Brief Communications, Vol. 1, book 2, p. 547.

SAMUELSON, E. G. & ULRICH, P. (1982) XXI Int. Dairy Congress, Moscow, Brief Communications, Vol. 1, book 1, p. 288.

SCHANKAR, P. A. & DAVIES, F. L. (1977) *J. Soc. Dairy Technol.* **30**, 31.

SCHULZ, M. E. (1966) *Milchwissenschaft* **21**, 68.

SEITZ, E. W., SANDINE, W. E., ELLIKER, P. R. & DAY, E. A. (1963a) *Can. J. Micr.* **9**, 431.

SEITZ, E. W., SANDINE, W. E., ELLIKER, P. R. & DAY, E. A. (1963b) *J. Dairy Sci.* **46**, 186.

SHARPE, E. M. (1979) *J. Soc. Dairy Technol.* **32**, 9.

SHIGAYEVA, M. Kh. & OSPANOVA, M. Sh. (1982) XXI Int. Dairy Congress, Brief Communications, Vol. 1, book 1, p. 308.

SPECK, M. L. (1975) *Cultured Dairy Prod. J.* **10**, 8.

SPECK, M. L. (1978) *Devel. Ind. Microbiol.* **19**, 95.

SPECKMAN, R. A. & COLLINS, E. B. (1968) *J. Bacteriol.* **95**, 174.

STANLEY, G. (1980) In *The Stability of Industrial Microorganisms*, B. E. Kirsop, Ed. Kew, Surrey, England, p. 20.

STOYANOVA, L. G., PONOMARYOVA, O. JA. & SPIRIDONOV, W. A. (1982) XXI Int. Dairy Congress, Moscow, Brief Communications, Vol. 1, book 1, p. 308.

SUPIŃSKA, J. & PIJANOWSKI, E. (1937) *Polish Agricultural and Forest Annual* **xxxviii**, 209.

TAMIME, A. Y. (1978) *Milk Industry* **80**, 4.

TAMIME, A. Y. & GREIG, R. I. W. (1979) *Dairy Industries International* **44**, 3.

TAMIME, A. Y. & ROBINSON, R. K. (1978) *Milchwissenschaft* **38**, 209.

TEPLY, M. (1970) XVIII Int. Dairy Congr., Sydney, p. 413.

TEPLY, M. (1978) *Vyživa Lidu* **33**, 107.

VAKIL, J. R. & SHAHANI, K. M. (1965) *Bacteriol. Proc.* 9.

VAYSSIER, Y. (1978) *Revue Laitiere Francaise*, 361, Fevrier, 1.

VEDAMUTHU, E. R. (1977) *J. Food Protection* **40**, 601.

VEDAMUTHU, E. R. (1979) *Devel. Ind. Microbiol.* **20**, 187.

VEDAMUTHU, E. R. (1982) Fermented milks. In: *Economic Microbiology*, Vol. 7, *Fermented Foods*, A. H. Rose, Ed. Academic Press, London, p. 199.

VINCENT, J. G., VEOMETT, R. C. & RILEY, R. F. (1959) *J. Bacteriol.* **78**, 477.

WACHOL-DREWEK, Z. & ROCZNIAK, B. (1982) XXI Int. Dairy Congress, Moscow, Brief Communications, Vol. 1, book 1, p. 309.

WEBB, B. H. & JOHNSON, A. H. (1965) *Fundamentals of Dairy Chemistry*. Avi Pub. Co., Westport, Conn., USA.

WHEATER, D. M., HIRSCH, A. & MATTICK, A. T. R. (1952) *Nature, Lond.* **170**, 623.

ZUBKOVA, Z. S. & MYTNIK, L. G. (1982) XXI Int. Dairy Congress, Moscow, Brief Communications, Vol. 1, book 1, p. 295.

Chapter 5

Fermented Protein Foods in the Orient, with Emphasis on Shoyu and Miso in Japan

TAMOTSU YOKOTSUKA

Kikkoman Corporation,
Noda-shi, Chiba-ken, Japan

1. INTRODUCTION

From ancient times, nations all over the world have inherited their own alcoholic beverages, which are prepared principally by converting the sugars involved in raw materials into alcohol by the action of yeasts. At the same time, vinegars have been made from almost all of these alcoholic beverages converting alcohol into acetic acid by the action of acetic acid bacteria. Thus, fruit wines have been made from sweet fruits such as grapes, apples, oranges, and so on. But, in the preparation of wines from starchy raw materials such as wheat, barley, rice, or corn, these raw materials must be degraded into sugars, mainly glucose, in order to ferment them by yeasts. It must be noted that there is a major difference between the saccharification process of Western countries and that of the Orient. The amylolytic enzymes used for the saccharification in Western countries have derived from malt, while in the Orient, *Aspergillus* or *Rhizopus* moulds have been utilised as the source of amylolytic enzymes. Accordingly, beer is prepared by first saccharifying the starch of barley by the use of malt, while in the preparation of alcoholic beverages from rice or wheat in the Orient, *Aspergillus* or *Rhizopus* moulds are cultured on part of these raw materials to produce amylolytic enzymes. These mould cultured materials are called 'koji' in Japan, and this koji is mixed with the other remaining parts of rice or wheat and water to make mash, which is then concurrently subjected to enzymatic saccharification, lactic fermentation, and yeast fermentation.

197

On the other hand, people in the world also have their own fermented foods and beverages, in preparations of which sugars are principally converted into lactic acid by the action of lactobacilli. Examples are lactic acid drinks, cheese, and pickles throughout the world, and some important fermented foods of Mid-Asia, the Middle East, and Africa, such as Idli, Kishk, Ogi, Mahewu, and so on. Lactic acid fermentation is important not only in the manufacture of these fermented foods or beverages, but also in the manufacture of alcoholic beverages in the Orient, because it prevents the undesirable acetic acid fermentation in the preliminary stage of manufacture of these comestibles.

Our ancestors also knew the techniques of enzymatically hydrolysing certain protein foods into amino acids and lower peptides to make them more appealing and more nourishing. For example, since ancient times people in the West have enriched the flavour of cheese by fermenting it with some *Penicillium* moulds. And the people in the Orient have enriched the flavour of fish and meat, proteinous beans, pulses, and some cereals, by fermenting them with the proteolytic and amylolytic enzymes produced by *Aspergillus* or *Rhizopus* moulds, and at the same time, sometimes fermenting them with lactobacilli and yeasts, in the presence of high salt concentrations. These foods formerly were called soy in English and can still be found in every Asian country including Japan. Those are believed to be the antecedents of shoyu and miso now in use, and their records date back 3000 years ago in China. The prototypes of these foods are believed to have been introduced from China to Japan 1300 or more years ago.

The typical traditional fermented foods in Japan are fermented soy sauce or shoyu, as we call it in Japan, fermented soybean paste or miso, fermented rice wine or saké, distilled saké mash or shochu, rice vinegar, amasaké, natto, pickles, and so on.

It is the common characteristic in the production of these fermented foods, except natto and pickles, to cultivate the moulds belonging to *Aspergillus* groups such as *Asp. oryzae*, *Asp. sojae*, or *Asp. niger* on some parts or on the total amount of raw materials to produce such plant tissue degrading enzymes as amylase, protease, lipase, cellulase, pectinase, and others. The mould cultured material is called koji in Japanese, and the koji is utilised for the degradation of raw materials in water with or without salt.

According to the old records such moulds as *Rhizopus* or *Mucor* were also used in China, and are still used in other Oriental countries, Taiwan and Indonesia, for example, but interestingly enough only *Aspergillus* moulds have been utilised in Japan.

Among Japanese fermented foods, shoyu or soysauce is prepared by digesting mould cultured soybeans and wheat in different ratios, usually almost fifty to fifty, in the presence of about 17 % salt, and concurrently fermenting the mash with lactobacilli and yeasts, and after 6 to 8 months the well-aged mash is pressed. The liquid part obtained is pasteurised to make the final product. The annual production of shoyu is about 1·2 million kilolitres in recent years, being estimated to be 1·19 million kilolitres in 1982. That means the average yearly consumption per capita is about 11 litres. The shoyu is the most popular liquid condiment used in Japanese cuisine as well as in the other Oriental countries.

Miso is prepared by enzymatically degrading a mixture of cooked soybeans and moulded rice, or barley, or wheat, in the presence of 8–12 % salt with a rather small amount of water, along with some lactic and yeast fermentations. The final product is used for cooking, mainly for making miso soup by diluting it with water and adding various kinds of vegetable, chicken, fish, or animal meat. The per capita consumption of miso is about one half of that of shoyu in weight. The annual production of miso in 1982 in Japan is estimated to be 578 000 tons.

Saké or rice wine is prepared by digesting a mixture of cooked rice and moulded rice (rice-koji) in water, concurrently fermenting the mash with lactobacilli and yeasts. The Japanese consumption of saké is 1 450 000 klitres, that is roughly about 120 % of shoyu in quantity. Shochu is a kind of rice 'brandy' containing 20–35 % alcohol, distilled from a mash in which rice or dried sweet potato is saccharified with the enzymes from yellow or black *Aspergillus* moulds and fermented with yeasts. Its annual production is about 240 000 klitres. Beer, whisky, and grape wine are also popular in Japan, and their consumption is increasing in recent years, contrary to those of saké and shochu, but a little more than 50 % of the Japanese intake of pure alcohol from the alcoholic beverages in general is still calculated to be from saké and shochu nowadays.

Mirin is a very sweet liquid containing about 35 % glucose and 12 % alcohol which is used mainly for cooking. It is prepared by digesting the mixture of rice and rice koji in water in the presence of 35 % alcohol. The annual production of mirin was about 67 000 klitres in 1981. A fairly large amount of saké is also utilised for cooking, but both saké and mirin are monopolised in Japan. The production of mirin-like and saké-like alcoholic seasonings containing some 5 % salt, which are free from the monopoly, has been rapidly increasing in recent years in Japan, reaching 58 000 klitres in 1981.

Amasaké is a kind of beverage prepared by saccharifying the mixture of cooked rice and rice-koji and is served after dilution with water.

TABLE 1
Per Capita Annual Consumption of Fermented Foods Prepared from *Aspergillus*
Moulds in Japan (1981)

Food	Per capita/year	Total production/year
1. Shoyu	10·1 litres	1 200 000 klitres
2. Miso	4·9 kg	572 000 tons
3. Saké	12·3 litres	1 445 000 klitres
4. Mirin	0·6 litres	74 000 klitres
5. Shochu	2·2 litres	260 000 klitres
6. Rice vinegar	0·25 litres	30 000 klitres
(Vinegar)	2·5 litres	305 000 klitres

Note:

Beer	39·5 litres	4 656 000 klitres
Whisky and other foreign alcoholic beverages	3·7 litres	445 000 klitres

Japanese population: 117 850 000 (Oct. 1, 1981).

The yearly production of vinegar in Japan is about 250 000 klitres, and about 10 % of it is prepared from rice wine or saké by acetic acid fermentation. The per capita annual consumption of these fermented foods prepared from *Aspergillus* moulds in Japan is summarised in Table 1.

2.   HISTORY

2.1. The History of Fermented Proteinous Foods in China
2.1.1.   Chu
The first documentation of *chu* was found in *Shu-Ching* written 3000 years ago in *Chou dynasty* (1121–256 BC), in which it is stated that chu is essential for making alcoholic beverages.

As we know it now, chu is the same as koji in Japanese, and it is speculated that it was naturally moulded grains such as wheat, barley, millet and/or rice that was utilised as the source of enzymes to degrade the complex plant tissue. It is speculated that man must have discovered chu 6000–7000 years ago. There were two different colours of chu, yellow and white. The most popular one, which had a yellow colour indicating perhaps *Aspergillus oryzae*, was called yellow robe. The white one is presumed to be *Rhizopus* or *Mucor* and was called white robe.

Chu was usually made in granular form, which was called *san-chu*. By the time of the *Han dynasty* (AD 947–979) chu in the form of cake was developed, which was called *ping-chu*. The growth of *Rhizopus* and yeast was much more abundant in *ping-chu* than that of *Aspergillus oryzae*. A book on agricultural technology entitled *Chi-Min-Yao-Shu* was written in the 6th century (AD 532–549), in which detailed descriptions of the preparation of several kinds of chu and other alcoholic fermented foods are found.

Huang-chu was widely used for alcoholic fermentation as well as for fermentation of soybean foods. Huang-chu was the first man-made chu with *Aspergillus oryzae* or perhaps *A. sojae*. Three types of Huang-chu were described, *Huang-yi*, *Huang-tcheng*, and *Nu-chu*. The raw material of *Huang-yi* was crushed wheat, which was washed, soaked in water until sour and then drained and steamed. After cooling, the steamed wheat was piled up to a thickness of about 6 cm and covered with some leaves. After 7 days, the wheat was covered with yellow mycelia and spores, which indicated the chu was prepared, and then the moulded wheat was dried in the sunshine.

In the preparation of *Huang-tcheng*, wheat flour and some water were made into a ball or cake, which was steamed, cooled, and then covered with leaves until it developed cultures of moulds. *Nu-chu* was made from cooked rice, which was shaped into a cake and then cultured with moulds.

According to *Chi-Min-Yao-Shu* in the 6th century and *Bei-Shau-Chiu-Ching* in the 12th century, wheat was the main grain used for making chu in the early times. Wheat chu originated in the northern part of China, while rice chu came from the south.

2.1.2. Chiang

Chiang has been the most common flavouring agent in China since ancient times. According to the book of *Rites in Chou dynasty*, there was a kitchen in which 120 jars of chiang were placed. The chiang at that time was prepared from animal meat, or bird flesh, or fish tissue together with millet-chu, salt, and alcoholic beverage, sealed in a jar, and stored for about 100 days. Alcoholic beverages were already popular at that time and were used as preservatives along with salt in this case. Soybeans are not described in the book as the raw materials of chiang, but it is known that soybeans were widely cultured in China 4000 years ago, and it is easily speculated that soybeans were also already used as the raw materials of chiang or other fermented protein foods. In the *Analects of Confucius* written 600 years later than the Chou dynasty, he spoke of chiang. These records suggest that chiang has a history of more than 3000 years.

Although four types of chiang were mentioned in the 2nd century book *Se-Min-Yue-Ling*, the method of preparation of chiang was first found in *Chi-Min-Yao-Shu* (AD 532–549), which tells us the method of making chiang from beans, fish, meat, or elm seeds. Following is the account of making *tou-chiang* from black soybeans. The beans were steamed, sun dried, and dehulled. The dehulled beans were then soaked in water, steamed again and cooled. The beans were mixed with *Huang-tcheng* (moulded cake of wheat flour) and salt in the ratio of 6:2:1. The mixture was tightly sealed in a jar and the materials were enzymatically digested and cultured perhaps a little with moulds until it became a solid mass; this took about a month. The fermented mass was cracked into small pieces and mixed with salt water and salt water extract of moulded cracked-wheat, then fermented for about 100 days with occasional stirring. When wheat was used for chiang, boiled wheat, huang-yi, salt, and water were fermented. When animal meat or fish tissues were used as raw materials, these were not cooked but were mixed with powder-chu, huang-tcheng, or huang-yi, and salt in the ratio in volume 10:5:1:2·5, and fermented for about 2 weeks until the odour of chu had disappeared. Alcoholic beverages were sometimes added to the mixture which was fermented at an elevated temperature to complete the fermentation earlier. It must be noted that in the *Chi-Min-Yao-Shu*, boiled soybeans were not cultured with moulds, but boiled soybeans and moulded wheat were mixed along with salt water and stored to make chiang.

2.1.3. Shi

The first written record of *shi* or *tou-shi*, meaning fermented beans, appears in *Shih-chi* written in the 2nd century BC, in which it states that shi was the most popular seasoning sold next to salt at that time.

The detailed method of preparing shi is found in the 6th century book, *Chi-Min-Yao-Shu*. The temperature was the most important factor in preparing shi, and June was the best season of the year for making it. Soybeans (yellow or black) are cooked, cooled, and placed in a pile on a straw mat, which is covered with straw. The pile is turned frequently to reduce the temperature and when the beans are covered with white mycelia of mould, the size of pile is reduced to increase the aeration and lower the temperature to promote the growth of yellow moulds. When the beans are fully covered with the yellow spores, they are transferred to a pit, and tightly covered with straw. The beans become black after 10–15 days and the shi is prepared, and then sun dried. The washing step of mould cultured materials to remove the mycelia and spores is essential to remove the bitter taste from the final product.

In *Ben-Chao-Gong-Mu* (1590), many types of shi are described. In more recent times shi can be classified into three types according to the kinds of mould employed:

1. *Aspergillus oryzae* type
    Pure cultures of *Aspergillus oryzae* are used and the fermentation is carried out at 25 °C in wooden barrels. In some cases, the washed moulded beans are mixed with 16–18 % salt and fermented at 35 °C for 30 days.

2. *Mucor* type
    This type of shi is usually made in *Szechwan* state. The cooked beans are packed in trays about 2–3 cm in depth and incubated at 10–15 °C for 1–2 weeks. When the beans turn white then grey with the growth of *Mucor racemosus*, the moulded beans are mixed with salt and distilled liquor, tightly packed into earthen jars, and sealed. After aging 6 months in a shady place, the shi is ready for sun drying. Another bean product of *Mucor* fermentation is known as *la-pa-tou*, which is made in December. Cooked beans are wrapped in straw and placed in a room for about 15 days. The fermented mass of beans is sliced, sun dried, and used as a flavouring agent or is consumed fresh.

3. *Bacillus* type
    Soaked and cooked soybeans are placed in a cloth bag, covered with straw and fermented for 1–2 days at 25–30 °C. When the beans are covered with viscous substances, *Shui-tou-shi* is prepared. The sticky beans are mixed with minced ginger and salt, and then tightly packed into jars. After aging for 1 week, they are ready for consumption. The organisms responsible for this fermentation have been identified as *Bacillus* species.

2.1.4. Chiang-Yu

Chiang-yu (soysauce) or *Tou-yu* is presumed to have derived from chiang. The name of chiang-ching is found in *Chi-Min-Yao-Shu* (AD 549); unfortunately there is no description of preparing chiang-ching in the book, but it is speculated to be the origin of chiang-yu from the meaning of chiang-ching (Wang & Fuang, 1981). The earliest known description of the method of preparing chiang-ching was in *Ben-Chao-Gong-Mu* (AD 1590). Boiled soybeans are mixed with raw barley flour in the ratio of 3:2, and pressed into cakes, which are left in the room until the cakes are covered with yellow mould growth. The moulded cakes or chu are mixed with salt and water, and aged under the sun. After pressing, the liquid is known as Chiang-yu. In more recent years, chiang-yu is made with pure cultures of *Aspergillus oryzae*, which are inoculated onto a mixture of cooked soybeans and roasted cracked wheat in a temperature controlled room.

2.1.5. Shi-tche

Shi-tche means the juice of shi. According to *Chi-Min-Yao-Shu*, shi-tche is obtained by extracting shi with boiling water, and was the most popular seasoning in the 6th century.

This section was based on material drawn from *Thirty-five Years History of Noda-Shoyu Company* (1955), *The History of Kikkoman* (1970), Sakaguchi (1979) and Wang & Fuang (1981).

2.2. The History of Shoyu and Miso in Japan

2.2.1. Hishio, or Sho, or Soya, or Soy

Chiang in Chinese, or *Hishio* or *Sho* in Japanese or Soya or Soy in English is the same Chinese character with different pronunciations. Hishio was made from fish and salt also at the beginning of Japanese history, and is generally believed to be the antecedent of the shoyu and miso now in use. Fish tissues were degraded by the enzymes released from the organs in the presence of high salt concentrations. Animal meat or bird flesh was also used for the same purpose. The hishio made from fish, bird or meat was called *Shishibishio*, which is found in many old Japanese books including *Manyoshu* (4500 songs sung during AD 350–759 which were compiled later in 8th century), *Reigikai* (AD 833), *Engikai* (AD 907), *Wamei-ruishu-sho* (AD 903–930), and others.

Fish or meat as raw materials of hishio was gradually replaced by beans or grains such as soybeans or wheat, perhaps by the influence of Buddhism which derived from China via Korea in AD 538. Buddhism had the principle of abstaining from fish and meat. References to several kinds of hishio made from soybeans or other beans or grains are found in many Japanese old books including *Manyoshu* (AD 350–759), *Todaiji-Shosoin-bunsho* (AD 730–748), *Seireishu* (AD 811); and others.

2.2.2. Miso or Misho

According to the oldest Japanese dictionary, *Wamei-ruishusho* (AD 931), by the time when soybean-hishio arrived from China in the Tang dynasty (AD 618–906), another sho was already in Japan; it derived from Korea and was named Koma (meaning Korea) -sho or *Misho*, or *Miso* in order to differentiate it from the former. Products which imitated these foreign products also appeared in Japan, and were called domestic-hishio. A Chinese Buddhist priest Ganjin (the name in Japan) brought hishio or chiang from China into Japan along with other foods including sugar in AD 754 but 50 years earlier than this the *Taiho-Laws* were enforced in Japan (AD 701), in which it is stated that there was a department in the Imperial court to deal with several kinds of hishio, miso, and shi or kuki. These foods were paid as a part of salary to the governmental officers along with rice, salt, soybeans, and other kinds of beans and grains. At the same time, sho-hishio and miso were widely sold in many stories in Kyoto, the capital city at that time (*Sandai-jitsuroku*, written in AD 886).

Miso is mainly used for preparing miso-soup, which is very popular among Japanese dishes, but not so popular among Chinese ones. The residue of miso or soybean-sho, from which the liquid part is separated is also used for the same purpose. Miso-soup is said to have first occurred in the Japanese diet around the Kamakura period (1185–1333).

2.2.3. *Tamari, Miso-damari, Tare-miso and Usudare*
The discriminations between these foods are not always clear, but, judging from old records, the clear liquid obtained from miso or sho was generally called by the different names as above. Literally, Tamari or Miso-damari, or Tare-miso means the clear liquid separated on the top of miso, or drained off from the bottom of the kegs in which miso or sho was stored, or filtered into a bamboo cage which is put into miso or sho. But according to such books as *Honcho-bunsho* (AD 1487), *Shijoryu-hochosho* (AD 1489) and others (AD 1504, 1537), Taremiso or Usudare seems to have been the name for the clear liquid drained off or press-filtered from the boiled mixture of miso or sho and salt water. But the name of *Shoyu* (the same as chiang-yu in Chinese) was not found in these books at the time.

2.2.4. *Shoyu*
The book in which the name of *shoyu* appeared for the first time in Japan was *Ekirinbon-Setsuyoshu* (AD 1598). Shoyu literally meant the clear liquid obtained from sho, but at the same time, the clear liquid obtained from miso or *Tamari* (moulded soybeans fermented in salt water) was also called shoyu in the beginning. And in a book (*Yoshu-fushi*, AD 1686), shoyu was defined as a common Shi-ju (Shi-tche in Chinese), while in another book, shoyu was defined as wheat-sho. Judging from these descriptions, shoyu had a broad meaning in the beginning, but later, shoyu became the name only for the clear liquid obtained from the mash in which moulded mixture of soybeans and wheat or barley was fermented with water in the presence

of high salt concentrations, and was differentiated from Tamari or a Shitche-like product made almost entirely from soybeans.

Great progress was made in the technology of preparing shoyu and its production scale was enlarged in the Edo era (1603–1867). Many books are found in this period dealing with the preparation of shoyu: *Ryori-monogatari-yorozu-kikigaku* (1643), *Yoshufushi* (1686), *Honcho-shokukan* (1692), *Wakan-sansaizue* (1715), *Mankin-sangyo-bukuri* (1731), *Zoshu-seiho* (1716), *Sake-shoyu-denjuki* (1785) and *Koeki-Kokusanko* (1844). The following is an abstract of these books regarding the preparation of shoyu at that time. The mixture of one part of soybeans and one part of wheat kernels or dehulled barley was used as raw materials of shoyu in the beginning, but later the superiority of wheat kernels over dehulled barley was gradually recognised from the point of view of the quality of shoyu. Soaked soybeans were boiled, while wheat kernels or dehulled barley were roasted and crushed, and the mixture of these two materials was put between straw mats or in wooden trays and was cultured with moulds. It took two or three days to finish the mould cultivation. The mould cultured materials were called *koji* (the same as chu in Chinese). They judged the quality of finished koji from its colour; white, or yellow, or brown was good, while blue or black was bad, which suggests to us that *Aspergillus oryzae* or *sojae* had already been selected to be the best starter of moulds. A small portion of good koji was usually used as starter mould for the next cultivation.

The best method of preparing mash or *Moromi* was found to be mixing the koji prepared from a mixture of one part of soybeans and one part of wheat kernels, with 2·2 parts of water, and 1·1 parts of salt. The mash or Moromi was stored for about 70 days in summer or 100 days in winter. Summer was believed to be the best season in the year to prepare koji and moromi. Amasaké or saccharified rice-koji with water was sometimes added to shoyu-mash to ameliorate the salty taste. Thus the characteristic procedures of *Koikuchi*-shoyu, which is the typical Japanese shoyu today made from soybeans and wheat, were established about 300 years ago.

The total population of Japan at that time was 30 millions, of whom about 1·2 millions lived in Edo (old name of Tokyo), and consumed much more shoyu per capita than is the case nowadays. One keg of shoyu at that time contained 14·4 litres, and this amount was said to be enough for consumption by one person in one year (Chohoroku, 1856, from *Shoyu-monogatari*, p. 5, written by N. Matsumoto, published by Kikkoman Shoyu Co. Ltd, 1976).

The centre of shoyu production was in Noda-city and Choshi-city, both of which were near to Tokyo, and shoyu production was begun in these cities in 1561 and 1616, respectively. About 1·6 million kegs of shoyu were consumed in Edo, of which 1·5 million kegs were transported from the above two cities, and the remaining 0·1 million from the western parts of Japan: Kishu, Tatsuno, and Shodo-shima. The light colour shoyu, named *Usukuchi-shoyu*, which was invented in Tatsuno-city in 1666, was prepared from almost the same raw materials as those of *Koikuchi-shoyu* but a slightly greater amount of salt water was added to koji to prepare the mash. Both kinds of shoyu, *Koikuchi* and *Usukuchi*, were differentiated from *Tamari* which was made almost entirely from soybeans, with a small amount of wheat or barley flour, The major areas for Tamari production have remained in the middle part of Japan near Nagoya-city until the present. In the preliminary stage of production of shoyu in Noda and Choshi, they called their products *Tamarishoyu*, but it is not clear whether these products were made from a mixture almost entirely composed of soybeans or from a mixture of equal parts of soybeans and wheat or barley in the beginning.

The Japanese shoyu was introduced to Europe together with soybeans (or soya-beans meaning shoyu-beans) by a Swedish botanist named Carl Thunberg in 1775. And moreover, there is an old record that Japanese shoyu was conveyed to Europe by the Dutch (1668) and may have been appreciated in the court of King Louis XIV in France. The pasteurised shoyu was bottled in a porcelain jar while it was hot, and then sealed with pitch, which was 50–100 years earlier than the invention of pasteurisation by L. Pasteur (1862) in France. In Japan, *Saké* or fermented rice wine had been widely pasteurised 200 or 300 years earlier than the above story of shoyu (K. Sakaguchi, 1979).

2.2.5. *Miso of Today*

Miso or *Koma-miso* which appeared in the Taiho-Laws (AD 702) is speculated to be the prototype of miso now in use, but judging from the fact that miso was prepared at that time in the Korean way from almost-moulded soybeans, it very much resembled Shi in China. This type of miso still remains in Aichi-Prefecture (central part of Japan) nowadays as soybean-miso, the amount of which is very small however. The miso in Japan nowadays is principally prepared by storing a mixture of cooked soybeans, moulded rice or barley, and salt. Thus this type of miso is rather similar to Chiang of old China, which was prepared by mixing cooked soybeans and moulded millet or other grains. It was in the 17th century (1645) when the miso of the modern type was for the first time industrially produced in Sendai-City in the northern part of Japan.

Foreign trade was generally forbidden in Japan by the government until the end of the Edo-era, with slight exception, via Nagasaki harbour, located in the westernmost part of Japan. Starting with the Meiji-era (1868–1912) continued by the Taisho-era (1912-1926), the industrial technology of shoyu and miso production made rapid progress, greatly affected by Western civilisation. Pure cultured *Aspergillus oryzae* or *sojae* began to be used as the starter mould for koji cultivation; soybeans were autoclaved under pressure instead of boiling in water, hydraulic pressure was applied for pressing of shoyu mash instead of a long wooden rod loaded with heavy stones in the end of it, utilising the principles of the lever and fulcrum; the raw shoyu was pasteurised through a closed tube heated with steam instead of heating in an open kettle; wooden kegs as the containers of shoyu were gradually replaced by glass bottles; and the quality of shoyu and miso was controlled not only by sensory tests but also by chemical and instrumental analyses.

3.   FERMENTED SOYBEAN FOODS IN THE ORIENT WITH THE EMPHASIS ON SHOYU AND MISO

Typical fermented soybean foods nowadays are shoyu, miso, tempeh, natto, and others. Shoyu is the Japanese name for soysauce in general, which is a salty fermented seasoning produced from soybeans with or without wheat, barley and/or rice. Many varieties of shoyu are produced in Japan and other Oriental countries. Their characteristics depend on the kinds and ratios of raw materials used, the kinds of microbes employed, and the conditions of preparation. Although most varieties are made from vegetable materials, fish soy is popular in Southeast Asian countries and is even produced in Japan in small amounts. The chemical analyses of soysauce in the Orient as compared with the other amino-acid containing seasonings in the world are indicated in Table 2. There are distinct differences of alcohol content among them, which indicate the amount of wheat used as raw material and the degree of alcoholic fermentation of the mash, and the latter relates to the contents of volatile flavorous ingredients of the products.

Miso is fermented soybean paste, which is popular in Japan, China, Korea, and some other countries. Cooked soybeans are mixed with moulded rice, or barley, and salt, and stored for fermentation. Miso is used for preparing miso-soup and for seasoning in general. To a small extent, moulded soybeans are stored with salt and a small amount of water for fermentation. On the other hand, soysauce made almost entirely from

TABLE 2
Top Grades of Amino Acid Seasoning in the World

	Be	NaCl	TN	RS(IS)	Alc.	Colour intensity
Koikuchi Shoyu (Japan)	23·6	17·0	1·70	5·07	2·50	+ +
Usukuchi Shoyu (Japan)	22·2	18·0	1·18	4·00	2·00	+
Soy sauce (Taiwan)	25·6	15·6	2·05	5·95	0·86	+ +
Soy sauce (Korea)	21·9	17·3	1·50	2·10	0·39	+ +
Soy sauce (Hong Kong)	28·5	26·2	1·54	4·22	0·00	+ + +
Soy sauce (Philippines)	23·3	24·7	0·76	1·06	0·01	+ +
Soy sauce (Singapore)	30·1	24·1	1·97	4·81	0·00	+ + +
Soy sauce (Malaysia)	23·9	18·3	1·17	8·50	0·03	+ + +
Soy sauce (Indonesia) (Kecap asin)	—	7·2	0·19	14·45	0·02	+ +
Soy sauce (Indonesia) (Kecap manis)	—	5·9	0·19	11·1 (58·1)	0·09	+ + +
Soy sauce (USA)	22·8	16·5	1·65	3·70	2·07	+ +
Chemical soy sauce (USA)	23·8	19·7	1·51	0·82	0·01	+ +
H.V.P. (Europe)	30·6	21·4	4·75	0·00	0·06	+
Fish sauce (Thailand)	26·8	27·6	2·25	4·81	0·02	+

Analysed by Kikkoman Corporation.
Be: specific gravity, Degrees Baumé, NaCl: Sodium chloride, TN: total nitrogen, RS(IS): reducing sugar (invert sugar), Alc.: alcohol.
NaCl, TN and RS(IS): g/100 ml, Alc.: ml/100 ml.

soybeans is popular in Southeast Asian countries such as Hong Kong, Singapore, Malaysia, Indonesia, and in Japan and Korea in small amounts. In this case, the residue remaining after soysauce has been taken from the salty mash by dripping off or by extraction with salt water is sometimes used as a lower grade of miso as seasoning.

Tempeh is very popular in Indonesia as the staple food. Cooked whole soybeans are cultured with *Rhizopus oligosporus*, while wrapped in banana leaves (Pisau Batu is the best species) for about 40 h at about 30 °C. The mould cultured materials are eaten fresh or after deep frying. The annual production of tempeh in Indonesia is about 80 000 metric tons in a year and 14 % of the soybeans produced in Indonesia are consumed for tempeh production. Between 20 and 120 g fresh tempeh is consumed per day by each person on Java Island. It was reported that they pay the same amount of money for tempeh as that paid for uncooked rice (Goan-Hong Lie, 1981).

Natto is popular in Japan, some parts of China and Thailand; it is prepared by culturing autoclaved whole soybeans with *Bacillus natto*, identified as *B. subtilis*, at over 40 °C for 12–40 h. It contains 0·1–0·8 % of viscous substances composed of a mixture of glutamic polypeptide and polymer of fructose, which are produced by *B. natto*. Its annual production in Japan is about 150 000 tons. It is a kind of side dish with cooked rice and is served in Japan with some shoyu, mustard, and chopped Welsh onion.

Sufu is a fermented soybean curd, which has a very long history in China. Similar products are found also in Vietnam, Philippines, and East Indies. The small cubes of soybean-curd or tofu are sterilised and then cultured with *Actinomucor elegans* at below 20 °C for 3–7 days, and the moulded cubes are then stored in strong salt solution containing 12 % salt and 12 % alcohol and aged for 1–2 months (Hesseltine & Wang, 1972). Cheese-like products produced by fermenting soybean curd by *Aspergillus* moulds have been reported recently.

3.1. Japanese Shoyu

The Japan Agricultural Standard (JAS) for shoyu recognises three kinds of production method of shoyu, as follows.

1. *Honjozo* or genuine fermented.
2. *Shinshiki-jozo* or semi-chemical. Genuine fermented shoyu mash or shoyu is mixed with chemical or enzymatic hydrolysate of plant protein, the amount of which is 50 or 30%, respectively, on a nitrogen basis, and fermented and aged for more than one month. Enzymatic hydrolysate here means plant protein degraded by the use of protease preparations.
3. *Amino acid-solution-mixed*. (1) or (2) is mixed with chemical or enzymatic hydrolysate of plant protein of which the amount is less than 50 or 30%, respectively, on a nitrogen basis.

According to JAS, in the production of genuine fermented shoyu, heat treated raw materials, soybeans and wheat, should be cultured with Koji moulds (*Aspergillus oryzae* or *A. sojae*) to make koji, and koji is mixed with salt water to make mash or moromi. Moromi is fermented with lactobacilli and yeasts and then well aged. The total amount of shoyu checked by JAS in 1981 was about 1·076 million klitres, of which 72·1 % was genuine fermented, 24·2 % was Shinshiki-jozo, and 3·7 % was amino acid-solution-mixed. The amounts of raw materials used for shoyu production in Japan in 1980 are indicated in Table 3. JAS recognises five kinds of shoyu, but fish soy is not included in the JAS. The names of the five kinds of shoyu and the amounts produced in 1981 are shown in Table 4, and their chemical compositions are in Table 5.

Eighty-five percent of all shoyu consumed in Japan is of Koikuchi type,

TABLE 3
Raw Materials Used for Shoyu Production in Japan, 1980

Wheat	181 637 tons
Defatted soybean	179 364 tons
Soybeans	6 657 tons
Salt	208 113 tons
Chemical hydrolysate of plant protein	87 206 klitres

which means dark in colour, and made from approximately equal parts of soybeans and wheat. The Koikuchi mash is subjected to vigorous lactic and alcoholic fermentations and the finished product is pasteurised at a rather high temperature of about 80 °C to give it a characteristic reddish brown colour and strong heat flavour.

Usukuchi shoyu is made from a mixture containing more wheat and less soybeans than the Koikuchi type. The saccharified rice-koji with water, which is called 'Amasake', is sometimes added to Usukuchi mash to ameliorate the salty taste. The nitrogen content of the finished product should not exceed 1·2 %. Usukuchi shoyu is used mainly for cooking when one wishes to preserve the original colour and flavour of the foodstuff.

Tamari shoyu is made mostly from soybeans with only a small amount of wheat with the ratio 10:1–2. Its nitrogen content is sometimes more than 2 % and there should be only a trace of alcohol.

TABLE 4
Production of Different Kinds of Shoyu in Japan, Recognised by JAS* in 1981**

Total production	1 076 224 klitres	100·0 %
Koikuchi	673 698 klitres	84·4
Usukuchi	83 609 klitres	12·8
Tamari	13 805 klitres	2·0
Shiro	2 782 klitres	0·5
Saishikomi	1 884 klitres	0·3

* JAS: Japan Agricultural Standard.
** From March 1, 1981 until February 28, 1982.
Note: Above figures were supplied by the Japanese Association for Shoyu Inspection. The total production of shoyu which was announced by the Ministry of Agriculture, Forest, and Fishery, Japan, was 1 190 618 klitres in 1981, and is estimated to be 1 190 000 klitres in 1982.

TABLE 5
Typical Composition of Different Kinds of Genuine Fermented Shoyu in Japan
(May, 1982)

		Baumé	NaCl*	TN*	FN*	RS*	Alc.**	pH	Colour***
Koikuchi	(1)	23·3	16·2	*1·94*	1·15	5·80	2·48	4·86	7
	(2)	22·7	16·9	1·68	1·00	4·75	2·37	4·74	10
	(3)	21·9	17·1	1·57	0·93	3·52	2·09	4·74	11
****	(4)	18·7	*13·2*	1·54	0·84	2·72	*3·20*	4·74	11
*****	(5)	16·6	*8·91*	1·56	0·94	4·10	*3·24*	4·84	13
Usukuchi	(1)	22·5	18·0	*1·50*	0·91	4·98	2·79	4·79	28
	(2)	22·4	19·3	1·19	0·73	5·02	2·63	4·84	28
Tamari		23·2	17·6	*1·85*	1·03	3·45	2·87	4·90	3
Shiro		25·0	18·0	*0·49*	0·23	*17·9*	*0·96*	4·62	46
Saishikomi		29·6	13·1	*2·01*	0·94	*14·3*	*1·07*	4·78	2

*   %(w/v), TN (Total nitrogen), FN (Formol Nitrogen), RS (Reducing Sugar).
**   %(v/v), Alc. (Alcohol).
***   Nos. of Shoyu Colour Standard.
****   Salt reduced by 20%.
***** Salt reduced by 50%.
Note: Very high values of alcohol (italic) may be because the shoyu is fortified
as a preservative. In other columns exceptional values are in italics (see text).
Cited from *J. Japan Soy Sauce Res. Inst.* **8**(4), 195 (1982).

Shiro shoyu is very light in colour and is made from wheat with very little
soybeans in the ratio 10:1–2. Saishikomi shoyu is made by enzymatically
degrading mould cultured soybeans and wheat in shoyu instead of the usual
salt water.

Good quality genuine fermented Koikuchi shoyu is 1·5–1·8% (w/v) total
nitrogen, 3–5% reducing sugar, mainly glucose, 2–2·5% (v/v) ethanol,
1–1·5% (w/v) polyalcohol, primarily glycerol, 1–2% organic acid,
predominantly lactic acid, 4·7–4·8 pH, 17–18% sodium chloride. In order
to achieve a palatable taste for a shoyu, about one half of its nitrogenous
compounds must be free amino acids, and more than 10% of the
nitrogenous compounds must be free glutamic acid.

The JAS specifies three grades for each variety of shoyu: Special, Upper
and Standard. The grade is determined by organoleptic evaluation, total
nitrogen content, soluble solids without sodium chloride content and
alcohol content. Only high quality shoyu made by fermentation can qualify
for the Special grade. About 60% of Japanese shoyu was Special grade in

1979. The JAS for the Special grade of Koikuchi shoyu is: more than 1·5 % total nitrogen, more than 16 % extract, and more than 0·8 % alcohol.

Blending fermented shoyu with not more than 50 % (on a nitrogen basis) of chemical hydrolysate of plant protein is permitted for Upper and Standard grades as long as the characteristic flavour of fermented shoyu is not spoiled. The annual consumption of shoyu per capita is about 10 litres, of which 4·4 out of 10 litres is consumed in the home and the remaining 5·6 litres institutionally and industrially. The shoyu manufacturers in Japan are assumed to be less than 3000 in number. The biggest five produce 50 % and the remaining big fifty produce 25 % of the total production. The names of the biggest five are Kikkoman, Yamasa, Higashimaru, Higeta and Marukin, all of which produce both genuine fermented Koikuchi and Usukuchi shoyu of the special grade of JAS. Kikkoman is the biggest among them and its annual production amount has been ranging between 360 000 and 400 000 klitres in recent years.

3.2. The Soysauce Produced in Oriental Countries other than Japan

The annual production of soybean sauce in Korea was 223 000 klitres in 1971, which included 107 000 klitres of industrially produced soysauce and 116 000 klitres of home-made product (Cherl-Ho Lee & Mogen Jul, 1981). The fermented soysauce industrially produced in Korea is of the Japanese Koikuchi type, but some 70 % of its production is estimated to be chemically hydrolysed soysauce. The home-made soysauce is prepared by a traditional method, in which cooked soybeans are mashed and made into small balls, and these are dried in the sun during the day and kept warm at night for several days in winter. Moulds grow on the surface of, and penetrate the interior of the balls, which are then called *Meju*. Sufficiently dried meju is packed in a rice-straw bag for aging for a few months. The aged meju balls are put into brine and kept in big china jars in the sunshine for several months for fermentation. The ripened meju-brine mixture is separated into supernatant liquid and the sediment residue. The liquid is soysauce and the residue is soybean paste. The residue is sometimes mixed with red pepper. In recent years, improved Meju is prepared industrially, in which cooked soybeans are inoculated with *Aspergillus oryzae* mould in a controlled fermentation room. The housewives take the improved meju home and put it in the brine to make soysauce and paste. The per capita daily consumption of soybean sauce (*Kanjang*), soybean paste (*Doenjang*), and red pepper soybean sauce (*Gochoojang*) were 23·3, 10·4 and 13·9 g, respectively, in 1971. The production of soybean products including 56 000 tons of the paste was 224 000 metric tons industrial-made and 168 000 tons of the home-made, and that of red pepper soybean paste was 112 000 tons including 23 000 tons of the industrial-made and 89 000 tons of the home-made in 1971 (Cherl-Ho Lee & Mogen Jul, 1981).

The annual production of soysauce in Taiwan was estimated to be 160 000 klitres in 1978, which is equivalent to 9 litres per capita consumption per year. About 80% is so-called *tou-yu* and made from soybeans and wheat originating from China. There were 433 soysauce plants in Taiwan in 1978, of which the eight largest producers occupied at least 45% of the local market. The soysauce products include genuine fermented soysauce (25%), chemically hydrolysed soysauce (5%), and blended soysauce (70%) (Yuan-Chi Su, 1980). Five to ten percent of Taiwan soysauce is estimated to be *in-yu*, which is made only from black soybeans and very much resembles Japanese *Tamari* made from only yellow soybeans. The black soybean koji is washed with water before it is mixed with salt water to make mash so as to remove the bitter taste of the product. There are three national standard grades of soysauce in Taiwan, and their total nitrogen percentages were $1·4$, $1·2$ and $1·0 \, g/100 \, ml$, respectively, in 1980.

Fermented soybean sauce similar to *in-yu* and *Tamari* is also being produced in the southern part of China and it seems to be the prototype of the soysauce prepared from only soybeans. Tamari mash is fermented usually in wooden kegs in Japan, but the soybean sauce in Taiwan, Thailand, Singapore, Malaysia, Indonesia, and the southern part of China is fermented in china jars of some 150 litres volume and in the sunshine.

There are about 10 big soysauce manufacturers in Singapore, which employ more than 50 workers. All are operated by the Chinese. The biggest is Yeo Hiap Seng Ltd, in which more than 10 000 klitres soybean sauce is prepared per year from soybeans and roasted wheat flour in the ratio 5:1, fermenting the salty mash in 10 klitres FRP tanks for 4 months in the sun. The total amount consumed by Singapore's population (2 400 000) is estimated to be 14 000 klitres, which is equivalent to about 6 litres per capita per year and is made from 3158 metric tons of soybeans (Ong Kim Lian, 1981).

In Singapore, Malaysia and Indonesia, two types of soysauce are being manufactured; a light soysauce (in Cantonese *sung-show* or in Hokkien *chiuw-cheng*), and a dark soysauce mixed with cane molasses (in Cantonese *low-chow* or in Hokkien *tau-iu*). In Indonesia, soysauce is called '*ketjap*' or '*kecap*', and similarly, two types of kecap are popular: *kecap-asin* of salty taste and *kecap-manis* of very sweet taste blended with a large amount of cane or palm sugar. The former is popular in Sumatra and the latter in Java. The per capita daily consumption of kecap in Indonesia is 10–15 ml

(Goan-Hong Lie, 1981). The kecap mash is washed with salt water twice and the mixed extract is concentrated in the sun. The residue from the extraction is used for *tauco* or *miso* of inferior grade, but the genuine tauco is made from soybeans and wheat flour cultured with *Aspergillus oryzae* mould. The mould cultured material or koji is dried in the sun, mixed with salt water, and fermented and concentrated in the sun for 3–7 weeks. Tauco is a slurry containing 10% protein and sold in glass bottles, thus differing from Japanese miso, which is a paste containing 25% of protein. In the above countries, the chemical acid hydrolysate of soybeans and the semi-chemical or shinshiki soysauce are also popular, but the exact amount produced is not known.

However, the soysauce in Peking and Shanghai nowadays is different from the above and is prepared as follows: the koji is prepared by a usual method on a big scale, culturing *Aspergillus oryzae* with a mixture of steamed soybeans and wheat or wheat bran (6:4), and the koji is mixed with salt water to make hard mash, of which the moisture content is about 80% and the salt concentration is about 6–7%. This hard and low-salt mash is kept at 45–50 °C for about 3 weeks for enzymatic digestion. The digested mash is extracted with hot salt water and then with hot plain water. The residue, being without salt, is therefore good for animal and bird feed. There is no alcoholic fermentation of mash or the pressing of mash as there is in the case of Japanese shoyu manufacture. The yield of soysauce on the nitrogen basis in 1979 was 75–80%, because the defatted soybean as raw material was cooked by the NK method. The highest governmental standard of soysauce is as follows: total nitrogen 1·6%, reducing sugar 4%, sodium chloride 19% or more, respectively. The chemical acid hydrolysis of plant protein for soysauce manufacture is forbidden by the law in China.

3.3. Miso

Miso is the Japanese name for a semi-solid salty food made from soybeans, rice, or barley, and salt by fermentation. Miso is classified into three types on the basis of raw materials: rice-miso made from rice-koji, cooked soybeans, and salt; barley-miso made from barley-koji, cooked soybeans, and salt; and soybean-miso made from soybean-koji and salt. These three types of miso are further classified into sweet, medium, and salty, according to their salt contents, and white, light yellow, and red, according to their colour. About 80% of the miso consumed in Japan is rice-miso in such varieties as White, Edo, Shinshu, and Sendai, and the constituents of some typical miso including the above are indicated in Table 6.

The amount of miso produced in Japan was 568 000 tonnes in 1979, but

TABLE 6
Constituents of Some Typical Miso

	Water %	pH	Salt %	Protein %	Fat %	RS* %
White miso	45	5·3	4·5	7·9	3·8	38
Edo sweet miso	49	5·4	5·8	11·0	4·5	15
Shinshu miso	48	5·2	12·0	11·4	5·5	12
Sendai miso	50	5·1	12·8	12·0	5·3	11
Barley miso (salty)	48	5·1	12·0	12·7	5·5	11
Barley miso (sweet)	47	5·2	9·5	10·0	4·9	17
Soybean miso	46	5·0	11·5	20·0	10·5	4

* Reducing sugar.
Cited fron Ebine (1980).

this has been decreasing in the last decade. The per capita consumption of miso is about one half that of shoyu in Japan. There are about 2000 miso producers in Japan. Miso is usually employed as an ingredient for miso soup and it is also used for cooking in general as a condiment.

The miso made almost entirely from soybeans, with only a small amount of wheat flour, is also very popular in the Asian countries, but in most cases, the soybean miso produced in countries other than Japan is a slurry instead of a paste and moreover it is used mainly for cooking instead of making soup as in Japan.

4.   MANUFACTURE

4.1. Koikuchi Shoyu

Japanese fermented shoyu of the Koikuchi type is prepared by five main processes. They are: the treatment of raw materials, the koji making, the mash making and aging, the pressing, and refining. One example of the preparation of Koikuchi shoyu is schematically indicated in Fig. 1.

4 1 1 Treatment of Raw Materials

Whole soybeans, or more commonly, defatted soybean grits, are moistened and cooked with steam under pressure. This process greatly influences the digestibility of soybean protein. Details will be described in a later section. Wheat kernels, the other half of the raw materials, are roasted at 160–180 °C for less than one minute, then coarsely crushed into four or five pieces.

Soybeans 400 kg*   Wheat 340 kg   Koji mould
    | | Seed culture
Soaking in water   Roasting   0·1–0·2 % weight
    | | of that of raw
Autoclaving   Crushing   materials

Mixing   Moisture content
| 40–45 %
Culturing mould   Moisture content
(koji making)   of koji 25–30 %,
Salt 276 kg _____| 48–72 h   pH 6·5–7·0
Water 1200 litres |

Mixing
(mash making)
|
Fermenting tank   2000 litres, 6–8 months
| (1) Enzymatic degradation of
| materials
| (2) Lactic acid fermentation
Aging   (3) Yeast fermentation
|
Pressing
|

Soy cake   Raw shoyu pH 4·8–5·0
220 kg, ca. | 1500–1600 litres
30 % moisture   Pasteurisation T.N. 1·6–1·8 %
|

* or Defatted soybean   Sediment   Refined shoyu
  330 kg, moistened | pH 4·7–4·9
  with 420 litres hot water   Bottling

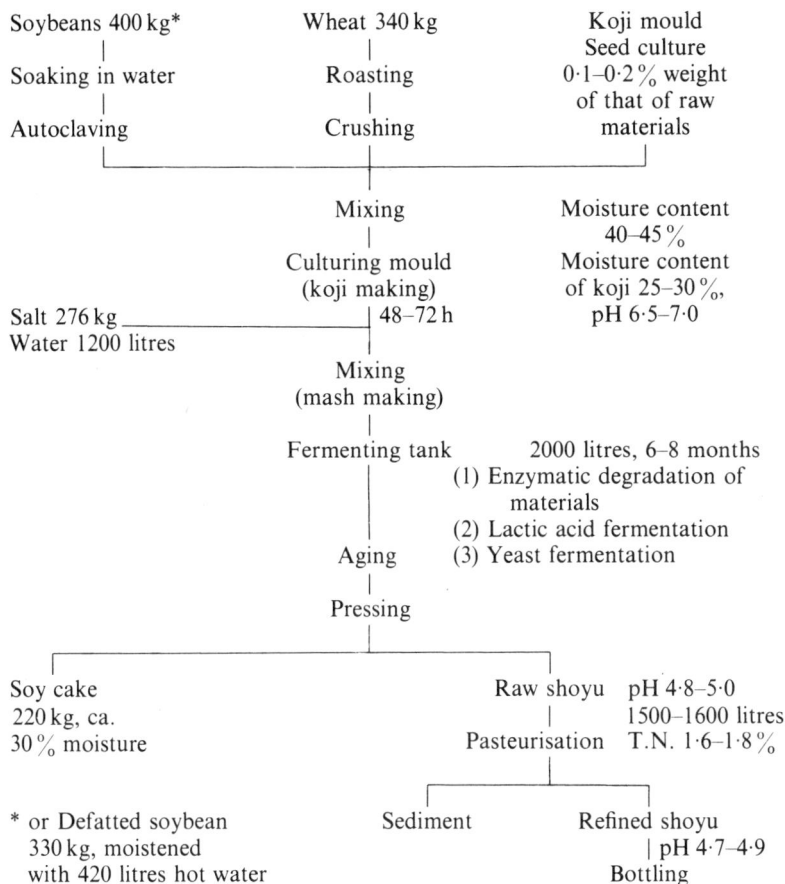

Fig. 1. Koikuchi shoyu fermentation.

4.1.2. *Koji Making*

These two materials are inoculated with a small amount of seed mould or a pure culture of *Aspergillus oryzae* or *A. sojae*. This mixture is spread to a depth of 30–40 cm on a large perforated stainless steel plate having a rectangular shape that is 5 m in width and 12 m in length, for example, or a doughnut shape with a diameter of 15–30 m. The heat treated raw materials are aerated for 2 or 3 days with temperature and moisture controlled air, which comes up from the bottom holes through the layer of fermenting material to give the proper conditions for mould cultivation and enzyme formation. The temperature of the materials is kept at around 30 °C and the 40–45 % moisture of the materials at the beginning of cultivation decreases to 25–35 % after 2 or 3 days. This allows the mould to grow throughout the mass and provide the enzymes necessary to hydrolyse the protein, starch, and other constituents of the raw materials. This mould cultured material is called 'koji'.

4.1.3. Mash Making and Aging

In making mash, the koji is mixed with saline water which has a 22–23 % salt content and 120–130 % volume of that of the raw materials. The mash or 'moromi' is transferred to the deep fermentation tanks. About 5–10 klitres capacity wooden kegs or 10–20 klitre concrete tanks are now being replaced by resin-coated iron tanks of 50–300 klitres capacity. The moromi is held for 4–8 months, depending upon its temperature, with occasional agitation with compressed air to mix the dissolving contents uniformly and to promote the microbial growth. During the fermentation period, the enzymes from koji mould hydrolyse most of the protein to amino acids and low molecular weight peptides. Around 20 % of the starch is consumed by the mould during koji cultivation, but almost all of the remaining starch is converted into simple sugars, more than half of which are fermented to lactic acid and alcohol by lactobacilli and yeasts, respectively. The pH drops from an initial value of 6·5–7·0 down to 4·7–4·9. The lactic acid fermentation at the preliminary stage is gradually replaced by yeast fermentation. Pure cultured *Pediococcus halophylus* and *Saccharomyces rouxii* are sometimes added to the mash. The salt concentration of mash stabilises at around 17–18 % (w/v) after 1 or 2 months. The high salt concentration of mash effectively limits the growth to a few desirable types of micro-organisms.

4.1.4. Pressing of Mash

An aged mash is filtered under a high hydraulic pressure through cloth. Usually 12–13 litres of shoyu mash is put on a square sheet of cloth of 100 × 100 cm and the four sides of the cloth are folded into a square of 70 × 70 cm and another smaller square sheet of cloth of 65 × 65 cm is put on it; this is done so as to wrap the mash and the second sheet of cloth covers it. The next portion of shoyu mash is put on another large cloth and wrapped in the same way as above. These operations are repeated in a wooden box until 300–400 sheets of folded cloth containing the mash are piled in it; they are then pressed for 2 or 3 days under hydraulic pressure. Sometimes a sheet of cloth twice as large as the above is used to wrap about

25 litres moromi. The pressure used for pressing is increased in two or three steps, sometimes reaching 100 kg/cm² at the final stage, which makes the moisture content of the press-cake less than 25 %. A diaphragm type of continuous pressing machine has recently been applied for shoyu-mash filtration instead of a batch-type hydraulic press as described above with the moisture content of the press-cake more than 30 %. The residue from the pressing of the shoyu-mash, or shoyu-cake, is used for animal feed for cows and ducks.

4.1.5. Refining

The liquid part of the mash obtained by pressing is stored in a tank and is divided into three layers; the sediment on the bottom, the clear supernatant of the middle layer, and the oil layer floating on top. The middle layer is sometimes further clarified by filtration with Kieselguhr as a filter aid in order to get the raw shoyu. After adjusting the salt and nitrogen concentrations to the standard, the clarified raw shoyu is pasteurised at 70–80 °C and stored in a semi-closed tank. After settlement of the coagulum produced by heating, the clear middle layer is bottled or canned, or sometimes spray-dried. An oil layer separates from the heated shoyu; it consists of free higher fatty acids and their ethyl esters derived from the yeast metabolism of soybean and wheat oils, and it is sometimes utilised by mixing with paint as an antifreezing agent.

4.2. Tamari Shoyu

A mixture of cooked soybeans or defatted soybean grits and roasted wheat (20:3) is treated with an extruder to make granules of 12–16 mm diameter. These granulated soybeans are inoculated with a mixture of seed moulds, *Aspergillus oryzae*, *A. sojae*, or *A. tamarii*, and the powder of roasted barley, of which the amount is less than 1·5 % that of the other raw materials. These materials are incubated at a rather lower temperature, 26–28 °C, for about 45 h to make koji. The moisture content of finished koji is preferably about 35 %, and its weight is about 120 % of that of the raw materials. This tamari-koji is sometimes dried so as to decrease the weight of koji by 7–8 % before the mash making. The koji is mixed with salt water, of which the volume is between 50 and 130 % of that of the raw materials, to make mash. The mash is usually too stiff to agitate, so the liquid part of the mash from the bottom is repeatedly spread over the top of the mash instead of agitating it with compressed air as is the case with Koikuchi mash. Genuine Tamari shoyu is rich in soluble solids and has little contamination from film-forming yeasts, so it is usual not to pasteurise the final product.

4.3. Miso

Whole soybeans are almost always used for the preparation of ordinary miso. Dehulled soybeans or soybean grits are sometimes employed for the production of rice-miso of white or light yellow colour. Soybeans are soaked in water until saturation, and then cooked in water for 30–60 min at atmospheric pressure, or steamed for 20 min at a pressure of 0·7 kg/cm^2 (115 °C). Milled rice or barley is soaked in water to absorb enough water and then steamed batchwise in an open cooker for 40 min or continuously on a net conveyor in a closed autoclave for 30–60 min. The koji cultivation on rice or barley with *Aspergillus oryzae* is conducted at 35–38 °C, sometimes with an increase of the temperature up to near 40 °C at the final stage, taking 40–48 h from the beginning. The finished koji is mixed with salt to stop any further mould growth. Various types of koji fermenter are employed nowadays. Cooked soybeans are mixed with salted rice or barley koji and with an inoculum of cultured yeast and lactic acid bacteria, if necessary. The mixture is packed in a tank for fermentation with a little weight from the top. The mash is removed from one tank to another at least twice during the fermentation period to mix the contents and to introduce

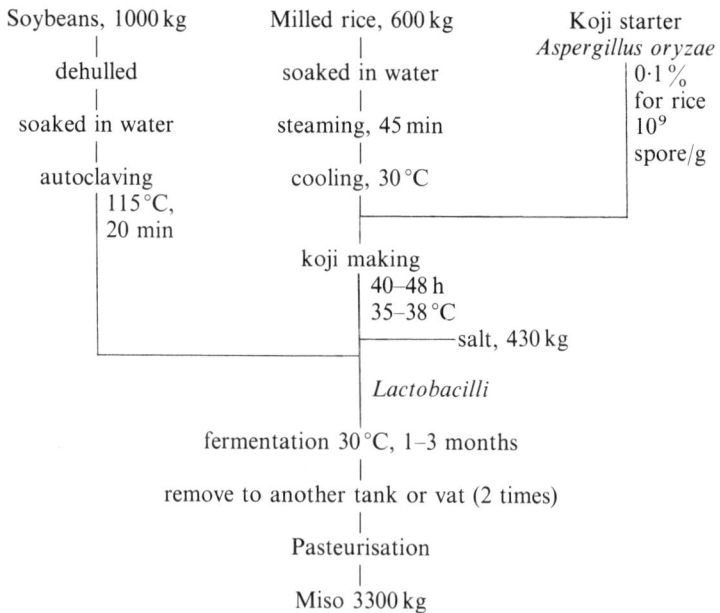

Soybeans, 1000 kg   Milled rice, 600 kg   Koji starter
Aspergillus oryzae

dehulled   soaked in water   0·1 %
for rice

soaked in water   steaming, 45 min   10^9
spore/g

autoclaving   cooling, 30 °C
115 °C,
20 min

koji making
40–48 h
35–38 °C
salt, 430 kg

Lactobacilli

fermentation 30 °C, 1–3 months

remove to another tank or vat (2 times)

Pasteurisation

Miso 3300 kg

Fig. 2.   Miso fermentation.

some oxygen, so promoting microbial growth. Fermentation is conducted at around 30 °C in a room at 20–25 °C for 1–3 months depending upon the kind of miso. Well-ripened miso is then blended and mashed, if necessary, and pasteurised through a tube heater or by heating in water after packaging. About 2 % alcohol is added to the product to stop the growth of yeasts. The production process for manufacturing salty rice miso is shown in Fig. 2.

5. RECENT PROGRESS OF RESEARCH AND TECHNOLOGY IN SHOYU AND MISO PRODUCTION IN JAPAN

5.1. Soybeans and Wheat as Raw Materials
5.1.1. Soybeans
Only whole soybeans were used as raw materials of shoyu and miso before World War II, but nowadays, defatted soybean grits, which are prepared by extracting the dehulled crushed whole soybeans with lower boiling hexane, are widely used. In the case of miso, however, a great part is still produced from the whole beans. The whole beans represented only 3·2 % of the total soybeans used for the production of shoyu in 1978.

The comparison between whole and defatted soybeans is based nowadays on the cost, enzymatic digestibility of proteins, fermentation period, relative difficulty in manufacturing, especially in koji making and mash controlling, and the quality of shoyu in terms of chemical components such as glycerol, alcohol, and lactic acid, organoleptic evaluation, and the stability of the product.

The enzymatic digestibility of the defatted bean for the fermentative production of shoyu has been much improved, due to the change of oil-extraction procedure from the pressing method carried out at rather higher temperature using an expeller to the solvent extraction at rather lower temperature, which resulted in less denaturation of protein than before. An NSI value of about twenty of defatted soybean is generally believed to be adequate for miso and shoyu production.

The glycerol contents of shoyu made from whole and defatted soybeans were reported to be 1–1·2 % and 0·6–0·7 %, respectively (Okuhara and Yokotsuka 1958, 1962, 1963), from which the glycerol derived from the degradation of soybean oil was calculated to be about 0·5 %. On the other hand, the glycerol was found to be produced also by yeast fermentation from glucose in the presence of high salt concentrations. Shoyu mash is nowadays subjected to much more vigorous yeast fermentation than before, which results in much more glycerol formation, sometimes reaching 1·5–1·7 %. Thus the difference between the glycerol contents of whole and defatted soybean shoyu has become much smaller than before. Nevertheless, it is true that the shoyu made from whole beans has some flavour characteristics different from that of the defatted soybean shoyu. This may account for the fact that some shoyu producers are still making their products from mixtures of whole and defatted soybeans.

5.1.2. Wheat

The ratio of soybeans and wheat as raw materials for Koikuchi shoyu ranges between 6:4 and 4:6. The proteins in wheat kernels are good sources of glutamic acid which is an important taste ingredient of shoyu; thus the high protein wheat kernels are preferred for shoyu production. Wheat bran is sometimes used instead of the whole or part of wheat kernels, but this decreases the alcohol content of shoyu, makes the colour of shoyu darker and the colour stability of shoyu inferior because of the increase of pentose sugars in the shoyu.

5.2. Treatment of Raw Materials

5.2.1. Soybeans

The protein in raw soybeans is native and not hydrolysed by the proteases in Koji. Therefore it is necessary to denature the soybean protein by some method so that it can be digested by the enzymes of koji mould to make shoyu or miso. Soybeans used as raw material for shoyu were, in the past, boiled in water at atmospheric pressure, but it was changed to autoclaving under pressure, in which well moistened soybeans were cooked at a gauge pressure of $0·8 \, kg/cm^2$ for about 1 h, and after stopping the steam, the cooked soybeans were kept in the kettle for several additional hours without opening the seal.

Tateno & Umeda invented (1955) the so-called NK-method of soybean cooking, in which thoroughly moistened soybeans were cooked in a rotary cooker at a gauge pressure of $0·8 \, kg/cm^2$ for about 1 h, and immediately thereafter the materials were cooled to below 40 °C by reducing the inside pressure with the aid of a jet condenser. The protein digestibility in shoyu manufacture, which is the ratio between the total nitrogen of a shoyu and that of the raw materials, was increased from 69 to 73 % by the NK-method as compared with the conventional cooking method, which is shown in Table 7. The importance was pointed out of containing a sufficient amount of water in cooked soybeans, that is usually about 58 % for whole beans and about 62 % for defatted beans.

TABLE 7

NK-Cooking Method of Soybeans as Compared to the Conventional
Method

Cooking method	Digestibility of proteins in mash, salt 18%, room temp. 1 year	Ratio between Formol N and total N	Ratio between glutamic N and total N
Conventional*	68·7%	49·4%	5·5%
NK-Method**	73·1%	53·8%	7·3%
Increasing ratio	106·4%	108·8%	135·4%

Tateno & Umeda (1955), Kikkoman Shoyu Co., Ltd.

* Cooked at $0·8 \, kg/cm^2$ for 1 h, the soy beans left in the autoclave for additional 12 h.

** Cooked at $0·8 \, kg/cm^2$ for 1 h, immediately thereafter the soybeans are taken out of the autoclave.

The treatment of soybeans with water containing methanol, ethanol, or propanol at its boiling point was found to give near 90% enzymatic digestibility of protein (Yamaguchi, 1954; Fukushima & Mogi, 1955, 1957). But these methods did not become industrially applied, mainly because of the difficulty of making koji and the inferior organoleptic quality of the final shoyu.

Yokotsuka *et al.* (1966) found it is useful to increase the enzymatic digestibility of cooked soybeans with a higher temperature and a shorter cooking time than the NK-method, as shown in Table 8. This method indicated the possibility of 92–93% protein digestion in shoyu production with a relatively better organoleptic quality of the final product (Yasuda *et al.*, 1973a, b). Similar research results were reported by Harada & Kawaguchi (1968), in which defatted soybean was cooked at a maximum pressure of $4 \, kg/cm^2$ for 3 min.

In the above cases, thoroughly soaked soybeans were cooked by using saturated steam. Aonuma *et al.* (1970, 1971) reported a new method of cooking soybeans and wheat used for brewing without adding moisture before cooking by super-heated steam at a pressure of $4–8 \, kg/cm^2$ or at 200–289 °C for not less than 15 s with almost the same protein digestibility as that obtained by saturated steam. This method has the advantage of making it possible to stock the heat-treated raw materials.

New high temperature/short time (HTST) cooking methods of raw materials inspired the development of several types of continuous cooker,

Tamotsu Yokotsuka

TABLE 8
Effect of the Cooking Conditions of Soybeans on the Enzymatic
Digestibility of Protein

Steam pressure (kg/cm^2)	Cooking time (min)	Digestibility of protein in enzyme solution $(salt\ 0\%,\ 37°C,\ 7\ days)$
0·9	45	86%
1·2	10	91
1·8	8	91
2·0	5	92
3·0	3	93
4·0	2	94
5·0	1	95
6·0	0·5	95
7·0	0·25	95

T. Yokotsuka *et al.* (1966) Japanese patent 929,910, Kikkoman Shoyu Co., Ltd.

which are indicated in Fig. 3. At the same time, the NK-method was also greatly improved toward the HTST method. Protein digestibility of 87·80 % was achieved by cooking soybeans at 1·7 kg/cm² for 8 min by using a NK-cooker as compared with 81·80 % obtained by the conventional NK-cooking conditions at 0·9 kg/cm² for 40 min (Iijima *et al.*, 1973). The time for cooling of autoclaved soybeans in a NK-cooker is closely related to their proteolytic digestibility (Yasuda *et al.*, 1973a). By enlarging the diameter of both the inlet and exhaust steam pipes of a NK-cooker in order

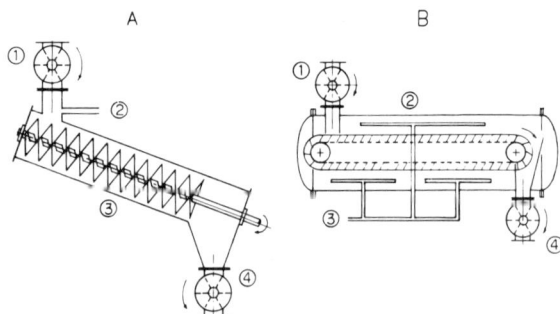

Fig. 3. Continuous soybean cooker. A, screw type; B, net conveyor type; 1, rotary valve (charge); 2, steam; 3, cooker; 4, rotary valve (discharge).

to give rapid rise in temperature at the beginning of cooking and rapid cooling of cooked soybeans, the protein digestibility increased by about 3 % under the same conditions (Eguchi, 1977).

Two things should be taken into consideration, especially in HTST cooking of soybeans for soysauce production as follows:

(1)   Avoid too much heating which results in the overdenaturation of protein and decreases the enzymatic digestibility of protein.

(2)   Steam the soybeans uniformly so as not to leave undenatured parts in the cooked soybeans, which go into the shoyu and produce turbidity when the shoyu is boiled or diluted with water.

In order to determine the digestibility of cooked soybeans by analysis, samples of cooked soybeans to be tested are digested by the enzyme extract from wheat-bran koji which has been cultured with *Aspergillus* moulds, the protein content in the filtrate of the digest is determined, and the ratio of solubilised protein to the total protein content of the cooked soybeans is calculated. The undenatured protein remaining in the cooked soybeans is determined by boiling the above filtrate from enzymatic digestion of the cooked soybeans. The formation of turbidity indicates that undenatured soybean protein remains in the cooked soybeans.

5.2.2. Wheat

Wheat kernels were roasted in an iron pan for shoyu production in the past. This method was replaced by roasting with sand in a rotary roaster at the beginning of the 1900s, in which only the heated sand is recycled in the oven. This method gives a relatively uniform roasting of wheat and is still popular.

In roasting wheat kernels for shoyu production, it is necessary to satisfy the following two contradictory factors:

(a)   to make the alpha-starch content or the enzymatic digestibility of starch a maximum;

(b)   to make the enzymatic digestibility of protein a maximum.

The trend is that the higher the temperature, the higher the alpha-starch content, but the lower the digestibility of protein. The alpha-starch content of roasted wheat kernels can be maximised by making the moisture content of wheat kernels before roasting 15–25 % (Yamaguchi *et al.*, 1961).

The same HTST cooking method as applied to soybeans with some 10 % of added moisture gives similar good results for the roasting of wheat kernels with some 10 % of added moisture (Yokotsuka *et al.*, 1974).

According to Aiba (1982), good results were obtained in the roasting of wheat kernels at atmospheric pressure when the wheat kernels contained more than 8 % moisture and were treated with hot air at more than 150 °C for less than 45 s.

5.3. Koji Moulds

The shoyu or miso manufacturers have been utilising the strains of *Aspergillus* mould which were selected by themselves or purchased in the market. The mould strains used for food fermentation should be selected from the following viewpoints: the flavour and the colour of the final product; good spore forming ability which is necessary to prepare the seed starter; strong and rapid growth; high enzymatic activity especially of proteolytic and macerating enzymes; lower consumption of starch during growth; genetic stability; length of stalk (short stalk strains are most suitable for mechanical koji cultivation); and no toxin production.

Terada *et al.* (1981) isolated 128 strains of koji moulds from the mould starters purchased in the Japanese market, which included 35 starters for shoyu production and 33 for miso production. Sixty-eight per cent of the starters for shoyu and 79 % for miso were composed of more than two kinds of koji mould. The starters for shoyu had the tendency to have short stalks and high production of spores. The starters for miso production were good producers of amylase. Sixty-five strains of koji mould used for shoyu were composed of 80 % of *Aspergillus oryzae* and 20 % of *A. sojae*, while 63 strains for miso were composed of 89 % of *A. oryzae* and 11 % of *A. sojae*.

About 80 % of protease produced by koji moulds is alkaline protease having optimum pH 9–10, but in addition, three kinds of acid protease (optimum pH 3), two kinds of neutral protease (optimum pH 6–7) and one semi-alkaline protease have been isolated (Nakadai, 1977).

The strong soybean-protein digesting ability of the neutral proteases I and II, especially of the former, has been pointed out (Sekine, 1972, 1976), but the percentages of neutral protease to the total protease of the *Aspergillus* moulds checked were 10–20 % (Tagami & Sugawara, 1977). Three kinds of aminopeptidase and 4 kinds of carboxypeptidase have also been isolated. These peptidases, especially leucine-aminopeptidase (optimum pH 7–8), are greatly associated with the enzymatic formation of Formol nitrogen and glutamic acid in shoyu mash (Iguchi & Nasuno, 1978).

The types of enzymes isolated from koji moulds and their molecular weights and isoelectric points are listed in Table 9 (Ohtsuki *et al.*, 1982).

The proteinases of koji moulds degrade protein into peptides and not

TABLE 9
The Kinds of Enzyme Isolated from Koji Mould

	Molecular weight × 10³	Isoelectric point
Leucine-amino-peptidase	26·5	3·3
	40	3·9
	61	4·1
	99	4·4
	145	6·1
Acid carboxy-peptidase	43	2·1
	61	4·2
	125	4·4
		6·0
Acid proteinase	36	3·4
	55	4·1
	120	4·6
Neutral proteinase I	45	4·3
Neutral proteinase II	19	5·8
Alkaline proteinase	22	7·8
Semi-alkaline proteinase	32	6·5
α-amylase	23	3·6
Glucoamylase	80	5·8
Carboxy methyl cellulase	17·5	3·6
	22	4·3
	31	8·5
	89	9·6
Glutaminase	81	3·9
		4·6

From Ohtsuki *et al.* (1982).

into individual amino acids. Glutamic acid and glutamine are separated from peptides by the action of carboxypeptidase and aminopeptidase, respectively. Glutamine is then converted into glutamic acid by the action of glutaminase of koji mould, of which the optimum pH value and temperature are around 7·0 and 40–45 °C, respectively. The glutaminase of koji mould is not heat tolerant in the new shoyu mash and is easily destroyed at temperatures above 25 °C (Kuroshima *et al.*, 1969), and moreover, the activity of glutaminase derived from koji mould is greatly lowered in the presence of high salt concentrations (Terada *et al.*, 1973). It was found that the amount of intercellular glutaminase of koji mould in the shoyu mash is ten times that of the extracellular one (Ohtaka & Hakai, 1972), and the former was more resistant to heat and pH than the latter (Shikata *et al.*, 1978).

Ishii *et al.* (1972) searched for the *Aspergillus* moulds having enzymes possessing strong plant tissue degrading activity, and found *Aspergillus sojae 48.* This activity was attributed to the pectinases produced by the mould and was found to be greatly lowered in the salt solution. Nevertheless, the shoyu mash prepared from the koji cultured with this strain of mould exhibited a greater digestibility of protein and carbohydrates and a lower viscosity as compared to those of the control mash prepared by the ordinary koji mould. And the amount of residue after pressing of this mash was smaller than the control. It is generally known that cellulase, hemicellulase, pectinase, β-galactosidase, and pentosan-degrading enzymes are involved in the enzymatic degradation of plant tissues of soybeans and wheat kernels in shoyu fermentation, which relates to the yield of shoyu, the feasibility of pressing of shoyu mash, and the quality of the final product.

The shoyu koji cultured with *A. sojae* has the characteristics as compared to the koji cultured with *A. oryzae* as follows (Terada *et al.*, 1979, 1981; Hayashi *et al.*, 1981):

1. higher pH value of koji due to the lower content of citric acid;
2. lower consumption of starch during koji making;
3. lower activity of α-amylase, acid protease, acid carboxypeptidase, and higher endo-poly-galacturonase in koji;
4. lower viscosity of mash or moromi;
5. lower enzymatic activity remaining in raw shoyu, which relates to the smaller amount of heat coagulated substances caused by pasteurisation;
6. lower content of reducing sugar, lactose, and ammonia, and lower pH value of raw shoyu.

The improvements in proteolytic activity of koji moulds have been achieved by induced mutation, crossing, or cell fusion. A 2–6 % increase in protein digestibility was reported in shoyu production by using an induced mutant of *A. sojae*, of which alkaline protease was increased by 6 times compared to that of the mother strain (Nasuno *et al.*, 1971a, b, c; 1972).

Many investigators have checked for the aflatoxin productivity of koji moulds, but so far, all results suggest that koji moulds do not produce aflatoxins. The investigators are Hesseltine and his colleagues in USA (1966), and in Japan, Aibara and Miyaki (1965), Masuda *et al.* (1965), Murakami *et al.* (1967), Manabe *et al.* (1968), and Kinoshita *et al.* (1968). We also could not find aflatoxin producers among 200 strains of *Aspergillus* mould used in Japanese food fermentations (Yokotsuka *et al.*,

1966, 1967a, 1968; Sasaki *et al.*, 1967, 1974). In the course of our research, 7 types of fluorescent and non-toxic pyrazine compound, lumichrome, and other kinds of unknown compounds, which are produced by moulds in general and on thin layer chromatography exhibit similar Rf values to those of aflatoxin B or G dependent upon solvent systems, were isolated (Fig. 4). So, in the detection and characterisation of mould samples thought to be contaminated with aflatoxins, Rf values should be determined with two or three solvent systems, and ultra-violet and infra-red spectral data should be used. This is most important in the discrimination of *A. sojae*, which is non-toxic, from *A. parasiticus*, which includes aflatoxin producers, because of their morphological similarities.

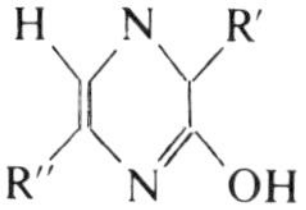

	R'	R''
1. Flavacol	I	I
2.	I	II
3.	I	III
4.	I	IV
5.	I	V
6.	II	II
7.	II	III

Structure with substituents:

I.   —CH$_2$CH(CH$_3$)$_2$
II. —CH(CH$_3$)C$_2$H$_5$
III. —C(OH)(CH$_3$)C$_2$H$_5$
IV. —CH(CH$_3$)$_2$
V.   —C(OH)(CH$_3$)CH$_3$

Fig. 4. Fluorescent pyrazine compounds exhibiting similar Rf values to those of aflatoxin B1 on TLC (Yokotsuka *et al.*, 1968; Sasaki *et al.*, 1968, 1970).

Twenty-nine strains among 69 strains of *Aspergillus* mould were found to be aspergillic acid producers, but the strongest producer among them did not produce aspergillic acid on a solid substrate composed of soybeans and wheat at least within 2 days which is the usual period of time for koji cultivation (Yokotsuka *et al.*, 1969).

The *Aspergillus ochraceus* which are rarely found in koji cultivation as contaminants in the southern part of Japan, sometimes produce ochratoxin and some fluorescent isocoumarine compounds having some toxicity.

Sasaki *et al.* (1970, 1980), and Yokotsuka & Sasaki (1980) were unable to detect aflatoxin, patulin, ochratoxin, sterigmatocystin, penicillic acid, and cyclopiazonic acid in 33 kinds of industrial *Aspergillus* mould, with the exception of a very few strains, which produced cyclopiazonic acid.

5.4. Koji Making
The quality of koji very much influences not only the degree and speed of

enzymatic degradation of raw materials in the salty mash but also the chemical and organoleptic quality of the final product. To prepare a good quality koji, it is necessary, (1) to obtain sufficient growth of mycelia, (2) to produce maximum amounts of enzymes needed, such as protease, amylase, and other plant tissue degrading enzymes, (3) not to destroy the activity of enzymes once produced, (4) to minimise the consumption of starch caused by the growth of mould, (5) to avoid the bacterial and mould contamination.

The starter mould is cultured so as to give the highest possible yield of viable spores. Wheat bran, crushed wheat, dehulled and pressed barley, rye, or crushed rice grains are used as raw materials for the cultivation of starter mould. These materials are moistened with 45–55 % water and are autoclaved for sterilisation. Then a pure culture of *Aspergillus* mould is inoculated and incubated at 25–30 °C for 75–100 h. The effective number of spores in the finished mould starter reaches $1-2 \times 10^9$ per gram. An absolutely sterilised room is often used for the inoculation and cultivation of seed mould. In addition, the sterilisation of raw materials, and inoculation and cultivation of mould are sometimes conducted in a large autoclave under automatically controlled temperature and moisture, and absolutely sterile conditions.

The mixture of cooked soybeans and roasted and crushed wheat kernels is mixed along with 0·1–0·2 % of starter mould, *Aspergillus oryzae* or *A. sojae*. The mixed materials were formerly cultured for 72 h or more in many small boxes or trays piled in a warm room, of which the temperature was controlled by windows. About one ton of raw materials was divided into about 1000 wooden trays with a thickness of 3–5 cm. During the incubation period, the materials were cooled (usually twice) by handmixing. The major effort was directed to get visibly good mycelial growth at around 35 °C, but it was difficult to keep to this temperature because of the operation by hand without mechanical cooling. The materials sometimes reached over 40 °C at that time. One example of the temperature change during koji cultivation in wooden trays is indicated in Fig. 5. It was found that a lower temperature around 20, 25, 30 or 35 °C is preferable for protease formation by koji mould, although around 35 °C is preferable for amylase formation (Yamamoto, 1957).

In miso production, cooked soybeans are mixed with rice or dehulled-barley koji along with salt, in which case a koji which is rich in amylase rather than protease is needed. This is why the cultivation of rice or barley koji for miso production takes place at around 35 °C throughout. In shoyu-koji cultivation, which needs to be rich in protease rather than amylase, the

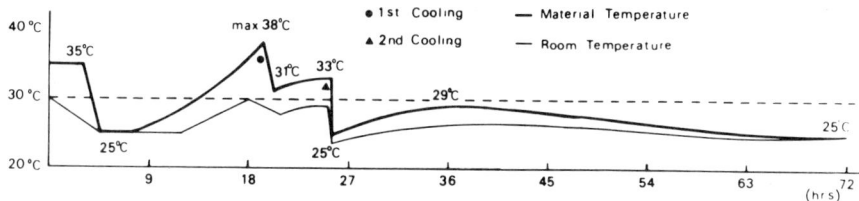

Fig. 5. Temperature change of materials during shoyu-koji cultivation by the conventional method using wooden trays (Shibuya, 1969).

temperature is kept at 30–35 °C at the preliminary stage for the mycelium formation, and at less than 30 °C, preferably around 25 °C, in the latter stage for the protease formation (Ohara *et al.*, 1959). Koji preparation at a constant temperature of 23–25 °C was also proposed to produce more protease and to avoid the inactivation of peptidase, which occurs at temperatures greater than 25 °C (Miyazaki & Honkawa, 1964; Tazaki & Watanabe, 1966; Imai *et al.*, 1969). The preferable temperature change of materials during shoyu koji cultivation is shown in Fig. 6, but in practice it is rather difficult to keep to this temperature change especially in the conventional hand-operated method of koji making.

The development of the so-called TF-method of mechanical equipment for koji cultivation has made it possible to obtain the desirable temperature and humidity of materials to be cultured with koji mould, and at the same time, it has greatly contributed to shortening the time required for koji cultivation from 72 to 48 h, to increasing the enzymatic activities of koji, to reducing the undesirable bacterial contamination in koji and to reducing the labour costs. For example, by reducing the temperature of materials after the second cooling of koji cultivation below 35 °C, the yield of shoyu increased by 7 % as compared to the conventional method (Harada *et al.*, 1951), and when the koji was cultivated at the constant temperature of 25 °C, the protein digestibility increased by 7 % as compared to the

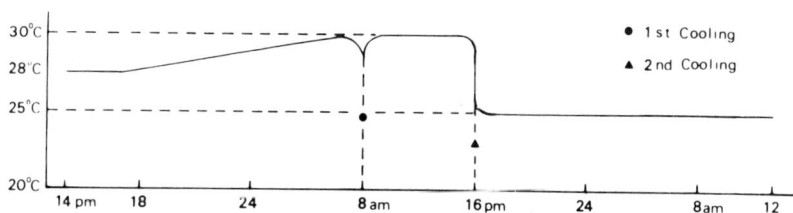

Fig. 6. Preferable temperature change of materials during 3-day shoyu-koji cultivation (Haga, 1968).

conventional wooden-tray method (Imai *et al.*, 1967). The moisture content of materials to be cultured with koji is very much related to the protease formation of koji. The preferable moisture content of materials is about 43 % at the beginning and about 30 % at the final stage. The higher temperature and humidity increase the consumption of starch by the growth of mould during the koji cultivation, and its average figures range from 20 to 30 %.

Although no hygienic hazard arising from bacterial contamination in koji has been reported in Japan to date, it sometimes reaches 10^{8-9} organisms per gram. Too much bacterial contamination in koji not only reduces the proteolytic activities of koji but also makes the quality of the shoyu inferior. The major contaminants in the koji cultivation in wooden trays with hand operation used to be *Bacillus subtilis* at too high temperature and *Rhizopus nigricans* at too low temperature. In the modern mechanical koji cultivation by the TF-method, the major contaminants in koji tend to be *Micrococcus*, which is aerobic and of lower optimum temperature than that of *Bacillus*. In addition, *Leuconostoc*, *Lactobacillus* and *Saccharomyces rouxii* are sometimes found as contaminants in koji. It is possible to reduce the bacterial contamination in koji to 10^6 or less organisms per gram by starting with 10^2 or less bacteria per gram of raw materials in the preliminary stage of koji cultivation. It is effective for the same purpose to reduce the moisture content of the surface of cooked soybeans by wrapping the soybean particles with roasted and then finely crushed wheat. Furthermore, the temperature effective in preventing bacterial contamination in koji production was reported to be below 34 °C (Ishigami & Ueda, 1965, 1967; Ueda *et al.*, 1972).

Mechanical equipment for koji cultivation is classified as follows:

(1) Through-flow system of aeration (Fig. 7).

    (a) Batch-type with a rectangular perforated plate.
    (b) Batch-type with a circular moving perforated plate.
    (c) Continuous-type with a circular moving perforated plate.

(2) Rotary drum.
(3) Surface-flow system of aeration:

    Temperature and moisture controlled air flows over the materials put in many trays. The traditional method.

(4) Liquid cultivation.

Nos (1a) and (1b) can deal with about 5–10 tons of raw materials in one batch, and No. (1c) 3–4 tons per hour. The rectangular perforated plate of

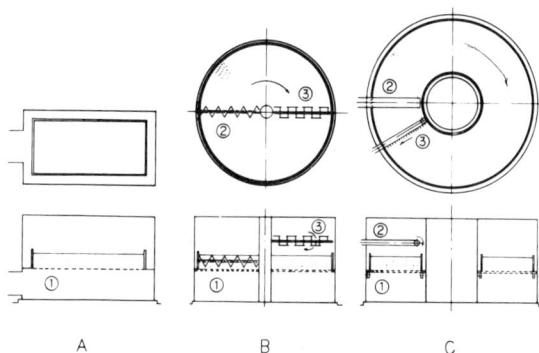

Fig. 7. Koji culturing machines with through-flow system of aeration. A, rectangular type; 1, perforated plate. B, circular type (batch); 1, perforated plate; 2, feed and discharge screw; 3, mixer. C, circular type (continuous); 1, perforated plate; 2, feed conveyor; 3, discharge conveyor.

apparatus (1a) was changed to a doughnut-shaped plate equipped with mechanical washer, material charger to the plate, a device to mix the materials, a discharger of finished koji, and automatic temperature and humidity controller, which greatly reduced the labour cost, and above all, improved the quality of the koji. This is the batch-type machine (1b), and the perforated plate is moved only when it is necessary to charge the materials on the plate, to mix the materials with the fixed mixer, and to discharge the finished koji. The continuous koji making machine equipped with a constantly moving doughnut-shaped perforated plate with a diameter of 33 m appeared 10 years ago, and it can deal with 50–100 tons of raw materials a day (Akao *et al.*, 1972). No. (2) is widely used for the production of rice-koji for making miso. No. (3) is not so popular nowadays. The application of liquid cultivation of koji for the protein food industries has not yet been successfully employed in practice, because of the high cost of facilities and the lack of flavour in the final products.

5.5. Mash Fermentation

5.5.1. Microbes in Mash

The pH value of shoyu mash starts at 6·5–7·0, depending upon the pH value of the koji, which is greatly affected by the extent of contamination by acid-forming bacteria such as *Micrococcus*. The water activity (A_w) of 18 % salt water is 0·88, and that of a typical well-aged mash is 0·80. The types of microbes which can grow in the shoyu mash are limited by 16–18 % salt concentrations, pH and A_w values as above. The non-salt-tolerant microbes derived from koji such as wild yeasts, *Micrococcus,* and *Bacillus* are destroyed or cease growing at the beginning of mash fermentation, and only salt-tolerant lactic acid bacteria and salt-tolerant yeasts are active in shoyu mash. The major lactic acid bacterium in shoyu mash was shown to be *Pediococcus soyae* (Kenji Sakaguchi, 1958), and it was morphologically identified as *Pediococcus halophylus* (Buchanan & Gibbons, 1974). It was found that its optimum pH is 5·5–9·0, A_w is more than 0·81, and that it can grow in 24% salt solution at highest rates in the temperature range 20–42 °C.

The initial pH value of shoyu mash rapidly decreases in accordance with the enzymatic degradation of proteins into lower peptides and free amino acids and with lactic acid fermentation. And at around the time when the pH value becomes 5·5 or less, the growth of the yeast *Saccharomyces rouxii* begins and takes the place of lactobacilli, and reaches a viable count of 10^6–10^7/ml. The dominant strains of yeast found in shoyu mash are *Saccharomyces rouxii,* but sometimes *Torulopsis* yeasts such as *T. versatilis* and *T. etchellsii* are found along with or continuing after *Saccharomyces rouxii* in shoyu mash fermentation. The A_w of *Saccharomyces rouxii* and *Torulopsis* yeasts are 0·78–0·81 and 0·84–0·98, respectively, and both of them can grow in up to 24–26% salt concentrations (Yoshii, 1979). These yeasts can grow at pH 3–7 in salt-free media, but this range is shortened to 4–5 in 18% salt solution (Onishi, 1957, 1963). The changes of microflora in shoyu mash are indicated in Fig. 8 (Tamagawa *et al.,* 1975).

5.5.2. Chemical Changes in Shoyu Mash Fermentation

The enzymatic degradation of proteins from the raw materials into lower peptides, free amino acids and ammonia almost stops in 2 or 3 months from the beginning, depending upon the temperature. The carbohydrates are hydrolysed to hexoses and pentoses, and these are metabolised partly into about 1% of lactic acid and other organic acids by lactobacilli and partly into 2–3% of ethanol and other minor flavorous compounds by yeasts, and 2–4% of glucose and trace amounts of xylose usually remain in the final mash. If the mash is adequately controlled, lactic and alcoholic fermentations are almost completed in 3–4 months from the beginning, but an additional 3–4 months are necessary to finish the mash fermentation or aging, which mainly consists of so-called browning reactions such as Strecker degradations and other reactions. The colour degree of shoyu mash becomes about double in this latter stage of fermentation, and the pH value ends up at around 4·8–5·0.

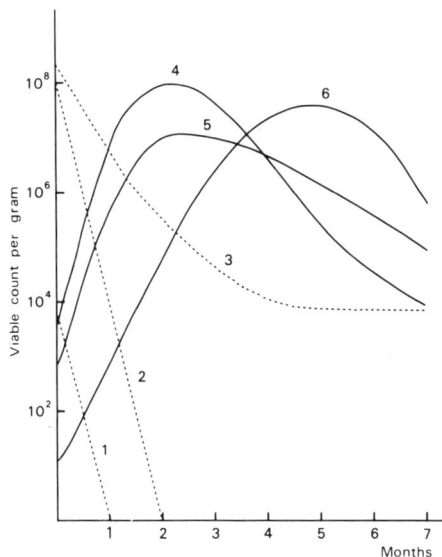

Fig. 8. Microflora changes in shoyu mash fermentation. 1, wild yeasts; 2, *Micrococcus* spp.; 3, *Bacillus* spp.; 4, lactobacilli; 5, *Saccharomyces rouxii*; 6, *Torulopsis* spp. (From Tamagawa *et al.*, 1975.)

The diversity of lactobacilli in shoyu mash which is related to the aroma, pH and colour of shoyu (Fujimoto *et al.*, 1978, 1980), metabolism of organic acids (Terasawa *et al.*, 1979), sugars and some amino acids such as arginine, histidine, tyrosine and aspartic acid (Uchida, 1978) have been pointed out. Uchida (1982) classified the lactobacilli in shoyu mash into 67 types of strain according to their metabolism of ten types of sugar including glucose, arabinose, lactose, melibiose, mannitol and sorbitol. In addition, it was found that some strains metabolise arginine into ornithine (Iizuka & Goan, 1973) or histidine into histamine, or tyrosine into tyramine, and so increase the pH value of the shoyu mash. Some other strains metabolise aspartic acid into alanine and carbon dioxide and increase the pH value of the mash. Some of them convert citric acid into acetic acid and malic acid, the latter of which is metabolised into lactic acid and acetic acid (Terasawa *et al.*, 1979).

5.5.3. Temperature of Mash

Under the natural temperature change, the shoyu prepared in summer had such characteristics as a smaller content of total nitrogen, amino nitrogen and glutamic acid; and a greater content of organic acids, and inferior organoleptic evaluation, as compared to shoyu prepared in winter. By reducing the temperature of the new mash, a 1–3% increase of protein digestibility is expected, because the lower temperature prevents the rapid decrease of pH value caused by rapid lactic fermentation, which inactivates the alkaline protease (Goan, 1957; Tazaki *et al.*, 1969; Imai *et al.*, 1969). The general method of mash making nowadays is to mix koji with saline water at about 0 °C, to keep the temperature of the new mash below 15 °C for several days and then gradually raise it up to 28–30 °C after 20–30 days from the beginning (Ebine *et al.*, 1976).

It has been pointed out that the glutaminase, which is derived from koji moulds, is rather sensitive to heat and its activity rapidly decreases in new mash (Kuroshima *et al.*, 1969). Adding salt- and heat-tolerant glutaminase of some strains of yeasts to the new mash is effective in increasing the glutamic acid content of the final product by some 20%, regardless of the temperature of the new mash (Yokotsuka *et al.*, 1968b, 1970, 1972; Iwasa *et al.*, 1972a, b).

5.5.4. Period of Mash Fermentation

Years ago, it was said that commercial shoyu was prepared by blending one, two, and three year mash in a certain ratio, because one year mash was good in flavour, two years mash good in taste, and three years mash good in colour. It took 18 months to attain the maximum content of glutamic acid in mash in 1931, 10 months in 1953, and now about 3 months. This period of mash fermentation in getting to the highest content of glutamic acid was utilised in judging the completion of fermentation. The remarkable increase of protein digestibility in shoyu production which is due both to the improvements in soybean cooking and to koji cultivation in recent years, has also contributed to the shortening of the fermentation period to less than one year.

Good results were reported by adding pure cultured lactobacilli to the new mash (Jose & Sugimori, 1973). Care must be taken not to add too much lactic starter which causes the rapid pH decrease and the decrease of protein digestibility.

To accelerate the alcoholic fermentation and to shorten its period, pure cultured yeasts, *Saccharomyces rouxii*, are sometimes added to the shoyu mash, when its pH value becomes about 5·3, usually 3–4 weeks after the mash making (Watanabe *et al.*, 1970). The addition of *Torulopsis* yeasts along with *Saccharomyces rouxii* was recommended to obtain a good volatile flavour in the finished product (Suzuki *et al.*, 1972).

The control of shoyu mash at lower temperature in the preliminary stage of fermentation sometimes limits the growth of yeasts and makes it necessary to add a pure cultured yeast starter. On the contrary, it is not always necessary to add lactobacillus starter in such a case. The adding of yeast starter, both of *Saccharomyces* and *Torulopsis*, sometimes becomes very important to the mash which is stored in the resin-coated iron tanks, because the natural starter of yeasts in these tanks is usually insufficient, a difference from the wooden kegs or the tanks made of concrete (Noda *et al.*, 1979, 1981a, b, 1982a, b).

The factors which limit the activities of lactobacilli and yeasts most significantly in shoyu mash were found to be its salt content for the former and its ether extract such as guaiacol and vanillin, and alcohol for the latter (Sakasai *et al.*, 1975a, b, c; Noda *et al.*, 1976a, b, c). Lactic acid fermentation is affected by the yeasts derived from koji and others (Kusumoto *et al.*, 1977; Fujimoto *et al.*, 1978).

5.6. Refining
5.6.1. Pressing of Mash
An aged mash is press-filtered through cloth under hydraulic pressure. Two types of new pressing machine for shoyu mash are becoming popular nowadays. In one case, the principle of pressing is the same as above but it uses a long sheet of filter cloth instead of separate sheets, and the mash is mechanically charged on to the cloth which is then folded in a tall cage and pressed. The use of long sheets of cloth is convenient for automatic removal of the residue from the cloth, for automatic washing of the cloth, and for folding the cloth into a roll. One machine can process 10–30 klitres mash a day. Another one is a diaphragm type of press filter with automatic devices. One machine can be charged with 10–100 klitres mash at one time. The pressing is finished within a day or two depending upon the pressure applied, which ranges between 50 and 100 kg/cm^2.

The difficulty in the pressing of shoyu mash has been much decreased in accordance with the increase of protein digestibility in recent years. The activity of plant tissue degrading enzymes involved in the koji is greatly associated with the decrease of viscosity and the amount of press-cake of shoyu mash. Pectin transeliminase was claimed to have the most important role in this case (Ishii *et al.*, 1972). On the other hand, the compounds which are most responsible for the difficulty in pressing of shoyu mash were found to be the acidic polysaccharides derived from soybeans (Kikuchi, 1975, 1979; Kikuchi *et al.*, 1976).

5.6.2. Pasteurisation
The filtrate of an aged mash is heated to 70–80 °C in order to stop the greater part of microbial and enzymatic reactions. The formation of an

agreeable brown colour, the separation of heat-coagulable substances, the increase of acidity, colour, clarity, and antiyeast potency, the full development of good shoyu flavour, the decrease of reducing sugar and amino acid content, and the evaporation of volatile compounds are major changes in the course of this heating (Yokotsuka 1954, Yokotsuka & Takimoto, 1956, 1958; Okuhara *et al.*, 1961, Ohnishi, 1970, 1971, 1972, 1975, 1976). Retarding alcohol evaporation during pasteurisation of shoyu was indicated to improve its organoleptic evaluation. In Japan, benzoic acid or butyl-*p*-hydroxybenzoate are legally added to the refined shoyu as preservative but the trend seems to be toward either aseptic bottling of shoyu, or bottling shoyu which is fortified with ethanol as preservative.

The coagulum produced by the heating of raw shoyu is equivalent to 10% in volume and 0·025–0·05% in weight of shoyu, and it consists of mainly proteins derived from the koji mould or 70–80% proteins and 15–20% sugars (Motai *et al.*, 1982). The protein molecules associate with each other through hydrophobic bonds by the action both of heat and proteases. The acid proteinase (optimum pH 5·0) mostly accelerates the coagulation on heating. Adding such kinds of protease, above all a heat tolerant one from outside, also accelerates this formation (Hashimoto & Yokotsuka, 1971, 1972, 1973, 1974, 1976).

On the other hand, it was reported that the alkaline protease mostly accelerated the heat coagulum formation of raw shoyu among the proteases of koji (Tamura *et al.*, 1982). Motai *et al.* (1982) reported that the alkaline protease accelerates the heat coagulum formation of raw shoyu, but the heat coagulum consisted of particles of very small size, which it was difficult to induce to sediment. This sedimentation in pasteurised shoyu was accelerated by the acid-protease of koji, not by amylase, and the alkaline protease hindered the sedimentation of coagulated substances. The volume of the sediment of heat coagulated substances at the bottom of containers of pasteurised shoyu very much influences the yield of refined shoyu. Noda *et al.* (1982) kept the aged shoyu mash at 40 °C for 120 h, or at 45 °C for 72 h, or at 50 °C for 24 h in order to reduce the activity of protease and amylase, thereby reducing the heat coagulum formation by 60%, or 84%, or 99%, respectively.

5.7. Product

5.7.1. Colour of Shoyu

The colour increase of shoyu by an oxidative reaction during consumption after opening a seal is an important problem, because some flavour deterioration is observed along with the colour darkening. Factors influencing the oxidative colour increase of shoyu which have been identified up to the present time include temperature, the initial colour degree, and the contents of such ingredients of shoyu as total nitrogen, sugars, carbonyls, peptides, amino acids, 3-deoxy-osones, Amadori compounds, reductones, organic acids, iron, copper, sodium chloride, etc. (Okuhara *et al.*, 1970, 1971, 1972, 1975, 1976; Hashiba, 1971, 1978, 1979).

5.7.2. Flavour Evaluation of Koikuchi Shoyu

The fragrance of a fermented shoyu was found to be roughly proportional to its ethanol content which is produced by yeast fermentation. A multivariate analysis indicated that the contributing proportion of the eleven chemical components to the preference of a shoyu was only 46·3 %. Among the partial correlation coefficients of the eleven chemical components such as alcohol, degrees Baumé (density), sodium chloride, reducing sugar, total nitrogen, formol nitrogen, titrable acidity and pH, the alcohol content had the highest value. Eleven types of odorous characters elucidated 96·5 % of preference of odour of shoyu by a multivariate analysis. Fragrance and alcoholic smell were positive contributions, while smell of chemical hydrolysate of plant protein mixed with fermented shoyu, oily smell, natto smell, abnormal smell, butyric acid smell, smell of shoyu mash fermented at too high temperature, cooked soybean smell, and mouldy smell were negative contributions to the preference in descending order. Nine types of characteristics regarding taste elucidated 97·6 % of the preference to taste of shoyu. Good after-taste, pure taste, and palatable taste had the highest positive correlation coefficients, while too sweet, too sour, abnormal taste, and the lack of harmony and body were the opposite. It was concluded that a good flavour shoyu must be made by a totally fermentative method, free from disagreeable odour derived from bacterial contamination, must be well fermented by yeasts, and its chemical components must be well balanced (Saito & Tanaka, 1967; Tanaka *et al.*, 1969a, b, 1970). According to the result of multivariate analysis, an organoleptically preferable shoyu has not only good harmony of taste components such as salty, acidic, sweet, bitter, and delicious, but good aroma (Mori, 1979).

5.7.3. Flavour Components of Shoyu

The importance of the volatile fraction of shoyu was indicated by the fact that the organoleptic ranking of two samples of shoyu could be reversed by exchanging their volatile fractions which were prepared by steam-distillation of the samples *in vacuo*, 15 mm Hg, at 40 °C.

Japanese investigators have identified nearly 300 kinds of volatile flavour compounds in the fragrance of Koikuchi shoyu, which include 51 carbonyls, 24 organic acids, 41 esters, 31 alcohols, 3 acetals, 11 sulphur compounds, 36 nitrogenous compounds, 17 phenols, and 62 others (Yokotsuka 1953, 1975, Yokotsuka & Takimoto, 1956; Asao *et al.*, 1958, 1967, 1977; Sasaki, 1975; Sasaki & Nunomura, 1978; Nunomura *et al.*, 1976, 1977, 1978a, b).

The most important part of the fragrance characteristic in shoyu seems to exist in its weak acidic fraction.

The important flavorous compounds isolated from the weak acidic fraction of Koikuchi shoyu are as follows:

(1) Methionol (3-methylthio-l-propanol)(Akabori & Kaneko, 1936).

(2) 4-Ethyl guaiacol and *p*-ethyl phenol (Yokotsuka, 1953; Asao & Yokotsuka, 1958).

(3) Phenol esters between phenolic compounds such as 4-ethyl guaiacol, vanillic acid, vanillin, and organic acids such as benzoic acid and acetic acid (Yokotsuka, 1953).

(4) Maltol (Kihara, 1940; Nunomura *et al.*, 1976) and 5-hydroxy maltol (Nunomura *et al.*, 1980).

(5) Hydroxy-furanones (Nunomura *et al.*, 1976, 1977, 1979).
   HEMF (4-OH-2(or 5)-Et-5(or 2)-Me-2(H)-furan-3one)
   HMF (4-OH-5Me-3(2H)-furanone)
   HDMF (4-OH-2,5,di Me-3(2H)-furanone)

(6) Cyclothen (2-OH-3Me-2-cyclopentene-1-one)

(7) Lactones such as 4-butanolide, 4-pentanolide, 2-Me-4-butanolide (Nunomura *et al.*, 1980), and 4-hexanolide (Liardon and Phillipposian, 1978).

About 25% of 50–70 samples of shoyu tested in 1964 contained 0·5–2·0 ppm 4-ethylguaiacol (4EG). The organoleptically best 10 samples except one, and only one sample among the remaining 40 samples contained 4EG (Yokotsuka *et al.*, 1967a). It was observed that 4EG also had the taste characteristic of fermented shoyu and moreover that it ameliorated the salty taste of shoyu. 4-ethylguaiacol and *p*-ethylphenol are produced by *Torulopsis* yeasts such as *T. etchellsii* and *T. versatilis*, and not by *Saccharomyces rouxii*, that is the predominant yeasts of shoyu mash (Yokotsuka *et al.*, 1967b; Asao *et al.*, 1967). The yeast flora in 35 kinds of shoyu mash obtained in Hokkaido (northernmost island of Japan) was investigated in 1960, and it was found that the organoleptically good mashes were well populated with *Torulopsis etchellsii* and *T. versatilis* (Sasaki & Yoshida, 1966, 1972; Yoshida, 1979).

The 4EG contents of three types of the popular brand of Koikuchi-shoyu were reported to be 1·0, 1·8 and 2·1 ppm, respectively, and those of three types of Usukuchi-shoyu were 0·5, 1·3 and 0·3 ppm, respectively (Noda & Nakano, 1979).

Hydroxy furanones such as HEMF, HMF and HDMF have a caramel-like flavour. HEMF seems to be the most important ingredient or the character impact component of fermented shoyu fragrance because of its high content of more than 100 ppm and its very low threshold value of 0·04 ppb or less in water (Nunomura *et al.*, 1976). Nunomura *et al.* (1978a, 1980) identified 70 kinds of pyrazine in shoyu. The contents of 4 major pyrazines and their significant increase in the course of pasteurisation were pointed out. The flavour differences among four major brands of shoyu from the Japanese market were explained by the differences in their volatile flavour contents among the proportions of isobutyl alcohol 0·43–1·99, n-butyl alcohol 0·46–1·48, isoamyl alcohol 1·08–3·63, acetoin 0·74–1·51, ethyl lactate 4·04–13·15, furfuryl alcohol 2·02–3·55, methionol 1·47–3·39, 2-phenylethanol 1·61–3·67, 4-ethylguaiacol 0·31–1·31 ppm (Sasaki *et al.*, 1975). According to Mori *et al.* (1982, 1983), the correlation coefficients between the 27 kinds of odour component and the sensory evaluation of shoyu was 0·313 at highest, which suggested that it was difficult to predict the scale value of shoyu by only one kind of odour component. The combination of 4-ethylguaiacol and methionol was found to have a kind of synergic effect resembling that of so-called blending effects which are recognised with many foodstuffs, and the combination was revealed as the most significant variable in the model which chiefly influences the variation of sensory data. The optimum contents of 4EG and methionol were found to be 0·8 and 3·9 ppm, respectively, which were confirmed by adding both materials to test shoyu.

5.7.4. Nutrition

According to the governmental report, each Japanese person consumed 18·6 g of miso and 30·0 ml of shoyu per day in 1974. The former was equivalent to 29·2 cal, 2·3 g protein, 0·6 g fat, and 1·86 g salt, and the latter was equivalent to 14·0 cal, 2·4 g protein, 0·2 g fat, and 5·46 g salt. The salt contents were calculated on the basis of 10 % for miso and 16 % for shoyu. From these figures, it is calculated that one Japanese person's daily salt intake from miso and shoyu is 7·32 g. The daily salt intake in Japan per person in 1972 was 14·5 g, while it decreased to 12·4 g in 1983, ranging from

10 g to over 15 g, depending upon the district, in 1983. On the other hand, a high incidence of high blood pressure, especially in the district of high salt consumption in the northern part of Japan, has been seriously pointed out. For these reasons, it is an urgent problem for the miso and shoyu producers to reduce the salt contents of their products. The production of less-salt miso and shoyu, in which the salt contents are cut by 20–50 %, has been gradually increasing in the Japanese market.

5.7.5. Safety Problems

Debates about the aflatoxin problem regarding shoyu and miso are not so heated as formerly, because almost all the research to date to detect aflatoxin producers among the Japanese food industrial moulds has yielded negative results and, at the same time, it has come to be widely known that the aflatoxin producing strains of the mould, *Aspergillus flavus*, can not grow in the districts where the average temperature in a year is below 16 °C. Nevertheless, we have to be very cautious about the toxin producing ability of *Aspergillus* seed starter.

The long term effect of Koikuchi shoyu (Kikkoman) on the gastric mucosa was assessed in intact rats and in those with a fundasectomy by MacDonald and Dueck in Canada (1976). The animals given shoyu for 29 months were smaller than the controls but healthier, more active and longer lived. Breast tumours developed in the control rats but none in those given shoyu. It was concluded that shoyu did not appear to be carcinogenic to the rats; its prolonged use impaired neither health nor longevity. In long term feeding tests of shoyu for mice and rats carried out by the Kikkoman Company, no carcinogenicity was observed, supporting the Canadian workers' results.

The mutagenicity of heated products of amino acids or proteins is widely known nowadays. Secliff and Mower (1977) reported that upon heating, soy sauce produces mutagens from glucose, galactose, and arabinose in it. Lin *et al.* (1978) reported that when treated with nitrite at the 2000 ppm level, soybean sauce produced a mutagenic substance as demonstrated using a *Salmonella*/mammalian microsome mutagenicity test. Nagahori *et al.* (1980) reported on a 60–80 % suppression of N-nitroso dimethylamine formation by adding 5–7 % fermented shoyu to a mixture of dimethylamine and nitrite at pH 3·6. They concluded that the nitrosamine-formation-hindering substances in shoyu were amino acids, which more easily react with nitrite than dimethylamine by the so-called Vanslyke reaction.

REFERENCES

AIBA, T. (1982) Proceedings of the 14th Symposium on Brewing, p. 20.

AIBARA, K. and MIYAKI, K. (1965) *Proc. Agr. Chem. Soc. Japan*, p. 86.

AKABORI, S. & KANEKO, T. (1936) *J. Chem. Soc. Japan* **57**(8), 828.

AKAO, T., SAKASAI, T., SAKAI, M., TAKANO, A. & YOKOTSUKA, T. (1972) First Pacific Chemical Engineering Congress, Kyoto, Japan. Oct. 10–14, pp. 127–8.

AONUMA, A., YASUDA, A., YUASA, T., ARAI, A., MOGI, K. & YOKOTSUKA, T. (1970, 1971) Japanese patent 794,915, and US patent 3,764,708.

ASAO, Y. & YOKOTSUKA, T. (1958) *J. Agr. Chem. Soc. Japan* **32**(8), 617, 622.

ASAO, Y., SAKASAI, T. & YOKOTSUKA, T. (1967) *J. Agr. Chem. Soc. Japan* **41**(9), 434.

ASAO, Y. & YOKOTSUKA, T. (1977) *Chemical Components in Fermented Foods*. Brewing Society of Japan, Takinogawa 2–6, Kitaku, Tokyo, Japan, p. 376.

BUCHANAN, R. E. and GIBBONS, N. E. (1974) *Bergey's Manual of Determinative Bacteriology*. The Williams & Wilkins Co., Baltimore, USA, p. 515.

EBINE, H. (1980) *Science of Foods*, **56**, 59.

EBINE, H., KIMURA, E., FUKUZAKI, K., FURUTA, T., MAEDA, H. & YOKOTSUKA, T. (1976) Standard production and circulation of shoyu. Bureau of Food, Japan, p. 73.

EGUCHI, U. (1977) *J. Brew. Soc. Japan*. **72**, 250.

FUJIMOTO, H., AIBA, T. & GOAN, M. (1978, 1980) *J. Japan Soy Sauce Res. Inst.* **4**, 191; **6**, 5, 10, 213.

FUKUSHIMA, D. & MOGI, M. (1955) Japanese patent 236,368, 238,805.

FUKUSHIMA, D. & MOGI, M. (1957) Japanese patent 248,103.

GOAN, M. (1957) *Seasoning Sci.* **7**(1), 7.

HAGA, H. (1968) *J. Brew. Soc. Japan* **63**(9), 931.

HARADA, Y. (1951) Report. Tatsuno Brewing Institute **2**, 51.

HARADA, Y. & KAWAGUCHI, S. (1968) Nihon Maruten Shoyu Co., Japanese patent, applied Feb. 26.

HASHIBA, H. (1971) *Seasoning Sci.* **18**(3), 9.

HASHIBA, H. (1978) *Agr. Biol. Chem.* **42**(4), 763.

HASHIBA, H. (1979) *J. Japan Soy Sauce Res. Inst.* **5**(4), 169, 295.

HASHIMOTO, H. & YOKOTSUKA, T. (1971, 1972, 1973, 1974) *J. Ferment. Technol.* **49**(7), 642; **50**(4), 257; **51**(9), 661; **52**(5), 328.

HASHIMOTO, H. & YOKOTSUKA, T. (1976) *J. Brew. Soc. Japan* **71**(7), 496.

HAYASHI, K., TERADA, M. & MIZUNUMA, T. (1981) *J. Japan Soy Sauce Res. Inst.* **7**(4), 166.

HESSELTINE, C. W. & WANG, H. L. (1972) 'Fermented Soybean Food Product'. In *Soybeans: Chemistry and Technology*. The Avi Publishing Company, Inc. Westport, Connecticut, USA, pp. 389–419.

HESSELTINE, C. W., SHOTWELL, O. L., ELLIS, J. J. & STUBBLEFIELD, R. D. (1966) *Am. Soc. Microbiol.* **30**(4), 795.

IGUCHI, N. & NASUNO, S. (1978) *J. Ferment. Technol.* **56**(5), 645.

IIJIMA, K., DEJIMA, M., TSUJI, A., WATANABE, T. & KAGAMI, T. (1973) *Seasoning Sci.* **20**, 13.

IIZUKA, K. & GOAN, M. (1973) *Seasoning Sci.* **20**(1), 17.

IMAI, S. & SUZUKI, K. (1967) *ibid.* **14**(2), 22.

IMAI, S., SUZUKI, K. & KANEKO, M. (1969) *ibid.* **16**(5), 1.

ISHIGAMI, T. & UEDA, R. (1965, 1967) *J. Ferm. Tech.* **43**, 165; **45**, 1003.

ISHII, S., KIKUCHI, T. & YOKOTSUKA, T. (1969, 1970) *J. Agr. Chem. Soc. Japan* **43**, 536, 544; **44**, 299, 306.

ISHII, S., KIKUCHI, T., OGAMI, T. & YOKOTSUKA, T. (1972) *J. Agr. Chem. Soc. Japan* **49**(7), 349.

IWASA, T., FUJII, S., KAKINUMA, T. & YOKOTSUKA, T. (1972a) Presented at the annual meeting of Agr. Chem. Soc. Japan at Sendai, April 2.

IWASA, T., FUJII, S. & YOKOTSUKA, T. (1972b) Presented at the 4th International Fermentation Symposium, Kyoto, Japan, Mar. 19–25.

JOSE, H. & SUGIMORI, T. (1973) *Seasoning Sci.* **20**(9), 19.

KIHARA, K. (1940) *J. Chem. Soc. Japan* **43**, 876.

KIKUCHI, T. (1975) *J. Agr. Chem. Soc. Japan* **49**(4), 231.

KIKUCHI, T. (1979) *J. Japan Soy Sauce Res. Inst.* **5**(2), 71.

KIKUCHI, T., SUGIMOTO, H. & YOKOTSUKA, T. (1976) *J. Agr. Chem. Soc. Japan* **50**(6), 279.

KINOSHITA, R., ISHIKO, T., SUGIYAMA, S., SETO, T., IGARASHI, S. & GOETZ, I. E. (1968) *Cancer Res.* **28**, 2296.

KUROSHIMA, E., OYAMA, Y., MATSUO, T. & SUGIMORI, T. (1969) *J. Ferment. Technol.* **47**, 693.

KUSUMOTO, E., INAMORI, K., UCHIDA, K. & YOSHINO, H. (1977) *J. Japan Soy Sauce Res. Inst.* **3**(6), 283.

LEE, CHERL-HO & MOGEN JUL (1981) The effect of Korean soysauce fermentation on the quality of soybean. The 8th ASKA meeting, Medan, Indonesia, February 9–15.

LIARDON, R. & PHILLIPPOSIAN, G. (1978) *Z. Lebensm. Unters. Forsch.* **167**, 180.

LIE, GOANG-HONG (1981) Nutritional aspects of fermented foods in Indonesia. Presented at the 8th ASKA meeting. Medan, Indonesia, February 9–15.

LIN, J. Y., WANG, H. I. & YEN, Y. C. (1978) *Consumer Toxicol.* **17**, 329.

MACDONALD, W. C. & DUECK, J. W. (1976) *J. nat. Cancer Inst.* **56**(6), 1148.

MANABE, M., MATSUURA, S. & NAKANO, M. (1968) *Nippon Shokuhin Kogyo Gakkaishi* **15**(8), 7.

MASUDA, G., MORI, K. & KURATSUNE, M. (1965) Paper presented at the annual meeting of the Japan Cancer Association, Fukuoka, Oct. 16.

MIYAZAKI, K. & HONKAWA, Y. (1964) *Seasoning Sci.* **11**(4), 21.

MORI, S. (1979) *J. Brew. Soc. Japan* **74**(8), 526.

MORI, S., NUNOMURA, N. & SASAKI, M. (1982) Proceedings of annual meeting, Agr. Chem. Soc. Japan, March 30th, at Kyoto, p. 34.

MORI, S., NUNOMURA, N. & SASAKI, M. (1983) Proceedings of annual meeting, Agr. Chem. Soc. Japan, April 1st, at Sendai, p. 236.

MOTAI, H., HAYASHI, K., ISHIYAMA, T. & MIZUNUMA, T. (1982) Proceedings of 16th meeting of Japan Soy Sauce Research Inst., pp. 9–10.

MURAKAMI, H., TAKASE, S. & ISHII, T. (1967) *J. gen. appl. Microbiol.* **13**, 323; **14**, 97, 251.

NAGAHORI, T., MOTAI, H. & OKUHARA, T. (1980) *Nutrition and Foods* **33**(3), 151.

NAKADAI, T. (1977) *J. Japan Soy Sauce Res. Inst.* **3**(3), 99.

NASUNO, S., OHARA, T. & IGUCHI, N. (1971a) *Agr. Biol. Chem.* **35**, 291.

NASUNO, S. & OHARA, T. (1971b) *ibid.* **35**, 836.

NASUNO, S. & NAKADAI, T. (1971c) *J. Ferment. Technol.* **49**, 544.

NASUNO, S. & ONO, T. (1972) *Seasoning Sci.* **19**(10), 41.

NODA, F., SAKASAI, T. & YOKOTSUKA, T. (1976a, b, c). *Nippon Shokuhin Kogyo Gakkaishi* **23**(2), 53, 59, 67.

NODA, Y., MINE, H. & NAKANO, M. (1982) *J. Japan Soy Sauce Res. Inst.* **8**(4), 176–181.

NODA, Y., NAKANO, M. *et al.* (1979, 1981a, b, 1982a, b) *J. Japan Soy Sauce Res. Inst.* **5**(6), 299; **7**(2), 64, (4), 173; **8**(1), 28, (3), 108.

NODA, Y. & NAKANO, M. (1979) *J. Japan. Soy Sauce Res. Inst.* **5**(6), 299.

NUNOMURA, N., SASAKI, M., ASAO, Y. & YOKOTSUKA, T. (1976) *Agr. Biol. Chem.* **40**(3), 485, 491.

NUNOMURA, N., SASAKI, M., ASAO, Y. & YOKOTSUKA, T. (1977) *J. Agr. Chem. Soc. Japan* **51**(12), 709.

NUNOMURA, N., SASAKI, M., ASAO, Y. & YOKOTSUKA, T. (1978a) *Agr. Biol. Chem.* **42**(11), 2123.

NUNOMURA, N., SASAKI, M. & YOKOTSUKA, T. (1978b) Presented at the annual meeting. Agr. Chem. Soc. Japan., Nagoya, Apr. 13.

NUNOMURA, N., SASAKI, M. & YOKOTSUKA, T. (1979) *Agr. Biol. Chem.* **43**(6), 1361,

NUNOMURA, N., SASAKI, M. & YOKOTSUKA, T. (1980) *ibid.* **44**, 399.

OHARA, H., MORIGUCHI, S. & NISHIYAMA, T. (1959) *Seasoning Sci.* **7**(3), 25, 35.

OHTAKA, H. & HAKAI, T. (1972) Proceedings of the annual meeting of Ferm. Techn. Japan, p. 39.

OHTSUKI, H., KANEMATSU, Y. & HONKAWA, Y. (1982) *J. Japan Soy Sauce Res. Inst.* **6**(6), 242–7.

OKUHARA, A. & YOKOTSUKA, T. (1958, 1961, 1962, 1963). *J. Agr. Chem. Soc. Japan.* **32**, 138; **35**, 447; **36**, 320; **37**, 255.

OKUHARA, A., TANAKA, T., SAITO, N. & YOKOTSUKA, T. (1970) *J. Ferment. Technol.* **48**(4), 228.

OKUHARA, A., SAITO, N. & YOKOTSUKA, T. (1971) *ibid.* **49**(3), 272.

OKUHARA, A., SAITO, N. & YOKOTSUKA, T. (1972) *ibid* **50**(4), 264.

OKUHARA, A., SAIKI, M. & SASAKI, S. (1975) *J. Japan Shoyu Res. Inst.* **1**(4), 185.

OKUHARA, A. (1976) *J. Brew. Soc. Japan* **71**(8), 603.

ONG-KIM LIAN (1981) Some traditional foods in Singapore. Presented at the 8th ASKA meeting. Medan, Indonesia, February 9–15.

ONISHI, H. (1957) *J. Agr. Chem. Soc. Japan* **21**, 137, 143.

ONISHI, H. (1963) *J. Brew. Soc. Japan* **58**, 602.

ONISHI, T. (1970, 1971, 1972). *Seasoning Sci.* **17**(4), 103; **18**(5), 46; **19**(2), 30.

ONISHI, T. (1975) *J. Brew. Soc. Japan* **70**(7), 471.

ONISHI, T. (1976) *J. Japan Soy Sauce Res. Inst.* **2**(6), 269.

SAITO, N. & TANAKA, T. (1967) *J. Ferment. Technol.* **45**(3), 246, 1023.

SAKAGUCHI, KENJI (1958) *Bull. Agr. Chem. Soc. Japan* **22**, 353.

SAKAGUCHI, KINICHIRO (1979) Search for the route of shoyu. *Sekai* **1**, 252–66.

SAKASAI, T., NODA, F. & YOKOTSUKA, T. (1975a, b, c) *Nippon Shokuhin Kogyo Gakkaishi* **22**(10), 474, 481, 530.

SASAKI, M. (1975) Proceedings of 7th symposium on brewing, Sept. 4, p. 30.

SASAKI, M. (1980) Unpublished data, Kikkoman Corp.

SASAKI, M., KIKUCHI, T., ASAO, Y. & YOKOTSUKA, T. (1967) *J. Agr. Chem. Soc. Japan* **41**(4), 154.

SASAKI, M., ASAO, Y. & YOKOTSUKA, T. (1968) *ibid.* **42**(5), 288, 351.

SASAKI, M., KANEKO, Y., OHSHITA, K., TAKAMATSU, H., ASAO, Y. & Yokotsuka, T. (1970) *Agr. Biol. Chem.* **34**(9), 1296.

SASAKI, M., KANEKO, Y., OHSHITA, K., TAKAMATSU, H., ASAO, Y. & YOKOTSUKA, T. (1974) *J. Agr. Chem. Soc. Japan* **48**(10), 569.

SASAKI, M., OHSHITA, K. & YOKOTSUKA, T. (1975) *ibid.* **49**(10), 553.

SASAKI, M., NUNOMURA, N., ASAO, Y. & YOKOTSUKA, T. (1975) Proceedings of the 11th Symposium on Brewing (T. Yokotsuka), Sept. 13, p. 62.

SASAKI, M. & NUNOMURA, N. (1978) *Chemy Ind.* **29**(10), 73.

SASAKI, M., NUNOMURA, N. & YOKOTSUKA, T. (1980) Proceedings of the annual meeting of Agr. Chem. Soc. Japan, p. 282.

SASAKI, T. & YOSHIDA, T. (1966) *J. Ferment. Technol.* **44**, 61, 158.

SASAKI, T. & YOSHIDA, T. (1972) Proceedings of Agr. Chem. Soc. Japan, p. 180.

SECLIFF, J. A. & MOWER, H. F. (1977) *Fed. Proc.* **36**, 304 (March).

SEKINE, H. (1972) *Agr. Biol. Chem.* **36**(2), 198, 207.

SEKINE, H. (1976) *ibid.* **40**(4), 703.

SHIBUYA, H. (1969) *Shoyu-Zukurino Jissai*, Chiqyu-Shokan, Ushigome, Tokyo.

SHIKATA, H., YASUI, T., ISHIGAMI, Y. & OHMORI, K. (1978) *J. Japan Soy Sauce Res. Inst.* **4**(1), 48.

SUZUKI, T., SHIBUYA, N., WATANABE, Y. & TAZAKI, R. (1972) *Seasoning Sci.* **19**(1), 30.

TAGAMI, H. & SUGAWARA, S. (1977) *J. Japan Soy Sauce Res. Inst.* **3**(3), 111.

TAMAGAWA, Y., YAMADA, K., TAKINAMI, K., KODAMA, K. & SUGA, T. (1975) Proceedings of annual meeting of Ferm. Tech, p. 212.

TAMURA, J., AIBA, T. & MOGI, K. (1982) Proceedings of annual meeting. Agr. Chem. Soc. Japan, p. 450.

TANAKA, T., SAITO, N. & YOKOTSUKA, T. (1969a) *J. Ferment. Technol.* **47**(12), 780.

TANAKA, T., SAITO, N. & YOKOTSUKA, T. (1969b) *Seasoning Sci.* **16**(3), 21.

TANAKA, T., SAITO, N. & YOKOTSUKA, T. (1970) *J. Ferment. Technol.* **48**(1), 56.

TATENO, M. & UMEDA, I. (1955) Japanese patent 204,858.

TAZAKI, R. & WATANABE, Y. (1966) *Seasoning Sci.* **13**(4), 1.

TAZAKI, R., WATANABE, Y., KUMAKI, T. & KOZAKI, M. (1969) *ibid.* **16**(4), 20.

TERADA, M., HAYASHI, K., MIZUNUMA, T. & MOGI, K. (1973) *Seasoning Sci.* **20**(2), 23.

TERADA, M., HAYASHI, K. & MIZUNUMA, T. (1979, 1981) *J. Japan Soy Sauce Res. Inst.* **6**(3), 75; **7**(4), 158.

TERASAWA, M., KADOWAKI, K., FUJIMOTO, H. & GOAN, M. (1979) *J. Japan Soy Sauce Res. Inst.* **5**, 15.

UCHIDA, K. (1978) Proceedings of annual meeting of Agr. Chem. Soc. Japan, p. 458.

UCHIDA, K. (1978) Proceedings. The 10th Symposium on Brewing, p. 77.

UCHIDA, K. (1982) *J. Gen. Appl. Microbiol.* **28**, 215, and Proceedings, 14th Symposium on Brewing, p. 67.

UEDA, R. *et al.* (1972) *Seasoning Sci.* **19**, 29, 31, 39.

WANG, H. L. & FUANG, S. F. (1981) History of Chinese fermented foods. Misc. Publ. FL-MS-33, NRRL, US Dept. Agriculture, Peoria, Illinois.

WATANABE, Y., ISHII, M. & TAZAKI, R. (1970) *Bull. Agr. Chem. Soc. Japan* **21**, 319.

YAMAGUCHI, S. (1954) Japanese patent 219,545.

YAMAGUCHI, S., OKUBO, K., IHO, K. & TATENO, M. (1961) Announcement. Japanese Patent Sho-36-346.

YAMAMOTO, K. (1957) *J. Agr. Chem. Soc. Japan* **21**, 319.

YASUDA, A., MOGI, K. & YOKOTSUKA, T. (1973a) *Seasoning Sci.* **20**, 20.

YASUDA, A., ARAI, A., TSUKADA, N., MOGE, K., AONUMA, T. & YOKOTSUKA, T. (1973b) *ibid.* **20**, 25.

YOKOTSUKA, T. (1953) *J. Agr. Chem. Soc. Japan* **27**(5), 276, (6), 334.

YOKOTSUKA, T. (1954) *ibid.* **28**(2), 114.

YOKOTSUKA, T. & TAKIMOTO, K. (1956) *ibid.* **30**(2), 66.

YOKOTSUKA, T. & TAKIMOTO, K. (1958) *ibid.* **32**(1), 23.

YOKOTSUKA, T., MOGI, K., FUKUSHIMA, D. & YASUDA, A. (1966) Japanese patent 929,910.

YOKOTSUKA, T. & SASAKI, M. (1980) Risks of mycotoxin in fermented foods, in: *Advances in Biotechnology*, Vol. II, ed. M. Moo-Young, Pergamon Press, Oxford, pp. 461–6.

YOKOTSUKA, T., SASAKI, M., KIKUCHI, T., ASAO, Y. & NOBUHARA, A. (1967a) *Biochemistry of some Foodborne Microbial Toxins*. R. R. Mateles and G. N. Wogan, Eds. The MIT Press, Cambridge, Mass., pp. 131–52.

YOKOTSUKA, T., SAKASAI, T. & ASAO, Y. (1967b) *J. Agr. Chem. Soc. Japan* **41**(9), 428, 442.

YOKOTSUKA, T., ASAO, Y., SASAKI, M. & OHSHITA, K. (1968a) Proceedings of the first US-Japan conference. Oct. 7–10, at Honolulu, Hawaii, p. 133. UJNR joint panel on toxic microorganisms and US Dept. of the Interior.

YOKOTSUKA, T., IWASA, T. & FUJII, S. (1968b) Japanese Patent 682,848.

YOKOTSUKA, T., OSHITA, K., KIKUCHI, T. & SASAKI, M. (1969) *J. Agr. Chem. Soc. Japan* **43**, 189.

YOKOTSUKA, T., IWASA, T. & FUJII, S. (1970) Japanese patent 753,376.

YOKOTSUKA, T., IWASA, T., FUJII, S. & KAKINUMA, T. (1972) Presented at the annual meeting of Agr. Chem. Soc. Japan, at Sendai, April 1.

YOKOTSUKA, T., AONUMA, T., YASUDA, Y., WATANABE, H., FUKUSHIMA, D. & MOGI, K. (1974) Announcement. Japanese Patent Sho-46-39074.

YOKOTSUKA, T. (1975) Proceedings of the 11th symposium on brewing, Sept. 13, p. 62.

YOKOTSUKA, T. (1977) Oral Presentation. 'Shoyu'. SCOGS Hearing. Hilton Hotel, Bethesda, Maryland, USA, July 26, Kikkoman Shoyu Co. Ltd.

YOSHIDA, T. (1979) Proceedings of the 11th symposium on brewing, p. 62.

YOSHII, H. (1979) *J. Ferm. Assoc.* **74**, 213.

YUAN-CHI SU (1980) Traditional fermented foods in Taiwan. Proceedings of the Oriental Fermented Foods, Taipei, Taiwan, Republic of China, pp. 15–30.

Chapter 6

Microbiology of Breadmaking

T. Frank Sugihara
*Western Regional Research Center,
US Department of Agriculture, Berkeley, California, USA*

1. INTRODUCTION

The 'roots' of modern breadmaking reach down to the Egyptians about
3500 years ago. They were the first to observe fermentation and leavening
when bread dough was allowed to stand for hours. This knowledge helped
them produce a spongy and tastier loaf of bread. The Romans were
probably the first to commercialise breadmaking by using yeast separated
from wine. It is estimated that 250 bakeries existed in Rome around 100 BC
(Pederson, 1971). The 'naturally' leavened bread of ancient times, like the
sour dough breads of today, relied on a mixed microflora of yeasts and
bacteria to produce alcohol, carbon dioxide, organic acids and other
compounds producing the flavour and texture of bread.

Most breads made today are fermented with commercial baker's yeast
(*Saccharomyces cerevisiae*). Since these yeast products contain, on the
average, 5% contaminating lactic bacteria, bacterial fermentations may
still play an important role in the flavour quality of the bread. Breads made
by the sponge and dough method definitely have the necessary time element
for the bacteria to produce organic acids, diacetyl and other flavour
compounds. For economic reasons, the trend has been toward less and less
fermentation time, even to the point of eliminating primary fermentation.
Doughs are mechanically developed and the function of the yeast is limited
to the final proofing of the dough. There is insufficient time for metabolic
reactions necessary for flavour development. The end result is a bland, soft-

textured, white bread that is used primarily as a carrier or wrapper for jams, jellies, meats, cheeses and other tasty items.

With the rapid rise in the standard of living, the demand for high-quality, flavoursome, variety breads has increased tremendously. Many of these breads are produced by bacterial fermentations or by a combination of yeast and bacteria, relying heavily on the bacterial metabolites for flavour.

2. SOUR DOUGH RYE BREAD

Over the years, the most studied bacterial bread fermentation is probably the sour dough rye bread process. The use of sour rye starter cultures goes back to 800 BC when the early Europeans made a flat sour rye bread (Pyler, 1952). Sour rye bread has survived the centuries and is still very popular in parts of Europe as well as in the USA. Spicher and his colleagues at Detmold have been studying the sour rye fermentation for over 25 years (Spicher, 1959; Spicher and Stephan, 1964, 1966; Spicher and Schröder, 1978, 1979, 1980a, b; Spicher *et al.*, 1979; Spicher *et al.*, 1980). They have

TABLE 1
Micro-organisms Isolated from Sour Rye
Starters (Spicher, 1959)

Bacteria:	*Lactobacillus plantarum*
	L. brevis
	L. casei
	L. fermenti
	L. pastorianus
	L. buchneri
	L. delbrueckii
	L. leichmannii
	L. acidophilus
	L. farciminis
	L. alimentarius
	L. brevis var. *lindneri*
	L. fermentum
	L. fructivorans
	Pediococcus acidilactici
Yeasts:	*Candida krusei*
	Saccharomyces cerevisiae
	Pichia saitoi
	Torulopsis holmii

isolated numerous species of lactic bacteria and yeasts. Table 1 lists the isolates from 'Reinzuchtsauer' (a starter culture) and other sour starters by Spicher *et al.* Amino acid requirement studies indicated that none of the sour dough bacteria required hydroxyproline, norleucine or norvaline. The homofermentative lactic acid bacteria do not require alanine and serine. All of the isolates studied required glutamic acid and valine. The majority required arginine, cysteine, leucine, methionine, phenylalanine, tryptophan and tyrosine. Some of the isolates required glycine, isoleucine, lysine, proline and serine. Significantly, the lactic acid bacteria with very high amino acid requirements (*Lactobacillus brevis* var. *lindneri*, *L. fructivorans* and *L. farciminis*) dominate the sour dough starter cultures.

Of the four species of yeast isolated from rye starters, *Candida krusei* was found to be the dominant one. It was also found to be the most acid tolerant and ferments at pH 3·6. The temperature ranges of the yeasts were 20–45 °C.

Baking tests were conducted using pure culture starters made from the isolates. The sour rye bread considered most similar to that made with 'Reinzuchtsauer' (a starter culture consisting of mixed species) was that of a pure culture starter of *Lactobacillus brevis* var. *lindneri*, plus *Candida krusei*. The trend in the USA is to add wheat flour, up to as much as 80 % of the total flour, to give a light-coloured and fine textured product. Since rye flour does not have the glutinous character of wheat flour, it will not hold carbon dioxide to give a light textured bread.

Dry chemical rye bread flavours (mostly lactic and acetic acids) are available but do not give the full-bodied flavour of microbiologically fermented rye bread.

3. THE SAN FRANCISCO SOUR DOUGH FRENCH BREAD PROCESS

One of the most unique starter cultures occurs in San Francisco (USA). This starter culture or 'mother-sponge' is used to make the famous San Francisco sour dough French bread (Kline & Sugihara, 1971; Sugihara *et al.*, 1971). Kline and Sugihara found that the ecosystem consists of one species of yeast and one species of bacteria. They always occurred in a ratio of 1:100. The yeast was originally classified as *Torulopsis holmii* (a non-spore-forming species of *Saccharomyces exiguus*) but was recently reclassified as a new species by Yarrow (1978) and named *Candida milleri*

TABLE 2

Formulations for San Francisco Sour Dough French Bread

Starter-sponge	Bread dough
100 parts of previous sponge (40% of final mix)	20 parts starter-sponge (11% of final mix)
100 parts flour (high-gluten)	100 parts flour (regular patent)
46–52 parts water	60 parts water
	2 parts salt
Starting pH 4·4–4·5	Starting pH 5·2–5·3
Final pH 3·8–3·9	Final pH 3·9–4·0

sp. nov. The bacteria was found to be a new species and was named *Lactobacillus sanfrancisco* sp. nov. This was later confirmed by Sriranganathan *et al.* (1973) using DNA–DNA hybridisation techniques.

The origin of this natural starter culture is not known but it has been used continuously for over 140 years. One theory is that the starter was brought over by a Basque immigrant. Table 2 shows the formulation used for this unique bread. Essentially, the starter sponge contains only flour and water with micro-organisms transferred from the previous starter. Of great importance here is the acidity or pH range of the system. The starter sponge begins with a pH of 4·4 and levels off at a pH of 3·9, an extremely acidic system. It is no small wonder that the starter has survived for so many years without being contaminated by other micro-organisms. It takes about 8 h for the starter to fully develop. It is then rebuilt in the same manner about three times a day, 7 days a week. The dough is formulated as shown in Table 2. After approximately 1 h of floor time, the dough is formed and placed on canvas for proofing. After approximately 7–8 h, it is ready for baking. The pH of the dough drops from about 5·3 to 3·9.

The mother-sponge or starter culture from five different commercial sour dough bread bakeries were examined. All were found to contain the same species of yeast, *Candida milleri* sp. nov., which was readily classified as shown in Table 3, in part by its inability to ferment or assimilate maltose and its ability to grow out well in the presence of Actidione (cycloheximide), an antibiotic inhibiting the growth of most yeasts. All five of the starter cultures were also found to contain the same bacteria, *Lactobacillus sanfrancisco* sp. nov. The unusual bacterium was found to utilise only maltose, required a fresh yeast extractive, unsaturated fatty acids, a carbon dioxide rich atmosphere and an acidic environment (pH 6·0 or lower) (Kline *et al.*, 1970; Sugihara *et al.*, 1970). The absolute requirement of the sour dough bacteria for maltose dovetails with the fact that the sour dough

TABLE 3

Fermentation Characteristics of Sour Dough Yeasts

Yeast	Glucose	Sucrose	Raffinose	Galactose	Maltose	Actidione*
Bakers	+	+	+	+	+	—
Sour dough No. 1	+	+	+	+	—	+
Sour dough No. 2	+	+	+	+	—	+
Sour dough No. 3	+	+	+	+	—	+
Sour dough No. 4	+	+	+	+	—	+
Sour dough No. 5	+	+	+	+	—	+

* Growth in the presence of 100 ppm actidione.

yeast does not utilise maltose. The two micro-organisms of the sour dough ecosystem are not competitive for the same carbohydrate source which, doubtless, has contributed to their ability to jointly survive in this system over so many years. Further nutritional studies were conducted by Sugihara and Kline (1975) to optimise the growth of *L. sanfrancisco* on a chemically defined medium. The basal broth medium used as a starting point consisted of maltose, $2 \cdot 0 \%$; yeast extract (Difco), $0 \cdot 3 \%$; freshly prepared yeast extract solids (FYE), $0 \cdot 5 \%$; Trypticase (BBL), $0 \cdot 6 \%$; and Tween 80 (sorbitan polyoxyethylene mono-oleate), $0 \cdot 03 \%$. The pH was adjusted to $5 \cdot 6$ with 1N to 6N HCl before autoclaving. The FYE were prepared by autoclaving a 20% suspension of commercial compressed baker's yeast in distilled water; the clarified supernatant was used directly or after freezing or freeze-drying. It was found that the FYE can be partially substituted by the addition of salts ($MgSO_4$, $MnSO_4$ and $FeSO_4$), Trypticase at a level of $1 \cdot 0 \%$ and a purine–pyrimidine mixture. The growth response was approximately 10 times the growth obtained on the basal medium without FYE and roughly equivalent to the growth stimulatory effect of $0 \cdot 5 \%$ FYE solids. Addition of $0 \cdot 5 \%$ FYE to this improved medium resulted in further doubling of the growth. Further substantial growth increments were observed as the FYE level was increased to $1 \cdot 5$ to $2 \cdot 0 \%$. The studies showed that the organic supplements tested only partially substituted the contributions of FYE. Recently, Berg *et al.* (1981) identified the growth stimulant in FYE for *L. sanfrancisco*. The stimulant was identified as a small peptide with a molecular weight of approximately 1065, containing aspartic acid, cysteine, glutamic acid, glycine and lysine. The stimulatory peptide may arise in the natural environment of the starter sponge by autolysis of *Candida milleri*, the yeast responsible for the leavening activity in San Francisco sour dough fermentation.

Pure starter cultures of *L. sanfrancisco* for commercial bakery use have been developed by Kline and Sugihara (1973, 1975). These cultures are grown in a chemically defined medium, concentrated by centrifugation, stabilised and either frozen as concentrates or freeze-dried. Kline (1981) developed a starter culture grown on a wheat flour and water slurry, stabilised with 6% disaccharide and then freeze-dried.

The San Francisco sour dough French bread was, until very recently, made only in the San Francisco area (USA). It accounts for approximately 20% of the total bread consumption in the area. Since the development of the pure starter cultures, it is now being made in many distant parts of the USA and also in Japan.

4. IDLI, PUTO AND KANON-TAN BREADS

A pancake-like bread called Idli is common in the southern area of India (Pederson, 1971). The bread is prepared from rice and black gram mungo (*Phaseolus mungo*), a legume. The rice and black bean are washed, soaked in water separately, then ground, mixed and finally allowed to ferment overnight. When the batter shows sufficient leavening, it is cooked by steaming and generally served hot. The bread has a very spongy and soft texture and a unique flavour and taste. Puto, a Philippines bread, is made in a similar way except that the dough is neutralised during leavening to reduce its acidity. The Kanon-tan, a bread made in Thailand, is also quite similar.

Microbiological studies by Mukherjee *et al.* (1965) found that the dominant heterofermentative lactic bacterium was *Leuconostoc mesenteroides*. There was a sequential change in the bacterial flora during fermentation, which included *Streptococcus faecalis* and *Pediococcus cerevisiae* but the predominant *L. mesenteroides* was responsible for the souring, strengthening (formation of dextrans) and leavening (carbon dioxide) of the bread.

The adaptation of this fermentation technique using rice flour, soy flour and other non-glutinous materials could possibly become a dietetic food item for the Western countries.

5. ARABIC AND MIDDLE EASTERN BREADS

A recent article by El-Gendy (1983) describes the production of breads in Egypt. There are three types, Balady bread, Fino bread and Shamsy bread.

Most commercially sold breads in Egypt are round-shaped, flat and varying in volume. There are two types of this bread made—the Balady type, which represents approximately 90 % of commercial production, and the Shamsy bread. The Fino bread is shaped like a tube. The Shamsy bread and the Fino bread represent 10 % of the commercial bread.

To make Shamsy bread, the dough is prepared by mixing flour with water, a small quantity of salt and some of the starter. The starter is made by mixing approximately 100 g of a fully fermented dough with about 2 kg of flour and half a litre of water. The starter sponge is fermented overnight in a warm location. The final bread dough is mixed with the starter by hand for approximately 25 min, allowed to rest for 45 min, and divided into appropriate pieces. The pieces of dough are placed onto boards covered with bran and allowed to ferment for 60 min in a warm location (second fermentation). The fermented pieces are then flattened to about 20 cm in diameter and allowed to ferment for another 60 min (third fermentation). The dough pieces are then turned over and left in a cooler location (shady) for 30 min (fourth fermentation). They are finally baked in a specially built clay oven.

The microbiology of the starter cultures for the Arabic breads has not been reported but undoubtedly consists of an ecosystem of sour dough yeasts and lactic bacteria.

A few interesting chemical analyses were reported. Shamsy bread was found to have a higher destruction of phytic acid (78·2 %) than the Balady bread (55·7 %) and the Fino bread (48·8 %). Losses in the essential amino acids during production were lower in the Shamsy bread. It was concluded that Shamsy bread has more nutritive value than Balady bread or Fino bread.

6. THE ITALIAN PANETTONE AND RELATED PRODUCTS

For centuries the Italians have been producing a sweet dough bread that relies on a lactic fermentation for its flavour and 'bouquet'. The most popular item is called Panettone which is enjoyed primarily around the Christmas holidays. The birthplace of this unique 'cake-like' bread is said to be the city of Milan in northern Italy. Panettone is still being manufactured today using the original 24-h fermentation schedule. The same starter-sponge and a similar formulation is used to produce an Easter holiday 'cake', Colomba, which is baked in the form of a dove and covered with whole almonds and confectioners' sugar. More recently, it has been covered with a chocolate icing and injected with a cream filling. Panettone dough is also used continuously during the year for the production of snack cakes and breakfast rolls.

Panettone dough fermentation is a complex microbiological pheno- menon. It involves a single sour dough yeast and two or more lactic bacteria in the ecosystem (Ottogalli & Galli, 1972). The sour dough yeast has been classified as *Saccharomyces exiguus* and the dominant lactic bacterium as *Lactobacillus brevis*. The starter culture has been perpetuated for centuries by careful maintenance in 'hospital-clean' facilities. Extraordinary care is taken in the preparation of the 'Madre' (mother-sponge or starter-sponge). Fermentation of the Madre is checked continuously by microbial counts, pH monitoring and measurements of total acidity.

Production of Panettone begins with a fully developed Madre (24-h starter-sponge) which consists of flour, water and the micro-organisms of the ecosystem. The Madre is used to inoculate a sour sponge which is rebuilt three times to obtain a sufficient quantity for making up the 'white- dough'. The 'white-dough' is made up by mixing the following items into the fully developed sour dough sponge—flour, butter oil, sugar and water. The 'white-dough' is allowed to ferment for about 8 h at 28 °C. The final dough ('yellow-dough') is made by adding the following ingredients to the fully fermented 'white-dough': flour, water, egg yolk, butter oil, raisins and candied citron peels. After mixing, the dough is divided, rounded, moulded and then placed into a parchment-paper dish. The dough is then proofed for 8–10 h at approximately 30 °C. The proofed dough is finally baked for 1 h in a moderate oven. In order to retain its shape, the Panettone is cooled slowly, up to 20 h, in an inverted position.

Another famous product of Verona, Italy, the Pandoro (a Christmas holiday cake) is also made by using the same Madre or starter-sponge. The formulation is much richer since it contains high levels of egg and butter (Zorzanello & Sugihara, 1982). The Pandoro requires special technology for its production. The mechanics of dough handling are very complex.

To reduce the time and cost of production, a pure culture 'liquid-sponge' technology has been developed (Sugihara, unpublished data). The culture consists of two micro-organisms in the ecosystem, the sour dough yeast, *Saccharomyces exiguus*, and a lactic bacterium, *Lactobacillus brevis*. Other species of lactic bacteria can be used to give the Panettone a special taste or flavour.

7. THE SODA CRACKER PROCESS

Soda crackers have been made for over 140 years but the fermentation of the process still relies on the contaminating micro-organisms. In the USA alone, production amounts to almost a billion US dollars in annual sales. With this huge production, it is hard to believe that pure culture technology has not been developed. Giant production facilities have been built incorporating the latest automation but still no pure culture fermentation.

Recently, Sugihara (1978a, b) studied the fermentation process of two different soda cracker production plants. He found that a fully developed soda cracker sponge had total microbial counts of 4–49×10^7 per gram (yeast counts were 1–15×10^7 and bacteria counts 1–41×10^7). A fully developed soda cracker dough sample showed total microbial counts of 9–90×10^7 per gram (yeast counts were 1–12×10^7 and bacteria counts 9–80×10^7). Since compressed baker's yeast was part of the formulation of the sponge, the yeasts were primarily *Saccharomyces cerevisiae*. The dominant lactic bacterium was found to be *Lactobacillus plantarum*. Two other species of lactic bacteria, *Lactobacillus delbrueckii* and *Lactobacillus leichmannii* were found in substantial numbers and proved to be essential for true flavour development. Using a 'liquid-sponge' technology, the conventional sponge time of 18 h was reduced to 4 h and the conventional dough time was reduced from 4 h to just 2 h. With the use of pure starter cultures, the conventional 24-h process has been reduced to an 8-h day process.

8. A MIXED CULTURE STARTER FOR A NEW FRENCH SOUR DOUGH BREAD

Recently, a French sour dough bread fermentation was studied in great detail by Hardy (1982). Hundreds of isolates were studied and finally culminated in the development of a unique mixed culture starter using one yeast, *Candida tropicalis* and one lactic bacterium, *Lactobacillus plantarum*. The unusual aspect of this culture technique is that both micro-organisms are grown together to produce a unique starter culture for the production of a sour dough bread.

The substrate for culturing the micro-organisms consists of an enzyme (amylase) treated flour, 100 g; wheat germ, 5 g; $(NH_4)_2SO_4$, 13·4 g; KH_2PO_4, 2·2 g; $MgSO_4$, 9·6 g; $CaCl_2$, 0·336 g; yeast extract 1 g; and water 1000 ml, pH 6·5.

The culture medium was inoculated with *Candida tropicalis* and *Lactobacillus plantarum* at a level of 2×10^7 per gram. It was then incubated for 17 h at 30 °C. After incubation, the counts for both micro-organisms were approximately 2×10^9 per gram. The liquid starter culture was stored at 4 °C and remained fully active for at least three weeks.

9. THE FUTURE OF BREADMAKING

Modern breadmaking to date has achieved technology for massive production of 'nutritious' bread for the masses. Bread dough can now be mechanically developed in a few minutes. New strains of commercial baker's yeasts are now more active and made easier to handle by the bakers. Bread can be made very cheaply and in great quantities. But the demand now, in many developed countries, is for tastier quality variety breads. Many of these types of product cannot be made by mass production at this time because of the complex microbial fermentations required. A few products have been successful by the use of scientific controls on the fermentation of the process. Some still use the centuries-old technique of using a 'mother-sponge' or 'starter-sponge' but combined with the use of scientific technology to control the ecosystem. Others have developed pure starter cultures for direct and exact control of the ecosystem. Both systems will survive over the years but pure culture will eventually become the standard procedure for the bakeries of the future. This is inevitable since it is the only way to cut the cost of labour, to ensure quality and dependability of the process.

REFERENCES

BERG, R. W., SANDINE, W. E. & ANDERSON, A. W. (1981) Identification of a growth stimulant for *Lactobacillus sanfrancisco*, *Appl. Environ. Microbiol.* **42**(5), 786–8.

EL-GENDY, S. M. (1983) Fermented foods of Egypt and the middle east, *J. Food Protection* **46**, 358–67.

HARDY, J. L. (1982) Mise au d'une technique de panification sur levain a partir de ferments cerealiers associes, Docteur Ingenieur, These, Universite de Technologie de Compiegne, France.

KLINE, L. (1981) US Patent No. 4,243,687 January 6.

KLINE, L. & SUGIHARA, T. F. (1971) Microorganisms of the San Francisco sour dough bread process, II. Isolation and characterization of undescribed bacterial species responsible for the souring activity. *Appl. Microbiol.* **21**, 459.

KLINE, L. & SUGIHARA, T. F. (1973) US Patent No. 3,374,743 May 22.

KLINE, L. & SUGIHARA, T. F. (1975) US Patent No. 3,891,773 June 24.

KLINE, L., SUGIHARA, T. F. & McCREADY, L. B. (1970) Nature of the San Francisco sour dough French bread process. I. Mechanics of the process, *Bakers Digest* **44**(2), 48–50.

MUKHERJEE, S. K., ALBURY, M. N., PEDERSON, C. S., VAN VEEN, A. G. & STEINKRAUS, K. H. (1965) Role of *Leuconostoc mesenteroides* in leavening the batter of Idli, a fermented food of India, *Appl. Microbiol.* **13**, 227.

OTTOGALLI, G. & GALLI, A. (1972) Istituto de Microbiologia Agraria e Tecnica, Universita di Milano, Italia, manuscript.

PEDERSON, C. S. (1971) *Microbiology of Food Fermentation*, Chapter 8, The Avi Publishing Co., Inc., Westport, Conn., USA.

PYLER, S. J. (1952) *Baking Science and Technology*, Siebel Publishing Co., Chicago, Illinois, USA. p. 3.

SPICHER, G. (1959) Die Mikroflora des Sauerteiges. I. Untersuchungen über die Art der in Sauerteigen anzutreffenden stäbchenförmigen Milchsäurebakterien (Genus *Lactobacillus* Beijerinck). *Zentr. Bakt. Parasitenkunde Infect. Hygiene* II Abt. **113**, 80–105 (German).

SPICHER, G. & SCHRÖDER, R. (1978) Die Mikroflora des Sauerteiges. IV. Untersuchungen über die Art der in 'Reinzuchtsauern' anzutreffenden stäbchenformgen Milchsäurebakterien (Genus *Lactobacillus* Beijerinck). *Z. Lebensm. Unters. Forsch.*, **167**, 342–54 (German).

SPICHER, G. & SCHRÖDER, R. (1979) Die Mikroflora des Sauerteiges. VI. Das Aminosäurebedürfnis der in 'Reinzuchtsauern' und in Sauerteigen anzutreffenden stäbchenformigen Milchsäurebakterien (Genus *Lactobacillus* Beijerinck). *Z. Lebensm. Unters. Forsch.* **168**, 397–401 (German).

SPICHER, G. & SCHRÖDER, R. (1980a) Die Mikroflora des Sauerteiges, VIII. Die Faktoren des Wachstums der im 'Reinzuchtsauer' auftretenden Hefen, *Z. Lebensm. Unters. Forsch.* **170**, 119–23 (German).

SPICHER, G. & SCHRÖDER, R. (1980b) Die Mikroflora des Sauerteiges, IX. Vergleichende Untersuchungen über die Säuerungsleistung der in 'Reinzuchtsauern' auftretenden Milchsäurebakterien (Genus *Lactobacillus* Beijerinck). *Z. Lebensm. Unters. Forsch.* **170**, 262–6 (German).

SPICHER, G. & STEPHAN, H. (1964) Die Mikroflora des Sauerteiges. II. Untersuchungen über die backtechnische Bedeutung der aus Sauerteigen isolierten stäbchenförmigen Milchsäurebakterien (Genus *Lactobacillus* Beijerinck), *Zentr. Bakt. Parasitenkunde Infect. Hygiene* II. Abt. **118**, 469–70 (German).

SPICHER, G. & STEPHAN, H. (1966) Die Mikroflora des Sauerteiges. III. Untersuchungen über die Art der in 'Spontansauerteigen' anzutreffenden Milchsäurebakterien und ihre backtechnische Bedeutung. *Zentr. Bakt. Parasitenkunde Infect. Hygiene* II. Abt. **120**, 699–701 (German).

SPICHER, G., SCHRÖDER, R. & SCHÖLLHAMMER, K. (1979) Die Mikroflora des Sauerteiges, VII. Untersuchungen über die Art der in 'Reinzuchtsauern' auftretenden Hefen. *Z. Lebensm. Unters. Forsch.* **169**, 77–81 (German).

SPICHER, G., SCHRÖDER, R. & STEPHAN, H. (1980) Die Mikroflora des Sauerteiges, X. Die backtechnische Wirkung der in 'Reinzuchtsauern' auftretenden Milchsäurebakterien (Genus *Lactobacillus* Beijerinck). *Z. Lebensm. Unters. Forsch.* **171**, 119–24 (German).

SRIRANGANATHAN, N., SEIDLER, R. J., SANDINE, W. E. & ELLIKER, P. R. (1973) Cytological and deoxyribonucleic acid-deoxyribonucleic acid hybridization studies on *Lactobacillus* isolates from San Francisco sourdough. *Appl. Microbiol.* **25**(3), 461–70.

SUGIHARA, T. F., unpublished data.

SUGIHARA, T. F. (1978a) Microbiology of the soda cracker process, I. Isolation and identification of microflora, *J. Food Protection* **41**, 977–9.

SUGIHARA, T. F. (1978b) Microbiology of the soda cracker process, II. Pure culture fermentation studies, *J. Food Protection* **41**, 980–2.

SUGIHARA, T. F. & KLINE, L. (1975) Further studies on a growth medium for *Lactobacillus sanfrancisco*, *J. Milk Food Technol.* **38**(LL), 667–72.

SUGIHARA, T. F., KLINE, L. & MCCREADY, L. B. (1970) Nature of the San Francisco sour dough French bread process. II. Microbiological aspects. *Bakers Digest* **44**(2), 51–3, 56–7.

SUGIHARA, T. F., KLINE, L. & MILLER, M. W. (1971) Microorganisms of the San Francisco sour dough bread process. I. Yeasts responsible for the leavening action, *Appl. Microbiol.* **21**, 456.

YARROW, D. (1978) *Candida milleri* sp. nov., *Int. J. System. Bacteriol.* **28**(4), 608–10.

ZORZANELLO, D. & SUGIHARA, T. F. (1982) The technology of Pandoro production, *Bakers Digest* **56**, 12–15.

EDITOR'S NOTE

While the evidence is far less complete than that gathered by Sugihara, Kline and their co-workers for the San Francisco sour dough fermentation, studies of the leavens used in Poland and by a Polish–Jewish bakery in Scotland give clear indications that these leavens have a microflora resembling the San Francisco rather than the Detmold type (Wood *et al.*, 1975; Wood, 1981). Current studies (Al-Armaghani, Allan & Wood, unpublished observations) on a leaven from a bakery near Agen in France, also show a San Francisco type of leaven. Studies in Poland, which are discussed in the papers referred to above, show the same pattern of mutual interdependence between the yeast and bacterium as that referred to by Sugihara, with the bacterium metabolising maltose with maltose phosphorylase (Wood & Rainbow, 1961) so releasing glucose which the yeast utilises, while in its turn the bacterium receives growth factor(s) from the yeast. This suggests that the San Francisco type of system is rather widespread in situations where a leaven is maintained in an unbroken line of succession for a long period.

In developing countries there is sometimes a problem with breadmaking in that the bakers are committed to using expensive imported dried baker's yeast, the country's economy being unable to support indigenous production and distribution of pressed yeast. The remarkable stability of the yeast/lactobacillus consortium in sour doughs, even under the very adverse conditions experienced by the Pioneers in the days of the settlement of the far West of the USA, suggests that it may be worthwhile to investigate the possibility that baking with sour doughs be adopted in those developing countries. The changes in dough rheology brought about by sour dough fermentation (Wood *et al.*, 1975) may also be of advantage in permitting the use of softer wheats than would otherwise be practicable.

REFERENCES

WOOD, B. J. B. (1981) The yeast/lactobacillus interaction; a study in stability. In *Mixed Culture Fermentations*, M. E. Bushell & J. H. Slater, Eds. Society for General Microbiology/Academic Press, London, pp. 137–50.

WOOD, B. J. B. & RAINBOW, C. (1961) The maltophosphorylase of beer lactobacilli. *Biochem. J.*, **178**, 204–9.

WOOD, B. J. B., CARDENAS, OLGA S., YONG, F. M. & McNULTY, D. W. (1975) Lactobacilli in the production of soy sauce, sour dough and Parisian barm. In *Lactic Acid Bacteria in Beverages and Food*, J. G. Carr, C. V. Cutting & G. L. Whiting, Eds. Academic Press Ltd, London, pp. 325–35.

Chapter 7

Yeast–Lactic Acid Bacteria Interactions and their Contribution to Fermented Foodstuffs

BRIAN J. B. WOOD and MARY M. HODGE*

*Department of Bioscience and Biotechnology,
University of Strathclyde, Glasgow, Scotland, UK*

1. INTRODUCTION

Throughout this book there are references to the presence of yeasts and lactic acid bacteria in fermenting foods. Although the text is intended to be biased toward practical rather than the more academic examination of topics related to food fermentation, the Editor has exercised his privilege and chosen to include a chapter which both deals with some fermented products not mentioned elsewhere, and reviews recent advances in the study of interactions between yeasts and lactic acid bacteria. Inevitably there is overlap to varying degrees with other chapters, but it is hoped that the reader will exercise tolerance in this matter in order that general principles may be explored.

Some of the processes utilising yeasts/lactic acid bacteria associations are among the oldest known food fermentations, including bread leavens; kefir and koumiss (milk products); ginger 'beer', kvass and some un-hopped ales (beverages). These fermentations long predate the recognition of the existence of micro-organisms, and their success depended upon the careful observance of traditional processes developed over centuries of experience. Not surprisingly, myth and legend accreted around them and today we are perhaps too ready to dismiss all claims of (for example) therapeutic uses of

* Present Address: Department of Microbiology, University of Surrey, Guildford GU2 5XH, UK.

these products as 'old wives' tales' without fully testing these claims in an objective manner. It is certain that these ferments exhibit great stability together with the ability to dominate over the wide variety of microbes which will inevitably be present in grains, etc., prepared by traditional methods without the benefits of modern cleaning and sterilising agents. Some typical examples of such products are listed in Tables 1 and 2.

Fermentations involving yeasts and lactic acid bacteria, and which are

TABLE 1

Examples of Beverages which Require (or are Thought to Require) for their Production the Involvement of Yeasts and Lactic Acid Bacteria

Name of product	Raw materials	Place of origin
Alcoholic Beverages		
Burukutu	Sorghum and cassava	Nigeria
Busa	Rice	Turkestan
	Millet and sugar	Tartars of Krum
Busaa	Maize	Kenya
Geuze Beer	Malted barley	Belgium
Ginger 'beer'	Ginger root, sugar	Various sources
Kaffir beer	Various grains	Africa
Kvass	Rye bread	Russia, E. Europe
Lambic beer	Malted barley	Belgium
Merissa	Sorghum	Sudan
Pulque	Agave juice	Mexico
Rum	Cane molasses	Caribbean
Saké	Polished rice	Japan
Sourmash bourbon	Cereals	USA
Stock beer	Malted barley	England
Tibi	Sucrose, figs	Mexico
Whisky	Malted barley	Scotland
Milk-based Beverages		
Continental acidophilus	Skim milk	USA
Dahi (dadhi)	Cows' or buffaloes' milk	India
Kefir	Goats', sheep's or cows' milk	Russia and E. Europe
Koumiss	Mares' or cows' milk	Russia
Kuban	Milk	—
Leben	Buffaloes', goats' or cows' milk	Middle East
Mazun	Buffaloes', goats' or cows' milk	Armenia
Taette	Cows' milk	N. Europe

carried out in closed vessels will rapidly become anaerobic, acidic, saturated with carbon dioxide and alcoholic. This combination of conditions will certainly be inhibitory to many spoilage micro-organisms including filamentous fungi and bacteria associated with various forms of food poisoning. Thus, as with pickling, the storage life and the safety to the

TABLE 2

Examples of Foods and Flavourings which Require (or are Thought to Require) for their Production the Involvement of Yeasts and Lactic Acid Bacteria

Names of product	Raw materials	Place of origin
Flavourings		
Miso	Soybeans	China, Japan,
	Alternatively soybeans plus rice or barley	S.E. Asia
Soy sauce	Soybeans	China, Japan,
	Alternatively soybeans plus wheat	S.E. Asia
Foods		
Jalebies	Wheatflour, yoghurt, sugar	Arabia or Persian origin
Kenkey	Maize	Ghana
Nan and related breads	Wheatflour	Indian sub-continent
Ogi	Maize	Africa
Parisian barm	Wheat	Scotland
Sour dough breads and related products	Wheat and rye	World-wide
Various cassava fermentations	Cassava	Africa, S. America

consumer of the product would be substantially improved by fermentations of these types. The fermentations to be discussed here will in many cases have higher water activity and/or lower concentrations of acid or alcohol than is the case with cheese, pickles, wine, etc., and the storage life would be correspondingly reduced; thus such factors as flavour- and texture-improvement were probably more important than improved storage life, although in the time before refrigeration, improvements in storage life of only a few days were probably not unimportant.

2. BEVERAGES

There are many beverages that require (or are thought to require) for their production the involvement of both yeasts and lactic acid bacteria; for simplicity these are separated into milk-based beverages and alcoholic beverages. The associations that occur between these organisms are important in the production of many of the beverages, therefore the latter part of this section is devoted to a more detailed examination of this aspect in a few of the systems.

2.1. Milk-based Beverages

According to the literature there are at least eight fermented milks that owe their production to both yeasts and lactic acid bacteria. A short description of each is given, with the micro-organisms involved being listed where known.

2.1.1. Kefir

Kefir is an acid-alcohol fermented milk which originated in the Caucasian Mountains of Russia. It is not a curdled product and is produced by adding kefir grains to the milk of the goat, sheep or cow (Kosikowski, 1977).

Bacteria and yeasts are thought to be involved in a symbiotic association in these grains, held together by a water soluble polysaccharide, called kefiran (La Riviere *et al.*, 1967). A more detailed discussion of these grains and the micro-organisms involved will be given in Section 2.3.1.

In Russia, where kefir is produced on a large scale, cows' milk is used; the final product contains approximately 0.8% lactic acid, 1% ethanol and carbon dioxide (Kosikowski, 1977). A good kefir milk foams and fizzes when agitated.

2.1.2. Koumiss

Koumiss is also a fermented milk containing both acid and alcohol. It originates from Southern Russia, its name being derived from a tribe called the Kumanes. Originally Koumiss was prepared by adding a small amount of previously fermented milk to mares' milk (Kosikowski, 1977). Koumiss, like kefir, is not a curdled product and foams and fizzes when agitated.

From the literature it is evident that many studies have been performed on the microbes involved, and nearly all indicate that it is a mixed fermentation involving yeasts and lactic acid bacteria.

In the manufacture of commercial Koumiss using mares' milk, the fermentation is brought about by *Lactobacillus bulgaricus* and a *Torula* yeast. It can be produced with varying concentrations of alcohol and lactic acid, plus carbon dioxide (Kosikowski, 1977).

The fermentation of cows' milk to produce Koumiss is now being attempted in Russia, it is brought about by *Lactobacillus bulgaricus, L. acidophilus* and *Saccharomyces lactis* (Kosikowski, 1977).

2.1.3. Continental Acidophilus

This fermented milk resembles koumiss and is produced in the US. It is made from skim milk and the organisms involved are *Lactobacillus acidophilus, L. caucasicus* and a yeast (Kosikowski, 1977).

2.1.4. Taette

Taette is a viscous, coagulated, acidic milk product of the Northern European countries. Scandinavian Taette is produced by inoculating sweet cows' milk with the leaves of butterwort (Heinemann, 1911). According to Olsen-Sopp (1912) the following organisms are necessary for the production of Taette, *Saccharomyces major taette, Lactobacillus taette* and *Bacillus acid actis longus* (*sic*). However, Foster *et al.* (1957) write that Taette is produced with a strain of *Streptococcus lactis* resembling *hollandicus* variety. No recent data on this fermented milk appears to be available, although it is reasonable to assume that the product referred to as 'Taet-mjölk' by Oberman (this volume) is the same.

2.1.5. Mazun

Mazun (Matsun, Matzoni) is a coagulated milk from Armenia, which is produced from cows', goats' or buffaloes' milk (Tanner, 1944). According to Duggeli (1905), the organisms present are rod-shaped bacteria and lactose fermenting yeasts; similar results were reported by Weigmann *et al.* (1907). Oberman (this volume) mentions *Streptococcus thermophilus*.

2.1.6. Leben

Leben (Lebneh) is a concentrated yoghurt resembling Kefir and is said (Vedamuthu, 1982) to have originated in the Tigris-Euphrates Valley; there is evidence that it was also consumed by the Egyptians (Tanner, 1944).

It can be prepared from the milk of the sheep, goat, cow or buffalo or a mixture of any of these (Vedamuthu, 1982), the fermentation being started by the addition of dried leben to milk which has been boiled and cooled (Tanner, 1944).

Rist and Khoury (1902) reported that three types of bacteria and two types of yeast were responsible for the fermentation; the yeasts were found to be unable to ferment lactose. However, Vedamuthu (1982) writes that the predominant organisms are *Streptococcus lactis*, *S. thermophilus*, *Lactobacillus bulgaricus* and lactose-fermenting yeasts.

2.1.7. Kuban

The only work on this fermented milk appears to be by Bogdanoff (1934). It is again an acid–alcohol fermented milk, the microflora consisting of an organism resembling *Streptococcus hollandicus*, an organism resembling *Lactobacillus bulgaricus* and three types of yeasts.

2.1.8. Dahi

Dahi is an Indian fermented milk and may be produced from cows' or buffaloes' milk or both (Vedamuthu, 1982). It is produced by boiling the milk, which is then cooled and inoculated with a small amount of dahi from a previous fermentation; if left overnight a coagulum is formed. In this fermentation, lactic acid is produced without the formation of alcohol (Ram-Ayyar, 1918).

The organisms involved, according to Ram-Ayyar, are a non-lactose fermenting yeast which is always associated with the two types of lactic acid bacteria in the dahi. The yeast grows only in curdled milk and consumes the lactic acid produced by the bacteria. The lactic acid bacteria were found to live longer when associated with the yeast, due to the prevention of accumulation of toxic quantities of acid. However, Vedamuthu (1982) states that the micro-organisms involved are lactose fermenting yeasts, *Streptococcus lactis*, *S. thermophilus*, *Lactobacillus bulgaricus*, *L. helveticus* and *L. plantarum*. From pure culture work however (Moniz *et al.*, 1976), it appears that the presence of yeast is not essential for the production of a good quality dahi.

2.2. Alcoholic Beverages

It is unnecessary and would be tedious to describe all of the alcoholic beverages given in Table 1 in detail, therefore only a representative selection are discussed.

2.2.1. Kaffir Beer

Various forms of Kaffir beer are produced and consumed in much of Africa, and in consequence it has many other different names (Hesseltine, 1979). It is prepared from Kaffircorn and other cereals, being produced by both village and industrial processes.

The beer is pink, opaque (due to suspended solids), has a yoghurt-like flavour, a thin consistency, is effervescent and alcoholic. It is consumed in an active state of fermentation and hence can only be kept for a few days (Hesseltine, 1979).

In the indigenous process, saccharification, souring and alcoholic fermentation proceed almost simultaneously. However, in the industrialised process, there are two distinct phases; the first is saccharification plus lactic acid souring and the second is the alcoholic fermentation (Novellie, 1968). Odunfa (q.v.) discusses this important food beverage in more detail elsewhere in this text (Vol. 2).

2.2.2. Busa

There appears to be some confusion as to whether this is a fermented milk or alcoholic beverage. Tanner (1944) writes that it is a fermented milk of Turkestan, and then proceeds to say that Chekan (1922) states that the raw material used is rice. The organisms responsible for the fermentation are reported as *Saccharomyces busae asiaticae* and *Bacterium busae asiaticae*. According to Hesseltine (1965, 1979) the Tartars of Krum prepared this fermented drink from millet and sugar, the organisms involved being *Lactobacillus delbrueckii* and *Saccharomyces busae asiaticae*. He also states that the busa of Turkestan is made from rice.

Busa appears to be the name given to a Kenyan opaque maize beer according to Nout (1980). Its microbial population is dominated by yeasts, *Lactobacillus* species and *Pediococcus* species. The alcoholic fermentation is principally by *Saccharomyces cerevisiae* and the lactic acid fermentation initiated by heterofermentative and homofermentative lactobacilli.

From the information obtained it seems probable that similar names for different products have evolved independently in the different regions.

2.2.3. Pulque

Pulque is a common beverage in Mexico. It is the product of the spontaneous fermentation of agave juice, which is obtained mainly from *Agave atrovirens* and *A. americans*. The juice is extracted from the plants when they have reached full maturity.

The organisms responsible for this product are *Saccharomyces carbajali* which is to be the principal alcohol producer, two *Lactobacillus* species which are thought to be responsible for the lactic acid produced and two species of *Leuconostoc* which are thought to be responsible for the viscosity of the product (Sanchez-Marroquin & Hope, 1953).

These workers found it possible to produce a good pulque by using pure cultures of *S. carbajali*, homofermentative *Lactobacillus* species, and the two *Leuconostoc* species. They found that successive inoculation with bacteria followed by yeast gave higher yields of pulque, than did simultaneous inoculation.

2.2.4. Kvass

Kvass is a refreshing, acidic, slightly alcoholic drink from Russia and Eastern Europe. Little by way of scientific information seems to have been published on it in the West so far as we can ascertain, although this seems to be surprising and rather improbable in view of its long history and popularity, particularly in Russia. Hearsay accounts of its preparation seem to be rather vague and variable, as might perhaps be expected. In some versions rye bread is the raw material. This is said to be toasted or to be baked in an oven until crisp, then crumbled into water and added to a container of already-fermenting material. Portions of the clearer liquid from the top of the fermentation are drawn off for consumption as required, and fresh additions of water and rye bread are made as necessary. In some accounts it is stated that a kvass fermentation can be started with an inoculum of bread leaven of the sour dough type used in the production of rye bread in Eastern Europe and Russia. The view that the kvass fermentation is dominated by yeasts and lactic acid bacteria is very reasonable and makes the idea of using a starter inoculum of sour leaven quite credible. In Poland, studies have been carried out with the intention of producing kvass in the form of a clear, bright, stable, pasteurised, bottled beverage (personal communications from staff of the Politechnika Łodzka). One of us (BJBW) has sampled their product; it was a sparkling, refreshing, acidic, brown liquid with a pleasing, slightly nutty flavour. The alcohol content was low.

Tradition describes this kvass as a very healthy and health-giving drink. There are reputed to be accounts of its use in the treatment of a variety of diseases but the 'references' offered to the authors in support of these claims are to obscure German language sources and we have so far been unable to examine them and assess their scientific worth.

According to Pederson (1979), other types of kvass are prepared from sprouted rice or barley or rye which is then milled, mixed with water and fermented, while in a Ukranian variety, beetroots are used in its preparation.

2.2.5. Ginger Beer and Bees' Wine

Ginger beer is a sparkling beverage, which is distinctly acidic, with a ginger flavour and containing a small amount of alcohol. The raw materials used are sugar solution (10–20%), a little cream of tartar and a few pieces of ginger; lemon may also be added. Pieces of ginger beer 'plant' are placed into this mixture and allowed to ferment for a day or two (Ward, 1892).

A typical traditional recipe requires that a portion of the 'plant' (actually a slimy, wet mixture of ground ginger and micro-organisms) be placed in a jar. To it is added about 2 cups of water and 2 teaspoonfuls each of sugar and ground ginger. The mixture is stirred. Thereafter the fermenting mixture is kept in a warm place and on each of the next twelve days it is 'fed' with a teaspoonful each of sugar and ground ginger, these additions being made with stirring. After the 12th day the feeding and stirring are discontinued, the mixture is allowed to settle for a day or two and the liquid layer is then decanted off. The 'plant' is divided into two halves, one being discarded, while the other half is treated as described above. The supernatant liquid is mixed with 7 pints of water, $3\frac{1}{2}$ cups of sugar and the juice of 3 lemons. The mixture is bottled and is ready for drinking after 10 days.

The origin of the ginger beer 'plant' appears to be unknown. Ward (1892), and Kebler (1921) who describe it by several different names, imply that it may have many different origins.

According to Ward (1892), the 'plant' consists of a yeast, *Saccharomyces pyriformis* and a bacterium, *Bacterium vermiforme*, which are held together by gelatinous sheaths produced by the bacterium. Other organisms are present from time to time, but he found these non-essential when he produced the ginger beer 'plant' from pure cultures of the above organisms. A symbiotic relationship appears to exist between the yeast and bacterium as Ward found that both function best when in the presence of each other.

A strange concoction known as 'bees' wine' has similarities with ginger beer (see Kebler, 1921). The 'bees' are small flecks of material which rise to the surface of the sugary liquid in which they are floating as their fermentation produces a bubble of gas. When one reaches the surface the bubble bursts and the particle sinks down, only to begin the process all over again. They are placed into a dilute sugar solution and fed every day for a week with sugar (and ginger in some recipes). The strained liquid is then mixed with sugar, acid and water and bottled as with ginger beer. A very unusual aspect is that the suspension of 'bees' is placed in a sunny window to 'work'. The 'bees' are thought to be a mixture of yeasts and lactic acid bacteria bound in a polysaccharide matrix.

2.2.6. Tibi

Tibi is an acidic, mildly alcoholic beverage which is produced from a sucrose solution to which is added a few Tibi grains; this is then allowed to ferment for a day or two (Horisberger, 1969); figs, dates, raisins or ginger-roots may be added to provide flavour and growth factors. These grains originate from Mexico where they occur on the leaves of the Opuntia plant (Lutz, 1899; Daker & Stacey, 1938), and according to Horisberger (1969) the grains are a symbiotic association of *Lactobacillus brevis*, *Streptococcus lactis* and *Saccharomyces cerevisiae*.

It is apparent from the literature that there exists some confusion as to whether the ginger beer 'plant' and the Tibi grain are the same grains (with different names) or not. Moinas *et al.* (1980) state that Ward (1892) and Kebler (1921) both described the Tibi grain, but neither of these workers mention the Tibi grain by name. Horisberger (1969) however, writes that Ward (1892), Stadelmann (1957) and Hesseltine (1965) believe the Tibi grain and ginger beer 'plant' to be similar. The situation is probably best summed up by Kebler (1921), 'The above synonyms indicate that these ferments are derived from various sources. They do not seem to have a common origin. Investigations show that, while the different specimens resemble one another in many respects, there appear to be fundamental differences', an observation which could be extended to include 'Bees' wine'. A more detailed discussion of these grains is given in sub-sections 2.3.2 and 2.3.3.

2.2.7. Other Alcoholic Beverages

For the beverages mentioned in Table 1 that are not discussed the interested reader is referred to the following: Lambic, Geuze and Stock beer, Lloyd-Hind, 1950; Whisky, Bryan-Jones, 1975; Merissa, Dirar, 1978; Burukutu, Faparusi, 1970; Saké, Steinkraus, 1980; Sourmash bourbon, Wood, 1981.

2.3. Associations of Yeasts and Lactic Acid Bacteria in the Kefir Grain, Tibi Grain and Ginger Beer 'Plant'

The Tibi grain and ginger beer 'plant' are described here separately despite the confusion over their identity or difference (see above).

2.3.1. Kefir Grain

Composition. The grains consist of a slimy material in which yeast and bacterial cells are firmly embedded (La Riviere *et al.*, 1967). They are irregular in shape, vary in size, most having a diameter of about 2–3 mm and they are mostly white in colour (Botazzi & Bianchi, 1980).

Several investigations have been carried out on the microflora of the Kefir grain and these show that the microflora is dominated by yeasts and lactic acid bacteria.

During the production of Kefir asepsis is not observed, and the process can be repeated *ad infinitum* (La Riviere *et al.*, 1967). It appears therefore, that the micro-organisms embedded in the grains are capable of surviving contamination from other organisms, selection taking place each time that the fermented milk is removed. The material responsible for embedding the organisms would appear to be an important factor in sustaining a favourable and specific ecological niche. It was found that a polysaccharide made up almost half of the embedding material of Delft Kefir grains; this polysaccharide was named Kefiran. Table 3 shows some of the characteristics of Kefiran. Polysaccharides extracted from grains from various sources showed similar properties to the polysaccharide from the grains maintained in Delft on which this work was performed.

TABLE 3
Characteristics of Kefiran

Test performed on Kefiran	Properties of Kefiran from Delft Grains
Hydrolysis	Glucose and galactose only
Extraction with:	
(i) Cold water	Dissolved slowly
(ii) Hot water	Dissolved rapidly
Galactose/glucose ratio	1
Optical rotation	$+ 68°$ $(c = 1, H_2O)$

After La Riviere *et al.* (1967).

These workers showed that rod-shaped organisms were responsible for the polysaccharide production. The capsulated organism was reported to be *Lactobacillus brevis*. Although capsulated in the Kefir grain, the bacterium apparently loses the ability to produce capsules when isolated and grown in pure culture. However, it was found that if Kefir grain extract was included in the isolation medium, capsulated organisms were obtained. However, Ottogalli *et al.* (1973) seem to think the *Lactobacillus acidophilus* may be responsible for the polysaccharide production.

A recent study (Kandler & Kunath, 1983) reports that the bacteria constitute a new species to which they give the name *Lactobacillus kefir*. These authors point out that confusion has surrounded the identity of the lactic acid bacterium (or bacteria) from Kefir for over a hundred years, with the earliest workers using '*caucasicus*' or some variant thereon as the species

name. The organisms isolated by different workers were variously homo-
and heterofermentative, able or unable to grow at temperatures above 40°,
and so forth. The use of DNA/DNA homology studies has shown that the
heterofermentative lactic acid bacteria isolated from various samples of
drink Kefir show a high degree of homology between each other but not
with strains of *L. brevis*. Kandler and Kunath therefore obtained Kefir
grains from private homes, from producers of Kefir starter cultures, and
from milk and dairy institutes in Germany, Poland and Finland (see also
Kunath, 1983). They then cultured the various grains on milk and plated
out both the resulting kefirs and homogenates of the various grains in order
to obtain isolates of lactic acid bacteria for detailed study. The bacterial
flora of the grains was dominated by Lactobacilli although Leuconostoc
was present at about 1% of the abundance of the Lactobacilli.
Homofermentative Lactobacilli accounted for 90% of the Lactobacillus
population in the grains and Streptococci accounted for less than 0·1% of
the total bacterial population. In the finished Kefir 80% of the Lactobacilli
were heterofermentative, Leuconostocs were as numerous as Lactobacilli
and Streptococci were 10 times more numerous.

All of 100 heterofermentative Lactobacilli isolated from Kefir grains and
finished kefir exhibited the same pattern of carbohydrate fermentation as
each other and as the organism now designated *L. brevis* (ATCC 8007),
which was originally isolated from Kefir by C. S. Pederson in 1944. For
three of the new isolates plus strain ATCC 8007, the cell wall composition,
electrophoretic mobility of the lactic dehydrogenase, G + C ratio of the
DNA and optimum growth temperature were also determined. They also
proved similar in all four organisms.

While similar in all other respects to *L. brevis* and *L. bachneri*, the
organisms from Kefir showed high DNA/DNA homology between each
other, but low homology with the two type strains. Additionally, the Kefir
isolates also differed 'from all the other heterofermentative species in regard
to their G + C content of DNA, their cell wall composition, and the
electrophoretic mobility of their D- and L-lactic dehydrogenases'. On
balance therefore the heterofermentative organism from Kefir has to be
regarded as a distinct species of Lactobacillus.

Kandler & Kunath (1983), in contrast to the work reported by La Riviere
et al. (1967), were unable to detect the formation of capsules by their
heterofermentative Kefir isolates when tested under the same conditions as
those applied by the latter group. It must be stressed that *L. kefir*, while the
major Lactobacillus in the Kefir, is only a minor component in the grain
and this may suggest that there is a need to investigate the Kefiran-forming

ability of the major bacterial component of the grain, especially since Rosi & Rossi (1978) reported that homofermentative organisms (described by them as 'atypical streptobacteria') formed the polysaccharide present in the Kefir grains. The situation is confused and requires further work to resolve it. It may even be that both groups of lactic acid bacteria play a part in the formation of kefiran. The literature which we have examined does not even rule out the possibility that the two groups of lactic acid bacteria may form different polysaccharides, unlikely though that seems.

Studies on Kefir grains using scanning electron microscopy by Botazzi & Bianchi (1980), showed that the yeast cells dominate the centre of the granule and that this part of the granule has a much smaller microbial population than does the peripheral region. The peripheral region was shown to consist mostly of rod-shaped bacteria and the median part of the granule was shown to have a spongy structure, consisting of extracellular material, which apparently holds the microbial populations together.

Proliferation and reconstruction. During the production of Kefir, the grains increase in size and multiply in the milk (Botazzi & Bianchi, 1980). Rosi (1978) suggested that where the largest concentration of yeast cells are found may be the site of proliferation. However, as Botazzi & Bianchi (1980) state, a better understanding of the reasons for the arrangement of the microbes within the grains is required before any advances can be made in the understanding of the proliferation of the grains.

The literature does not appear to contain any reports of obtaining new Kefir granules from crude or pure cultures of the micro-organisms involved. Hence the conditions necessary for formation may be different from those required for propagation.

The association. In milk the main carbon and energy source available for micro-organisms is lactose, hence microbes which can utilise lactose will have a competitive advantage over other organisms present (Vedamuthu, 1978). Many investigators (Freudenreich, 1897; La Riviere, 1969; Ottogalli *et al.*, 1973; Rosi, 1978) found the predominant yeasts in the Kefir grain to be non-lactose fermenters. Therefore the bacteria present, which can utilise lactose, would appear to have a competitive advantage over the yeasts. However, the association has been described by many workers (Freudenreich, 1897; La Riviere, 1969; Kosikowski, 1977) as symbiotic. Therefore the yeasts are presumably using bacterial products as a carbon and energy source, with the bacteria being dependent on the yeasts in some way. La Riviere (1969) found that the predominant Lactobacillus requires yeast autolysate to grow in milk, and that the yeasts and Lactobacilli are mutually dependent and grow in balanced proportions in the Kefir grain.

The extraordinary claim by Ram-Ayyar (1918) that the yeast found in Dahi (see above) is not able to ferment lactose but consumes the lactic acid produced by the Lactobacilli also present in the fermentation, seems to be refuted by Vedamuthu's (1982) report that the yeasts present in the product do ferment lactose.

Progress in understanding the nature of any interaction between microbes must depend at least in part on the completeness of our understanding of the biochemical activities of the organisms involved. The discussion of the Kefir lactic acid bacteria shows that while distinct progress is being made, puzzles and contradictions still remain. Information on the yeast(s) involved seems to be even scarcer than that on the lactic acid bacteria. Whereas Freudenreich (1897) described the yeast as *Saccharomyces kefir*, La Riviere *et al.* (1967) reported the presence of *Torulopsis holmii* and *Saccharomyces delbrueckii*, while Oberman (this volume) refers to the presence of *Saccharomyces florentinus*, *S. kefir* and *Torula kefir* in Kefir, and *S. lactis* plus *T. koumiss* in koumiss; she also cites several reports of 'lactose fermenting yeasts' in the numerous fermented milks which she discusses.

2.3.2. Ginger Beer 'Plant'

The only published work performed on this 'plant' appears to be by Ward (1892). However we have had access to a more recent study carried out as an Honours Year project by Mr Philip Voysey, at the University of Surrey, which has some useful information.

Composition. Ward describes the 'plant' as a white, semi-translucent, irregularly shaped mass, which is of a gelatinous nature. The 'plant' was found to consist of several organisms, two of which were always present and necessary for its formation and action. The other organisms present were probably due to the lack of asepsis during the production of ginger beer, although two other types of organisms were found constantly but these were non-essential for the formation of the 'plant' and hence for the production of the beverage.

The two organisms always present were a yeast which he called *Saccharomyces pyriformis* and a bacterium which he described as *Bacterium vermiforme*. The bacterium was found to be capable of producing gelatinous sheaths which enclose the yeast cells in the 'plant'. On isolation however, the bacterial cells were unable to produce capsules, they were 'naked'. However, it was found that the isolated bacteria could produce capsules in a medium that was acidic, free of oxygen, contained carbon dioxide and contained carbohydrates, preferably cane sugar.

This resembles the results on Kefiran production by La Riviere *et al.* (1967).

The association. Ward found that the 'plant' could be produced by using pure cultures of the above organisms and that their activities were enhanced when they made contact. The synthesis of the plant was most readily brought about when yeast cells were added to an advanced culture of the bacterium. Formation of the plant was also achieved from unsterilised ginger and sugar after 10 weeks.

Ward put forward an hypothesis as to the type of symbiosis present—the bacterium may benefit from substances released by the yeast and the yeast in turn benefits from the removal of these, or vice versa. Thus there are many similarities in the microbiology and biochemistry of the microbes in Kefir and the ginger beer 'plant'.

In the study by Voysey referred to above, he started his ginger beer with an inoculum of *Saccharomyces cerevisiae* plus whatever organisms were present in the ground ginger, sugar and water used in the fermentation. The *S. cerevisiae* seems to have maintained a steady population, not increasing in number, during the 'feeding' stage. On bottling, however, its numbers declined sharply. Other yeasts were detected at later stages of the fermentation. He found that *Bacillus* spp. were well-represented throughout the fermentation, which is not too surprising given the abundance of *Bacillus* spores on most spices. Lactic acid bacteria appeared only after the fermentation had been in progress for a few days, but were fairly numerous. This is somewhat different from the situation described by Ward and discussed above.

When fermentations were set up using established ginger beer 'plants', their micro-organisms, a yeast (one type only, judged on colony morphology) and lactic acid bacteria (number of species not determined), dominated the fermentation. Voysey was able to carry out very little by way of identification studies on the microbes which he isolated, but he obtained evidence from sugar fermentation tests that the Lactobacilli in 'plants' from two different sources resembled *L. buchneri* and *L. vermiforme*.

2.3.3. Tibi Grain

Composition. Tibi grains are translucent, tough and contain a matrix of dextran (Horisberger, 1969). They are irregular in shape and are reported (Porchet, 1934; Stadelmann, 1957) to have a maximum diameter of 8–10 mm.

It appears (Daker & Stacey, 1938) that the bacterium isolated from the Tibi grain by Meyer (unpublished work) is identical to that isolated from the ginger beer 'plant' by Ward (1892) and called *Betabacterium vermiforme* (Ward–Meyer). Horisberger (1969) refers to this organism as *Lactobacillus brevis*, and reports that the Tibi grain is a symbiotic association of *L. brevis, Streptococcus lactis* and *Saccharomyces cerevisiae*.

The bacterium isolated by Meyer was found to synthesise a polysaccharide from sucrose (Daker & Stacey, 1938). This polysaccharide was found to consist of a backbone of alpha 1-6 glucose units and to give an optical rotation of +1800 (water). Horisberger (1969) found the grains to contain a matrix of dextran which consisted mainly of alpha-D-(1-6) linked glucopyranosyl residues with 1-3 linked side chains and to have an optical rotation of +206° (NaOH). The organism responsible for this polysaccharied is not specified, however Moinas *et al.* (1980) state that the Lactobacilli generate the dextran.

The structural organisation of the grain was revealed by the work of Moinas *et al.* (1980). With phase contrast microscopy the outer layer was shown to be more densely populated by micro-organisms embedded in the polysaccharide than is the inner layer. Scanning electron microscopy showed the grain to be hollow, presumably due to carbon dioxide formed during fermentation, and the dense outer layer was shown to contain Streptococci, Lactobacilli, yeasts and the dextran. The outer layer was shown to contain less dextran than the inner layer by fluorescence microscopy.

Proliferation and reconstruction. Like Kefir grains, the Tibi grains increase in size and divide in the growth medium, the fission being determined by the inner pressure of carbon dioxide (Moinas *et al.*, 1980). The literature does not appear to contain any reports of attempts to reconstruct the grain from its component parts.

The association. Fermentation and transfer of grains can be carried out under non-sterile conditions without any extensive growth of undesirable organisms. For example the grains used by Moinas *et al.* (1980) had been sub-cultured from the original grains for 10 years, hence the association would appear to be very stable. Although the Tibi grain has been referred to as a symbiotic association of *Lactobacillus brevis, Streptococcus lactis* and *Saccharomyces cerevisiae*, no information appears to be available as to the biochemical or other basis of this relationship.

3. FOODS

Only a few of the foods mentioned in Table 2 are described. For a description of Jalebies and Nan and related breads see Batra (1980), and for soybean products see Yokotsuka (this volume) and Hesseltine (1979). Odunfa (Vol. 2) discusses African foods in greater detail.

3.1. Fermented Maize Products

3.1.1. Ogi

Ogi is a fermented maize product of Africa, however it appears that sorghum and millet may also be used as the raw materials (Banigo & Muller, 1972). Although it is still produced traditionally (Fig. 1) a few investigations have been made to find the most suitable organisms for the industrial manufacture of ogi; Akinrele (1970) found the most important and desirable organisms in the souring process to be *Saccharomyces cerevisiae, Aerobacter cloacae* and *Lactobacillus plantarum.*

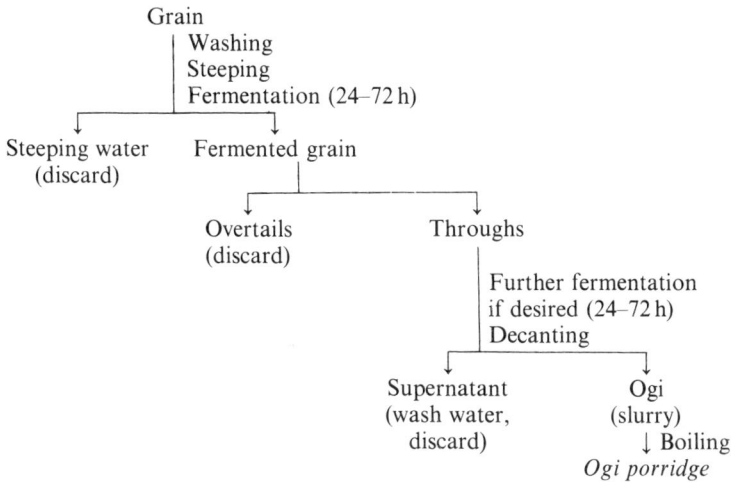

```
                    Grain
                     │ Washing
                     │ Steeping
                     │ Fermentation (24–72 h)
           ↓                     ↓
   Steeping water        Fermented grain
    (discard)                   │
                     ↓                          ↓
                  Overtails                  Throughs
                  (discard)                     │
                                     │ Further fermentation
                                     │ if desired (24–72 h)
                                     │ Decanting
                           ↓                          ↓
                      Supernatant                   Ogi
                     (wash water,                 (slurry)
                       discard)                   ↓ Boiling
                                               Ogi porridge
```

Fig. 1. Flow sheet for traditional preparation of Ogi (adapted from Banigo *et al.*, 1974).

However, Banigo *et al.* (1974) using high lysine corn for the manufacture of ogi, found the most successful combination of organisms to be *Lactobacillus plantarum, Streptococcus lactis* and *Saccharomyces rouxii.* This new ogi processing system (Fig. 2) was found to be nutritionally superior to the existing traditional process.

3.1.2. Kenkey

Kenkey is a fermented maize dumpling from Ghana. During the process (Fig. 3) *Aspergillus* and *Penicillium* species which predominate initially,

Grain
| cleaning

Tempering or conditioning
dehulling (Palyi mill)
Air separation
Screening

Hulls   Grits, fines and germs
(discard)   (combined)

Milling   Milling
(laboratory   (laboratory
hammer mill)   hammer mill)
Plus further size   Plus further size
reduction (roller mill   reduction (roller mill
with smooth rolls)   with smooth rolls)

Whole corn flour   or   Dehulled corn flour
                   | Mixing (with water)

Inoculation   Cooking
                                               Cooling
Incubation   Inoculation
at 32 °C   Incubation at
(24–28 h)   32 °C (24–28 h)

Fermented Ogi   or   Fermented Ogi
(uncooked)   (partially cooked)

Boiling | Drying
with water   Dried instant Ogi
                                           | Mixing (with water)
   Ogi porridge ←

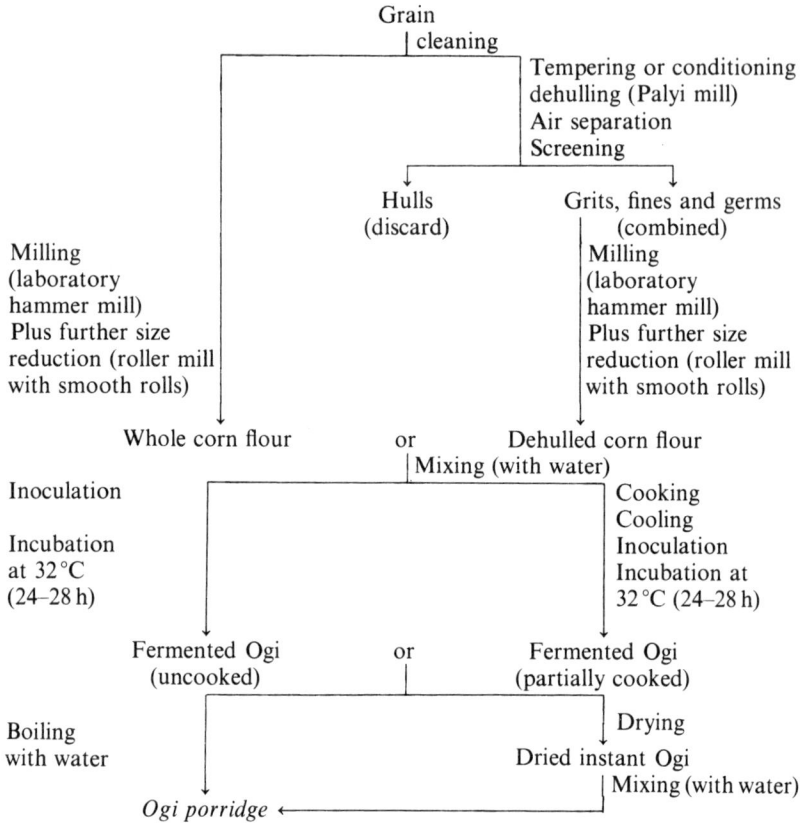

Fig. 2. Flow sheet for new approach to Ogi manufacture (adapted from Banigo
et al., 1974).

soon decline. Lactic acid bacteria start to multiply rapidly after 9 h
fermentation, reaching a peak between 24 and 36 h. These bacteria,
together with wild yeasts, form the predominant microflora during the
latter phase of fermentation.

3.2. Sour Dough Breads

Breadmaking is one of the oldest arts known to man. Traditionally bread
leavens involved lactic acid bacteria and yeasts, and the preparation of the
barm (sour ferment) was more of an art than a science. Although
commercial breadmakers now use compressed pure yeast preparations

Maize grain   (winnowed and washed)
↓
Soaked   1–2 days at 30 °C
↓
Dough   Spontaneous fermentation, 2–3 days
↓
Dough divided ⌐
Water   ↓ |
Slurry |
Boiled   ↓ |
(Porridge)   'Aflata' ←——┘
Divided, shaped
into balls and
wrapped in leaves
↓   Boiled
Kenkey

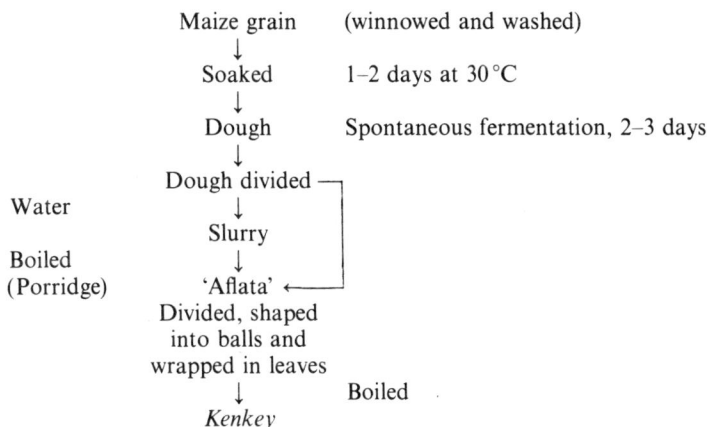

Fig. 3. Kenkey process (after Muller & Nyarko-Mensah (1972).

these arts were never totally lost (the exception being the Parisian Barm of Scotland; Bennion, 1954). The areas continuing to produce sour dough bread are Central and Eastern Europe, the Scandinavian countries and North America. Sugihara (this volume) discusses the topic in detail and we summarise the situation for completeness.

3.2.1. Sour Dough French Bread
Probably the best known sour dough is the San Francisco sour dough French bread. A 'starter' is rebuilt every 8 h with fresh flour and water. This 'mother-sponge' when fully developed serves as the inoculum for each batch of dough. In this way the process has been made continuous for over a century (Sugihara *et al.*, 1971). Although the process is carried out under hygienic conditions, the system is far from aseptic, thus demonstrating the remarkable stability of the micro-organisms involved (Kline & Sugihara, 1971).

The souring is brought about by bacteria (Kline *et al.*, 1970; Sugihara *et al.*, 1970) and these bacteria were isolated and characterised (Kline & Sugihara, 1971) as *Lactobacillus sanfrancisco*. The predominant yeast responsible for the leavening action was identified as the imperfect form of *Saccharomyces exiguus* (*Torulopsis holmii*); other yeasts isolated were *Saccharomyces inusitatus* (Sugihara *et al.*, 1971) and *Saccharomyces uvarum* (Ng, 1976).

Two of the strains of *Torulopsis holmii* isolated by Sugihara *et al.* (1971) have now been designated (Yarrow, 1978) as a new species *Candida milleri*, due to having a higher guanine plus cytosine content than *Torulopsis holmii*; physiological differences were also observed.

3.2.2. Rye Sour Dough

In the rye sour process, three lactic acid bacteria are considered to be of major significance, *Lactobacillus plantarum*, *L. brevis* and *L. fermentum* (Schulz, 1966). Other workers (Spicher & Schröder, 1978, 1979a, b, 1980; Spicher *et al.*, 1980) also found a more diverse group of bacteria than that present in the San Francisco sour dough. It was found that different bacteria predominate in different leavens. Kosmina (1977) reported that the best quality bread is obtained by using mixed cultures of homo- and heterofermentative bacteria.

The yeasts also exhibited a similar diversity (Spicher *et al.*, 1979); isolated from the leavens of two bakeries were *Candida krusei* (27 strains), *Saccharomyces cerevisiae* (11 strains), *Pichia saitoi* (2 strains) and *Torulopsis holmii* (4 strains).

Rye sours are also used to produce certain varieties of crispbread (Oura *et al.*, 1982). The USA and German pumpernickels are both made by the rye sour dough process (Drews & Seibel, 1976).

3.2.3. 'Panettone' Cake

This is a popular Italian Christmas fruit cake which is still produced by the traditional 24 h natural fermentation process. The microflora was found to be represented mainly by yeasts and lactic bacteria, being similar to that of the San Francisco French bread type and rye bread (Galli & Ottogalli, 1973); Sugihara, who has done much to advance our understanding of this product, discusses it in detail in his contribution to the present volume.

3.2.4. Soda Cracker

The manufacture of the soda cracker has been reported (Sugihara, 1978a) to depend primarily upon chance contamination. The microflora of the sponge and dough was found to consist of *Saccharomyces cerevisiae* (part of standard formulation), *Lactobacillus plantarum*, *L. delbrueckii* and *L. leichmannii* (Sugihara, 1978a).

In pure culture studies Sugihara (1978b) found that the use of these three Lactobacilli as a starter culture reduced the overall time from 24 to 8 h.

3.3. Interactions Between the Yeasts and Lactic Acid Bacteria During the Production of Fermented Foods

The production of many of the fermented foods requires specific associations of the organisms involved. These associations in many instances are very stable and are apparently able to resist contamination from other organisms. This is perhaps especially true of the sour dough ferment and it will therefore be used as an example.

It has been suggested (Sugihara *et al.*, 1970, 1971; Saunders *et al.*, 1972) that the predominant organisms *Saccharomyces exiguus* and *Lactobacillus sanfrancisco* live in a sort of 'symbiotic' association in the San Francisco sour dough.

Properties of the predominant microflora. The yeast isolated from the San Francisco sour dough by Sugihara *et al.* (1971) was found to have the following properties:

(1)   Unable to assimilate maltose, but assimilates glucose.
(2)   Resistant to cycloheximide.
(3)   Tolerant to acetic acid.

The bacterium isolated from sour dough (Kline & Sugihara, 1971), *Lactobacillus sanfrancisco*, was found to have a requirement for maltose, with poor or no growth on glucose. Wood *et al.* (1975) reported that bacteria from a Glasgow sour dough had the enzyme maltose phosphorylase.

The system. Numerous reports (Sugihara *et al.*, 1971; Kline & Sugihara, 1971) make it clear that sour dough starters resist invasion by other organisms. This apparently is not just due to the anaerobiosis and low pH of the system, as it has been found (Kline & Sugihara, 1971) that only cycloheximide resistant yeasts can survive significantly in the system. Looking at the system in detail:

(1)   Maltose is the main carbohydrate present in the medium, due to the action of amylases on starch in the grain. The bacteria exhibit a high requirement for maltose (Kline & Sugihara, 1971) and possess the enzyme maltose phosphorylase (Wood *et al.*, 1975). Presumably the bacteria are therefore using the maltose phosphorylase pathway, with glucose being excreted into the environment:

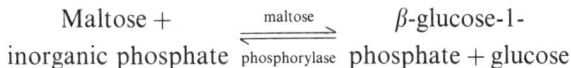

$$\text{Maltose} + \text{inorganic phosphate} \underset{\text{phosphorylase}}{\overset{\text{maltose}}{\rightleftharpoons}} \beta\text{-glucose-1-phosphate} + \text{glucose}$$

(Wood & Rainbow, 1961).

The yeast cannot utilise maltose but can utilise other non-maltose carbohydrates present (Sugihara *et al.*, 1971) including the glucose excreted by the bacteria. The two organisms are therefore not competing for the same carbohydrate.

(2)   The yeast is tolerant to the acetic acid and resistant to an antibiotic produced by the bacteria (Sugihara *et al.*, 1971).

(3)   It seems that the yeast supplies the bacteria with essential nutrients for growth (Wlodarczyk, unpublished work, personal communication), supplementing the nutrients supplied by the flour.

The system would thus appear to be self-protecting and self-regulating.

From the evidence cited in the discussions above of other similar associations it seems to be probable that similar relationships will be demonstrated for some at least of the many associations which await detailed biochemical scrutiny.

4. FLAVOURING AGENTS

4.1. Fermented Soybean Products

Soy sauce and miso are flavouring agents which have their origins in the Orient.

4.1.1. Soy Sauce

Soy sauce is a dark brown liquid with a pleasant aroma and salty taste. In China, most of the soy sauce is made from soybeans or from a mixture of soybeans and wheat (with a higher percentage of soybeans), whereas in Japan, it is made from equal amounts of soybeans and wheat (Yong & Wood, 1974). In the Orient it is still produced traditionally in the home, as well as industrially.

The production of soy sauce consists of a two-stage process, the first is an aerobic process and the second (moromi) stage is an anaerobic fermentation. The moromi undergoes fermentation by lactic acid bacteria and yeasts.

The review by Yokotsuka (this volume) shows that a consortium of yeasts is found in the moromi, while *Pediococcus* and *Lactobacillus* species have been reported to be the main lactic acid bacteria present.

4.1.2. Miso

Miso is used as a flavouring agent in soup, meat, fish and vegetables and is also used as a spread. As with soy sauce, it is prepared both on a factory scale and in the home.

The production of miso is very similar to soy sauce production (Abiose *et al.*, 1982; Yokotsuka, this volume) in both technique and microbiology, the main difference being that miso can be prepared with a variety of substrates, e.g. beans and rice, beans and barley or beans alone, and with a greater diversity in the relative quantities of beans, grain and salt used in the mixture.

4.2. Interactions Between Yeasts and Lactic Acid Bacteria During the Production of Flavourings

4.2.1. Moromi Stage of Soy Sauce Production

It is now clear that the lactic acid fermentation occurs before yeast fermentation. Thus, Yong & Wood (1976), using pure cultures of *Saccharomyces rouxii* (strain NRRLY-1096) and *Lactobacillus delbrueckii* found that after the addition of salt to the koji, the lactic acid bacteria grew up rapidly, lowering the pH and permitting yeast growth to take place when the pH fell below 5·5. During these studies it was also found that the sterile soy mash underwent a drop in pH from 6·5 to 4·5, after a couple of weeks; the reason for this is not known. A reasonable soy sauce was also achieved when no lactic acid bacteria were added, but the mash was adjusted to pH 4·5 with lactic acid and inoculated with *S. rouxii*. This however produced lower quality soy sauce than that produced with lactic acid bacteria and yeast (Yong & Wood, 1976, 1977). Detailed studies on the interaction between pH, salt concentration and the growth of *S. rouxii* are reported by Yong *et al.* (1978). It appears that the main function of the lactic acid bacteria is to bring about quickly the lowering of the pH and hence the yeast fermentation. However, this appears not to be their only role, judging by the organoleptic assessment of soy sauce quality. From the pure culture work a sequential relationship of lactic acid bacteria followed by yeasts would seem to exist but as is the case with all mixed cultures, a complex situation of interactions probably exists in the natural (uninoculated) mash. For example, in a study by Noda *et al.* (1980), it was found that osmophilic yeasts such as *Saccharomyces rouxii* and *Torulopsis holmii* were inhibited by a metabolite produced by *Pediococcus halophilus*. The primary inhibitor seemed to be acetic acid, although lactic acid was also slightly inhibitory.

4.2.2. Moromi Stage of Miso Production

Although the microbiology is very similar to that involved in soy sauce production, development of the appropriate microflora is aided by adding a portion of miso from a previous fermentation to the raw materials. The main bacteria involved are lactic acid bacteria and the yeast of choice is *Saccharomyces rouxii* (Abiose *et al.*, 1982).

Although many lactic acid producing bacteria are said to develop in miso, it is not certain that they are essential for the fermentation, and Hesseltine & Shibasaki (1961) report that a satisfactory miso can be produced with a pure culture strain of *Saccharomyces rouxii*.

5.   MEDICAL ASPECTS OF THE FERMENTED PRODUCTS

5.1. Medicinal Uses of the Fermented Products

There are many traditions asserting that kvass, kefir and koumiss confer benefit upon the user in a variety of ways. In Russia, koumiss has been used widely in treating pulmonary tuberculosis (Kosikowski, 1977) and kvass has'been reported to benefit the digestive tract and possibly to afford some protection against cancer. Sour leavens have also been claimed to benefit the digestive tract, but whether these claims would survive Western medical investigation is unknown.

5.2. Antibiotic Production

Certain lactic acid bacteria produce antibiotics, for example *Lactobacillus acidophilus* produces the antibiotic acidolin (Hamdan & Mikolajcik, 1974) in skim milk. Acidolin exhibits antimicrobial activity against Gram positive and Gram negative bacteria including enteropathogens and sporeformers. It has only limited activity against lactic acid bacteria and is not active against the organism that produces it.

Fermented milk containing viable *L. acidophilus* is reported as being beneficial to those suffering from disorders of the digestive tract. Only some strains of *L. acidophilus* are implantable (that is to say can become permanently established) in the human intestinal tract, and it is the consumption of milk cultured with these strains which is beneficial to sufferers from disorders such as constipation and diarrhoea (Pederson, 1979), suggesting that the organisms take up residence in the intestine and exert a continuing effect by competing and interacting with other microbes present in, or gaining access to, the intestine, so regulating and harmonising the intestinal microflora. Elsewhere in this volume Oberman discusses the benefits resulting from the consumption of various types of fermented milks in Eastern Europe, the Mediterranean area and Africa. Topical application for the relief of skin diseases has also been beneficial according to reports which she cites. An attractive feature of therapy with fermented milks is that it is highly unlikely to do any harm, even if the benefits prove to be more limited than some traditions suggest.

Furthermore it would not be expected to interfere with the action of medicinals prescribed in accordance with conventional medical practice.

6. DISCUSSION

In many of the systems described here, the fermentation is started by inoculating the raw materials with a small portion from a previous fermentation, or by awaiting spontaneous fermentation of the raw materials. Only in a small number of cases, for example koumiss, is the traditional fermentation started by precise and deliberate inoculation of the desired organisms to the raw materials, under controlled conditions. Therefore in the majority of the products control is limited to maintaining a balance between the micro-organisms involved, which is generally achieved by manipulation of the cultural conditions. This is changing as foods such as yoghurt develop into commercial products.

Although the micro-organisms responsible for the fermentations are known in many of the systems, information pertaining to the associations between the organisms is rather limited. The understanding of the physiology and biochemistry of these interactions appears to be an essential prerequisite to a fuller and more controlled utilisation of the desired fermentation. The pure culture work on soy sauce moromi highlights this aspect of an understanding of the organisms' interactions leading to a more controlled fermentation. The extent to which the system simulates the actual moromi conditions is questionable; however, a soy sauce with good organoleptic quality can be obtained.

Not only would the understanding of these interactions provide better control over the systems, but it would be interesting to find the reasons why many of these systems remain remarkably constant in composition, when faced with continuous infection. The grains described in Section 2.3 highlight this aspect of constant composition. Although the ecology of the grains has been studied in detail very little appears to be known about the actual bases of the associations.

This has probably been hindered by the fact that the Lactobacilli, which produce the embedding material, lose this ability when cultured under laboratory conditions, the synthetic capacity being unstable (Dunican & Seeley, 1965). This probably hinders the reconstruction of the grains. It is also interesting to note that *Lactobacillus brevis* is reported to be responsible for the production of the embedding material in each of these grains, a different polysaccharide being produced under different environmental conditions, although this view is under increasing challenge as the identity of the Lactobacilli is reassessed using modern methods (e.g. Kandler & Kunath, 1983).

Therefore the reasons for the stability of most of these systems appear to be unknown. However, it is apparent that many of the organisms are highly adapted to their environments and to each other. An interesting example of this is the partnership between *Lactobacillus bulgaricus* and *Streptococcus thermophilus* in yoghurt (Bautista *et al.*, 1966) where the release of glycine and histidine by the Lactobacillus promoted more rapid acid production by the Streptococcus.

This dissertation has dealt only with products edible by humans but it should be noted that the associations between yeasts and lactic acid bacteria are found in other environments. Hrubant (Vol. 2) draws attention to their importance in converting animal 'feedlot' waste into a form acceptable to farm animals as part of their diet. He also perceives that this type of fermentation will contribute to the understanding of the biochemistry of the interactions between the organisms involved.

This short survey therefore shows that stable mixed cultures of yeasts and lactic acid bacteria are found in many different environments. This stability allows the fermentations to be maintained safely and successfully when facing continuous infection. However, if their interactions were studied in greater detail, more controlled fermentations could be achieved, so increasing their benefits to humanity.

As therapeutic claims have been made about some of these products it may prove worthwhile for investigations to be made into this aspect. The available evidence also suggests that many of these products should be examined for the occurrence of antibiotics.

REFERENCES

ABIOSE, S. H., ALLAN, M. C. & WOOD, B. J. B. (1982) Microbiology and biochemistry of miso (soy paste) fermentation. *Adv. appl. Microbiol.* **28**, 201–37.

AKINRELE, I. A. (1970) Fermentation studies on maize during the preparation of a traditional African starch-cake food. *J. Sci. Food Agric.* **21**, 619–25.

BANIGO, E. O. I., DEMAN, J. M. & DUITSCHAEVER, C. L. (1974) Utilization of high-lysine corn for the manufacture of ogi using a new, improved processing system. *Cereal Chem.* **51**, 559–72.

BANIGO, E. O. I. & MULLER, H. G. (1972) Carboxylic acid patterns in ogi fermentation. *J. Sci. Food Agric.* **23**, 101–11.

BATRA, L. R. (1980) Fermented cereals and grain legumes of India and vicinity. In *Advances in Biotechnology*, M. Moo-Young & C. W. Robinson, Eds. Pergamon Press, Toronto, Canada, pp. 547–53.

BAUTISTA, E. S., DAHIYA, R. S. & SPECK, M. L. (1966) Identification of compounds causing symbiotic growth of *Streptococcus thermophilus* and *Lactobacillus bulgaricus* in milk. *J. Dairy Res.* **33**, 299–307.

BENNION, E. B. (1954) *Breadmaking, its Principles and Practice.* Oxford University Press, Oxford, pp. 119–22.

BOGDANOFF (1934) *J. Dairy Res.* **5**, 153–9. Cited by Tanner (1944).

BOTAZZI, V. & BIANCHI, F. (1980) A note on scanning electron microscopy of micro-organisms associated with the Kefir granule. *J. appl. Bacteriol.* **48**, 265–8.

BRYAN-JONES, G. (1975) Lactic acid bacteria in distillery fermentations. In *Lactic Acid Bacteria in Beverages and Foods*, J. G. Carr, C. V. Cutting & G. C. Whiting Eds. Academic Press, London, pp. 165–75.

CHEKAN (1922) *Centralblatt für Bakteriologie Pt 2* **78**, 74–93. Cited by Tanner (1944).

DAKER, W. D. & STACEY, M. (1938) Investigation of a polysaccharide produced from sucrose by *Betabacterium vermiforme* (Ward-Meyer). *Biochem. J.* **32**, 1946–8.

DIRAR, H. A. (1978) A microbiological study of Sudanese merissa brewing. *J. Food Sci.* **43**, 1683–6.

DREWS, E. & SEIBEL, W. (1976) Bread baking and other uses around the world. In *Rye: Production, Chemistry and Technology*, W. Bushuk Ed. American Association of Cereal Chemists, Inc., St. Paul, Minnesota, p. 127.

DUGGELI (1905) *Centralblatt für Bakteriologie Pt 2* **15**, 577–600. Cited by Tanner (1944).

DUNICAN, L. K. & SEELEY, H. W. (1965) Extracellular polysaccharide synthesis by members of the genus *Lactobacillus*: conditions for formation and accumulation. *J. gen. Microbiol.* **40**, 297–308.

FAPARUSI, S. I. (1970) Sugar changes during preparation of Burukutu beer. *J. Sci. Food Agric.* **21**, 79–81.

FOSTER, E. M., NELSON, F. E., SPECK, M. L., DOETSCH, R. N. & OLSEN, J. C. (1957) *Dairy Microbiology*. Prentice-Hall, Inc., New Jersey, USA, pp. 318–33.

FREUDENREICH, E. (1897) *Centralblatt für Bakteriologie pt 2* **3**, 47–54. Cited by Tanner (1944).

GALLI, A. & OTTOGALLI, G. (1973) The microflora of the sour dough of the 'Panettone' cake. *Annali di microbiologie ed Enzimologia* **23**, 39–43. Cited in *Microbiology Abstracts A. Industrial and Applied Microbiology* (1976) **11**, 11A, 108.

HAMDAN, I. Y. & MIKOLAJCIK, E. M. (1974) Acidolin: an antibiotic produced by *Lactobacillus acidophilus*. *J. Antibiot.* **27**, 631–6.

HEINEMANN (1911) *Science* **33**, 630. Cited by Tanner (1944).

HESSELTINE, C. W. (1965) A millenium of fungi, food and fermentation. *Mycologia* **57**, 149–97.

HESSELTINE, C. W. (1979) Some important fermented foods of Mid-Asia, the Middle East and Africa. *J. Am. Oil Chemists Soc.* **56**, 367–74.

HESSELTINE, C. W. & SHIBASAKI, K. (1961) Miso III. Pure culture fermentation with *Saccharomyces rouxii*. *Appl. Microbiol.* **9**, 515–18.

HESSELTINE, C. W. & WANG, H. L. (1967) Traditional fermented foods. *Biotechnol. Bioengng* **9**, 275–88.

HORISBERGER, M. (1969) Structure of the dextran of the Tibi grain. *Carbohyd. Res.* **10**, 379–85.

KANDLER, O. & KUNATH, P. (1983) *Lactobacillus kefir* sp. nov., a component of the microflora of Kefir. *System. appl. Microbiol.* **4**, 286–94.

KEBLER, L. F. (1921) Californian Bees. *J. Am. pharmaceut. Assoc.* **10**, 939–43.

KLINE, L. & SUGIHARA, T. F. (1971) Micro-organisms of the San Francisco sour dough bread process. II. Isolation and characterization of undescribed bacterial species responsible for the souring action. *Appl. Microbiol.* **21**, 459–65.

KLINE, L., SUGIHARA, T. F. & McCREADY, L. B. (1970) Nature of the San Francisco sour dough French bread process. I. Mechanism of the process. *Bakers' Digest* **44**, 48–50.

KO, S.-D. (1982) Indigenous fermented foods. In *Economic Microbiology Vol. 7, Fermented Foods*, A. H. Rose Ed. Academic Press, London, pp. 15–38.

KOSIKOWSKI, F. V. (1977) *Cheese and Fermented Milk Foods*, 2nd edn. Edwards Bros. Inc., Ann Arbor, Michigan, pp. 40–6.

KOSMINA, N. P. (1977) *Biochemie der Brotherstellung*. VEB Fachbuchverlag, Leipzig. Cited by Oura *et al.* (1982).

KUNATH, P. (1983) Die mikroflora von kefir. Dissertation der Facultät für Biologie der Ludwig-Maximilians-Universität, München.

LIPATOV, N. N. (1978) Fermented milks other than yoghurt. XXth International Dairy Congress, Paris. 43ST.

LLOYD-HIND, M. (1950) *Brewing Science and Practice*, Vol. II. Chapman and Hall, London, pp. 647–648.

LUTZ, L. (1899) Recherches biologiques sur la constitution du Tibi. *Bulletin de la Société Mycologique de France* **15**, 68–72. Cited by Moinas *et al.* (1980).

MOINAS, M., HORISBERGER, N. & BAUER, H. (1980) The structural organization of the Tibi grain as revealed by light, scanning and transmission microscopy. *Arch. Microbiol.* **128**, 157–61.

MONIZ, L., GURAO, M. G. & PATIL, B. D. (1976) Studies on utilization of colostrum for making a good quality dahi. *J. Maharashtra agric. University* **1**, 31–3.

MULLER, H. G. (1982) Fermented cereal products of tropical Africa. In *Advances in Biotechnology*. Vol. II, pp. 501–46. M. Moo-Young & C. W. Robinson, Eds. Pergamon Press, Toronto.

MULLER, H. G. & NYARKO-MENSAH, B. (1972) Studies on Kenkey, a Ghanaian cereal food. *J. Sci. Food Agric.* **23**, 544–5.

NG, H. (1976) Growth requirements of San Francisco sour dough yeasts and bakers' yeast. *Appl. environ. Microbiol.* **31**, 385–98.

NODA, F., HAYASHI, K. & MIZUNUMA, T. (1980) Antagonism between osmophilic lactic acid bacteria and yeasts in brine fermentation of soy sauce. *Appl. environ. Microbiol.* **40**, 452–7.

NOUT, M. J. R. (1980) Microbiological aspects of the traditional manufacture of Busaa, a Kenyan opaque maize beer. *Chemie Mikrobiologie Technologie der Lebensmittel* **6**, 137–42. Cited in *Microbiological Abstracts A. Industrial and Applied Microbiology* (1980) **15**, 11073-A15.

NOVELLIE, L. (1968) Kaffir beer brewing: ancient art and modern industry. *Wallerstein Laboratory Communications* **31**, 17–19.

OLSEN-SOPP, O. J. (1912) *Centralblatt für Bakteriologie II* **33**, 1–54. Cited by Hesseltine (1965).

OTTOGALLI, G., GALLI, A., RESMINI, P. & VOLONTERIO, G. (1973) Composizione microbiologica, chimica ed ultrastruttura dei granuli di Kefir. *Annali di*

Microbiologia ed Enzimologia **23**, 109. Cited in *Microbiology Abstracts A. Industrial and Applied Microbiology* (1976) **11**, 11A-1224.

OURA, E., SUOMALAINEN, H. & VIKSKARI, R. (1982) Breadmaking. In *Economic Microbiology, Vol. 7, Fermented Foods*. A. H. Rose Ed. Academic Press, London, pp. 87–146.

PEDERSON, C. S. (1979) *Microbiology of Food Fermentations*, 2nd Edn. AVI Publishing Co. Inc., Westport, Conn., USA. p. 295.

PORCHET, B. (1934) Etude d'une boisson fermentée à base de figues. *Mitteilungen Lebensmittelunters Hygiene* **25**, 235–44. Cited by Moinas *et al.* (1980).

RAM-AYYAR, C. S. (1918) *Agric. J. India* **23**, 107–10. Cited by Tanner (1944).

RIST, E. & KHOURY, J. (1902) Etudes dur un lait fermenté comestible. Le Leben d' Egypte, *Annales de l' Institut Pasteur* **16**, 65–84.

RIVIERE, J. W. M., LA (1969) Ecology of yeasts in the Kefir grain. *Antonie Van Leeuwenhoek* **35** (Suppl.), D15-D16.

RIVIERE, J. W. M., LA, KOOIMAN, P. & SCHMIDT, K. (1967) Kefiran, a novel polysaccharide produced in the Kefir grain by *Lactobacillus brevis*. *Archiv Mikrobiologie* **59**, 269–78.

ROSI, J. (1978). The Kefir micro-organisms: the yeasts/I microorganismi del Kefir: I Lieviti. *Scienzae Tecnica Lattiero-Cesearia* **29**, 59–67. Cited in *Microbiology Abstracts A. Industrial and Applied Microbiology* (1979) **14**, 179–A14.

ROSI, J. & ROSSI, H. (1978) I microorganismi del Kefir: I fermenti lattici. *Scienzae Technica Lattiero-Cesearia* **29**, 291–305. Cited in Kandler & Kunath (1983).

SANCHEZ-MARROQUIN, A. & HOPE, P. H. (1953) Agave juice: fermentation and chemical composition studies of some species. *J. Agric. Food Chem.* **1**, 246–9.

SAUNDERS, R. M., NG, H. & KLINE, L. (1972) The sugars of flour and their involvement in the San Francisco sour dough French bread process. *Cereal Chem.* **49**, 86–91.

SCHULZ, A. (1966) *Bakers' Digest* **40**, 77. Cited by Oura *et al.* (1982).

SPICHER, G. (1959) Die mikroflora des sauerteiges, I. Untersuchungen uber die art in sauerteigen anzutreffenden stabchenformigen milchsaure-bakterien (genus *Lactobacillus* Beijerinck). *Zentralblatt für Bakteriologie, Parasitenkunde, Infektionskrankheiten und Hygiene* **113**, 80–106.

SPICHER, G. (1974) Brot und andere backwaren. In *Ullmanns Encyklopadie der Technischen Chemie 4, Neubearbeitete und Erweiterte Auflage, Band 8, Antimon bis Brot.* Verlag Chemie, Weinheim, pp. 702–30.

SPICHER, G. & SCHRÖDER, R. (1978) Die Mikroflora des sauerteiges, IV. Untersuchungen uber die art in 'Reinzuchtassuern' ansutreffenden stabshenfor-migen milchsaurebakterien (genus *Lactobacillus* Beijerinck). *Zeitschrift für Lebensmittel-Untersuchung und—Forschung* **167**, 342–54.

SPICHER, G. & SCHRÖDER, R. (1979a) Die mikroflora des sauerteiges, V: Das vitaminbedurfruis der in 'Reinzuchtsauern' und in sauerteigen anzutreffenden stabchenformigen milchsaurbakterien (genus *Lactobacillus* Beijerinck). *ibid.* **168**, 188–92.

SPICHER, G. & SCHRÖDER, R. (1979b) Die mikroflora des sauerteiges, VI. Das aminosaurebedurfnis der in 'Reinzuchtsauern' und in sauerteigen anzutreffeden stabchenformigen milchsaurbakterien (genus *Lactobacillus* Beijerinck). *ibid.* **168**, 397–401.

292   *Brian J. B. Wood and Mary M. Hodge*

SPICHER, G. & SCHRÖDER, R. (1980) Die mikroflora des saurteiges, VIII Die faktoren des wachstaums der in 'Reinsuchtsauern' auftretenden hefen. *ibid.* **169**, 397–401.

SPICHER, G., SCHRÖDER, R. & SCHÖLLHAMMER, K. (1979) Die mikroflora des sauerteiges, VII. Untersuchungen uber die art der in 'Reinzuchtsauern' auftretenden hefen. *ibid.* **168**, 77–81.

SPICHER, G., SCHRÖDER, R. & STEPHAN, H. (1980) Die mikroflora des saurteiges, X. Die backtechnische wirkung der in 'Reinzuchtsauern' auftretenden milchsaure-bakterien (genus *Lactobacillus* Beijerinck). *ibid.* **171**, 119–24.

SPICHER, G. & STEPHAN, H. (1964) Die mikroflora des sauerteiges, II. Unter-suchungen uber die backtechnische bedeutung der aus sauerteigen isolierten stabchenformigen milchsaurebakterien (genus *Lactobacillus* Beijerinck). *Zentral-blatt für Bakteriologie Parasitenkunde, Infektionskrankheiten und Hygiene*, II **118**, 453–71.

SPICHER, G. & STEPHAN, H. (1966) Die mikroflora des sauerteiges III. Untersuchungen uber die art der in 'spontan sauerteigen' anzutreffenden milchsaurebakterien und ibre backtechnische beduetung. *ibid.* **120**, 685–702.

STADLEMANN, E. (1957) Die symbiose Tibi. *Bull. Soc. Fribourgeoise Sci. Nat.* **47**, 16–19. Cited by Moinas *et al.* (1980).

STEINKRAUS, K. H. (1980) Industrialisation of home and village food fermentation. In *Advances in Biotechnology* Vol. II, M. Moo-Young & C. W. Robinson Eds. Pergamon Press, Toronto, Canada, pp. 473–8.

SUGIHARA, T. F. (1978a) Microbiology of the soda-cracker process I. Isolation and identification of microflora. *J. Food Protection* **41**, 977–9.

SUGIHARA, T. F. (1978b) Microbiology of the soda-cracker process II. Pure culture fermentation studies. *ibid.* **41**, 980–2.

SUGIHARA, T. F., KLINE, L. & McCREADY, L. B. (1970) Nature of the San Francisco sour dough French bread process II. Microbiological aspects. *Bakers' Digest* **44**, 50–2.

SUGIHARA, T. F., KLINE, L. & MILLER, M. W. (1971) Micro-organisms of the San Francisco sour dough bread process, I. Yeasts responsible for the leavening action. *Appl. Microbiol.* **21**, 456–8.

TANNER, F. W. (1944) *Microbiology of Foods*, 2nd edn. Garrard Press, Champaign, Illinois, pp. 569–94.

VEDAMUTHU, E. R. (1978) Natural (unhydrolyzed) milk versus lactose hydrolyzed milk for cultured dairy products—physiological and practical implications for starter industry. *J. Food Protection* **41**, 654–9.

VEDAMUTHU, E. R. (1982) Fermented milks. In *Economic Microbiology, Vol. 7, Fermented Foods*, A. H. Rose Ed. Academic Press, London, pp. 199–226.

VOYSEY, P. (1983) The Microbiology of Ginger Beer. B.Sc. Project, Dept. of Microbiology, University of Surrey, Guildford, England.

WANG, H. L. & HESSELTINE, C. W. (1979) Mould modified foods. In *Microbial Technology*, 2nd edn, Vol. II. H. J. Peppler & D. Perlman Eds. Academic Press, New York, pp. 95–129.

WARD, H. M. (1892) The ginger-beer 'plant', and the organisms composing it: a contribution to the study of fermentation—yeasts and bacteria. *Phil. Trans. R. Soc.* **183**, 125–97.

WEIGMANN, GRUBER & HUSS (1907) *Centralblatt für Bakteriologie* Pt. 2 **19**, 70–87. Cited by Tanner (1944).

WOOD, B. J. B. (1981) The yeast/lactobacillus interaction: a study in stability. In *Mixed Culture Fermentations*, M. E. Bushell & J. H. Slater Eds. Academic Press, London, pp. 137–150.

WOOD, B. J. B. (1982) Soy sauce and miso. In *Economic Microbiology, Vol. 7, Fermented Foods*, A. H. Rose Ed. Academic Press, London, pp. 39–86.

WOOD, B. J. B., CARDENAS, O. S., YONG, F. M. & McNULTY, D. W. (1975) Lactobacilli in the production of soy sauce, sour dough bread and Parisian barm. In *Lactic Acid Bacteria in Beverages and Food*, J. G. Carr, C. V. Cutting & G. C. Whiting Eds. Academic Press, London, pp. 325–35.

WOOD, B. J. B. & RAINBOW, C. (1961) The maltophosphorylase of beer lactobacilli. *Biochem. J.* **78**, 204–9.

YARROW, D. (1978) *Candida milleri* sp. nov. *Int. J. system. Bacteriol.* **28**, 608–10.

YONG, F. M., LEE, K. H. & WONG, H. A. (1978) Study of some factors affecting the growth of soy yeast (*Saccharomyces rouxii* NRRLY 1096). *J. Food Technol.* **13**, 385–96.

YONG, F. M. & WOOD, B. J. B. (1974) Microbiology and biochemistry of soy sauce fermentation. *Adv. appl. Microbiol.* **17**, 157–94.

YONG, F. M. & WOOD, B. J. B. (1976) Microbial succession in experimental soy sauce fermentation. *J. Food Technol.* **11**, 525–36.

YONG, F. M. & WOOD, B. J. B. (1977) Biochemical changes in experimental soy sauce moromi. *ibid.* **12**, 263–73.

Chapter 8

Biology and Technology of Mushroom Culture

W. A. HAYES

Department of Biological Sciences,
University of Aston in Birmingham, UK

1. INTRODUCTION

In its simplest form, the life cycle of a mushroom may be traced (Fig. 1)
from a spore, which under favourable conditions germinates to form a mass
of branched hyphae or mycelium, which colonises a compatible substrate.
This represents the vegetative stage of growth. When a given substrate is
fully colonised with mycelium, i.e. when vegetative growth ceases, typically
some hyphae making up the mycelium form aggregations or initials, to
which a flow of water and nutrients are translocated from the established
mycelium to form primordia or fundaments, which are the beginnings of
the reproductive stage. These develop further to form the stipe (stalk), the
pileus (cap) of the fruitbody, which, when mature, exposes the gill tissue or
generative tissue, on the underside, from which spores are liberated, so that
the life cycle is perpetuated.

Although a mushroom fruit is a macrostructure and clearly visible, the
spore and hyphae are microscopic and dominate the time scale of the life
cycle. The cultivation of edible mushrooms is one of the few examples of
microbial culture in which the micro-organism cultured is used directly as a
human food.

To the uninitiated, the methods of artificial culture at first appear to be
complex but they follow closely standard laboratory techniques for the
culture of other micro-organisms. For example distinct stages may be
identified: (i) the production of pure culture inoculum or spawn, (ii)

295

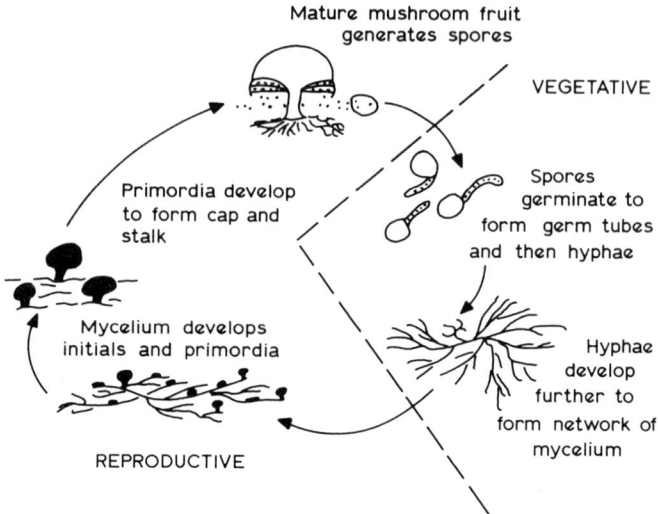

Fig. 1. The life cycle of a mushroom.

inoculation onto a medium or substrate, (iii) incubation, (iv) harvesting, and (v) terminal disinfection and disposal of the culture.

There is however a fundamental difference, in that culturing micro-organisms in the laboratory usually requires aseptic techniques, but in the mass culture of mushrooms no sterile methods are adopted. Indeed, for some species, including the most widely cultivated species, *Agaricus bisporus*, other micro-organisms play an essential role, without which the life cycle cannot be completed. The culture is thus a mixed culture fermentation and for the commercial production of fruits, the substrates are in the solid state, which contrast with other well known mixed culture fermentations, e.g. brewing.

A wide range of species are now cultivated but production is dominated by the white cultivated mushroom *Agaricus bisporus*, or as it is sometimes known, the 'Champignon de Paris'. The main feature of the method of culture is the requirement for a composted substrate and a second substrate, a capping or casing soil, which overlays the compost substrate, without which fruits will not form. Micro-organisms are intimately associated with both vegetative and reproductive stages of the life cycle. Other less widely cultivated species which require a casing soil include *Coprinus comatus*, the shaggy cap and *Stropharia raguso-annulata*, a species cultivated by amateur gardeners in Hungary and Poland.

(a)

(b)

Fig. 2. (a) *Agaricus bisporus* growing in compost and cased with peat–limestone soil. (b) Beds are arranged in portable trays in layers in a growing house in which the environmental conditions are controlled. (Courtesy I. Whitehall.)

A second group, which is rapidly gaining prominence in the world mushroom markets, are those which have a specific light requirement in order to induce fruit formation. There are two species: *Lentinus edodes* or the Japanese Forest Mushroom, which is widely cultivated on wood logs, and *Volvariella volvaceae*, the Chinese Straw Mushroom, which is grown on rice straw in tropical countries. Both species are predominantly cultivated in the Orient, but *Lentinus edodes* is now more widely cultivated in Europe, Canada and the United States.

Oyster mushrooms also belong to this group which have a light requirement for fruit formation. Traditionally, these mushrooms which include a number of species within the genus *Pleurotus*, have been part of Italian and Indian cuisine for many decades, but are now being exploited extensively in other parts of the world, particularly in developing countries. Relatively simple techniques of culture may be applied to this species and a wide range of agro-industrial wastes may be used as substrates.

Most of our knowledge on the biology of cultivated mushrooms is based on the cultivated white mushroom *A. bisporus* (Fig. 2) for which techniques of artificial culture have been practised for three centuries. However, research on other edible species has intensified over the last decade and for some species the future prospects for more extensive culture worldwide are promising.

2. *AGARICUS* AND OTHER SPECIES WHICH REQUIRE A CASING SOIL

Stages in the culture process of *Agaricus* are illustrated in Fig. 3 and in modern culture much stress is placed on maintaining maximum control of the cultural conditions. Typically, the commercial process, a batch fermentation, takes approximately 11 weeks from the time substrates are inoculated with spawn—a pure culture of *Agaricus bisporus* on grain. Preparation of the compost substrates, which precedes the cultural stages, may take up to 3 weeks to complete and the minimum time for the establishment of mycelium on grain for the production of spawn is also three weeks.

In commerce therefore it is usual to organise a continuity of output, by maintaining at least a once weekly input of substrate and for every given growing structure, at least five batches can be accommodated per annum.

The sequence of stages for *Coprinus* and *Stropharia* follow closely those for *Agaricus* culture, but in the case of *Stropharia* the reproductive stage or

Spawn manufacture   Composting

         → Spawning ←

                    Incubation at 25 °C for 14 days

        Casing

                    Incubation at 25 °C for 10 days.
                    Ventilate and further incubation

Trays and   at 14–18 °C for 11 days
shelves reused

        First harvest

        Second harvest

     6–7 harvests in 6 weeks

      — Terminal disinfection

                      Polythene sack
                 → culture disposed
                      (fertiliser)

      Disposal of used substrate
      (fertiliser)

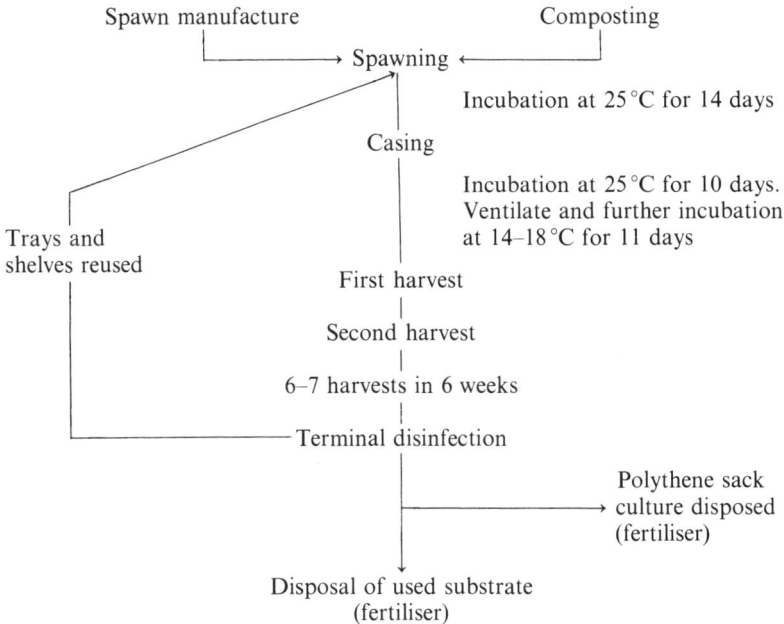

Fig. 3. Summary of stages in the culture of *Agaricus bisporus.*

fruit formation generally takes several weeks longer than for *Agaricus.* There are fundamental differences in the biology of the three species and this is reflected principally in the methods adopted for substrate preparation. Although specific information on the function of the casing layer in *Coprinus* and *Stropharia* culture is lacking, from the information available it appears to be similar in function to *Agaricus* culture. The activity of micro-organisms in the casing layer is known to be essential in the cultivation of *A. bisporus* and *Stropharia.*

2.1. Nutrition and Substrates
2.1.1. Agaricus and Coprinus
For *Agaricus* and *Coprinus*, the main source of nutrients is provided as composts, which traditionally are prepared from mixtures of wheat straw and horse manure. Spawn will develop mycelium in unfermented horse manure, but satisfactory development is prevented by the natural self-generation of heat and from competition by other micro-organisms. It is therefore necessary to ferment or compost the straw mixture in order to produce a medium which will remain stable and in which the amount of

available nutrients for competing organisms is reduced to low levels (Fig. 4).

Preparing such composts is the most difficult step in mushroom growing and satisfactory composts are obtained only after much experience.

Modern systems of composting follow a consistent pattern. Straw, or a mixture of straw, manure and fertilisers, or 'activators', is arranged in stacks of about 2 m in cross-section and is wetted or turned at 2 or 3 day intervals over a period of 10–12 days. This first stage is followed by a

Fig. 4.   Preparing a mushroom compost from straw in Taiwan.

controlled pasteurisation in which the composting mixture is placed in trays or shelves for a further stage of composting in a specially constructed heat room, designed to maintain aerobic conditions by the provision of fresh air and the exhaust of stale air from the room. The temperature is also precisely controlled so as to effectively kill all pest and pathogen contaminants and to select for a microbial population which rapidly utilises free ammonia. When free ammonia is completely utilised microbial activity subsides and the compost is cooled to 23–28 °C before inoculation with spawn.

As a result of these two distinct stages in composting, there are marked changes in the physical, chemical and biological characteristics, all of which contribute to a compost being not only a source of nutrients, but also a substrate which favours the inoculated mushroom at the expense of other competing micro-organisms, i.e. it is selective for *A. bisporus* and *Coprinus comatus* (Fig. 5).

During composting there is a loss of volume and density caused by the loss of dry matter such as carbon dioxide, ammonia and water. Studies by Waksman and co-workers related these changes to microbial activity and their work also demonstrated that *A. bisporus* derived most of its nutrients from lignin, cellulose, hemicellulose and protein (Waksman & Nissen, 1932). Later work by Gerrits *et al.* (1967) confirmed these findings using composts prepared according to modern methods and they also showed that during composting there was a substantial change in the C:N ratio from about 30 or above to about 15:1.

The sequence of the microbial changes in composting was defined by

Fig. 5. *Coprinus comatus* or the Shaggy Mane. An edible mushroom not cultivated extensively but it grows on a compost cased with a peat–limestone soil. Culture methods are comparable to those for *Agaricus* mushrooms. (Courtesy BC Research, Vancouver, Canada.)

Hayes (1969, 1977). At the commencement of composting the aerobic thermophilic bacteria dominate while in the later stages bacterial numbers decline and actinomycete populations increase. Conventional plate techniques reveal only minor changes in the number of fungus propagules. Changes in the composition of the microflora were also noted (Table 1) and these changes, together with the changes in number, could be related not only to the composition of the mixtures but also to the temperatures recorded within the compost at various stages of the process.

TABLE 1

Summary of Changes in the Dominant Thermophilic and Thermotolerant Flora During Composting (after Hayes, 1969)

	Species dominant at	
	Beginning	*End* *(when ready for spawning)*
Bacteria	*Bacillus subtilis* *Flavobacterium* spp.	*B. stearothermophilus* *Pseudomonas* sp
Actinomycetes	*Streptomyces* *thermovulgaris*	*S. thermovulgaris* *S. rectus*
Fungi	*Mucor pusillus* *Aspergillus fumigatus* *Humicola languinosa*	*H. griseus* *Torula thermophila*

This ecological study highlighted the importance of different microbial groups in the process of composting and in the subsequent nutrition of *A. bisporus*. Particular relevance was given to the importance of thermophilic bacterial populations in the productivity of the crop and led to the conclusion that the mass of dead thermophilic bacteria or 'biomass' contributed to the nutrition of the crop (Hayes 1969, 1978). In later studies, Eddy & Jacobs (1976) and Fermor & Wood (1979) provided further evidence that bacterial biomass was an important nutrient source for *A. bisporus*.

Following the inoculation of compost with spawn, temperatures are maintained within the mesophilic range, at 25 °C and encourage the growth of the mushroom mycelium from spawn, which, after a period of about 14 days, fully colonises and dominates the microbial activity of the substrate. Mesophilic bacteria and fungi are however present in large numbers and may flourish to dominate the compost at the expense of the inoculated *A. bisporus*, if composts are not adequately prepared.

Before mushroom fruits are formed it is necessary to 'cap' or 'case' the colonised compost with a layer of soil, referred to as casing. Many different materials may function as a soil, but a mixture of peat neutralised with chalk or limestone, is most commonly used in commerce. Mushroom mycelium readily colonises this layer, and when growth reaches the surface, temperatures are reduced to 15–18 °C and the growing house atmosphere is maintained fresh by ventilation.

Although the function of the casing layer is thought to be primarily one of providing support for the developing fruits and to maintain a constantly moist culture, the transition from vegetative (mycelium) to reproductive growth (fruits) is known to be associated with bacterial activity in the casing layer (Eger, 1961; Hayes *et al.*, 1969; Hayes, 1974). Bacterial numbers increase following the application of the casing soil, rising to a maximum level at about 10 days (Hayes, 1974); Hayes & Nair, 1977) after application, a time which coincides with the mycelium forming aggregates or initials, on or near the surface. As a proportion of these initials develop further into fruits their numbers decline slightly. Hayes *et al.* (1969) and Hayes & Nair (1977) showed that bacterial populations were dominated by *Pseudomonas putida* and Pseudomonads Group IV and were found to be particularly effective in stimulating the formation of fruits when added singly to axenic cultures of *A. bisporus*. Studies by Cresswell & Hayes (1979) show the possibility of the migration of mesophilic bacteria from the surface of the compost into the casing layer, following its application.

The function and role of the casing layer in the artificial culture of *Coprinus comatus* has not been studied.

Studies on the enzymology of *A. bisporus* in straw-based composts were carried out by Turner (1974) and Turner *et al.* (1975). There was a high level of laccase activity in compost during its colonisation by the mycelium, but cellulase activity was at a low level during this stage, and increased dramatically at about the time of fruit maturation. This, it is thought, reflects a change in the nutrition of the fungus at this time. These changes in extracellular enzyme activity at the time of fruit formation were later confirmed by Wood & Goodenough (1977) using axenic cultures, arrested at various stages of fruitbody development, and cellulase activity was shown to remain at a low level for the remainder of cropping, by these workers.

A characteristic feature of fruit formation in artificial mushroom culture is the formation of 'flushes' or 'breaks' at regular intervals. In the case of *Agaricus* and *Coprinus* flushes occur at about 6–12 day intervals (Fig. 6).

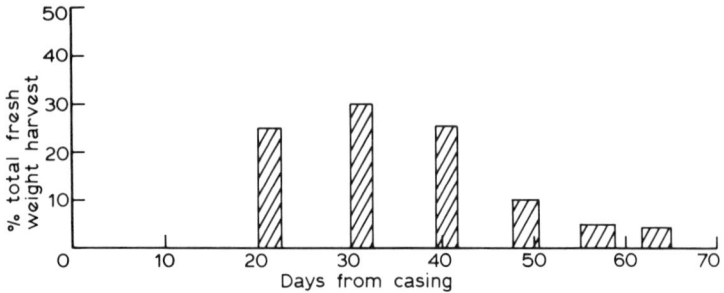

Fig. 6. Typical pattern of 'flushing' of *Agaricus bisporus* fruits in commercial mushroom culture.

Environmental and genetic factors are known to be responsible for variations in time but the controlling factors of flushing are not understood. In practice it is usual for the number of fruits forming at each flush to decline to an uneconomic level after 4–6 weeks. Compost nutrients are by this time depleted and the movement into the casing layer is also thought to be inhibitory.

2.1.2. *Stropharia raguso-annulata*
This mushroom, although not extensively studied and not cultivated on a large scale is thought to have a potential particularly in both Western and Eastern Europe, where there is a limited demand for a more extensive range of mushroom species, rather than the traditional species *Agaricus bisporus*.

Like *Agaricus* and *Coprinus* it requires a casing soil for fruit formation, but its nutritional requirements are less exacting. It grows specifically on fresh straw prewetted to a water content of about 70 %. Flax, wheat and rice straw are known to be the best, but if allowed to decompose, productivity is greatly reduced. Szudyga (1978) describes in detail its cultivation by amateur growers in allotment gardens and suggests that its productivity is closely associated with the cellulose content of straw, the component which is partially lost during decomposition.

Supplementation of straw with nitrogen or artificial fertilisers, or any form of composting, inhibits the development of mycelium.

The composition of the casing soil is also known to be extremely critical in the formation of fruits. Addition of limestone is extremely harmful and the use of a soil as a partial or total component of a casing mixture appears to be stimulatory to yield. Recent studies by Okwu and Hayes (in press) demonstrate the requirement for micro-organisms in the casing layer for fruit formation to occur, as in *Agaricus bisporus* culture. A mixture of peat and humus soil at pH 6·0 is the most productive casing soil known at present.

2.2. Environmental Factors

Temperature, the gaseous composition of the growing atmosphere and relative humidity are the main factors of the physical environment which governs both vegetative and reproductive growth in mushrooms. However, as is the case with most aspects of mushroom research, studies on environmental aspects have been confined to the most extensively cultivated species, *Agaricus bisporus*. Although both *Stropharia* and *Coprinus* may be regarded as biologically similar since a casing soil is required to induce fruit formation, it cannot be assumed that the environmental factors discussed here are generally applicable. Also, it must be stressed that within the species *A. bisporus* there are a wide range of varieties and strains which show a high degree of variation in their response to environmental factors. Such variations are exploited in commerce to allow for seasonal and other variations in growing environments.

2.2.1. Temperature

Different stages of the life cycle require different temperatures for optimum growth and for most temperate species the optimum for vegetative growth is 25 °C. For fruitbody formation the optimum ranges from 14 to 18 °C for *Agaricus bisporus* and *Coprinus comatus*. Cultivated strains of *Stropharia raguso-annulata* fruit between 10 and 20 °C.

The requirement for a different temperature for both stages of the life cycle dictates to a large extent the design of growing structures and also the system of growing.

For most climates, seasonal variations in temperature dictate the construction of insulated growing structures which are artificially heated for cold seasons and for warm weather artificial cooling is justified. Such sophistication allows cultivation on a continuous basis irrespective of climate.

In contrast, in many countries mushroom cultivation is restricted to one or two crops per annum, so that high expenditure in equipment and energy inputs for air heating and cooling are avoided (Kim, 1978).

2.2.2. The Gaseous Environment

Carbon dioxide is stimulatory to the vegetative stage but is inhibitory to the reproductive fruit forming stage of the life cycle (Tschierpe, 1959;

Tschierpe & Sinden, 1964; Long & Jacobs, 1968). While strains may vary in their response to carbon dioxide, levels in the atmosphere above 0·15 % are normally inhibitory to fruit formation. Thus in intensive systems, artificial methods of ventilation are essential for the initiation and formation of fruits.

Other gaseous by-products of metabolism have also been implicated in the growth process. For example, micro amounts of ethanol, acetone, ethylene, acetaldehyde and other organic volatiles may be detected in atmospheres in which *A. bisporus* mycelium is actively growing. These volatile compounds have been shown to be important in the ecology of the bacteria in casing soils which are stimulatory to fruit formation (Hayes *et al.*, 1969; Hayes, 1972, 1978).

2.2.3. Relative Humidity
The relative humidity of the atmosphere immediately above the casing soil is also known to be an important environmental variable. Flegg & Gandy (1962) for example, showed that at high relative humidities (80–90 %) the onset of fruiting tended to be earlier in *A. bisporus* and the weight of mushrooms greater than at low humidities (40–50 %). According to Storey (1972), at very high humidities evaporation from the casing layer is decreased, causing water to condense from the air onto the casing soil, resulting in delayed or in extreme cases, the inhibition of fruit formation.

Relative humidity also assumes importance in the incidence of certain disease organisms (see next section).

2.3. Competitors, Pests and Disease
Continuous and intensive cultivation of organisms inevitably results in the occurrence of other undesirable organisms in close association with the cultivated organism. These are disease causing organisms and pests which, if allowed to perpetrate, will cause severe losses in production.

Another group of organisms, known as competitors or 'weeds' are also encountered in the mass culture of organisms. In mushroom culture, imperfections in the methods and husbandry of the culture will result in loss of production due to competition by such contaminants. They are avoided by rectifying the imperfection and unlike diseases and pests, their numbers are proportional to the degree of imperfection, rather than to their direct association with the growth of mushrooms.

2.3.1. Disease Organisms
Bacteria, fungi and viruses infect mushrooms and cause disease. Fungus

pathogens are most commonly encountered and include soil borne species, *Verticillium fungicola* and *Mycogone pernicicosa* and severe infections cause malformations of the stipe and fruitbody. Both species produce large numbers of spores which are readily spread to establish secondary infections and if either of these hyperparasitic fungi are allowed to establish, losses can be severe. The use of selective fungicides is necessary to check severe infections, but measures aimed at preventing the initial establishment of these organisms are nowadays an integral part of the process of mushroom culture. For example, the application of the correct pasteurisation procedures to both compost and casing, which may serve as primary sources of the infecting organisms, is essential if such diseases are to be prevented.

The most common bacterial disease is caused by *Pseudomonas tolaasii*, which causes a superficial brown 'blotching' of the fruit pileus. High relative humidity of the growing atmosphere and temperatures above 18 °C are conducive to the multiplication of this bacterium, which is a common inhabitant of the soils used for casing mushroom beds. Pseudomonads are also thought to be responsible for a disease known as 'mummy', which causes fruits to become moribund, with a characteristic dry chalky texture. Schisler *et al.* (1968) reported on the intracellular occurrence of pseudomonads in diseased material and it is thought that the rapid spread of this disease is brought about by the movement of bacteria within the mycelium.

Viruses are also potent disease agents, being the cause of a range of disorders known as La France, Watery Stipe, X disease and dieback disease. Six virus particles have been isolated from diseased mushrooms, five of these are polyhedral, being 19, 25, 29, 35 and 50 μm diameter and one bacilliform measuring 19×5 μm. Mycelium, spores and spawn are known to transmit virus particles and although up to a decade ago virus disorders were major causes of crop loss, with modern techniques of pasteurisation and disinfection their occurrence now is rare. Particularly important is the disinfection of not only the culture, but also the entire growing structure at the termination of the crop cycle. This terminal disinfection is achieved by the use of live steam or by fumigating with methyl bromide.

2.3.2. Competitor Organisms

The commonly encountered competitors are fungi and are usually the result of defects in composting techniques or faulty pasteurisation. An olive green mould *Chaetomium oliveceum* colonises compost when the complete microbial transformation of ammonia and amines is not achieved during the composting process. This may be due to inadequate aeration during the pasteurisation stage or to insufficient available nutrients for microbial activity.

Similarly the presence of 'Ink Caps', species of *Coprinus*, results from a short composting time, again reflecting a restricted microbial activity.

Establishment of *Papulospora byssina* and *Scopulariopsis fimicola*, known as brown and white plaster mould respectively, reflects an over-composted substrate. Occasionally, common soil fungi invade mushroom substrates, such as *Diheliomyces microspores* and *Chrysosporium luteum*. Such invasions are the result of either faulty pasteurisation or post-pasteurisation contamination with soil or dust particles.

2.3.3. Pests

The highly organic nature of the substrates used in mushroom culture are attractive breeding places for a number of flies and mites. Sciarids, cecids, phorids and mites are the common pests of mushroom cultivation (see Hussey *et al.*, 1969; Hussey, 1972). Sciarid larvae burrow into the stipe and pileus and devour the mycelium in the casing soil. The less damaging phorids are attracted to mushrooms by volatiles evolved by growing mycelium. Mites, while not generally troublesome, are often associated with the occurrence of weed fungi in composts.

Nematodes are also found in compost and casing soil and if pasteurisation procedures are faulty, their numbers can increase to damaging proportions. Some species are mycelial feeders and if present in large numbers, substantial crop loss can be expected.

Rodents (mice and rats) are also a pest of mushroom culture, being attracted to the grain used as a base medium for spawn.

As with the microbial pathogens, pest control is primarily concerned with the adoption of sound pasteurisation procedures for compost and casing soil substrates and terminal disinfection procedures. Chemical pesticides are also used to minimise damage when infections do occur.

3. *LENTINUS, VOLVARIELLA* AND *PLEUROTUS* SPECIES WHICH REQUIRE LIGHT

Cultivated species belonging to this group, *Lentinus edodes*, *Volvariella volvaceae* and species of *Pleurotus*, represent about one quarter of the total mushrooms cultivated in the world. Biologically, they may be distinguished from other species cultivated by the requirement for cultures to be exposed to light in order to induce fruit formation. It is surprising that in view of its importance to the normal development of these mushrooms very few critical investigations of light action have been done. Much of the information available is based on the data of Aschan-Aberg (1960) for *Flamulina velutipes*, a mushroom species which is not generally cultivated to any extent. His data indicate that the effective light is of wavelengths between 435 and 470 nm for this species. Badham (1979) investigated a non-cultivated species *Psilocybe cubensis* and found that more primordia were formed in blue and ultra-violet light, with peaks at 370, 440 and 460 nm. Red, infra-red and green light having wavelengths greater than 510 nm were ineffective. Very short exposure times are thought to be effective in providing the stimulus for fruit formation, but in practice exposure times corresponding to a normal light day are given. Daylight or artificial light from fluorescent tubes is adequate. The light from an incandescent source needs to be very bright to be adequate.

While light is stimulatory to the formation of fruits, exposure of the mycelium to light before a substrate is fully colonised may retard the rate of vegetative growth. For a strain of *Pleurotus sajor-caju* for example (Okwu and Hayes, unpublished) growth rate per day was reduced by over 50 % when exposed to continuous light, compared with continuous darkness.

Although a casing layer is not required in the culture of this group of fungi, some investigations suggest that the application of a casing layer may benefit the culture process (Lim & Hayes, 1979). There is no evidence to suggest that any benefits are due to micro-organisms in the casing layer, as is the case in *Agaricus* and *Stropharia* culture.

Another contrasting feature of the methods adopted for the artificial culture of this group relates to the nature and preparation of substrates. *Lentinus edodes*, the forest mushroom or Shiitake, is grown principally in Japan and other countries of the Orient, on wood substrates. *Volvariella volvaceae*, the straw mushroom, is a tropical species, grown in the Orient on rice straw, while the range of *Pleurotus* spp., known collectively as Oyster mushrooms, are adapted to grow on a wide range of substrates derived from vegetable matter, including wood, cereal straw, cotton wastes, sugar cane wastes, etc.

Methods also vary considerably according to substrates used and locality. Generally, the methods are less sophisticated than those applied to intensive *Agaricus* culture, but there is considerable scope for improvements to the technology of culture and a more widespread application to countries where cultivation of *Agaricus* is traditional.

3.1. Forest Mushrooms or Shiitake on Wood Substrates

This mushroom is cultivated on logs and in a detailed account of the methods, Ito (1978) lists *Quercus sernata* and *Q. acutissima* as the most suitable species. Others, less suited, include Chestnut (*Castavea crenata*), hornbeams (*Carpinus tschonoskit*, |C|. *laxiflora* and *C. japonica*) and Shii (*Catanopsis cuspidata*), the tree which confers the local name, Shiitake, to the mushroom. Holes are cut in the log and spawn prepared on sawdust or pieces of wood are inserted at several positions, so that total colonisation of the log is achieved as quickly as possible.

Logs are incubated out of doors in special laying yards where particular attention is given to maintaining the correct moisture content and temperature conditions, 24–28 °C being optimal. In recent years, simple protective screens or the use of twigs and reeds as a cover, have been successful in creating the right environmental conditions for mycelium establishment, the most vulnerable stage of the process.

After about 8 months the logs are transferred to what are termed raising yards, which are usually in forested areas where there is shade and high humidity. Fruits develop from the logs at temperatures between 12 and 20 °C. Logs are watered at regular intervals and fruits develop in the spring and autumn over a period of about 6 years.

These methods have evolved over many centuries and to date attempts at intensifying culture by using sawdust as a base substrate have been only partially successful, due to the high cost involved in sterilising sawdust substrates. Also the fruits formed on these media lack the flavour and texture of those produced by the traditional extensive methods.

In Japan this mushroom is consumed as a 'health' giving food. There are over 230 000 producers located primarily in the rural areas, but cultivation is also practised in suburban areas in glasshouses. When harvested it is usually air dried and reconstituted in boiling water before consumption. Large quantities are exported, especially to Hong-Kong, Western Europe and the USA and Canada.

Little is known of the pests and pathogens of this mushroom, but it is known that viruses infect many of the strains in cultivation. The micro-organisms which compete with the inoculated mycelium in the laying yards are thought to be the most damaging to production and include common wood inhabiting species of *Trichoderma*, *Poria* and *Merulius*.

3.2. Rice or Padi Straw Mushroom

Outdoor growing of *Volvariella volvaceae* has been practised for many centuries in China and nowadays cultivation in the tropical and sub-tropical zones of the Orient is extensive, particularly in China, Indonesia,

Thailand, Malaysia, Hong Kong and Singapore. Although traditionally grown on padi straw (Fig. 7) other vegetable wastes are being successfully exploited as substrates. These include cotton wastes (Chang, 1974), water hyacinth (Cheng & Mok, 1971), oil palm pericarp waste (Young & Graham, 1973), banana leaves and sawdust (Chua & Ho, 1973), sugar cane rubbish (Hu *et al.*, 1973).

In the traditional method, bundles of wet straw are arranged into a small stack on an elevated soil base, usually in a rice field between successive rice crops. Spawn is prepared on chopped rice straw and is placed between the bundles during the preparation of the stacks and various methods are adopted to maintain moist conditions. Temperatures within the stack increase to 40–50°C and fruits form in about 12–14 days on the top and sides. Successive flushes develop over a 40–50 day harvesting time after which the exhausted beds are harvested.

Productivity under such systems is extremely variable and dependent on outside weather conditions. Extremes of temperature, heavy rains or low humidities contribute to low yields or even total crop failure. While recognisable disease organisms are not prevalent, rodents, snails and slugs are significant pests.

Over the last decade there has been some progress towards a more industrialised approach to cultivation. Indoor growing on straw beds is practised in Hong Kong, Taiwan and the Philippines. Simple, naturally ventilated growing houses prepared from bamboo frames, covered with leaves or polythene film are cheap and provide adequate protection. The light requirement is provided artificially by fluorescent lamps, and by introducing short pasteurisation procedures additional nutrients may be supplemented to rice straw to improve yields, e.g. rice bran, molasses and distillery wastes. A partial composting process has also been shown to be successful (Hayes & Lim, 1979; Chang, 1979).

Considerable scope exists for the industrialisation of *Volvariella* culture.

3.3. Pleurotus or Oyster Mushrooms

A large number of *Pleurotus* species are edible and because of their ability to colonise a wide range of substrates over a range of temperatures, cultivation is done both in temperate and tropical climates (Table 2). When compared with the methods applied to *A. bisporus* culture the requirements are simple and less costly. Despite these advantages, world production amounted only to 35 000 tonnes in 1983, about 3% of the world's total production.

Methods for growing oyster mushrooms on tree stumps and logs were known in the early part of this century, but cereal straw has traditionally

(a)

(b)

Fig. 7. *Volvariella volvaceae* or the Chinese or Padi-straw mushroom. This tropical species is grown extensively in the Orient, usually on rice straw. (a) Fruits developing on the surface of the straw. No casing soil is required. (b) A stack of rice straw being prepared before inoculation with *Volvariella* spawn.

TABLE 2
Cultivated Species of *Pleurotus* or Oyster Mushrooms (Source: Zadrazil, 1978)

	Species	Suitable temperature for fructification (°C)
1.	*Pleurotus oestreatus*	15–20
2.	*Pleurotus* sp. *florida*	20–27
3.	*Pleurotus eryngii*	20–28
4.	*Pleurotus cornucopiae*	16–25
5.	*Pleurotus sajor-caju*	16–30
6.	*Pleurotus* sp. *abalone*	25–28
7.	*Pleurotus tuber-regium*	25–33
8.	*Pleurotus flabellatus*	20–28

been used for small scale culture (Fig. 8). In the last decade or so, a wider range of materials have been shown to be suitable, including sawdust, cotton waste, banana stems, sugar cane trash, bagasse and fibrous sludges from pulp and paper mills. In nature, the cultivated *Pleurotus* species are primary saprophytes and natural decomposers of vegetable wastes, but for most commercial culture systems, additional protein is required to obtain a profitable yield level.

For most systems a pre-fermentation and/or pasteurisation of the substrate ingredients is necessary, but some substrates may not require any form of heat treatment, e.g. cotton wastes and some pulp mill sludges. Straw substrates invariably require pasteurisation, so that competitor organisms are controlled.

Low cost systems are applicable to this species, but in recent years some advances have been made in the industrialisation of production methods. The most common systems are based on the use of polythene sacks, arranged in layers in an environmentally controlled growing room, in which temperature, aeration and humidity can be controlled. When incubated at the optimum temperature for mycelial growth, colonisation of the substrate is rapid, varying from 10 to 20 days according to species.

When substrates are fully colonised, the plastic containers are opened, exposed to light, the growing room aerated and temperatures adjusted to the optimum for fruit formation, which varies according to species. Relative humidity in the growing atmosphere is also important and is maintained between 80 and 95% RH.

Pleurotus can also be cultivated in trays or shelves as for *Agaricus*

(a)

(b)

Fig. 8. *Pleurotus* or Oyster mushrooms. (a) *Pleurotus* mushrooms growing on bundles of rice straw—a technique used in village culture in developing countries. (Courtesy Z. Bano.) (b) Oyster mushrooms *Pleurotus sajor-caju* growing on pulp mill sludges contained in a bucket-like plastic container. (Courtesy BC Research, Vancouver, Canada.)

bisporus, or by the compression of spawned substrates into blocks covered with plastic foil. Bulk pasteurisation in tunnels also offers the opportunity of incubating spawned substrates in the same tunnels, then to be cropped in trays, shelves or polythene sacks. Such methods, however, require large investments in construction and machinery.

Fruits are harvested before maturity, so as to avoid the saturation of the atmosphere with spores, which can cause allergic reactions to some people. As in other mushrooms the fruits form in a sequence of flushes 7–10 days apart. Seldom is cropping extended beyond three flushes and in some commercial situations one flush only is harvested before substrates are discarded.

Up to the present, no significant pest or disease has been reported, but faulty techniques result in the colonisation of substrates with competitor organisms, such as *Trichoderma* spp. and *Penicillium* spp., and are the most serious hazard in cultivation.

Interest in cultivating this species is rapidly gaining momentum and is likely to figure prominently in the future development of mushroom culture in developing countries.

4. CONCLUDING REMARKS AND FUTURE PROSPECTS

Over the last two decades the production and consumption of mushrooms worldwide has increased from about 250 000 tonnes per annum in 1960 to over 1 million tonnes in 1980. This growth is indicative not only of a more general scientific understanding of the factors which govern growth and development of this fungus but also of changing attitudes to mushrooms as a food.

Traditionally, they have been regarded as a luxury food, consumed only by the high income consumers, but nowadays they are consumed by people in the lower income groups and increasing attention is being given to their value as a food (Hayes, 1976). Significant also is the potential of mushrooms as health foods. They have figured in some folklore remedies for a number of ailments and some potentially useful substances have been discovered, which suggests that further research may prove fruitful (Cochrane, 1978). It must be stressed however that there is no clinical evidence to advocate their inclusion in diets as therapeutic or prophylactic agents.

Mushroom culture is essentially a solid state fermentation in which the objective is to maintain the dominance of the inoculated mushroom species over other organisms. The technology involved is basically concerned with the application of microbiology, fermentation and bio-engineering to the propagation of micro-organisms in a large scale agricultural process.

Spawn and substrate manufacture are technically the most demanding of the stages while subsequent stages are by comparison less demanding on technical skills. Systems in the intensive production units of the industrialised western countries are, however, moving towards a higher degree of sophistication, particularly in regard to mechanisation (Fig. 9) and automatic computerised control of culture environments.

Fig. 9. Mechanical harvesting of *Agaricus* mushrooms is technically feasible. A mechanical cutting knife is drawn along the surface of a shelf bed. The cut mushrooms are transferred to a horizontal moving belt to be collected on the opposite side of the bed. (Courtesy H. Tschierpe.)

These methods contrast markedly with the outdoor systems adopted for the cultivation of *Lentinus edodes* and *Volvariella* in the Orient. Similar low cost systems are being applied in developing countries where mushroom cultivation is seen as an important activity in the programmes aimed towards the development of rural communities. In the remote regions of the Western Himalayas for example, cultivation is being developed as a cottage industry, where it is practical to grow *A. bisporus* throughout the year without heating or cooling the growing atmosphere. Important to the success of mushroom growing in these countries has been the separation of the two levels of technology required; spawn and substrate manufacture, a high technology, and growing, a relatively low technology in climatically favourable zones.

A scheme recently launched by the State Government of Himachal Pradesh, with the assistance of the FAO of the United Nations incorporates this concept of the separation of technologies. By centralising spawn and compost manufacture, the required high technology is maintained in what is termed a 'mother' unit, which supplies a culture fully prepared for cropping to a large number of satellite units, located in nearby villages—low technology. This has not only provided a new food which is complementary to the predominantly cereal Indian diet, but provides a new source of income for marginal farmers who have organised market outlets for fresh mushrooms in the large towns and cities. *Agaricus* mushrooms are in greatest demand, followed by Oyster mushrooms.

Mushrooms convert waste materials into a nutritious foodstuff and this attribute is particularly attractive in a future world of increasing population and declining resources. Although progress in research and in the application of mushroom science has resulted in a diversification of methods applicable to a wide range of locations and circumstances, there are a number of constraints to a more extensive exploitation of the edible fungi. Especially significant are:

(1)   Substrates are bulky and costly to transport to centres of production.

(2)   In most parts of the world the required environmental conditions can only be achieved by the construction of environmentally controlled growing houses.

(3)   Despite high yields of dry matter (540 tonnes per hectare) and protein (160 tonnes of dry protein per hectare) that can be achieved per annum, the biological efficiency in the conversion of substrates is low (at best 20–25% fresh product to fresh substrate).

(4)   Mechanical harvesting of fruits is not yet practical and thus hand harvesting is required, which in Western countries represents about 40% of the production costs.

In view of the above constraints it would seem that future expansion of cultivation will occur in developing countries adopting simple and unsophisticated systems of growing. Mechanisation is minimal and buildings made from locally available wood, thatch or mud provide sufficient protection (Fig. 10). Costs are low in comparison with Western

Fig. 10.   A low cost mushroom growing house made of thatch. Such structures are used in developing countries where environmental conditions are suitable.

countries largely because of the availability of labour at low cost. Substrates therefore assume the greatest share of production costs.

Current strategic research in genetics, breeding and the physiology of mushrooms will undoubtedly lead to improvements, but new concepts (Hayes, 1976) based on the utilisation of residual substrates after growth of one species for the growth of another edible species may improve on the biological efficiency of the system. This essentially permits the practice of crop rotation, an established practice in other forms of crop production.

Alternatively, utilisation of the used substrates in horticulture and/or other income generating activities, e.g. vermiculture, could substantially improve the biological and economic efficiency of the waste conversion system (Hayes & Hand, 1984). In this way costs of mushrooms as a food may be competitive with vegetables and fruits from conventional agricultural practices.

REFERENCES

ASCHAN-ABERG, K. (1960) The production of fruitbodies in *Collybia velutipes*, III. Influence of the quality of light. *Physiologia plantarum* **13**, 267–79.

BADHAM, E. R. (1979) The effect of light upon Basidiocarp initiation in *Psilocybe cubensis*. *Mycologia* **71**, 136–42.

CHANG, S. T. (1974) Production of the straw-mushroom (*Volvariella volvacea*) from cotton wastes. *The Mushroom Journal* **21**, 348–53.

CHANG, S. T. (1979) Cultivation of *Volvariella volvacea* from cotton waste compost. *Mushroom Sci.* **10**(2), 609–18.

CHENG, S. & MOK, S. H. (1971) Preliminary experiment of water hyacinth used as a medium for the cultivation of padi straw mushroom. *J. hortic. Soc. China* **17**, 194–7.

CHUA, S. E. & HO, S. Y. (1973) Fruiting on sterile agar and cultivation of straw mushrooms (*Volvariella* species) on padi straw, banana leaves and sawdust. *World Crops (London)* **25**, 90–1.

COCHRANE, K. W. (1978) Medical effects. In *The Biology and Cultivation of Edible Mushrooms*, Chapter 7, S. T. Chang & W. A. Hayes, Eds. Academic Press, New York.

CRESSWELL, P. A. & HAYES, W. A. (1979) Further investigations on the bacterial ecology of the casing layer. *Mushroom Sci.* **10**(1), 347–59.

EDDY, B. P. & JACOBS, L. (1976) Mushroom compost as a source of food for *Agaricus bisporus*. *The Mushroom Journal* **38**, 56.

EGER, G. (1961) Untersuchungen uber die Funktion der Dechschicht bei der Fruchtkoerperbildung des Kulturchampignons. *Archiv. Mikrobiolog.* **39**, 313–39.

FERMOR, T. R. & WOOD, D. A. (1979) The microbiology and enzymology of wheat straw mushroom compost production. In *Straw Decay and its effects on Disposal and Utilisation*, E. Grossbard, Ed. John Wiley and Sons, Chichester.

FLEGG, P. & GANDY, G. (1962) Controlled environment cabinets for experiments with the cultivated mushroom. *J. Hortic. Sci.* **37**, 124–33.

GERRITS, J. P. G., MÜLLER, F. M. & BELS-KONING, H. C. (1967) Changes in compost constituents during composting, pasteurisation and cropping. *Mushroom Sci.* **6**, 225.

HAYES, W. A. (1969) Microbiological changes in composting wheat straw/horse manure mixtures. *Mushroom Sci.* **7**, 173–86.

HAYES, W. A. (1972) Nutritional factors and their relation to mushroom production. *Mushroom Sci.* **8**, 663–674.

HAYES, W. A. (1974) Microbiological activity in the casing layer and its relation to productivity and disease control. In *The Casing Layer*, Proceedings of the Aston Seminar in Mushroom Science, Vol. 1, 37, MGA, London.

HAYES, W. A. (1976) A new look at mushrooms. *Nutrit. Food Sci.* **42**, 2–6.

HAYES, W. A. (1977) Mushroom nutrition and the role of micro-organisms in composting. Proceedings of the Aston Seminar in Mushroom Science Vol. 2, 1–20. MGA, London.

HAYES, W. A. (1978) The biological nature of *Agaricus bisporus* Lange (Sing). In *The Biology and Cultivation of Edible Mushrooms*, Chapter 8, S. T. Chang and W. A. Hayes, Eds. Academic Press, New York.

HAYES, W. A. & LIM, W. C. (1979) Wheat and rice straw composts and mushroom production. In *Straw Decay and its Effect on Disposal and Utilisation*, E. Grossbard, Ed., John Wiley & Sons, Chichester.

HAYES, W. A. & NAIR, N. G. (1977) Effect of volatile metabolic by-products of mushroom mycelium on the ecology of the casing layer. *Mushroom Sci.* **9**, 259–68.

HAYES, W. A. & HAND, P. (1984) Utilisation of vermicomposts in mushroom production. Proceedings of the International Conference on Earthworms, Cambridge University Press, Cambridge (in press).

HAYES, W. A., RANDLE, P. E. & LAST, F. T. (1969) The nature of the microbial stimulus affecting sporophore formation in *Agaricus bisporus* (Lange) Sing. *Ann. appl. Biol.* **64**, 177–86.

HU, K. J., SONG, S. F. & LIU, P. (1973) Experiments on Chinese mushroom cultivation. I. Comparison of cultivating materials. *J. Taiwan agric. Res.* **22**, 145–8.

HUSSEY, N. W., READ, W. H. & HESLING, J. T. (1969) *The Pests of Protected Cultivation.* Edward Arnold, London.

HUSSEY, N. W. (1972) Pests in perspective. *Mushroom Sci.* **8**, 171–81.

ITO, T. (1978) Cultivation of *Lentinus* edodes. In *The Biology and Cultivation of Edible Mushrooms*, Chapter 22, S. T. Chang & W. A. Hayes, Eds. Academic Press, New York.

KIM, D. S. (1978) Cultivation in Asian countries: growing in temperate zones. In *The Biology and Cultivation of Edible Mushrooms*, Chapter 14, S. T. Chang & W. A. Hayes, Eds. Academic Press, New York.

LONG, P. & JACOBS, L. (1968) Some observations on carbon dioxide and sporophore initiation in the cultivated mushroom. *Mushroom Sci.* **7**, 727–31.

OKWU, C. I. S. & HAYES, W. A. (1984) The casing layer in the cultivation of the edible mushroom, *Stropharia raguso-annulata. Biologia Africana* (in press).

SCHISLER, L. C., SINDEN, J. W. & SIGEL, E. H. (1968) Etiology of mummy disease of cultivated mushrooms. *Phytopathology* **58**, 944–8.

STOREY, I. F. (1972) Recent trends in crop production methods as affected by environmental conditions. *Mushroom Sci.* **8**, 95–102.

SZUDYGA, K. (1978) *Stropharia raguso-annulata.* In *The Biology and Cultivation of Edible Mushrooms*, Chapter 26, S. T. Chang & W. A. Hayes, Eds. Academic Press, New York.

TSCHIERPE, H. E. (1959) Die bedentung des Kohlendioxyds für des Kultur-champignon. *Gartenbauwissenschaft* **24**, 18–75.

TSCHIERPE, H. E. & SINDEN, J. W. (1964) Weitre Untersuchungen Kohlendioxyd für die Fruktifikgation des Kulturchampignons. *Ag. campestris*, var. *bisporus* (L) Lge. *Archiv. Mikrobiol.* **49**, 405–25.

TURNER, E. M. (1974) Phenoloxidase activity in relation to substrate and development stage in the mushroom *Agaricus bisporus.* *Trans. Brit. mycol. Soc.* **63**, 541.

TURNER, E. M., WRIGHT, M., WARD, T. & OSBORNE, D. J. (1975) The production of ethylene and other volatiles and changes in cellulase and laccase activities during the life cycle of the cultivated mushroom *Agaricus bisporus. J. gen. Microbiol.* **91**, 167–76.

WAKSMAN, S. A. & NISSEN, W. (1932) On the nutrition of the cultivated mushroom *Agaricus campestris* and the chemical changes brought about by this organism in the manure compost. *Am. J. Bot.* **19**, 514.

WOOD, D. W. & GOODENOUGH, P. (1977) Fruiting of *Agaricus bisporus.* Changes in extracellular enzyme activities during growth and fruiting. *Archiv. Mikrobiol.* **114**, 164.

YOUNG, Y. C. & GRAHAM, K. M. (1973) Studies on the padi mushroom (*Volvariella volvaceae*). 1. Use of oil palm pericarp waste as an alternative substrate. *Malay agric. Res.* **2**, 15–22.

ZADRAZIL, F. (1978) Cultivation of *Pleurotus*. In *Biology and Cultivation of Edible Mushrooms*, Chapter 25, S. T. Chang & W. A. Hayes, Eds. Academic Press, New York.

Chapter 9

Bio-enrichment: Production of Vitamins in Fermented Foods

KEITH H. STEINKRAUS

Institute of Food Science, Cornell University,
Geneva/Ithaca, New York, USA

1. INTRODUCTION

Less than a hundred years ago, vitamin deficiency diseases were common in the United States. Unfortunately hundreds of millions of people still suffer from a variety of vitamin-deficiency diseases in the developing world. Each year millions of children become permanently blind via xerophthalmia caused by a lack of vitamin A in the diet. Surrounded by quantities of green and leafy vegetables, no child should be lacking vitamin A and have to suffer life-time blindness. Lack of proper nutrition education is the problem.

Thiamine deficiency leading to polyneuritis and muscular weakness characteristic of beri-beri is common among those subsisting primarily on highly polished rice and systems have been devised to enrich polished rice with thiamine. The problem would not exist if people were willing to consume brown or less highly polished rice; however, those eating predominantly polished rice are very sensitive and do not like the flavour or texture of rice retaining portions of the bran. Also, the keeping quality of brown rice is poorer. Insects rapidly invade the more nutritious brown rice.

People subsisting primarily on maize are in danger of niacin deficiencies leading to pellagra characterised by dermatitis, diarrhoea and dementia. Ascorbic acid deficiency leads to bleeding gums, loss of teeth and scurvy. Riboflavin deficiency leads to fissures at the corners of the mouth and abnormalities of skin and mucous membranes. Vitamin D deficiency leads to rickets in children. Exposure of infants to sunlight would generally prevent this but mothers in certain parts of the world prefer to protect their infants from sunlight. Deficiency of vitamin B_{12}—cobalamin—leads to pernicious anemia. This is rare in people consuming milk and meats. With the increase in vegetarianism, the incidence of B_{12} deficiency is increasing in the United States. Except for those people who follow unusual diets, for example, vegetarian diets for religious or personal reasons or those who follow weight reduction diets or for the poor and particularly the aged poor, vitamin deficiency diseases in the developed world have been largely eliminated by enrichment or fortification of the basic foods.

2. ENRICHMENT/FORTIFICATION

The process of adding nutrients to processed foods to restore the nutrient to its original level is called 'restoration' (LaChance, 1978). An example is the addition of ascorbic acid to 'instant' dried potatoes.

'Enrichment' in the Western world is the process of adding nutrients to selected formulated or manufactured foods as a public health measure. Examples are the addition of vitamin D to milk, vitamins A and D to margarine, and riboflavin to bread. 'Fortification' is the process of adding nutrients to levels coinciding with the image or place of the food in the diet. Thus, fruit juices may be fortified with ascorbic acid. Adding vitamin A to margarine is fortification based upon its relation to butter (LaChance, 1978).

Present levels of enrichment in the United States are presented in Table 1.

The National Academy of Sciences, National Research Council

TABLE 1
Levels of Enrichment of Several Cereal Products in the
United States (Bender, 1973)

Food	Thiamine	Riboflavin mg/100 g	Niacin
White flour	0·44–0·55	0·26–0·33	3·5–4·4
Bread	0·24–0·40	0·16–0·35	2·2–3·3
Corn meal	0·44–0·66	0·26–0·40	3·5–5·3
Rice	0·44–0·88	0·26–0·53	3·5–7·0

TABLE 2
Levels of Vitamins Recommended
for Fortification of Cereal-Grain
Products by the National
Academy of Sciences (NAS/NRC,
1974)

Vitamin	mg/100 g
A	0·48
Thiamine	0·64
Riboflavin	0·40
Niacin	5·29
Pyridoxine	0·44
Folic acid	0·07

recommends that cereal-grain products be fortified to vitamin levels indicated in Table 2.

Vitamins are available for enrichment of food products in the Western world as shown in Table 3.

Vitamin A, Vitamin C, thiamine, riboflavin, niacin and pantothenate are all quite inexpensive by Western standards, costing less than 10 cents (US) per 1000 mg.

TABLE 3
Availability and Prices of Selected Vitamins

Vitamin	Price per gram* $ (US)
Vitamin A	0·053
Vitamin D (ergocalciferol)	4·80
Vitamin C (L-ascorbic acid)	0·019
Thiamine	0·076 5
Riboflavin	0·098 4
Niacin (Niacinamide)	0·015 4
(Nicotinic acid)	0·011 5
Biotin	17·80
Vitamin B_{12}	20·50
Pyridoxine	0·223 5
Pantothenate	0·078
Folic acid	0·42

* Sigma Chemical Corp., St. Louis. February 1983.

TABLE 4
Recommended Daily Allowances of Selected Vitamins for Adult
Males (NAS/NRC, 1980)

Vitamin	Recommended daily consumption	Approximate cost per adult year $ (US)
Vitamin A	1 000 μg	0·019 3
Vitamin D	7·5 μg	0·013 1
Vitamin C	60 mg	0·416 1
Thiamine	1·5 mg	0·041 9
Riboflavin	1·7 mg	0·061 0
Niacin	19 mg	0·106 8
Pyridoxine	2·2 mg	0·179 5
Pantothenic acid	4–7 mg	0·199 3
Vitamin B_{12}	3 μg	0·022 4
Folacin	400 μg	0·061 3
Biotin	100–300 μg*	1·95
	Total	$3·07/year

* Not established, but 100–300 μg is probably sufficient.

The recommended daily allowances of selected vitamins for adult males are given in Table 4.

The prices of vitamins are low enough so that foods in the Western world can be enriched at a rather insignificant increase ($3·07/adult/year) in the cost of the food (Table 4). Eliminating biotin, the cost of vitamins for a year would be only $1·12 for an adult. At times it has been suggested that foods such as bread in India be enriched to eliminate some of the vitamin malnutrition in that country. However, when the daily requirements of particular vitamins are multiplied by 800 000 000 consumers, the total cost becomes prohibitive.

3. SOURCES OF VITAMINS

Thiamine was first isolated from rice polishings (bran). Niacin is synthesised during the germination of oats, barley, wheat and maize. It is also synthesised in commercial quantities by *Xanthomonas pruni* (Davis *et al.*, 1951). The only vitamins produced commercially in significant quantities by fermentation are riboflavin and vitamin B_{12}.

Present world consumption of riboflavin is about 1·25 million kg (Lago & Kaplin, 1981). Although riboflavin is produced by *Candida* yeasts, solvent producing bacteria such as *Clostridium acetobutylicum, Escherichia coli, Aerobacter aerogenes, Azotobacter* and *Mycobacterium*, the principal species used in commercial production are *Ashbya gossypii* and *Eromothecium ashbyii*, two closely related *Ascomycetes. E. ashbyii* has yielded as much as 2·2 mg riboflavin per ml on whey, skim milk, sucrose medium (Hendrickz & de Vleeschauwer, 1955). Superior cultures of *Ashbya* that produce 11 times more riboflavin under commercial conditions have been produced by chemical mutation (Lago & Kaplin, 1981).

Total sales of vitamin B_{12} in 1980 were estimated to be about 5000 kg (Lago & Kaplin, 1981). Merck and Co. use a selected strain of *Pseudomonas denitrificans* which produces 30 times the amount of cyanocobalamin produced by the original culture. *Propionibacterium shermanii* is also utilised for commercial production of vitamin B_{12}. *Streptomyces olivaceus* produces 55–66 µg vitamin B_{12} per gram mycelium (Pfeifer *et al.*, 1954). *Bacillus megaterium* also produces yields of 0·5 µg/ml vitamin B_{12} and higher (Garibaldi *et al.*, 1953).

Most of the other vitamins are chemically synthesised.

Modern food technology uses enrichment or fortification to improve nutritive value of foods (Harris, 1959). It is possible to accomplish much the same enrichment by use of suitable fermentations. Platt (1946, 1964) coined the phrase 'biological ennoblement' for the latter. This paper deals with a number of foods in which there are striking examples of 'biological ennoblement'.

The vitamin content of selected yeasts is given in Table 5.

Fermentations which involve yeasts and particularly those in which the yeasts are consumed along with the substrate tend to be enriched in the B vitamins. These include the primitive beers and wines which will be used as the first examples of bio-enrichment.

3.1. Kaffir (Sorghum) Beer

Kaffir beer is an alcoholic beverage with a pleasantly sour taste and the consistency of a thin gruel. It is the traditional beverage of the Bantu people of South Africa. Alcohol content may vary from 1 to 8 % v/v. Kaffir beer is generally made from kaffircorn (*Sorghum caffrorum*) malt and unmalted kaffircorn meal. Maize or finger millet (*Eleusine coracana*) may be substituted for part or all of the kaffircorn depending upon the relative cost (Schwartz, 1956). Even cassava and plantains may be used (Platt, 1964).

Keith H. Steinkraus

TABLE 5
The Vitamin Content of Some Selected Yeasts

Yeast type	Thiamine	Riboflavin	Nicotinic acid	Pyridoxine	Pantothenic acid	Folic acid	Biotin	Reference
				mg/100 g dry yeast				
Brewers	10·4–25	2·5–8·0	30–62·7	2·3–4·0	7·2–8·6	1·9–3·0	0·11	Peterson (1948)
Saccharomyces cerevisiae	2·8–4·1	3·9–6·2	27·7–56·8	—	—	1·9–3·6	0·045–0·36	Peterson (1948)
Torulopsis utilis	3·5–3·8	5·4–6·2	51·1–60·0			1·0–1·5		Agarwal et al. (1947)
Candida arborea	3·1–3·3	5·2–6·9	49·2–58·0			1·5–1·6		Agarwal et al. (1947)

The kaffircorn grain is steeped for 6–36 h. It is then drained and placed in layers and germinated with periodic moistening for 4–6 days. Germination continues until the plumule is 1 in (2·5 cm) or longer in length. It is then sun-dried. Over 80 % of the malt is sold for home brewing of kaffir beer.

The essential steps in brewing are: mashing, souring, boiling, conversion, straining and alcoholic fermentation. Mashing is carried out in hot (50 °C) water. Proportions of malted to unmalted grains vary but 1:4 is satisfactory. One gallon of water is added for about every 4 pounds of grain. Souring begins immediately due to the presence of lactobacilli. A temperature of 50 °C favours development of *Lactobacillus delbrueckii*. Souring is complete in 6–15 h. Water is added and the mixture is boiled. It is then cooled to 40–60 °C and additional malt is added. Conversion proceeds for 2 h and then the mash is cooled to 25–30 °C. Yeasts present on the malt are responsible for the natural fermentation. However, *Saccharomyces cerevisiae* isolated from kaffir beer is frequently inoculated in the more modern breweries. Kaffir beer is ready for consumption in 4–8 h. It is drunk while still actively fermenting. This state may continue for up to 40 h. Ethanol content is generally from 2 to 4 % w/v. The beer also contains from 0·3 to 0·6 % lactic acid and 4–10 % solids.

TABLE 6
Comparison of Diet With and Without Maize Beer*

Food item	Amount of food eaten	
	Diet without beer	Diet with kaffir beer
Maize, wholemeal	350 g	137·5 g
Maize, 60 % extraction	350 g	137·5 g
Maize beer	—	5 pints (2 840 ml)
Vegetables	130 g	130 g
Sweet potatoes	470 g	470 g
Kidney beans	30 g	30 g
Calories	3 016	2 979
Vitamin B_1	2·00 mg	1·95 mg
Riboflavin	1·13 mg	2·32 mg
Nicotinic acid	11·70 mg	20·30 mg

* Platt (1964).

Consumption of 5 pints of kaffir beer which requires approximately 425 g of grain is not at all unusual for a working man each day. The question has been raised, how does the consumption of the beer diet compare in nutrient intake with a diet in which the grains were consumed directly. Platt (1964) compares the two diets in Table 6.

It is seen that caloric content of the two diets is quite similar. Only 37 calories are lost in the diet containing the beer. However, most notable is the doubling of riboflavin and near doubling of nicotinic acid content of the diet containing beer due to synthesis of vitamins during malting and fermentation. Pellagra, which is relatively common in people subsisting on maize diets, is never noted in those consuming usual amounts of Kaffir beer (Platt, 1964).

The infants in the villages are given the dregs which contain very little alcohol, are rich in vitamins and protein content and are very likely highly beneficial to infants' nutrition.

TABLE 7

Effect of Germination on the Vitamin Content of Kaffircorn and Maize*

Sample		Vitamin content in µg per g (dry basis)			
		Moisture %	Thiamine	Riboflavin	Nicotinic acid
Kaffircorn	Grain	11·6	3·34	1·29	35·1
	Malt	10·7	1·73	2·41	34·1
Maize	Grain	12·1	3·50	1·46	19·6
	Malt	8·6	2·32	2·02	29·1

* Goldberg & Thorp (1946).

The effect of germination on vitamin content of kaffircorn and maize is presented in Table 7. Thiamine decreases; riboflavin shows a substantial increase; nicotinic acid remains nearly constant in Kaffircorn but increases by about 50% in maize. Thus, the micro-organisms involved in the fermentation must be contributing additional thiamine, riboflavin and nicotinic acid to the product.

Novellie (1966a, b) has found that the content of thiamine, riboflavin, and niacin in kaffir beers has tended to decrease (Table 8). The proportion of sorghum to maize used in brewing has decreased concomitantly from 4·9:1 to 1·2:1 or less. Following analyses of brewing practices and changes

TABLE 8

Average Vitamin Values for Kaffir Beer Produced in Large-scale Breweries in the Years 1954, 1959 and 1963

Year	Average vitamin content ($\mu g/100\,ml$)		
	Thiamine	Riboflavin	Nicotinic acid
1954	153	95	494
1959	80	34	194
1963	32	36	189

Source: Novellie (1966b). Reprinted from *Food Technology* **20**, 1607–8, 1966, Copyright by Institute of Food Technologists.

in vitamin contents during fermentation, Novellie (1966b) concluded that the change in substrate ratio was the primary factor responsible for the loss in vitamins. In particular, one brewery that was late in changing to low sorghum/maize ratios was also late in producing low-vitamin beer (Table 9). Changes in brewing practices have probably played a minor role.

This illustrates very well that modification and modernisation of traditional fermented foods should only be undertaken when the nutritional value can be maintained. Kaffir beer is a very important source of nutrition to the indigenous people. It would be a tragedy if modernisation of kaffir brewing were accompanied by a higher incidence of malnutrition among the Bantus.

TABLE 9

The Vitamin Content of Kaffir Beer Made at a Municipal Brewery

Year	Brewery	Sorghum/ maize ratio	Vitamin content ($\mu g/100\,ml$)		
			Thiamine	Riboflavin	Nicotinic acid
1954	old	high	226	171	600
1959	old	high	176	45	289
1963	old	6:1	150	87	480
1964	old	3:1	121	48	328
	new	0·875:1	29	35	233

Source: Novellie (1966b). Reprinted from *Food Technology* **20**, 1607–8, 1966. Copyright by Institute of Food Technologists.

TABLE 10
Composition of Municipal Kaffir Beers*

	Range	Mean	No. of analyses
pH	3·2–3·7	3·4	10
Alcohol (% w/v)	1·8–3·9	3·0	17
Solids (% w/v)			
Total	3·0–8·0	5·4	17
Insoluble	2·3–6·1	3·7	6
Nitrogen (% w/v)			
Total	0·059–0·137	0·093	16
Soluble	0·010–0·017	0·014	9
Thiamine (μg/100 ml)	20–230	93·0	21
Riboflavin (μg/100 ml)	27–170	56·0	21
Nicotinic acid (μg/100 ml)	130–660	315·0	21
Ascorbic acid (mg/100 ml)	0·01–0·15	0·04	7

* Aucamp *et al.* (1961).

Aucamp *et al.* (1961) reported chemical analyses of municipal kaffir beers (Table 10). The content of ascorbic acid in kaffir beer is negligible. However, 2 litres of beer per day, which is a rather common level of consumption, would supply 140 %, 72 % and 36 % of the US recommended allowance for adult males (Food and Nutrition Board, 1974) of thiamine, riboflavin and nicotinic acid, respectively (Table 11).

Kaffir beer nutritionally is a very important part of the South African village diet.

TABLE 11
Amounts of B Vitamins Supplied by $\frac{1}{2}$ gallon (US) of Kaffir Beer (calculated from values in Table 10)

	Thiamine mg	Riboflavin mg	Nicotinic acid mg
Minimum	0·38	0·51	2·5
Maximum	4·4	3·2	12·5
Mean	1·8	1·1	6·0
Minimum daily requirement*	1·0	1·2	10·0
Recommended allowance**	1·5	1·7	19·0

* Harris (1959)
** Adult males, NAS/NRC, 1980.

3.2. Palm Toddies

Palm sap is a sweet, clear and colourless liquid containing about 10–12% sugar and neutral in reaction (Okafor, 1975b).

Palm wine is essentially a heavy milky-white, opalescent suspension of live yeasts and bacteria with a sweet taste and vigorous effervescence (Okafor, 1975a, b).

The yeast *Saccharomyces cerevisiae* seems to be always present whereas *Lactobacillus plantarum, Leuconostoc mesenteroides* and other bacterial species vary (Okafor, 1972; Faparusi, 1973). Van Pee & Swings (1971) also reported the discovery in palm wines of a motile rod-shaped high alcohol producing anaerobic bacterium closely related to *Zymomonas mobilis*.

An enormous amount of palm wine is consumed in Southern Nigeria. Four million people each drink approximately half a litre per day which contains approximately 300 calories from the sugar and alcohol, 0·5–2 g of protein and important amounts of water soluble vitamins. During the first 24 h, there is as much as 83 mg ascorbic acid/litre. This declines later. Thiamine increases from 25 μg to 150 μg/litre. Riboflavin content increases from 35 to 50 μg/litre in the first 24 h. Pyridoxine increases from 4 to 18 μg/litre. Vitamin B deficiencies are particularly widespread among pregnant women and teenagers. Palm wine is an important addition to their diets (Bassir, 1968).

Van Pee & Swings (1971) reported that palm juice and wines also contain vitamin B_{12} as follows:

Fresh palm juice (26 samples)	17–180 pg/ml Vitamin B_{12}
Palm wine (12 h fermentation)	140–190 pg/ml Vitamin B_{12}
Palm wine (24 h fermentation)	190–280 pg/ml Vitamin B_{12}

The vitamin B_{12} content is very important for people consuming primarily vegetarian foods. The fact that the fresh palm juice contains vitamin B_{12} suggests that there is bacterial growth in the fresh juice before it is 'fermented'.

The major nutrients in palm wine are sugars and B complex vitamins, and the cheapest source of B vitamins in Ghana is palm wine (Nyako, 1977). During the first 3–4 days, the B vitamins increase in concentration, after which no further increase takes place (Faparusi, 1977). As palm wine is undrinkable after 3 or 4 days, the vitamin content at 24 h is more representative of the vitamins actually consumed. Bassir (1968) and Faparusi & Bassir (1972) have reported the following for 24-h oil and raphia palm wines: thiamine 8–25 μg/litre, riboflavin 8–35 μg/litre, pyridoxine 4–30 μg/litre, ascorbic acid 7·4–9·0 mg/100 ml, a decrease from about 11 mg/100 ml in fresh sap. Vitamin B_{12} increases with time up to 190–500 ng/litre at 24 h (Okafor, 1978).

The following vitamins were found in the microbial cells and fluid of fermenting coconut toddy (Leong, 1953): thiamine (23·9 μg/100 ml), riboflavin (10·8 μg/100 ml), and nicotinic acid (369 μg/100 ml).

Palm toddies play an important role in nutrition among the economically deprived in the tropics.

3.3. Pulque

Pulque is the national drink of Mexico where it was inherited from the Aztecs (Goncalves de Lima, 1975). It is produced by fermentation of the juices (called aguamiel) of certain cactus plants of the Genus *Agave*. The Agave plants grow on very poor soil and consumption of pulque is of particular importance in the diets of the poor and low income people.

Pulque is a cloudy, white, viscous alcoholic beverage produced by the natural fermentation of aguamiel.

In the traditional process, the floral stem of mature plants 8–10 years old is cut off and the juice accumulates in the cavity. The juices are collected daily by oral suction and the juice is then fermented in wooden, leather or fibre-glass tanks with capacity of about 700 litres. The inoculum is pulque from a previous fermentation. Fermentation time is 8–30 days depending upon temperature and the season. Generally 30–70 litres of fresh juice are added to a tank and an equal amount is withdrawn. Thus, the process is semi-continuous.

The essential organisms are homofermentative and heterofermentative *Lactobacillus* sp., *Leuconostoc* sp. (closely related to *Leuconostoc dextranicum* and *Leuconostoc mesenteroides*), *Saccharomyces carbajali* (closely related to *Saccharomyces cerevisiae*), and *Pseudomonas lindneri*. The *Leuconostoc* sp. produce bacterial polysaccharides or dextrans which are responsible for the characteristic viscosity of pulque.

Because of problems controlling the natural fermentation, pure culture techniques have been developed in recent years (Sanchez-Marroquin, 1953).

The pulque fermentation has been modernised (Sanchez-Marroquin, 1977). Mechanical presses are used to collect the juice which is then treated to remove impurities, filtered and pasteurised. Pure cultures are used for the fermentation. A separate fermentation with *Leuconostoc* sp. is utilised to provide the desired degree of viscosity in the product. Fermentations are carried out in fibre-glass tanks. Optimum fermentation temperature is 28 °C and optimum pH is 5·0. The overall result is a higher quality pulque produced in 48–72 h versus 8–30 days required for natural fermentations.

The vitamin contents of traditional and modern pilot plant produced pulque are given in Table 12. It is seen that modernising the production of pulque has not decreased the vitamin content. Pulque continues to be an important source of nutrition among the economically deprived.

TABLE 12
B Vitamins in Traditional and Pilot Plant Pulque

Number of samples	Vitamins	Traditional[a,b] (tinacales)	Pilot plant[a,b]
10	Thiamine	5·2–29·0	10·2–38·0
10	Niacin	54·0–515·0	115·0–635·0
10	Riboflavin	18·0–33·1	19·4–35·6
10	Pantothenic acid	60·0–355·0	72·0–392·4
5	p-Aminobenzoic acid	12·3–20·7	15·9–32·2
5	Pyridoxine	14·2–33·4	19·1–36·4
5	Biotin	9·1–32·2	11·0–35·3

[a] Range of values obtained.
[b] $\mu g/100$ ml.
Source: Sanchez-Marroquin (1977).

3.4. South American Chicha

Chicha is a fermented beverage which is produced traditionally among the Indians of the Andes by pre-chewing maize, yuca, mesquite, quinoa, or plantain. Salivary diastase is the amylolytic agent. Well-made chicha is an attractive beverage, clear and effervescent, resembling apple cider in flavour. It generally contains 5 % or less ethanol with a range of 2–12 % (Cutler & Cardenas, 1947).

It would be expected that the nutritive value of chicha would be relatively high. The alcohol supplies calories; the micro-organisms, if consumed with the chicha, would be rich in B vitamins and protein. Escobar *et al.* (1977) reported that riboflavin doubled while thiamine and niacin remained fairly constant during fermentation. Their results were obtained using a pure culture of *S. cerevisiae*. It would be worthwhile to study the vitamin contents of traditional chichas.

3.5. Indonesian Tape Ketan

Indonesian tape ketan is a sweet-sour, alcoholic rice food in which an amylolytic mould *Amylomyces rouxii* and at least one yeast of the *Endomycopsis burtonii* type hydrolyse steamed rice starch to maltose and glucose and produce ethanol and organic acids which provide an attractive flavour and aroma. If yeasts of the genus *Hansenula* are present, the acids and ethanol are esterified producing highly aromatic esters. Fermentation time is 2–3 days at 30 °C. With continued incubation, the product becomes more liquid.

Detailed studies have been made of the biochemical and nutritional changes that occur during tape fermentations (Ko, 1972; Cronk *et al.*, 1977).

The ethanol (up to 8·5 % v/v) serves as a source of calories and probably helps prevent transmission of disease or toxin-producing micro-organisms in tape. The protein content of rice, which generally is about 7–8 %, rises to a maximum of 16 % in tape (dry solids basis) due to losses of total solids and synthesis of protein by the micro-organisms (Cronk *et al.*, 1977). Lysine, the first limiting amino acid in rice, is selectively synthesised and increases by 15 % in tape ketan. *A. rouxii* by itself or in combination with *E. burtonii*, *Candida lactosa*, *C. melinii*, *C. parapsilosis*, *Hansenula anomala*, *H. malanga* or *H. subpelliculosa* raises the thiamine content from 0·04 mg/100 g to 0·11–0·13 mg/100 g, a 300 % increase of great nutritional importance for people subsisting principally on polished rice (Cronk *et al.*, 1977).

3.6. Acid-leavened Bread and Pancakes

Foods of the Indian idli type, acidified and leavened through fermentation by heterofermentative lactic acid bacteria, constitute a very interesting group of cereal-based foods of considerable potential importance in the developing and also the developed world where they are largely unknown (Ramakrishnan, 1979; Steinkraus, 1983). Idli is closely related to sour dough bread of the Western world, but it does not depend upon wheat or rye as a source of protein to retain the carbon dioxide gas during leavening. Leavening is produced by bacterial rather than by yeast activity.

White polished rice and dehulled black gram are soaked separately for 5–10 h during the day. In the evening, the rice is drained and coarse ground and the black gram is drained and finely ground. They are then combined with 1 % salt and sufficient water to make a relatively thick batter. The batter is incubated overnight, during which time *Leuconostoc mesenteroides* produces acid and CO_2 leavening the batter, and *Streptococcus faecalis* produces additional acid. The batter is steamed in the morning yielding acidified, leavened bread-like cakes or the batter can be made thinner and fried as a pancake (then called dosai) (Mukherjee *et al.*, 1965). Proportions of rice to black gram can vary from about 4:1 to 1:2 and still yield a satisfactory texture and flavour. Soybean cotyledons can be used to replace the black gram dhal.

Rajalakshmi & Vanaja (1967) reported that thiamine and riboflavin increase during fermentation (Table 13). Fermentation results in an

TABLE 13
Composition of Fermented and Unfermented Idli

Food	Amount in 100 g dry material[a]		
	Protein (g)	*Thiamine (mg)*	*Riboflavin (mg)*
Unfermented idli	13·9	0·21	0·25
	(13·7–14·9)	(0·20–0·25)	(0·24–0·29)
Fermented idli	14·0	0·58	0·54
	(13·9–14·1)	(0·51–0·64)	(0·43–0·60)

[a] Values are means of 4–7 determinations with range shown in parentheses. Adapted from Rajalakshmi & Vanaja (1967).

increase in both free and total niacin (Rajalakshmi *et al.*, 1964). In addition Akolkar (1977) reported increases in thiamine, riboflavin and niacin during the idli fermentation (Table 14). Rajalakshmi & Vanaja also reported improvements in weight gain per gram protein intake and increases in the liver contents of thiamine, riboflavin, xanthine oxidase, and succinic dehydrogenase in rats fed fermented idli. These results were consistent with the findings of higher thiamine and riboflavin levels in fermented idli and the observed increases in nitrogen retention and riboflavin content of idli fed rats.

The changes in thiamine, riboflavin and niacin contents were higher with fermentation by pure cultures than with natural fermentation. This bonus in vitamins is largely retained during short-term autoclaving of idli batter (Table 14). A loss of less than 15% has been associated with ordinary steaming.

3.7. Indonesian Tempe

Centuries ago the Indonesians, without modern chemistry and microbiology, developed a meat analogue by a fermentation process in which

TABLE 14
Vitamin Changes in Naturally Fermented, Experimentally Fermented and Steamed
Soy Idli Batter[a]

	Raw mixture[b]	Fermented batter[a]			
		Control[c]	Uninoculated, unautoclaved	Inoculated[d]	Steamed[e] inoculated
Thiamine (mg)	0·45	0·56	0·89	1·03	1·00
	(0·44–0·47)	(0·54–0·58)	(0·87–0·97)	(1·02–1·05)	(1·00–1·02)
Riboflavin (mg)	0·46	0·53	1·47	1·85	1·55
	(0·44–0·48)	(0·50–0·56)	(1·45–1·50)	(1·80–1·94)	(1·45–1·63)
Niacin (mg)	3·2	3·34	4·68	5·61	4·85
	(3·19–3·23)	(3·28–3·36)	(4·66–4·70)	(5·43–5·84)	(4·80–4·86)

[a] Values per 150 g raw ingredients; average of three trials; range given in parentheses.
[b] Rice meal (100 g) and soy dhal flour (50 g).
[c] Autoclaved batter incubated without inoculation.
[d] Autoclaved batter inoculated with mixture of L. mesenteroides, L. fermenti, L. delbrueckii and Bacillus sp.
[e] Autoclaved at 5 lb/in^2 for 5 min.
Source: Akolkar (1977).

soybeans are soaked, dehulled, partially cooked and inoculated with moulds belonging to the genus Rhizopus. Incubated in a warm place (30–33 °C), the soybean cotyledons are knitted into a compact cake by the fibrous mould mycelium in 1–3 days. The product, called 'tempe kedele', can be sliced thinly and deep-fat fried or cut into chunks and used in place of meat in soup and other dishes. Tempe contains over 40 % (w/w) protein (dry solids basis) and a flavour and texture which appeals to the consumers. It is a good substitute for meat and it has begun to serve the same role in diets of American vegetarians (Steinkraus et al., 1960; Hesseltine, 1961; Saono et al., 1977; Shurtleff & Aoyagi, 1979, 1980; Wang & Hesseltine, 1979).

The essential micro-organism for the production of the typical tempe bean cake is a mould belonging to genus Rhizopus. A number of species can complete the essential step of knitting the soybean cotyledons into a firm cake. These include Rhizopus oligosporus, R. stolonifer, R. oryzae and R. arrhizus (Hesseltine et al., 1963; Dwidjoseputro & Wolf, 1970). The best of the moulds so far discovered is Rhizopus oligosporus, Northern Regional Research Laboratories (NRRL) strain 2710. This strain was originally isolated by Keith H. Steinkraus at Cornell University from dried powdered tempe brought to the United States by Miss Yap Bwee Hwa in 1958 and identified by Dr C. W. Hesseltine in the Northern Regional Research Laboratories, Peoria, Illinois.

Steinkraus *et al.* (1960) reported that the only essential micro-organism in the tempe fermentation was the mould. Subsequently, however, it was found that tempe contained vitamin B_{12} (Steinkraus *et al.*, 1961). When a search was made for the source of the vitamin B_{12}, it was found that all commercial tempes studied contained a Gram-negative rod along with the mould. This rod produced the vitamin B_{12} (Liem *et al.*, 1977). Tempe made with the pure mould contains no vitamin B_{12} activity. The Gram-negative rod was subsequently identified as a non-pathogenic strain of *Klebsiella pneumoniae* (Curtis *et al.*, 1977). Since vitamin B_{12} is so important in the diets of vegetarians, from the nutritional viewpoint, it must be considered that *Klebsiella pneumoniae* is essential in the tempe fermentation.

Microbiological assays indicated that the vitamin content of tempe is higher than the starting soybeans in certain cases and lower in others (Steinkraus *et al.*, 1961; Roelofsen & Talens, 1964; Napavarn *et al.*, 1977). Riboflavin doubles, niacin increases 7 times, and vitamin B_{12} activity increases 33 times. Thiamine unfortunately decreases (Table 15) (Steinkraus *et al.*, 1961). Pantothenate has been reported to stay approximately the same (Steinkraus *et al.*, 1961) or to double or quadruple (Murata *et al.*, 1967, 1968). Murata *et al.* (1967) reported increases of riboflavin from 8 to 47 times, pyridoxine from 4 to 14 times, and niacin from 2 to 5 times in tempes manufactured and sun-dried in Indonesia.

Biotin and total folate compounds were respectively 2·3 and 4–5 times higher in tempe than in unfermented soybeans (Murata *et al.*, 1970). The increases in riboflavin, niacin, pyridoxine and vitamin B_{12} activity are of

TABLE 15
A Comparison of Certain Vitamins in Soybeans and in Tempe

Vitamin	*Concentration*	
	In soybeans per gram	*In tempe per gram*
Riboflavin	3 μg	7·0 μg
Pantothenate	4·6 μg	3·3 μg
Thiamine	10·0 μg	4·0 μg
Niacin	9·0 μg	60·0 μg
B_{12}	0·15 ng	5·0 ng

Source: Steinkraus *et al.* (1961).

considerable importance nutritionally. In the Western world, the consumer gets vitamin B_{12} from milk or meats, while vegetarians usually have to find alternative sources of B_{12}, often a vitamin capsule. Tempe serves not only as a protein-rich meat substitute but also as a source of vitamin B_{12}.

It has been shown that *Klebsiella pneumoniae* isolated from Indonesian tempe can be inoculated into Indian idli and enrich it with vitamin B_{12} (Parekh, 1979).

The above are examples of bio-enrichment through fermentations that are well-accepted by millions of consumers. There are numerous other food fermentations used in many parts of the world. Most of these have been inadequately studied to determine what are the synthetic capabilities of their essential edible micro-organisms. With further study, other methods of bio-enrichment may become known and available for enhancing the vitamin content, essential amino acid contents and related nutritional qualities of man's foods.

4. SUMMARY

While the affluent Western world can afford to enrich its basic foods with chemically available vitamins, most of the developing world must rely upon biological enrichment of foods through fermentation. Every culture studied to date has its own food fermentations which are accomplished at costs within the financial means of most of the people. While some of the indigenous food/beverage fermentations, for example those reported in this chapter, have been extensively studied, there are numerous fermentations that have not been sufficiently studied to determine the essential micro-organisms, their sequences, their synthetic capabilities, particularly of vitamins, essential amino acids, protein and other biochemical/nutritional changes occurring in the substrate.

There is a potential gold-mine of information awaiting discovery in the indigenous food/beverage fermentations that will enable the world's people to bio-enrich their basic foods at relatively low cost in the coming years when world population reaches 6 billion about the year 2000 and 8–12 billion in the 21st century.

REFERENCES

AGARWAL, P. N., SINGH, K., KING, P. S. & PETERSON, W. H. (1947) Yield and vitamin content of food yeasts grown on different kinds of molasses. *Arch. Biochem.* **14**, 105–15.

AKOLKAR, P. N. (1977) Studies on soyidli fermentation. PhD Thesis. M. S. University of Baroda, Baroda, India.

AUCAMP, M. C., GRIEFF, J. T., NOVELLIE, L., PAPENDICK, B., SCHWARTZ, H. M. & STEER, A. G. (1961) Kaffircorn malting and brewing studies. VIII. Nutritive value of some kaffircorn products. *J. Sci. Food Agric.* **12**, 449–56.

BASSIR, O. (1968) Some Nigerian wines. *West Afr. J. biol. appl. Chem.* **10**, 42–5.

BENDER, A. E. (1973) *Nutrition and Dietetic Foods.* Chemical Publishing Co., New York.

CRONK, T. C., STEINKRAUS, K. H., HACKLER, L. R. & MATTICK, L. R. (1977) Indonesian tape ketan fermentation. *Appl. Environ. Microbiol.* **33**, 1067–73.

CURTIS, P. R., CULLEN, R. E. & STEINKRAUS, K. H. (1977) Identity of a bacterium producing vitamin B-12 activity in tempe. Symposium on Indigenous Fermented Foods, Bangkok, Thailand.

CUTLER, H. C. & CARDENAS, M. (1947) Chicha, a native South American beer. *Bot. Mus. Leafl., Harv. Univ.* **13**(6), 33–60.

DAVIS, B. D., HENDERSON, L. M. & POWELL, D. (1951). Production of Niacin by *Xanthomonas pruni. J. Biol. Chem.* **189**, 543–9.

DWIDJOSEPUTRO, D. & WOLF, F. T. (1970) Microbiological studies of Indonesian fermented foodstuffs. *Mycopathol. Mycol. Appl.* **41**, 211–22.

ESCOBAR, A., GARDNER, A. & STEINKRAUS, K. H. (1977) Studies on South American Chicha. Symposium on Indigenous Fermented Foods. Bangkok, Thailand, Nov. 21–27.

FAPARUSI, S. I. (1973) Origin of initial microflora of palm wine from oil palm trees (*Elaeis guineensis*). *J. appl. Bacteriol.* **36**, 559–65.

FAPARUSI, S. I. (1977) Nigerian palm wine-emu. Symposium on Indigenous Fermented Foods, Bangkok, Thailand.

FAPARUSI, S. I. & BASSIR, O. (1972) Factors affecting the quality of Palm-wine 2. Period of storage. *West Afr. J. biol. appl. Chem.* **15**, 24–8.

GARIBALDI, J. A., IJICHI, K., SNELL, N. S. & LEWIS, J. C. (1953) *Bacillus megatherium* for biosynthesis of cobalamin. *Ind. Engng Chem.* **45**, 838–946.

GOLDBERG, L. & THORP, J. M. (1946) A survey of vitamins in African foodstuffs. VI. Thiamin, riboflavin and nicotinic acid in sprouted and fermented cereal products. *S. Afr. J. med. Sci.* **11**, 177–85.

GONCALVES DE LIMA, O. (1975) 'Pulque, Balche Pajauaru.' Univ. Fed. Pernambuco, Recife, Brasil.

HARRIS, R. S. (1959) Supplementation of foods with vitamins. *Agric. Food Chem.* **7**(2), 88–102.

HENDRICKZ, H. & DE VLEESCHAUWER, A. (1955) Production of riboflavin by *Eromothecium ashbyii. Meded. Landb Hoofesch. Gent.* **20**, 229–35.

HESSELTINE, C. W. (1961) Research at Northern Regional Research Laboratory on fermented foods. In: *Proceedings of Conference on Soybean Products for Protein in Human Foods.* USDA, Peoria, Illinois, pp. 67–74.

HESSELTINE, C. W., DE CAMARGO, R. & RACKIS, J. J. (1963) A mould inhibitor in soybeans. *Nature, Lond.* **200**, 1226–7.

Ko, S. D. (1972) Tape fermentation. *J. appl. Microbiol.* **23**, 976–8.

LACHANCE, P. A. (1978) Enrichment, restoration, fortification and nutrification. In: *Encyclopedia of Food Science*, M. S. Peterson & A. H. Johnson, Eds. AVI Publishing Co., Westport, Conn., pp. 232–7.

LAGO, B. D. & KAPLAN, L. (1981) Vitamin fermentations: B_2 and B_{12}. In *Advances in Biotechnology. Vol. III. Fermentation Products*. General Editor M. Moo-Young, C. Vezina and K. Singh, Eds. Pergamon Press, Oxford.

LEONG, P. C. (1953) The nutritive value of coconut toddy. *Br. J. Nutr.* **7**, 253–9.

LIEM, I. T. H., STEINKRAUS, K. H. & CRONK, T. C. (1977) Production of vitamin B-12 in tempeh, a fermented soybean food. *Appl. Environ. Microbiol.* **34**, 773–6.

MUKHERJEE, S. K., ALBURY, M. N., PEDERSON, C. S., VAN VEEN, A. G. & STEINKRAUS, K. H. (1965) Role of *Leuconostoc mesenteroides* in leavening the batter of idli, a fermented food of India. *Appl. Microbiol.* **13**, 227–31.

MURATA, K., IKEHATA, H. & MIYAMOTO, T. (1967) Studies on the nutritional value of tempeh. *J. Food Sci.* **32**, 580–6.

MURATA, K., MIYAMOTO, T. & TAGUCHI, F. (1968) Biosynthesis of B vitamins with *Rhizopus oligosporus*. *J. Vitaminol. (Kyoto)* **14**, 191–7.

MURATA, K., MIYAMOTO, T., KOKUFU, E. & SANKE, Y. (1970) Studies on the nutritional value of tempeh. III. Changes in biotin and folic acid contents during tempeh fermentation. *J. Vitaminol. (Kyoto)* **16**, 281–4.

NAS/NRC. (1974) Proposed Fortification Policy for Cereal-Grain Products. Food and Nutrition Board, National Academy of Sciences National Research Council, Washington, D.C.

NAS/NRC. (1980) Recommended Dietary Allowances. Committee on Dietary Allowances. Food and Nutrition Board, Washington, D.C.

NAPAVARN, N., CHALOTHORN, T. A. & SOMARI, S. (1977) Factors affecting fermentations and vitamin B-12 content in tempeh and tempeh-like products. Symposium on Indigenous Fermented Foods, Bangkok, Thailand.

NOVELLIE, L. (1966a) Bantu beer—popular drink in South Africa. *Int. Brewer and Distiller* **1**, 27–31.

NOVELLIE, L. (1966b) Biological ennoblement and kaffir beer. *Food Technol.* **20**, 1607–8.

NYAKO, K. O. (1977) Palm wine—an alcoholic beverage of Ghana. Symposium on Indigenous Fermented Foods, Bangkok, Thailand.

OKAFOR, N. (1972) Palm-wine yeasts from parts of Nigeria. *J. Sci. Food Agric.* **23**, 1399–1407.

OKAFOR, N. (1975a) Preliminary microbiological studies on the preservation of palm wines. *J. appl. Bacteriol.* **38**, 1–7.

OKAFOR, N. (1975b) Microbiology of Nigerian palm wine with particular reference to bacteria. *J. appl. Bacteriol.* **38**, 81–8.

OKAFOR, N. (1978) Microbiology and biochemistry of oil-palm wine. *Adv. appl. Microbiol.* **24**, 237–56.

PAREKH, B. J. (1979) Personal communication. M. S. University, Baroda, India.

PETERSON, W. H. (1948) Yeasts in feeding. Proceedings of the Symposium, Nov. 1948, p. 26; abstracted in *Wallenstein Lab. Comm.* **13**(43), 401 (1950).

PFEIFER, V. F., VOJNOVICH, C. & HEGER, E. N. (1954) Vitamin B_{12} by fermentation with *Streptomyces olivaceus*. *Ind. Engng Chem.* **46**, 843–9.

PLATT, B. S. (1946) 'Nutrition in the British West Indies,' Colon. Rep. No. 195. HM Stationery Office, London.

PLATT, B. S. (1964) Biological ennoblement: Improvement of the nutritive value of foods and dietary regimens by biological agencies. *Food Technol.* **18**, 662–70.

RAJALAKSHMI, R., NANAVATY, K. & GUMAZHA, A. (1964) Effect of cooking procedures on the free and total niacin content of certain foodstuffs. *Ind. J. Nutr. Diet.* **1**, 276–80.

RAJALAKSHMI, R. & VANAJA, K. (1967) Chemical and biological evaluation of the effects of fermentation on the nutritive value of foods prepared from rice and gram. *Br. J. Nutr.* **21**, 467–73.

RAMAKRISHNAN, C. V. (1979) Studies on Indian fermented foods. *Baroda J. Nutr.* **6**, 1–57.

ROELOFSEN, P. A. & TALENS, A. (1964) Changes in some B vitamins during molding of soybeans by *Rhizopus oryzae* in the production of tempeh kedelee. *J. Food Sci.* **29**, 224–6.

SANCHEZ-MARROQUIN, A. (1953) The biochemical activity of some microorganisms of pulque. *Mem. Congr. Cientif. Mex.*, 4th Centenario Univ. Mex., pp. 471–84.

SANCHEZ-MARROQUIN, A. (1977) Mexican pulque—a fermented drink from Agave juice. Symposium on Indigenous Fermented Foods, Bangkok, Thailand.

SAONO, S., BROTONEGORO, S., BASUKI, T., SASTRAATMADJI, D. D., JUTONO, BADJRE, I. G. P. & GANDJAR, I. (1977) Tempe. Symposium on Indigenous Fermented Foods, Bangkok, Thailand.

SCHWARTZ, H. M. (1956) Kaffircorn malting and brewing studies. I. The kaffir beer brewing industry in South Africa. *J. Sci. Food Agric.* **7**, 101–5.

SHURTLEFF, W. & AOYAGI, A. (1979) *The Book of Tempeh*. Harper and Row, New York.

SHURTLEFF, W. & AOYAGI, A. (1980) *Tempeh Production*. New Age Foods, Lafayette, California.

STEINKRAUS, K. H. (1983) Lactic acid fermentation in the production of foods from vegetables, cereals and legumes. *Antonie van Leeuwenhoek* **49**, 337–48.

STEINKRAUS, K. H., YAP, B. H., VAN BUREN, J. P., PROVIDENTI, M. I. & HAND, D. B. (1960) Studies on tempeh—An Indonesian fermented soybean food. *Food Res.* **25**, 777–88.

STEINKRAUS, K. H., HAND, D. B., VAN BUREN, J. P. & HACKLER, L. R. (1961) Pilot plant studies on tempe. In: Proceedings of Conference on Soybean Products for Protein in Human Foods. USDA, pp. 75–84.

VAN PEE, W. and SWINGS, J. G. (1971) Chemical and microbiological studies on Congolese palm wines (*Elaeis guineensis*). *East Afr. Agric. For. J.* **36**(3), 311–14.

WANG, H. L. & HESSELTINE, C. W. (1979) Mold-modified foods. In: *Microbial Technology*, 2nd edn, H. J. Peppler and D. Perlman, eds. Academic Press, New York, Vol. 2, pp. 95–129.

Chapter 10

Production of Industrial Enzymes and Some Applications in Fermented Foods

A. GODFREY

*Biocatalysts Ltd, Grand Metropolitan Biotechnology Division,
South Ruislip, Middlesex, UK*

1. INTRODUCTION

The widespread use of isolated industrial enzymes for the processing of foodstuffs is very ancient in its origins. Many traditional fermentations rely upon the hydrolytic influences of indigenous or deliberately added enzymes generally deriving from the metabolic activities of acceptable microbial invasion of the substrates. In recent and scientifically informed times, these activities have been identified and often refined by the use of separately extracted or fermented enzymes.

This chapter begins with a very brief account of the development of that knowledge and the evolution of the Industrial Enzyme Industry as it is today. There follows a discussion of the extraction of animal and plant enzymes of particular interest to the food processor, and continues into an account of the principles of the production of fermentation enzymes.

The concluding section of this chapter outlines the extensive use of industrial enzymes for the efficient conversion of fermentation feedstocks and describes some of the main features of their applications. A few selected examples of the more diverse uses of enzymes in food fermentation processes indicate the trends for the future.

In addition to the references drawn upon in the text several additional bibliographical references to useful accounts of industrial enzyme production are given.

2. SHORT HISTORY OF INDUSTRIAL ENZYMES

The absolute origins of the industrial use of enzymes remain clouded in the depths of ancient history and the concept of industrial processes is not really applicable until the late 19th century. The production of fermentable materials and their conversion to foods and beverages has been part of human endeavour for vastly longer than true industrialisation. The curdling of milk for cheese making is referred to in the ninth song of the Homeric Odyssey and again in the fifth song of the Iliad, where several uses for an extract of the fig are described and almost certainly represent applications of the proteolytic enzyme Ficin.

At the time that the human race had established cultivation of crops, the modification of cereals to induce alcoholic fermentation was also developed. In his splendid treatise, *The Ascent of Man*, Dr Jacob Bronowski indicates that the turning point for the development in agriculture occurred in the region of the ancient settlements at Jericho around 8000 BC in the Christian calendar. The natural chances of genetic hybridisation produced a cross between wild goat grass and wild wheat to give the plump headed cereal that had lost the natural wind-induced shedding of its grains. Man could harvest the grain and at the same time became responsible for its survival by sowing a portion for the next season's crop.

Rice and starchy roots such as manioc were also used to produce alcoholic beverages wherever they grew. The starch conversion was brought about by the action of mixed cultures of micro-organisms deliberately introduced to moist mashes of the starchy materials. The improved fermentations that were achieved if the starchy substances were first chewed can now be seen to have benefitted from the action of salivary amylases and the microbial contributions will have been extracellular carbohydrases and proteases.

Thus we can see that for every incidence of ancient food fermentations, there was an element of enzymic hydrolysis of complex natural polymers, coupled with either deliberate or inevitable inoculation with yeasts or bacteria that subsequently yielded a stable material of a nutritious and palatable nature.

The preparation of concentrated and more specific sources of these enzymes forms the basis for the expansion of fermentation products for many centuries, leading to the cultures for Koji and Saké fermentations in the Orient; the preparation of tea and coffee; the development of fish and soy condiments; the spread and diversification of cheeses and baked products; the expansion of bacterial acid fermentations of vegetables and proteins; and the development of the fermentation industries around cereals, and particularly their expansion following the discovery of the malting process to give a self-digesting cereal product.

By the middle of the 19th century, detailed investigation of the activities of micro-organisms was established and in 1878 the German chemist, Willy Kühne, had coined the term 'enzyme' to describe the chemical entities that were responsible for continued catalysis of cell free extracts of yeast. About the same time the industrial commercialisation of an enzyme, rennet, extracted from calf stomachs, had begun under the direction of the Dane, Christian Hansen.

By the turn of the present century, the Japanese scientist Takamine had isolated fungal carbohydrases and proteases, which rapidly improved on the traditional rice Koji for fish and soya conversions. The product 'Takadiastase' is still used as a digestive aid and the surface culture methods still find commercial application for the production of industrially significant enzymes, particularly the pectinolytic products used by wine and fruit processors. Pancreatic enzymes were isolated by Dr Otto Röhm around 1913 and soon became effectively used in the leather industry as popular replacements for animal dung.

The remaining progress in industrial enzyme research and commercial development derives largely from the knowledge of large scale microbial fermentations that was created by the discovery and rapid expansion of antibiotics. From the work of Fleming in the 1930s until around 1955, the transfer of technology to the enzyme industry was gradual, but by 1965 huge quantities of bacterial amylases and proteases were being produced in submerged fermentations. Progress since 1965 has been rapid and diverse, so that there are now commercially available enzymes for most hydrolytic processes of relevance to industrial needs. Most recently there have been developments in enzyme technology that have yielded continuous process possibilities using both soluble and immobilised forms. The economy of continuous processing is significant in times of high labour and energy costs and great progress has been made in starch conversion along this route.

Although much has been claimed for the benefits of the use of immobilised enzymes, either as stirred reactions or fixed beds in tubes or columns, there are as yet only limited examples that show truly worthwhile benefits of this technique. The production of fructose from glucose with immobilised glucose isomerase and the manufacture of certain highly valuable amino acids for nutritional needs have proved economic, although it can be seen that the technological problems that immobilisation overcomes may be the most significant feature in these instances.

The history of industrial enzymes is summarised in Table 1.

TABLE 1
Summarised History of Industrial Enzymes

Pre-history	Cheese production
	Carbohydrate fermentation for beverages
Pre-biological sciences	Oriental fermentations—beverages, sauces, pickles
	Wines, beers, malting of cereals, pickles, milk and cheese products
1874	Chr. Hansen—commercial rennet
1878	W. Kühne—term 'enzyme' proposed
1890	Takamine—takadiastase
1900–1930	Malt extract for textile desizing
	Developing animal enzyme extraction
1930	Pectinases in fruit processing
1954	Submerged fermentation—proteases for detergents; amylases for textile and starch industries
1960s	Diversification of fermented enzymes—wider range for starch and detergent industries
1970s	Further range expansion from fermentations; immobilised enzymes; thermostable and thermolabile specialities
1980s	New refined enzymes; application of specific combination enzyme products; energy saving systems; biofuels production; chemicals synthesis with enzymes; environmentally significant applications

It is currently estimated that industrial enzymes are produced by some 25 companies in the Western world, with almost half of the 65 000 tonnes of annual production being in Denmark. Holland produces a further 20 % and the remainder is from Japan, West Germany, Switzerland, France, the USA and UK.

For a full discussion of industrial enzymes, producers and applications, the reader is referred to Godfrey & Reichelt (1982).

3.   MODERN APPROACH TO ENZYME PRODUCTION

There are now almost 50 different enzymes available in commercial quantities, although researchers have identified more than 2500. The majority of the industrial enzymes are of microbial origin and the most significant developments in the past 30 years have been with this group.

Some consistently important enzymes are still extracted from animals and higher plants (Table 2).

TABLE 2
Enzymes for Food Use from Animals and Plants

Enzyme	Source
Alpha amylase ⎫ Protease ⎬ Lipase ⎬ Lecithinase ⎭	Pancreatic glands Bovine/Porcine
Rennets	4th stomach of lamb, kid and calf
Esterases	Parotid gland of lamb, kid and calf
Catalase	Bovine liver
Lysozyme	Hen egg albumen
Alpha and beta amylases	Malted cereals, soya bean, barley
Peroxidase	Horse radish root (*Armaracia rusticana*)
Urease	Jack Bean (*Canavalia ensiformis*)
Proteases	Papain (*Papaya*) Ficin (*Ficus carica*) Bromelain (*Bromus*)

4. ENZYMES FROM ANIMAL MATERIALS

Almost exclusively, animal enzymes of commercial interest are proteases extracted from intestinal tissues or pancreatic glands.

Pepsin (EC 3.4.23.1) is the carboxyl-acid protease extracted from porcine gastric mucosa. It is noted for its very acid pH optimum, lying between 1·8 and 2·0.

Rennet (Chymosin) (EC 3.4.23.4) is another carboxyl-acid protease with extremely high specificity at neutral pH, used almost exclusively for milk coagulation and extracted from the abamosum of unweaned ruminants, notably calf, kid and lamb. The majority is extracted from calves, but the extracts from kid and lamb may be produced to contain additional lipase activity which is relevant to the production of special cheese varieties (see Chapter 3, Cheese Fermentations).

Pancreatin is a mixed enzyme preparation obtained by the extraction of bovine or porcine pancreatic glands and contains the proteases Trypsin (EC 3.4.21.14) and Chymotrypsin (EC 3.4.21.1), together with Fatty Acid Esterase (EC 3.1.1.1) and Amylase (EC 3.2.1.1). The two proteases are also prepared as single and mixed entities of higher purity on a commercial scale.

4.1. Source Materials

Generally the appropriate tissues are excised from healthy animals, fit for human consumption, immediately post slaughter and rapidly deep frozen to aid the accumulation of sufficient bulk for transport to the processing factory.

During thawing, the frozen material is roughly broken in a coarse mincing or grinding machine and then, when completely thawed it is further subjected to grinding or comminution whilst still very cold.

4.2. Extraction

For rennets, it is considered important to avoid the release of large amounts of non-specific proteases that would interfere with cheese quality by excessive protein degradation. This is achieved by less complete homogenisation of the tissues and the extraction is achieved by washing with chilled aqueous solutions of common salt (food grade) ranging from 1 to 5 % in strength and containing dilute hydrochloric acid to activate the enzyme. The saline extract is recovered by filtration using plate and frame or rotary vacuum equipment. The fluid is combined with any subsequent washing liquors that have been applied to the filter cake or resuspended materials and concentrated to a commercial strength. Concentration may be achieved by vacuum evaporation at low temperature or, more economically in terms of yield and power consumption, by membrane techniques.

The concentrate will then be adjusted to commercial strengths by the addition of salt solutions such that the activity meets the required use rates for the intended markets and the salt level is sufficient to ensure microbial stability of the concentrate, typically 15–18 % by weight. The pH is raised to between 5 and 6 for stability. Where permitted, the addition of preservatives and caramel colouring is made at this stage.

In the case of the pancreatic enzymes and the preparation of pure pepsin and rennet, the extraction will utilise an appropriate dilute buffer to maintain the maximum enzyme activity and to limit the solubilisation of other tissue components. The first liquor separated from the tissues will then be treated to separate the desired enzymes as insolubles, or to precipitate unwanted materials, leaving the target enzymes in solution. Various concentrations of inorganic salts such as sodium sulphate, ammonium sulphate and sodium chloride are typically employed for this stage. A further purification of the enzyme can be obtained by repeated salting-out by these materials or the careful addition of chilled solvents such as ethanol or acetone. Finally the precipitated enzymes can be carefully dried under vacuum and standardised with carriers such as sodium chloride or lactose or dissolved in a stabilising solution usually containing sodium chloride and permitted preservatives. Some solid preparations are prepared by gentle spray or freeze drying from liquid concentrates followed by standardisation.

Throughout the procedures, great care is taken to keep the enzyme extracts cold and to avoid dramatic changes of pH or concentration of added chemicals. This is achieved by the use of chilled liquids and the continuous stirring of preparations when additions are being made.

It is seen from many published technical data on industrial enzymes that the pH at which an enzyme is most stable is not necessarily the same as the pH for optimum activity. It is therefore necessary to ensure that preparations are at the best pH for stability and that statements of activity are clearly identified with regard to the physical conditions of the assay employed.

For maximum activity of extracted animal enzymes, it is generally necessary to activate the precursor zymogen by addition of acid, alkali or proteases to the extracting buffers.

5.   ENZYMES FROM PLANT MATERIALS

Traditionally there are three classical proteases produced from the extraction of plant tissues, Bromelain, Ficin and Papain. Malted cereals have been used to obtain concentrated carbohydrases of which alpha and beta amylase are the most common. Malted wheat and barley are the main sources of both of these, although a very useful beta-amylase is obtained from the soya bean. With appropriate activation, it is also possible to obtain beta-amylase from unmalted barley.

The proteases are all of the thiol type and are restricted to applications under reducing conditions, since they are inactivated by oxidising agents. They are extracted from the plant tissue by processes that essentially parallel those for animal enzymes. Bromelain (EC 3.4.22.4) is obtained from the juices resulting from crushing either the stems or the fruits of various species of pineapple. The enzymes from stem and fruit have slightly different characteristics regarding the specific bonds they will hydrolyse, but both are active between pH 5 and 8 and have a thermal limit for effective use of 55 °C.

Ficin (EC 3.4.22.3) is extracted from the latex sap that is expressed from wounds made to the stem of the fig tree. The pH optimum lies between 5 and 7 and the maximum performance temperature is 65 °C.

Papain (EC 3.4.22.2) is obtained from the fruits and latex of species of papaya and has characteristics very like ficin, although it exhibits the broadest action of the three enzymes. Traditionally it is the most widely accepted and used of these plant enzymes.

Application to food processing requires the approval of legislative bodies in many countries and it should be noted that bromelain and papain are obtained from edible portions of the plant, whilst ficin is from the non-edible part. It is normally found that ficin is either prohibited or not advised for use in food applications.

Alpha Amylase (EC 3.2.1.1) and Beta Amylase (EC 3.2.1.2) from cereals are extracted by the application of the typical 'mashing systems' of the brewing industry, with careful attention to reduced temperature limits to avoid inactivation. The cereals are milled in the typical brewery manner and then mashed with warm water in the range 40–50 °C. After a period at this temperature, the liquor is drained from the cereal and then concentrated by vacuum evaporation.

Separation and purification of the two amylases can be achieved by raising the temperature to 60 °C when the beta amylase is more rapidly in-activated, or lowering the pH to 4, which more rapidly inactivates the alpha amylase. Concentration and standardisation can produce liquid products that require addition of permitted preservatives and stabilising salts or sugars, or powdered products by spray or freeze drying.

A number of enzymes for more specialised applications are also extracted from plant tissues and include pectin-degrading systems from citrus fruits, some fat splitting lipases from oil bearing seeds and lipoxygenases from soya and certain species of pea.

6. PRINCIPAL STEPS IN EXTRACTION OF ANIMAL AND PLANT TISSUES

1. Collection or harvesting must take into account the need for accurate identification of plant species and the selection of the appropriate enzyme bearing portion. For animal tissues, the careful selection of the appropriate organ or tissue is equally essential, and the animal must have been fit for human consumption.

2. Storage prior to extraction will relate to the potential of microbial spoilage and also the loss of the target enzyme activity. General autolysis of most tissues will be accompanied by the proliferation of micro-organisms that were naturally present and may have been introduced during stage

one. Careful drying of plant tissues often enables storage to be practicable for many months and freezing is very appropriate for animal materials.

3. Preparation for extraction generally requires the material to be crushed, milled, ground or comminuted in an appropriate aqueous buffer and usually under chilled conditions around 0–4 °C. The equipment for the method of choice is varied and can generally be developed by small modifications of traditional food processing plant. The maintenance of low temperatures is the most important modification.

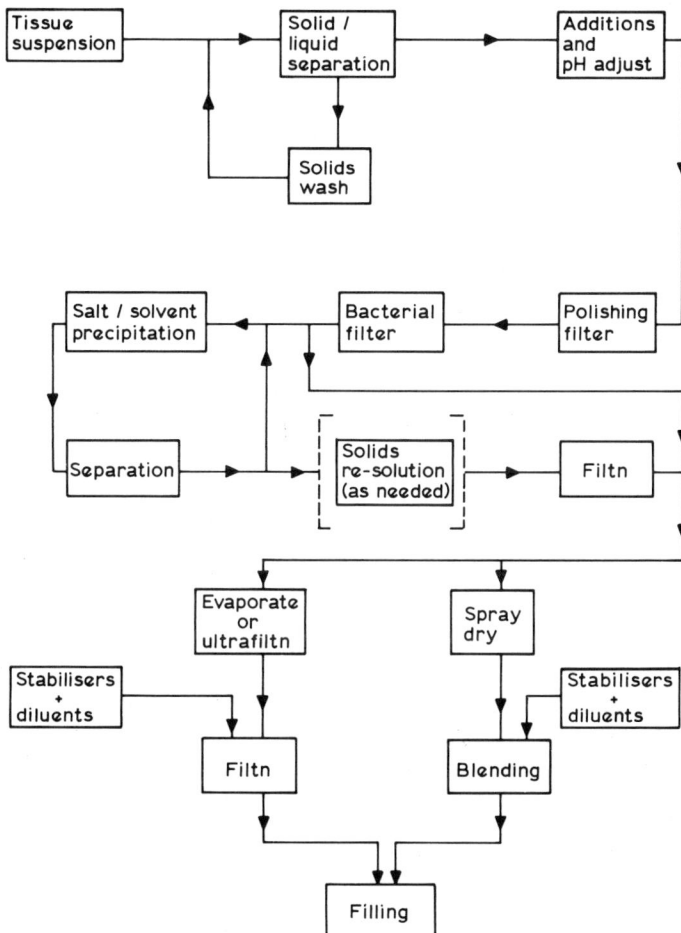

Fig. 1. Schematic flow diagram for the recovery of animal and plant enzymes.

4. Enzyme extraction (Fig. 1) generally consists of the solubilisation of the target enzyme, together with many other substances that are soluble in the liquid phase adopted, and the subsequent concentration and purification of the extract. Primary purifications are achieved by salting out or solvent precipitation and more intensive purifications involve further selective precipitations with the possible addition of bulk chromatography to specifically adsorb and remove impurities, or adsorb and desorb the target protein.

5. Presentation for market and application will require concentration and standardisation of the enzyme. Spray or freeze drying methods are suited to thermosensitive enzymes when dry products are needed. The standardisation is normally by dilution of the finished material with an appropriate carrier material such as lactose, salt and in some instances, starch or sugar. For liquid products it may be possible to evaporate the extract to a standard potency, but increasingly the concentration is achieved by ultrafiltration membrane systems that require only modest pressures and no heating.

The addition of permitted preservatives may be necessary to maintain the stability of the finished liquid product even after due account of the total solids content to restrict microbial growth has been considered.

7.   ENZYMES FROM MICROBIAL SOURCES

The participation of many, and largely unspecified, enzymes in the processes of fermentation of foods makes abundant explanation for the interest in having industrial food grade enzymes for the further development of food processing, with or without a fermentation stage.

In the general case, the micro-organisms of the fermentation utilise the nutrients available by the action of extracellular (secreted) enzymes that hydrolyse natural polymers. The resulting small fragments or individual molecular components so produced are then suitable for transport into the cells of the microbes and participate in the internal metabolism.

Thus it can be seen that the participation of micro-organisms parallels the digestive actions of higher animals and man. Industrial exploitation of this external digestive competence has been extensive since the mid-1960s, resulting in a valuable collection of hydrolytic enzymes now being available in bulk (Table 3).

In addition, there are now a number of other enzyme types produced in industrial quantity for a wide variety of applications, both food and non-food qualities, and some in the physical restricted presentations collectively

TABLE 3
Enzymes for Food Use from Micro-organisms

Enzyme	Source genus	Enzyme	Source genus
Amylases (diastases)	*Aspergillus* *Bacillus* *Endomyces*	Glucose oxidase	*Aspergillus* *Penicillium*
		Hemicellulase	*Aspergillus*
Amyloglucosidases	*Aspergillus* *Rhizopus*	Invertase	*Aspergillus* *Saccharomyces*
Beta galactosidases (lactase)	*Aspergillus* *Bacillus* *Saccharomyces* *Kluyveromyces*	Lipases	*Aspergillus* *Bacillus* *Candida* *Mucor* *Rhizopus*
Beta glucanases	*Aspergillus* *Bacillus* *Penicillium* *Saccharomyces*	Macerases	*Aspergillus* *Rhizopus* *Trichoderma*
		Peroxidases	*Aspergillus* *Penicillium*
Catalase	*Aspergillus* *Penicillium* *Micrococcus*	Pectinases	*Aspergillus*
		Proteases Acid	*Aspergillus* *Endothia* *Mucor* *Rhizopus*
Cellulase	*Aspergillus* *Penicillium* *Trichoderma*	Neutral	*Aspergillus* *Bacillus*
Dextranase	*Penicillium* *Klebsiella*	Alkaline	*Aspergillus* *Bacillus* *Rhizopus*
Glucose Isom.	*Actinomyces* *Bacillus* *Streptomyces*	Tannase	*Aspergillus*
		Xylanase	*Aspergillus*

called immobilised enzymes. A thorough discussion of the many applications of industrial enzymes together with extensive indexes of suppliers and biochemical details will be found in the text *Industrial Enzymology* (Godfrey & Reichelt, 1982).

The investigations of the internal metabolism of micro-organisms over the last 30 years have also made available a modest number of enzymes extracted from their internal systems. There are virtually no current examples of the application of these enzymes in the production of fermented foods, but examples of extended shelf-life of many food products by the action of one such enzyme, glucose oxidase, have been noted. The production of these intracellular enzymes has been described by M. D. Lilly in *Applied Biochemistry and Engineering Vol. 2* (Academic Press, 1979).

Similarly, the production of extracellular enzymes was also described by K. Aunstrup in the same volume, to which the reader is referred for more extensive discussion than that presented here.

8.   GENERAL PRINCIPLES FOR INDUSTRIAL PRODUCTION OF MICROBIAL EXTRACELLULAR ENZYMES

Very little specific information has been presented in the public domain that details the particular methods applied to the production of any one enzyme. This is largely due to the extremely competitive state of enzyme production and marketing resulting in very real differences in the way each producer arrives at a cost effective process for his products.

8.1. The Production Strain
Table 4 shows the principal micro-organisms that have found acceptance for production of industrial enzymes. The species listed are generally considered to present the least risk of toxin production during fermentation as well as being non-pathogenic to man.

Bacillus species are comparatively easy to isolate and despite the problems associated with spore formation, many have been isolated as non-sporing strains. The *Aspergilli* are similarly placed amongst the fungi, although the formation of conidial spores is desirable for the ease of inoculation of large scale fermentations. In every case, the strain selected for production will have a highly improved enzyme producing capability compared with the wild strains and will have undergone stringent screening to ensure that it does not produce toxins or antibiotics in order to meet

TABLE 4
Micro-organisms Used for the Industrial Production of Food Enzymes

Genus	Species	Genus	Species
Actinomyces	*missouriensis*	*Micrococcus*	*lysodeikticus*
Aspergillus	*niger* *ochraceus* *oryzae* *phoenicis* *saitoi* *sojae* *wentii*	*Mucor* *Penicillium*	*miehei* *pusillus lindt* *emersonii* *funiculosum* *glaucum* *lilacinum* *notatum*
Bacillus	*amyloliquefaciens* *amylosaccharicus* *cereus* *circulans* *coagulans* *fastidiosus* *licheniformis* *megaterium* *subtilis* *thermoproteolyticus*	*Rhizopus* *Saccharomyces* *Streptomyces*	*arrhizus* *delemar* *niveus* *carlsbergensis* *cerevisiae* *fragilis* *lactis* *albus* *olivaceus* *griseus*
Candida	*lipoytica*	*Trichoderma*	*reesei* *viride*
Endomyces	spp.		
Endothia	*parasitica*		
		Kluyveromyces	*fragilis* *lactis*
		Klebsiella	*aerogenes*

increasingly stringent standards for food applications of the enzyme product.

8.2. Fermentation

The choice of fermentation method lies between 'solid state' (which is also called semi-solid) and submerged or 'deep' fermentation. In rare cases the organism will dictate the choice by virtue of either non-production or low yields by one method. Generally, however, the nature of the final enzyme product and its designated performance objective determine the method. Enzymes from solid state cultivation are generally found to be complex mixtures, often including amylase, proteases, lipases and non-starch carbohydrases in definite proportions that are regulated by the cultivation. If a high level of a single activity is desired, it is commonly produced by submerged fermentation.

Semi-solid fermentations represent a degree of refinement of the traditional oriental 'Koji' systems described elsewhere in this book (Vol, 2, Chapter 9). Essentially used for fungal enzyme cultivation, they are typically used for non-starch carbohydrases such as cellulases and pectinases, some alpha-amylases and gluco-amylases, neutral and acid proteases, lipases and lactases.

The main characteristic of this process is the very flexible scale and comparative simplicity of the production plant that can be effectively employed. The fungus is grown on a moist but particulate mash substrate using wheat, soya or rice as the primary material. The cultivation is often performed in trays having shallow layers of the medium up to 10 cm deep and stacked in suitable boxes or rooms that permit moist air to be circulated over the trays.

Alternatively, the medium may be contained in rotating cylinders with fine mesh screens for the walls that permit free circulation of moist air as the drums rotate and tumble the medium.

The use of the tumble method has not proved particularly successful on a commercial scale. More significant developments have been achieved using forced aeration of comparatively deep beds of solid medium up to 2 m in depth. Care is required to ensure that humidity is maintained throughout the bed but that the mash remains sufficiently open for complete and even passage of moist air.

Each specific organism and selected medium will require optimisation to find the most productive method or combination of methods.

The amount of air and the temperature at which it enters the cultivation chambers is regulated according to the moisture levels required and the amount of heat to be taken out of the culture. In some cases, very rapid fermentation can yield considerable excess heat and positive cooling may have to be incorporated in the chamber design.

The medium is prepared to contain a large amount of the least costly source of carbohydrate and protein such as wheat bran, rice bran, soya bean meal and supplements of soluble trace elements, phosphates and in some cases additional nitrogen sources such as ammonia. In specific cases, the yield of a particular enzyme may be raised by the addition of specialised substances. In general these are not inducers of the enzyme directly, since the production strain will be selected to be capable of constitutive enzyme synthesis (Table 5).

TABLE 5
Representative Media for Semi-solid Fermentations for Enzyme Production

Enzyme type	Medium Component	Parts
Lactase	Wheat bran	100
	0·2N HCl (containing traces of Zn, Fe and Cu)	60
Lipase	Wheat bran	3
	Soya bean meal	1
	Water	3
Carbohydrases/ Proteases	Wheat bran	3
	Rice bran	2
	Soya bean meal	1
	Water	4

Sterilisation of the medium prior to inoculation is usually by live steam injection to the whole mash in a rotating screw cooker. Inoculation is generally achieved by further tumbling of the cooled medium and the introduction of spore suspensions before filling of trays or the deep bed chamber.

Submerged 'deep' fermentation has been adopted as the most economic route for the preparation of bulk industrial enzymes. Suspended insoluble nutrients and inexpensive additional sources of nitrogen, phosphate and trace elements in soluble forms are used. The medium selected must support good growth of the micro-organism and be as inexpensive as possible. Soybean meal, starch and starch hydrolysates and corn steep

liquor dominate the list of typical ingredients. The specific additional
growth and enzyme synthesis stimulating requirements are determined for
each organism selected as a production strain (Table 6).

Despite very great developments of sophisticated instrument monitoring
of research fermentations, the industrial enzyme fermentation system
utilises basic but large fermentation equipment. Main vessels can reach

TABLE 6

Representative Media for Submerged Fermentations for Enzyme
Production

Enzyme type	Medium component	g/litre
Bacillus protease	Starch hydrolysate	50
	Soya bean meal	20
	Casein	20
	Na_2HPO_4	3·3
	Ground barley	100
	Soya bean meal	30
	Na_2CO_3 (to adjust pH to 9–10)	
Fungal protease	Starch	30
	Corn steep liquor	5
	Soya bean meal	10
	Casein	12
	Gelatin	5
	Distillers dried solubles	5
	KH_2PO_4	2·4
	$NaNO_3$	1
	NH_4Cl	1
	$FeSO_4$	0·01
Bacillus amylase	Potato starch	100
	Ground barley	50
	Soya bean meal	20
	Sodium caseinate	10
	$Na_2HPO_4.12H_2O$	9
Fungal amylase	Corn starch	24
	Corn steep liquor	36
	NaH_2PO_4	47
	$CaCl_2$	1
	KCl	0·2
	$MgCl_2.6H_2O$	0·2

150 m^3 in practice and they are an essential feature of the economics of bulk processing. Controls to monitor pH, temperature and in some cases dissolved oxygen, are typical. Where the use of suspended medium is encountered, it is often necessary to have efficient foam detection and antifoam treatment as an extra control facility. Bulk medium is generally prepared separately in tanks that allow pH adjustment and direct or heat exchange steam sterilisation. Most systems pump the sterile medium into the fermentation vessels that have been previously sterilised with live steam.

There is generally a requirement for aeration in enzyme fermentations and this is provided by a supply of sterile filtered compressed air and combined with stirring of the fermentation. The design of the stirring configuration and the choice of rate of air input represents a major section of skilful economic engineering technology making a significant contribution to the successful production of enzymes.

Care in the selection of medium components also relates to the downstream separation systems for enzyme recovery. Trial fermentations are always involved in making this choice, having viscosity, total solids levels, cell mass, efficient utilisation of medium components as major considerations for the end of the fermentation itself.

It is also common that the organism produces the desired enzyme at the end of the major growth stage and this has tended to restrict processes to batch operation. Where the target enzyme can be induced by addition of specific compounds, usually the actual enzyme substrate or a derivative of it, it is sometimes convenient to run a two stage fermentation. The inducing substrate is added to the vessels when the culture is approaching maximum cell density in the growth phase.

In recent years, the expansion of application challenges from process industry has stimulated researches into the production of intracellular enzymes in bulk. The fermentation systems are essentially the same as for batch production of extracellular enzymes with the operation concentrated on the maximum cell mass at economic operating and medium costs. In a few exceptional cases, feeding of the fermentation to create a continuous system has been adopted and the enzyme either fully extracted from the cells, or the cell walls binding the enzyme used as the basis for immobilisation.

Enzyme recovery is necessary to ensure that the final preparation is sufficiently pure and stable to enter the intended market and application. The number of stages and the loss of activity are both kept to a minimum. Throughout the recovery system attention is paid to the prevention of contamination by toxic substances or harmful micro-organisms.

The equipment used for the various unit processes is almost entirely represented by traditional food machinery and the comparable hygiene constraints in the two industries are usually incorporated in the designs.

Semi-solid extraction is based on the assumption that the enzyme is produced extracellularly and the primary operation is the washing out of solubles from the bran ferment. Countercurrent and percolation systems are used, with the minimum amount of aqueous buffer of pH and ionic strength determined as appropriate for the enzyme in question. It is common to use a chilled solution in the range 5–10 °C. In some cases, a prior drying of the fermented bran allows a more concentrated extract to be obtained. Once the bran is extracted to an aqueous fluid subsequent stages are essentially the same as for the submerged fermentations of extracellular enzymes.

8.3. Broth Purification

Figure 2 illustrates the main unit operations in the processing of enzyme products to a stable commercial form.

The bran extract or fermentation broth contain the enzyme, residues of the suspended medium components, the soluble medium components and the cells of the fermented micro-organism. Initially, the solids are removed by filtration or centrifugation aided by the use of flocculants to increase the particle size, e.g. calcium salts, polyelectrolytes and aluminium salts typified by modern water treatment methods. It is common to load a proportion of diatomaceous earth or other filter aid into the stirred broth before filtration, which is most often performed on rotary vacuum filters. Where centrifugation is adopted, the high-speed disc machine with continuous operation is preferred.

Concentration of enzyme liquids is a compromise between energy efficiency and activity loss. Low temperature vacuum evaporation is most commonly applied to stable enzymes and ultrafiltration is used for the more sensitive products, since it can successfully be performed at temperatures around 5 °C.

Purification is usually necessary both to eliminate micro-organisms and to reduce the preparation to the lowest practical contamination with other enzymes produced by the fermentation. Polishing and germ filtration steps are able to remove micro-organisms and a series of precipitations may be performed to select the desired enzyme. The addition of an inorganic salt such as sodium or ammonium sulphate to a specified concentration will precipitate a range of proteins which may include the desired enzyme or leave it in the soluble phase. Further solution and precipitation stages may

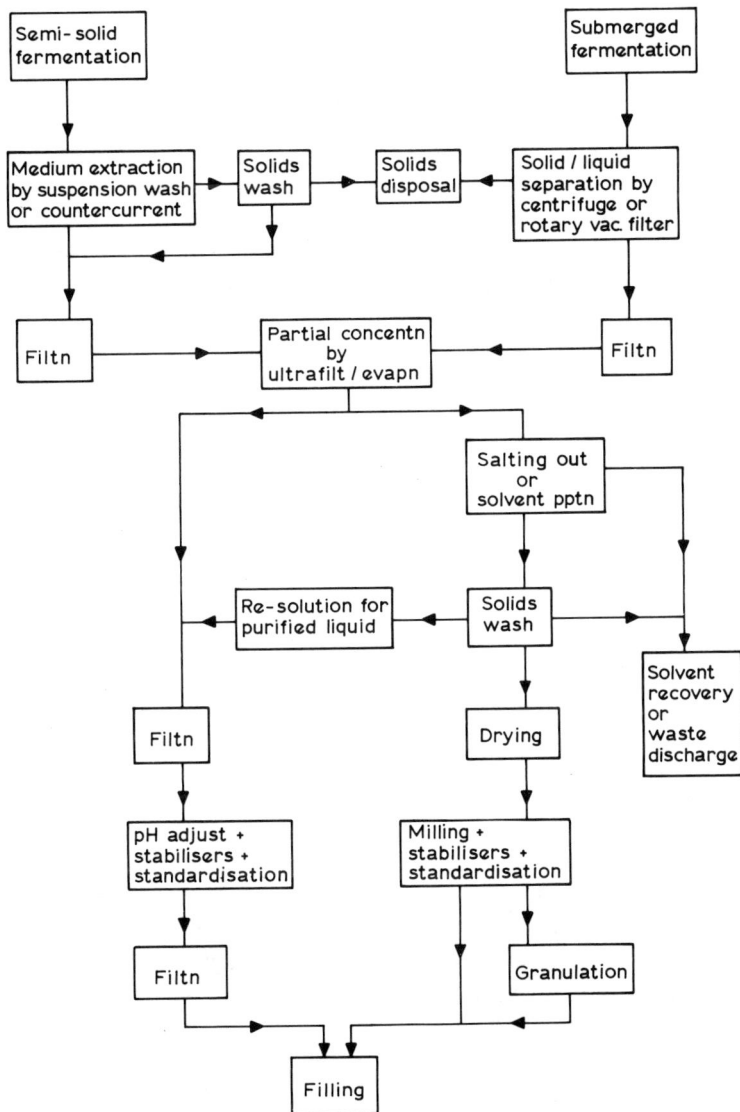

Fig. 2. Schematic flow diagram for extracellular microbial enzyme recovery.

be performed with different concentrations of precipitant to achieve a desired purification. Organic solvents that lower the dielectric constant of the system and so reduce the solubility of proteins are also used to precipitate enzymes. The most effective treatments are performed using chilled solvents and adding them to the aqueous broth, whose pH has been adjusted to the isoelectric value for the enzyme being processed.

Purified liquid enzymes are standardised by dilution and the diluents generally include stabilising salts, polyalcohols or sugars and any permitted preservatives deemed necessary. In the limited applications where a dry enzyme product is required, it is now recognised that the spray drying should include a granulation to minimise the potential hazards of dusty, dry products. The inhalation of any protein dust is likely to increase the risk of allergic response to further exposures to the same protein and it is recommended to take full precautions when handling enzymes in powder form. Granulation will follow standardisation with acceptable materials such as sugars, starch, flour or inorganic salts.

9.   INDUSTRIAL ENZYMES IN FERMENTED FOOD PRODUCTION

Fermentation processes utilise a wide spectrum of enzyme-mediated conversions carried out by the active organisms of the ferment. Some of the gross effects of these conversions can also be performed without the use of the whole organism but rather by the introduction of industrial enzymes under appropriate conditions. In other circumstances, an exaggerated extension of the traditional fermentation products can be created by enzyme additions to the whole system. Flavour, aroma and texture changes are examples of this effect.

The single major application for enzymes in the production of fermented foods lies in the preparation of the substrates for those fermentations. A variety of economically important cereal based fermentations produce alcoholic beverages and vinegars, whilst dough fermentations are important for many baked goods. Where the fermentation is to be performed by micro-organisms other than brewer's or baker's yeasts, the substrates vary more widely to include soya bean and fish proteins for many sauces and condiments, milk for cheese production, fruit and vegetable materials for wines and pickles and special treatments in producing tea and coffee.

9.1. Substrates for Alcoholic Fermentation
The traditional sources for enzymic hydrolysis of starches to fermentable

sugars have been Koji and malted cereals. The complexes of enzymes produced by these materials are used to hydrolyse further quantities of less costly starches deriving from cereals and such roots as cassava.

For many countries, the production of these enzyme sources is costly even if the appropriate raw materials are available. This is especially the situation regarding the provision of good quality malting barley and usually necessitates the importation of malt.

The hydrolysis of starch follows a series of steps that begins with a heating stage that ensures the gelatinisation and physical modification necessary to permit enzyme action. The first enzymic stage is accomplished by the action of alpha-amylase, which hydrolytically depolymerises the starch to soluble dextrins. The second enzymic stage utilises beta-amylases or other saccharifying enzymes to yield fermentable sugars as a mixture of glucose and maltose.

These steps are accomplished in the traditional malt brewery by a simple infusion mashing of milled malt with warm water at approximately 63–65 °C for a period of between 2 and 3 h (Fig. 3). If malt is available only of low quality or the economics of selecting a lower quality malt are desired, it is practicable to introduce a number of industrial enzymes to aid the release of a satisfactory fermentable wort (Fig. 4). Alpha-amylases obtained from *Bacillus subtilis* together with bacterial beta-glucanases, fungal glucanases and a bacterial neutral proteinase are used to supplement the malt enzymes in the mash at doses in the range of 0·2–1·5 kg per tonne malt. The proteinase ensures adequate release of soluble nitrogen for colour, flavour and yeast nutrition to remain satisfactory. In most cases, the

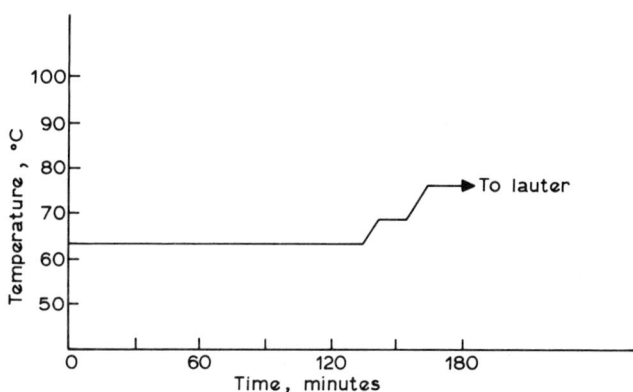

Fig. 3.   Mashing diagram for an all-malt mash.

A. Godfrey

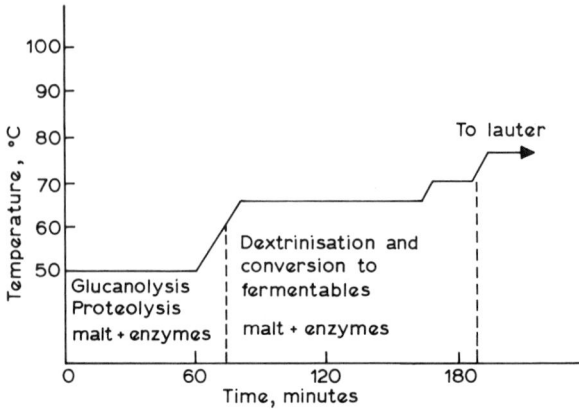

Fig. 4. Mashing diagram for enzyme aided malt or malt and barley mashing.

requirement for the saccharifying enzymes such as amyloglucosidase from *Aspergillus niger* is minimal unless highly fermented products or distillery alcohols are required. For these processes, the amyloglucosidases are added at from 0·5 to 1·5 litres per tonne starch in the system.

The most significant economic improvements will be achieved when beers are produced with a substantial replacement of the malt by other starches such as maize, rice, barley, wheat or cassava.

For these replacement mashes, it is generally accepted to process them separately by performing a decoction mash programme in which the finely ground materials are mashed and heated in the presence of a thermostable bacterial alpha-amylase (Fig. 5). This may be performed in a

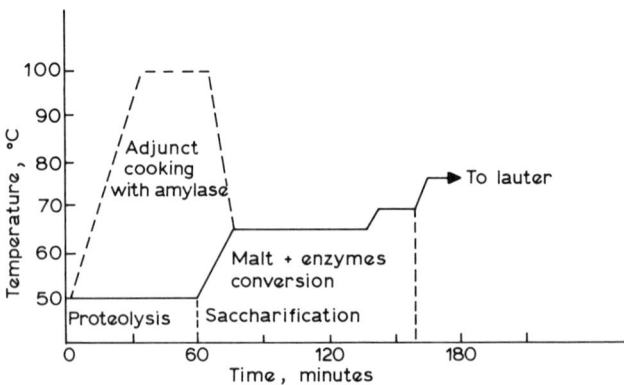

Fig. 5. Mashing diagram for an adjunct decoction mash.

batch cooker, or, most effectively, by direct steam injection into the slurry through a jet cooker. In some cases, the batch cooking is performed at high pressures (e.g. grain distilleries) and the mash is cooled to around 80 °C before the addition of a less thermostable amylase for the dextrinisation stage.

For beer production, the liquefied, dextrinised mash is combined with a malt mash to obtain saccharification before wort is separated for fermentation. In distillery operations, the mash is cooled to around 60 °C

TABLE 7

Microbial Enzymes Applied to Distilling and Brewing Practice

Distilling		kg enzyme/tonne starch
Liquefaction	Bacterial alpha amylase	1·5–2·0 (batch)
	Bacterial alpha (thermostable)	0·2–0·6 (batch)
	Bacterial alpha (thermostable)	0·2–0·3 (continuous)
Saccharification	Fungal alpha amylase (maltogenic)	0·1–0·2
	Fungal amyloglucosidase	1·5–3·0

Brewing		kg enzyme/tonne grain
Malt Improvement	Bacterial alpha amylase	0·5–1·0
	Bacterial beta glucanase	0·5–1·0
	Bacterial neutral protease	0·3–1·5
	Fungal beta glucanase	0·2–0·5
High adjunct content mashing		
	Bacterial alpha amylase	2·0–3·0
	Bacterial beta glucanase	2·0–3·0
	Bacterial neutral protease	1·2–1·5
	Fungal beta glucanase	1·5–2·5
	Fungal amylase	1·0–3·0
	Fungal glucoamylase	2·5–6·0
Adjunct cooking	Bacterial amylase (thermostable)	0·2–0·6

and dosed with amyloglucosidase to give a partial saccharification before cooling and fermenting. In other operations, the mash may be cooled directly to fermentation temperature and the amyloglucosidase and yeast added together.

In all cases of the use of non-malt adjuncts, it is necessary to monitor the amount of soluble nitrogen in the fermentation and adjust this upward by adding neutral bacterial proteinase to the retained malt mash to raise the levels as required.

Some examples of enzymes for alcohol production are given in Table 7.

9.2. Vinegar Fermentations

The production of an alcoholic feedstock for vinegar fermentation from starch sources follows the processes outlined in the preceding section. In some countries other materials such as bananas or pineapple canning wastes can be utilised for vinegar production. The starch and partially degraded polymers of under-ripened bananas can be effectively released as fermentables for alcohol production by treatment of the pulped material with amyloglucosidases. These enzymes typically act well at the pH and temperature of the yeast fermentation, which can be initiated directly on the pulp suspension. The added enzymes release sugars steadily throughout the fermentation.

Where further release of starch and sugars from the structural tissues is required in processing bananas and pineapple or similar fruit wastes, the pulp can be effectively treated with pectinolytic enzymes. These enzymes are generally of *Aspergillus* spp. origin and they function well under the acid conditions of these fruit pulps.

Processing of *coffee* has also utilised the pectinases in accelerating the fermentation stage to remove the mucilage coat before drying the beans. Dilute solutions of these enzymes are sprayed onto the gum covered cherries at rates of 2–10 g per tonne at 15–20 °C. The fermentation is more rapid and is complete in about 20 h. In *tea* fermentation an acceleration is similarly achieved, although the quantity of enzyme has to be carefully regulated to avoid excessive damage to the leaf structure.

The yeast fermentation of *bakery doughs* also relies upon the release of fermentable sugars from the flour starch. Traditionally the additional use of malt flour at the milling stage or malt extract at the bakery has been the method of supplementing and standardising the amylase content of bread flours. It is now regular practice to incorporate fungal amylase from *Aspergillus oryzae* into flour to ensure adequate release of sugars from damaged starch granules. The regulation of this gassing power for bread flours is essential for efficient performance of automatic, large-scale bakeries.

9.3. Cheese Production

Mention must be made here of the use of a variety of rennet enzymes for the coagulation of milk for cheese production, although the subject of cheese production itself has been covered thoroughly in Chapter 3.

Chymosin (calf rennet) is the traditional coagulant for cheese milk. It is sometimes mixed with or replaced by similar extracts of lamb or kid stomachs to provide the appropriate coagulum for special and highly flavoured cheeses. Additionally, the dilution of calf rennet, due to its high cost, with adult bovine pepsin or porcine pepsin is a regular practice. In recent years some extremely successful and economic replacements for these animal enzymes have been prepared from a number of micro-organisms.

Many micro-organisms produce proteinases that can be demonstrated to coagulate milk, but most of them are non-specific in their action and continue to hydrolyse the casein of the curd to yield unacceptable flavours and textures and even complete solution. A small number of fungal enzymes have, however, proved to perform in a manner that imitates the action of calf rennet on the kappa casein particles and to proceed no further. Notable examples of these come from *Mucor miehei, Mucor pusillus lindt* and *Endothia parasitica*. From the cheesemaker's point of view, these enzymes are available in bulk, at equivalent strength to calf rennet (or multiples of that strength), in powder or liquid form with excellent stability during storage and at substantially lower cost. For practical application they are used precisely in the same way as the traditional animal extracts.

Where animal lipases are used for certain cheeses, these are extracted from young lambs or goats together with the chymosin. Microbial alternatives, from fungi, are now under development with promising results that again propose economy and the flexibility in choice of the coagulant as a separate item.

9.4. Other Protein-based Fermentations

The production of soya bean and fish protein fermented foods requires the modification of the proteins to facilitate the nutrition of the micro-organisms of the fermentation which in turn impart the characteristic texture and flavour to the product. In each case, the ingredients of choice are finely ground and mixed with an appropriate amount of water. Inoculation with cultures and a lengthy fermentation then create the product.

Increased protein conversion and accelerated fermentation can be brought about by the application of plant proteases such as bromelain and papain to these mashes. Similarly, but more recently, the use of microbial proteases has been found to give a much lower contamination with unwanted microbes that are often associated with plant protease preparations. By varying the amount of added enzyme, the degree of solubilisation before and during fermentation can be regulated to produce both pastes and sauces.

9.5. Related and Experimental Applications

9.5.1. Cheese Ripening and Flavours

The enhancement of cheese flavours using microbial esterases from *M. miehei* has been investigated by Huang & Dooley (1976), who were interested in creating the characteristic flavour of Italian cheeses.

Trials have proved encouraging in the use of neutral proteases in the salting stage of cheddar cheese production to give accelerated ripening in store (Law & Wigmore, 1982).

9.5.2. Dairy Products

The use of lactases in low pH dairy foods such as buttermilk, yoghurt and sour cream, in which the lactose is converted to glucose and galactose, has been examined (Crisan & Sorenson, 1977). The final products can show improved taste without added calories.

The production of low lactose yoghurts by simultaneous hydrolysis of lactose and bacterial fermentation has been discussed (Dariani *et al.*, 1982).

9.5.3. Bakery products

These include improved sour dough flavours in baking and a dried sour dough ingredient containing rennet from lactic bacterial fermentation of skim milk (Luksas, A. J., US Patent 3,615,695).

9.5.4. Soya Fermentations

The partial hydrolysis of unwanted and unacceptable carbohydrates in soya beans (and peas and beans) has utilised various enzymes of the pectinase type. Further carbohydrate is removed by yeast fermentation to give a good quality protein concentrate (Gay, M. M., US Patent 3,958,015).

A fermented type of soy sauce can be prepared from fluid cheese whey by addition of lactase enzyme and fermentation with yeast. The intensely flavoured product is combined with non-fermented sauce or hydrolysed vegetable protein (Luksas, A. J., US Patent 3,552,981).

9.6. Future Developments

The increased pressure for natural colourings and flavourings should stimulate technical developments in their extraction. It can be seen that the complex carbohydrates of plant tissues will be gently hydrolysed by enzymic methods for higher yields and more efficient purifications. Similarly, the enzymic degradation of plant proteins will free desirable carbohydrates. The selection of enzyme and treatment conditions will have to be made by careful collaboration between chemist and enzymologist to ensure that the integrity of target molecules is maintained. However, the use of selected fermentations to further remove unwanted components from such hydrolysed extracts is very attractive.

A very similar series of concepts is now being applied to the processing of animal feeds via the silage fermentations, and a number of development products that add hydrolytic enzymes at the initial stages are showing promise in regard to accelerated fermentation and better nutritive value in the feeds.

The use of enzymes to selectively hydrolyse components of food processing wastes is also developing rapidly. Subsequent fermentation for biomass as human or animal feed seems to be the likely first option for upgrading such wastes from bakery, confectionery and vegetable operations.

REFERENCES AND BIBLIOGRAPHY

ATKINSON, B. & MAVITUNA, E. (1982) *Biochemical Engineering & Biotechnology Handbook*. Macmillan Press, London.

AUNSTRUP, K. (1979) *Applied Biochemistry & Bioengineering, Vol. 2, Enzyme Technology*. Academic Press Inc., New York.

BARFOED, H. C. (1981) In *Essays in Applied Microbiology*, J. R. Norris & M. H. Richmond Eds. John Wiley, London.

BOING, J. T. P. (1982) In *Prescott & Dunn's Industrial Microbiology*, 4th edn, H. Reed Ed. Macmillan Press, London.

BRONOWSKI, J. (1973) *The Ascent of Man*. British Broadcasting Corporation, London.

CRISAN, E. V. & SORENSEN, S. G. (1977) US Patent 4,007,283.

DARIANI, D. N., FRANK, J. F. & Loewenstein, M. J. (1982) *Cultured Dairy Products*, **17**, 2, 18.

GODFREY, A. & REICHELT, J. R. (1982) (Eds.) *Industrial Enzymology—the Application of Enzymes in Industry*. Macmillan Press, London.

HUANG, H. T. & DOOLEY, J. G. (1976) *Biotechnol. Bioengng* **18**, 909.

LAW, B. A. & WIGMORE, A. S. (1982) *J. Soc. Dairy Technol.* **35**(2), 75.

MEYRATH, J. & KOLAVSEK, G. (1975) Production of microbial enzymes. In *Enzymes in Food Processing*, 2nd edn, G. Reed Ed. Academic Press Inc., New York.

Index to Volumes 1 and 2